A SHEARWATER BOOK

AGAINST THE MACHINE

AGAINST the MACHINE

The Hidden Luddite Tradition in Literature, Art, and Individual Lives

NICOLS FOX

ISLAND PRESS / Shearwater Books

Washington / Covelo / London

For Kathryn and Sam

A Shearwater Book
Published by Island Press

©2002 Nicols Fox

Library of Congress Cataloging-in-Publication Data
Fox, Nicols.
Against the machine : the hidden Luddite tradition in literature, art,
and individual lives / Nicols Fox.
p. cm.
Includes bibliographical references and index.
ISBN 1-55963-860-5
1. Technology—Social aspects. 2. Technology and civilization.
3. Luddites. I. Title.

T14.5.F66 2002
303.48'3—dc21   2002009913

British Cataloguing-in-Publication Data available.

Printed on recycled, acid-free paper. ♲

Manufactured in the United States of America

09 08 07 06 05 04 03 02   8 7 6 5 4 3 2 1

Contents

Prologue

One-third of computer users admit to physically attacking a computer. More than 70 percent confess they swear at them. Frustration, anger, and exasperation—minus the swearing and the hitting—affect 67 percent. Or so revealed a study commissioned by the software company Symantec in 1999. Observation and personal experience indicate no improvement. The sticky mouse, a freeze, or a crash provokes the most anger.

The problem goes by several names: tech rage, desk rage, web rage, or simply CRAP—for Computer Rage, Anxiety, and Phobia—and the phenomenon follows closely on the heels of growing incidences of road rage and air rage. Today, as the threat of terrorism hangs in the air, the consequences of air rage can be more serious—even as tensions connected with flying increase. Now "airport rage" is barely contained as a new layer of anxiety is imposed over the everyday stress of modern mass transportation.

Our relationship to technology has become complex, a mixture of adulation, dependency, frustration, and rage. Clearly, in technology's ability to do what could only be fantasized in years past, it is a marvel. Its appeal and usefulness need no reinforcement from me. It is its own witness in that regard.

Yet, in all its various associated frustrations—traffic, crowds, herding, waiting; one's sense of being merely a small cog in a huge machine, of having to rely absolutely upon systems that are not absolutely reliable, of powerlessness so cunningly disguised as power that one labors under a persistent sense of unreality—it is plainly driving people crazy.

The solution to computer rage, a technical magazine suggests, is for people to change their habits. There are sensible suggestions to clean out surplus files so that crashes occur less frequently, to have realistic expectations about what machines can do, to develop patience. People must, in other words, adapt to the machine. The idea that it should be the other way around—that machines should adapt to humans—seems not to have occurred to anyone. And yet it would seem obvious. Who, after all, is in control here?

Do we really want the answer to that question? Of late the balance has shifted, and the answer is no longer as clear as it might once have been.

Technology delights us as much as it frustrates and complicates the lives into which we have willingly invited it. Our childlike needs for pleasure and excitement have been cheerfully accommodated by our high-tech industries. Our desire for comfort and ease has been catered to. Glittering material goods are available and cheap. The longed-for magic of the sorcerer now leaps from the laptop. The fantasies of comic books and science fiction are now everyday realities.

For the past two hundred years, technology has been creeping up on us slowly, seductively, incrementally, until it now dominates our thinking, our expectations, and our actions in ways that could not have been anticipated and of which we are scarcely aware. It has, in a manner not consciously or carefully considered, reshaped and reordered the world around us to its own measure. Over those two centuries, the relationship between human and tool has shifted dramatically. The extent to which we now attempt to adapt our lives to the requirements of the machine is unacknowledged. We adjust automatically, willingly, bravely: remembering our identification numbers, fitting our hands to the keyboards, fixing our eyes not on the horizon or the movement in the bush but on the screen; our ears tuned not to the sound of the wind and the rustle in the grass but to the whirs and chirps and hums and pings of the machines. But the struggle to adjust is not without consequences. It manifests itself in our stress, our discomfort, our rage.

And we should not be surprised. It should only be expected: machines and humans are basically incompatible. Humans are not machines. We don't naturally think or act like machines. Our bodies are not shaped and suited to the machine. Thus our attempts to reshape ourselves are doomed to frustration. It is an awkward, clumsy match. We are everything the machine is not: creatures of emotion and sensation with minds that are creative and imaginative. We act in unpredictable ways, we are naturally suited to nature—not to a world of electronic impulses. And this is nothing to apologize for. These are the traits of our successful endurance and adaptability, and if these qualities are now demeaned, it is the machine and its unnatural demands that have demeaned them. The struggle to adapt to the requirements and uncomfortable standards of the mechanical—to act in orderly, regimented, predictable ways—is creating more societal stress than anyone might have expected. Frustration is common as we struggle to fit our concept of ourselves into the blanks on forms; as we reluctantly press 3 for the selection that doesn't really answer our need or our question; as we sit for hours in front of digitized electronic impulses while outside the birds and the sunshine are calling; as we eat foods that suit the marketplace more than they suit our bodies—bodies that are essentially unchanged from the ones that survived nicely a thousand years ago or two thousand years ago. In this awkward process of adaptation, we fight our preferences, control our impulses, manage our emotions, and hide our intuitions in a world in which these qualities are unwelcome and discouraged, in a world shaped by a force that has none of these qualities and, in fact, denigrates them. Technology has reduced a thousand ordinary actions to numbers, to flashes of light or sound, to an overly simplified yes or no that has nothing to do with the complexity and subtlety that is humanness—or that is the world around us, for that matter. It is an artificial construct into which the natural world is being shoved, the round peg into the square hole. It will go, but it's not a good fit.

And yet, despite the accumulated frustration and rage, genuine resistance to the machine is relatively rare. Our preconditioning to favor novelty keeps us fascinated by the machines. Generally people try bravely, even enthusiastically, to accommodate themselves. They are not sure why they are consequently unhappy. They do not blame the machines, for we have convinced ourselves—or been convinced by advertising and promotion—of their marvelous natures and of our great need for them. We have created dependency where none existed, forgetting that we survived and thrived as a species for hundreds of thousands of years without the internal combustion engine or the cell phone. Now too many of us feel lost and inadequate and frightened if the lights go out. We love our machines, after all—as we would a spouse in an enduring bad marriage, whose flaws are so familiar, whose irritating voice is so much a part of the background that it is impossible to conceive its not being there. Alternatives are not even imagined.

But resistance to technology does exist, and it is not new. It emerged simultaneously with the machine itself, increased as the industrial revolution gained strength, and has remained a persistent, if underrecognized, presence even as the world has become a highly technical place. It endures for one reason: we are not the people we pretend to be. There has been no time to adapt in the evolutionary sense. We struggle in the twenty-first century with first-century bodies and minds and wonder why it is a challenge, and we assume that the problem is individual, personal, and fixable. We blame ourselves for our failure to keep up, for our failure to adapt.

Some people have always known what the problem is. In 1811 they were the followers of Ned Ludd and were called Luddites, and their anger welled and overflowed into a rebellion against the mechanical weaving machines that were taking their jobs and disrupting and destroying their communities and their lives. But resistance to the machine did not end there. It persisted, and it can be found as a strain of thinking that, if it has not dominated, if it has not even been entirely visible, has nevertheless endured, expressed through literature, art, philosophy, and ways of living that deliberately challenge the mechanical with an alternative that emphasizes what the machine is not.

The followers of Ned Ludd took up weapons against the machines that were destroying their lives, but the essence of Luddism is not violence. Far from it. It is a respect for and a confidence in those things that make us human, with a concomitant rejection of the mechanistic approach to being that devalues our humanity. It is a philosophy that respects tradition, intuition, spirituality, the senses, human relationships, the work of the hand, and the disorderly and unpredictable nature of reality, as opposed to a mechanistic or reductionist construct of the world. It questions the domination of science and the elevation of efficiency to a superior value. It rejects materiality.

Luddism, then and now, favors a thoughtful use of appropriate technologies that does not damage the relationships we hold dear. It cherishes the natural world from which we attempt to separate ourselves only at our peril.

I first heard about the Luddite Rebellion in an English history class in college. The idea of rebelling against technology appealed to me at once. My preferences for the old, the natural, the handmade, the traditional were already set—or inborn, a stray gene from some similarly fusty ancestor, perhaps, for my parents were more than half-infatuated with the new. I loved signs of wear in natural materials, the mark of the hand, evidence of a good age. For me it confirmed a past and promised a future; it represented time unfolding, a heritage. I loved the old ways, the old songs, things that had endured. If a carving knife worked well, why would we want something as silly as an electric one? I had never even seen a computer, but I knew I wouldn't like it. At nineteen I was a curmudgeon, an old fogy, a technology resister, a neo-Luddite. Since then, every mention of the word Luddite has made me sit up and listen.

I can recall the precise moment I decided to take up the research that led to this book. It was in 1995 and I was reading Kirkpatrick Sale's *Rebels Against the Future: The Luddites and Their War on the Industrial Revolution.* What caught my attention was his reference to a tradition of resistance to technology that had persisted just beneath the surface of general awareness since the rebellion. Sale dropped hints but didn't elaborate: Byron, Brontë, Thoreau. At that moment I began a search. If there was a literature of Luddism, if there was possibly a living tradition of resistance to technology, I aimed to dig it out.

History is a telescope that the present turns on the vastness of the past. The Present—let's personify it as a tall, darkly clad figure standing on a hill —turns slowly with the telescope, finds an agreeable view, then tightens the focus. History is necessarily a selective process, and what is selected is what seems pleasant, agreeable, suitable, and convenient to the Present. It is what the Present demands, a past that supports the prevailing, dominant view.

The rest of the past remains where it is, unchanged but unnoticed, until the figure with the telescope is replaced—or, awakened to the possibility of another view, turns the telescope elsewhere. This book is an invitation to the figure with the telescope to shift the gaze and tighten the focus on a neglected aspect of the past, to be aware that what is convenient to the Present is only half the story or less—a fraction, the easiest part—and that there is more: less convenient, but important nevertheless.

There is a discernible history in which the machine was questioned, challenged, and occasionally rejected entirely. We don't—in our love affair with the new, enthralled by novelty, seduced by the tantalizing but dubious promise of Progress—hear much about it. The democratic tradition has a flaw, I think. It conditions us to think in terms of winners and losers. The candidate who loses an election, even if by only a single vote, becomes not the individual who has the support of nearly half the population, but the loser, dishonored and ignored. We replay this way of thinking again and again in our culture: games, contests, awards. And yet the fact is that the principles and ideas of the loser remain, as a recognizable—if not a dominant—force or presence in society.

And so it was that the Luddites lost their fight against the machines. And so it was that everyone who has challenged the machine has lost. And yet they have not lost, for they represent a solid body of thinking that deserves to be reconsidered and appreciated as an alternative to the present domination of technology: an option, a value system that continues to throb beneath the shroud prematurely placed over it. It is possible to challenge the mechanistic approach to living and working; it is permissible to question whether it prevails with humans in mind or dominates for other reasons; and it is appropriate to envision, to consider, even to create and nourish alternatives.

Sale's book seemed, at the time, to fit neatly into a faint yet growing public frustration and concern with the impact of technology, coupled with an increase in actual resistance. A year or so earlier, Jerry Mander's *In the Absence of the Sacred: The Failure of Technology and the Survival of the Indian Nations* had openly advocated both a questioning *and* a rejection of technologies that were having an adverse impact on the environment and on human society. Problems with technology were obvious: the persistent threat of nuclear annihilation; the new realities of biochemical weapons; the industrial wastes that contaminate soil, rivers, and groundwater; the disasters of Chernobyl and Bhopal that poisoned so many and so much; the high probability that the climate is being changed by our addiction to fossil fuels—to cars, airplanes, and overheated houses—the problems of waste disposal, the diseases of modernity: the increasing cancers, diabetes, asthma and other lung disorders. A friend tells me she loves technology: she is wearing a complicated implanted device, she explains, that monitors and supplies insulin as she needs it to treat her diabetes. As I say nothing and slightly widen my eyes, she blushes and acknowledges, without my suggestion, that it is probably the modern diet that gave her diabetes in the first place. We seldom think how much of what we consider technological innovation is actually a response to a problem technology has created. Coping keeps the economy thriving.

Then there are the more subtle but immediate and personal challenges technology presents: the frustrations of adaptation; the repetitive-motion injuries; the stresses of urban or even suburban living; the noise; the trash; the traffic, the traffic, the traffic—and the parking. In our good dreams the telephone is not ringing.

It was in 1993 that Bill Henderson, editor of the Pushcart Press, organized the Lead Pencil Club after what was intended as a joke had to be taken seriously. After he published an op-ed essay in the *New York Times* describing his dislike of the computer, the mere mention of such an organization in print prompted hundreds of responses from individuals around the globe who also hated their computers and wanted to become members. This led to his editing a book, *Minutes of the Lead Pencil Club: Pulling the Plug on the Electronic Revolution*, which brought together letters, commentary, cartoons, and essays that collectively represent a range of reactions from outrage to dismay at our subservience to the mechanical. Sven Birkerts, in *The Gutenberg Elegies: The Fate of Reading in an Electronic Age*, wrote in 1994 of his concern that the computer was changing writing and thinking in ways that had not been carefully considered and which would damage important aspects of our ways of viewing reality. Langdon Winner's *The Whale and the Reactor* had already, in 1986, tapped into the powerful emotions generated by the battle between the natural world and the technological leviathan. Thomas Berry's *The Dream of the Earth*, published in 1988, considered the deteriorating connection between human-generated technologies and the damaged environment from a spiritual perspective. Gradually, a body of contemporary work was emerging that could be grouped under a heading that some people were already calling neo-Luddite. A passing reference in yet another magazine led me to a back issue of the *Utne Reader* containing Chellis Glendinning's *Luddite Manifesto*. Her program for the future includes dismantling nuclear, chemical, computer, electromagnetic, and genetic-engineering technologies, and it is important to consider this as a possibility. I identify with Mary McCarthy, who in her essay *My Confession* remembered, "It irritated me to be told that 'you could not turn the clock back.'" Obviously one cannot go back, but one can go forward, applying the understanding and accumulated wisdom of our technological experience. It is important to accept that we are still in control and that our unquestioning

worship of science and our imprisonment in a technological paradigm is a
choice that we have made, if not entirely conscious of the ramifications,
then willingly. That which we have created can be transformed, if we have
the desire and the will to do so. It is important that we not abrogate control
over our present situation, leaving the future to . . . what? To some indefin-
able, unnamed force that we confess in our supplicant's posture is not ours
to manage?

In all these sources were references to Wendell Berry, a farmer, essayist,
and poet whose common-sense approach to resisting technology has earned
him devoted fans around the globe. In fact, I was beginning to sense that
questioning technology seemed to strike a chord with individuals everywhere who had, at some point, felt the urge to take a blunt instrument to
some balky marvel of ingenuity that failed to keep its promise. The faster the
pace of life, the more insistent the hum of background motors; as more and
more things that individuals truly value are allowed less and less space in
modern life, the questioning becomes louder.

The characteristics that define Luddism can be discovered in the Romantic poets, in the writings of Thomas Carlyle, John Ruskin, Ralph Waldo
Emerson, and Henry David Thoreau. The Arts and Crafts movement was an
outright rejection of industrialized production. The same principles can be
found in the lives and work of potters such as Bernard Leach and his followers. Resistance to technology is a thread that winds through the writings
of the Southern Agrarians and the novels of such diverse authors as Wallace
Stegner, E. M. Forster, and John Fowles. It appears in the work of such
recent cult figures as Robert Persig and Edward Abbey. Modern poets from
Gary Snyder to W. S. Merwin express their anger at the technological juggernaut that rampages across the landscape. Environmentalism has its roots
in resistance to this same ruthless domination and those who use it to conquer and subdue nature—a sentiment that has its beginning in the writings
of John Muir and Aldo Leopold and evolves into the deep ecology of Arne
Naess. Behind the modern Luddite movement is a solid body of philosophical writing. Jacques Ellul and Lewis Mumford construct a base upon which
present-day ecophilosophers such as Edward Goldsmith build. And it is
possible to reread old favorites with a new awareness: to see Dickens's
Dombey and Son or *Hard Times,* for instance, not simply as entertaining
Victorian novels but as forceful protests against the machine, understood as
such (all too well, in some political circles) by their contemporary readers.

Luddites today are self-selecting. There is no litmus test. You may live in a mud hut, carry water, and chop wood by choice, or simply hate your computer, yearn to outdistance your cell phone, and wish you could buy a car without automatic windows. But at bottom you feel some identification with all those who are apprehensive about and resistant to the domination of the machine in our society, in our work, and in our individual lives. Luddism is neither conservative nor liberal: both capitalism and Marxism are committed to the concept of industrial progress, the wisdom of which Luddites question. It is, however, a conscious approach to living. Luddites —or neo-Luddites, if you prefer—carefully evaluate what contributes to the considered life and what does not. They do so to the degree they find personally appropriate. We must think about the "encompassing technocratic, manipulative world that we have established," writes Thomas Berry in *The Dream of the Earth*. "We must not over-romanticize primitivism . . . yet when we witness the devastation we have wrought on this lovely continent, and even throughout the planet, and consider what we are now doing, we must reflect."[1] Such reflection is, in fact, part of a tradition that is strong and enduring and today more important than ever.

The Machine, by which I mean all the agencies of order, regularity, and efficiency, whether social or technical. . . .

Lewis Mumford, *In the Name of Sanity*

AGAINST
the MACHINE

CHAPTER ONE

The Kellams and Their Island

AMONG THE MANY ISLANDS OFF THE COAST OF Maine there is one called Placentia. The odd-sounding name—pronounced without the final "ia" by the natives—is thought to be a corruption of the French word *plaisance,* or pleasure. It sits just off the much larger Mount Desert Island in a cluster that includes Black Island and the Gotts, Great and Little. The islands in this group are small, as close together as kin, and except for Great Gott, which still has a summer community, mostly tree-covered. The trees, dark and heavy conifers, are not old. These islands were long ago clear-cut for firewood. The grazing of sheep kept them bare until about sixty years ago.

Placentia wasn't always as pleasant as it seems today. The name may have been meant ironically, or perhaps optimistically, as it was once the place the indigents were sent—the strangers who appeared in the Tremont community on Mount Desert Island with no visible means of support. These rejected souls pried a living of sorts from the thin soil, growing what they could, raising a few animals, and cutting down everything that would burn to warm the long winters.

Today no one lives on the island, but its deserted state is recent. Nan Kellam lived there by herself for three years until 1989; before that, she and her husband Arthur had lived there for forty years. They weren't indigents. Arthur was an engineer employed by Lockheed during World War II doing work that was not to be talked about: the company supplied aircraft bodies to the War Department. The couple's desire to keep to themselves and stay close to nature was not a new one. During those war years, they had lived in California, in an isolated cabin up a long canyon. After the war, they bought Placentia and came here to live.

OUR VESSEL, *Poor Richard,* is a converted Ralph Stanley lobster boat, 36 feet long, broad-bottomed and sturdy. Gussied up with brightwork and chrome—a "lobster yacht," it is called—it is owned and captained by Rick Savage. It can carry twenty-five on excursions, although Rick limits it to twenty for reasons of safety and practicality. There are only nine of us today: seven guests, sitting on the wooden seats that run along the back and sides beneath the chrome railing, and forward, the captain and the single crew. We trail a tender, essential to our undertaking, bobbing behind us like an annoying but persistent child.

It is September. The sky is spotted with clouds, but the air is warm. With mountains behind us and the sails of the regular Saturday racers skimming the bright water ahead, it is the kind of day when the harmony of water, mountains, sunlight, and wind fills one with fluid contentment.

The sea grows rougher as we near the island, the spray drenching the passengers in the back from time to time. The timid among us shift to stand closer to the center of the boat. There is little or no danger. The *Poor Richard,* beyond its workaday sturdiness, is equipped with a Global Positioning System (GPS) that shows its precise location in the water, a dot in a flashing circle on a screen, moving across a measured and charted sea. It does this by intercepting signals from high-altitude satellites, a system that can position us to within a hundred meters no matter where on the globe we might be. Radar shows grainy pictures of the approaching shore. The days of paper charts are over, says Rick, although he keeps them tucked away on board just in case. Even on this small vessel, we are surrounded and kept safe by modern technology; the dangers inherent in sea travel reduced to a minimum.

We come up behind the island and anchor off a long pebble beach where the currents are docile, and are rowed ashore by Rick's assistant in groups of three. We all have different reasons for coming. Four of us are curious about water and islands, ready for anything; three of us want to see the Kellam house before it meets whatever fate the Nature Conservancy has in store for it—which some suspect is destruction, probably by burning.

A path leads from the beach past the rotten shell of a rowboat the Kellams used to get to Mount Desert Island; both of them at the oars, braving rough seas if Arthur was inconveniently out of cigarettes, accepting a tow from a fishing boat if they got into trouble. A badly weathered flagpole still stands beside the boat. Never used, it was there to signal trouble: an insurance policy of sorts. There was an agreement with their neighbors on nearby Gotts Island that if a flag appeared, help was needed.

When the Kellams first moved to the island, the house was visible from the sea. Now the woods are thick; the trees tall. The trail, no wider than a man, threads in worn permanency among them, the forest floor sometimes strewn with pine needles, sometimes soft with moss, the damp spots built up with stones laid like cobble paving by someone for whom time was not a problem. There is the smell of decaying vegetation and cedar, and there is silence except for our soft footfalls.

We come suddenly upon a clearing. There are several large trees that seem to have been planted by someone—not the sort that just grow here: a walnut, a fruit tree, something else I can't identify, and just past them the gray-shingled house. There is a shed, grayed and tilting, and around what was once a garden, a half-collapsed rail fence.

I am a year too late. The house is still standing, but until a year ago it remained exactly as the Kellams had left it, Rick tells us. None of the island's occasional visitors had touched a thing—not the books and papers, not the tools, not the baskets or the old shaker boxes. Then someone, relatives I am told, took away most of the books and anything else of value and piled what was left in a heap in one corner. Those who want to preserve the Kellam house have warned me that it is a heap that loudly says, "bonfire." There is tension between those who want places to revert completely to unspoiled nature and those who think some signs of an unusual human endeavor—or merely an ordinary one if it is old enough—are worth saving.

To the left of the entrance, the front porch—its roof sagging, its supports leaning, grass growing between the stones of its floor—still holds up a sturdy, homemade swing. On the terrace are two wheelbarrows. A small stoop just in front of the door is laid of rough island stones. Tacked to the door frame, just inside and protected from the weather, are two notes: one says, "In the bandstand, Nan," and the other, written in a heavy pen on a piece of curling birch bark, "Back Soon."

The front door opens easily. Inside, in the tiny entrance hall, there is a stairway leading straight up to a small bedroom. To the right there is a step down into what was the workshop with its now missing tools, although there are still the worn brooms and on a hook an old straw hat. To the left is a step down into the living room, piled now with debris, the detritus of two lives. Behind a narrow door just to the right is a tiny bathroom complete with shower and flush toilet, water furnished by a push-pull pump that used pressure to fill a tank. Off the sitting area is a one-person-sized kitchen with rough pine cupboards and, in the sink, a single tap.

There is no electricity, no telephone, no signs of more than rudimentary conveniences, no solar panels, no windmill. In the pile of things to be discarded are several kerosene lamps. The heat came from the wood-fired stove in the corner, old and battered and inefficient; a stove that needed feeding several times a night, a friend of theirs tells me. Perishables were kept cool by lowering them into the well in a bucket. The Kellams wanted no machinery that would require fuel beyond the kerosene and gas lamps. On the cold cement floor is a worn Oriental carpet.

We paw with a kind of reverential timidity through what is left—the dusty boxes, the old file folders—looking at a letter here, a receipt there, postcards from friends in the 1940s and 1950s; picking up the books thought too worthless to take: an airplane design manual; a series entitled *Finding One's Place in Life: The Foundation Stones of Success,* printed in 1917 by the Howard Severance Co.; *Marius the Epicurean* by Walter Pater, MacMillan and Co., Limited, London, 1924. An essayist, critic, and scholar, Pater was a leading figure in the Victorian aesthetic movement.

Inside Pater's book, on a yellowed order blank for the *Atlantic Monthly,* there is a pencil notation: "Pt.4-Chapter 20 p. 244." I am looking now for clues to what made them come here, what kept them here, what ideas or principles shaped their lives. I turn to the page, anticipating a revelation, and read:

> A highly refined modification of the acroama—a musical performance during supper for the diversion of the guests—was presently heard hovering round the place, soothingly, and so unobtrusively that the company could not guess, and did not like to ask, whether or not it had been designed by

their entertainer. They inclined on the whole to think it some wonderful peasant music peculiar to that wild neighborhood, turning, as it did now and then, to a solitary reed-note, like a bird's, while it wandered into the distance. It wandered quite away at last, as darkness with a bolder lamplight came on, and made way for another sort of entertainment. An odd, rapid, phantasmal glitter, advancing from the garden by torchlight, defined itself, as it came nearer, into a dance of young men in armour.

What does it mean? What did they need from that passage?

Here they lived; on this small island where they vowed not to cut a living tree or harm an animal, and so used only the trees the wind had blown down for firewood, letting the deer roam free and posting signs against poachers. Here they lived. In this tiny cramped space. The two of them. Winter and summer. Day after day. On peanuts and sardines, if their rubbish is to be believed, and on what they grew in the garden—although I am told that they did not like gardening or fighting the deer for their produce and eventually gave it up, relying on canned goods and the bread Nan made as Arthur read to her.

Their allegiance to frugality was impressive. A friend tells me of metal measuring spoons that were mended and remended with solder and small rivets; of the bedspread that wore patches on patches, as did their clothing. Nothing wasted. Scavenging the harvest of the sea on the stone beaches. Reshaping found objects for their use.

They were not unsociable. They welcomed the visitors they knew. They asked that someone come ahead of the party so that, forewarned, they could change into better clothing. From time to time friends brought ice cream, or chocolate, which they loved. Then they were alone again. Alone with the books they read over and over; with Walter Pater's solitary reed-note, like a bird's, phantasmal glitter in the garden by torchlight and the impression of young men in armor; and with each other. Alone with the memories of the things Arthur had done in the war that he couldn't or wouldn't talk about. Alone here, and in the bandstand.

Rick promises to show it to us as we leave. A friend brought them a primitive sawmill, and from fallen logs they fashioned the boards from which it is built. They used it for picnics and allowed intrepid visitors to sleep there from time to time. It is best seen, he says, from the water.

Before leaving the island, we wander to the end of the fine pebble beach. Two currents meet here, forming a sharp line of foam. Beneath the water, white barnacle-covered rocks look like pale apparitions. This land has been pushed, not simply into a geographical point, but into a powerful place where the energy from the currents and the winds meets and the pulse quickens. Off to the left is Great Gott, with its comfortable cluster of white frame cottages—almost within yelling distance, but not quite.

As we pull away, Rick points to a low cliff where an octagonal gazebo sits with a full view of the beach and Great Gott and the island-dotted sea: The Bandstand.

When Arthur was taken seriously ill with pneumonia, Nan thought of the flagpole. For the first time, they needed help. She went to the shore with their flag but couldn't raise it: the mechanism had rusted. She stood helpless, wondering what to do. The captain of the small ferry that delivers goods and mail to Gotts Island looked up on his return trip, saw her there, and radioed for help. A doctor was sent, and Arthur was eased down the path in a wheelbarrow, across the cobbled wet spots, through the moss and the pine needles to the tender; rowed out to the boat; and then, on Mount Desert Island, taken to the hospital where he had a stroke and died almost at once.

Nan stayed on in the house after Arthur's death, but he had taken such care of her that she didn't know even how to replace a flashlight battery. A friend installed a solar panel to give her a light she could switch on. Fishermen ferried supplies. She held out for three years, doing what she had always done. When her mind and body grew undependable, friends took her to a nursing home where she has a view of the sea.

I FIRST HEARD about the Kellams in 1987, when Nan was still by herself on the island. One evening, while I ate a late supper in a neighborhood restaurant, the owner's brother sat down and told me the essence of their story. Of course I was intrigued. The idea of living a simple, solitary life has universal appeal, if only to judge by the enduring popularity of Thoreau's *Walden*. But few have the courage to take up such a life or the fortitude to stick with it.

I said at once that I would like to talk to her, and he drew back a bit, concerned that he might have said more than he should to a person "from away," as I would likely forever be classified, having moved to Maine only a year earlier. I didn't press, but the story stayed in the back of my mind as one of those strands that just might one day fit somewhere. Almost twelve years would pass before I would visit Placentia.

It would have been so easy to get the story right then. Now, when it was most important, I was reduced to picking at the frayed threads of the Kellam's lives, turning over scraps in a deserted house, foraging for clues in the memories of those who had known them. That was a discovery in itself: finding all their plentiful friends, many of whom did not know the others existed, but all of whom felt close to this unusual couple.

Then I discovered that Nan was still alive. One of my good friends had not only known her for years but took a proprietary interest in her well-being still, and visited her frequently in the nursing home where she now lived.

She created silence around her there, complaining of the television and the intercom announcements and "the white people," named for their uniforms. She would like to leave, I was told. No one who went to see her, and I was discovering almost daily more and more who did so, was quite sure how clear her mind was now. Some days were better than others. I took a chance and made my own visit.

She sat at a table in the dining room, waiting for a meal that would be served in an hour or so, a small, plumpish woman wearing a nondescript sweatshirt I felt could never have been her own choice. Introducing myself and hoping that she would not be frightened, I attempted—total stranger that I was—to engage her in conversation. The results were mixed. Her voice was so low as to be nearly inaudible, but her answers, when she chose to give them, were perfectly reasonable. We spoke of their daily life, of making bread and other things. I came away glad I had made the effort and feeling I had a better—if still imperfect—idea of what their lives had been like.

I discovered that my friend had photographs of Nan and Art and the house in better days. She had visited them on the island a number of times. She invited me over, made tea, and we looked at snapshots.

There was Nan, not the almost bloated woman she seems now, fleshed out from bad food and inactivity, but a tiny woman with the carriage of a dancer and that birdlike, upturned tilt of the head often seen in people who spend their lives looking up. And Art, cigarette between fingers, in a denim jacket that looks like a seventies castoff, has a lean and weathered face and the look of a good mechanic, or one of those infamous American soldiers in wartime Europe who could repair a jeep with a bobby pin.

There are photographs of the front of the house, with ferns growing lushly around the porch, flowers in a border. A view of the back of the house shows a fenced-in yard with a wonderful, rustic gate made, it seems, of bent alders. The grass is neatly mown.

The pictures transformed what had been the scent of decay and abandonment into something that once again felt alive. Of course, I needed and
wanted more. Frustration gnawed. I was too late. The details of meaning
and motivation were missing, perhaps forever lost. Why had the engineer,
the designer of warplanes, the technologist, left technology behind?

When I had asked why she and Arthur moved to a remote Maine island
after the war, Nan had uttered a single, cryptic sentence: "He had government papers." When pressed, she began to make a repetitive sound, as if
sorry she had spoken. It was not an answer, simply another missing piece.

Then my friend admitted that she had been entrusted with Nan's diaries.
They were clearly meant for publication. My friend allowed me a look. I
pored greedily over Nan's clear, unaffected script, reliving, as she had
intended her future readers to do, the couple's thoughts and emotions as
they prepared to change their lives. What they wanted, she wrote, was "to
leave behind the battle for non-essentials and the burden of abundance and
to build in the beauty of this million-masted island a simple home and an
uncluttered life."

They planned their adventure, Arthur collecting U.S. Ordinance Survey
maps. They spotted Swans Island—then found Placentia. It had everything
they thought they would need: fresh water, a good building site. They could
see by the brown shading on the map that it had interesting contours and at
its highest point rose 135 feet above sea level. It was a half-mile from the
next island; far enough from the mainland to offer privacy; and, most important, "free of the black dots that meant habitation." That Christmas they
tied the deed to the top of their Christmas tree.

Months were spent in preparation, selling what they wouldn't need and
buying the basic tools and supplies they would need. Finally, "at three
o'clock on the twenty-third of May, Art cashed in his last salary check, then
we made a little round of calls, paying respects to civilization before turning
our backs upon it. About midnight, still going smooth and steady, we crossed
the first state line, the same two people on the way to a different world."

In this new life, "there would be room enough and time for unscheduled
work and lots of solitude where the spending of the days would become a
spontaneous, not a socially controlled affair. We hoped to build a simple
house and a simple life, to learn to appreciate fundamental things and carry
on without the expensive diverting complications of modern civilized existence. Hard work and thrift could lead to peace."

Forty years of solitude. Forty years of winter storms and late springs and hungry mosquitoes. Forty years of canned sardines. Forty years of reading to each other.

"What did he read to you?" I had asked her.

"It was always the right thing," she answered.

When it was over—my visit with Nan had confirmed what I already suspected—there was only the longing to have it last forty more.

CUT OFF so sharply from comfort and community, Nan and Arthur Kellam would have seemed odd, even genuinely eccentric, in any age. They seem especially so in ours, when reliance on technology is so universal, so unquestioningly accepted by most people as an important part of who we are. The Kellams had reduced their lives to a level of primitivism—living without electricity, telephone, refrigerator, without internal-combustion engines of any sort—that most Westerners today would find inconceivable. Most of our lives are so intertwined with the mechanical that it is often difficult to decide where one leaves off and the other begins. The driver and the car move with a fluid synchronicity, not two things, but a unit; the nail gun becomes an extension of the carpenter's hand; the computer and the mind tango. From morning until the electric light is snapped off and on into darkness, from refrigerator to furnace to alarm clock, the motors hum and whir, never far away—the background music of modernity.

In the life they chose to lead on Placentia Island, the Kellams can be counted as an extreme example of individuals who consciously and determinedly turn their backs on that familiar world; who actively resist the lure of the mechanical and the ease it can provide, and who spurn the seductive consumer culture. Intentionally distancing themselves from the "diverting complications of modern civilized existence," as Nan Kellam called them, they lived alone on their island. Yet they did not so much reject technology as *choose* simplicity and independence. They did so as part of a principled approach to what they considered the serious and worthy business of living the examined life. It was a practice that had moral overtones and was carried out with a level of commitment that seems almost religious in spirit— although religion, in its traditional forms, had little or no place in their lives.

I had been interested in the Kellams for years, but so had many others. "She kept them alive," someone told me, dramatically, about a woman who visited them often. Thinking their diet nutritionally poor, she made it her business to bring them better, healthier food. Others watched out for them in various ways, helping them to get what they needed, willing to lend a hand when necessary, all from a respectful distance. The Kellams had a cushion, quietly arranged by others, that made their lives a bit easier. It was as if these supporters had an investment in the experiment on Placentia, and in this interest and support, I believe, there was more than simply curiosity. People liked the Kellams; liked being with them; felt it an honor, even, to be counted as their friends. Perhaps the Kellams were doing what their admirers had thought about doing, what they might have done if they had not been tied so tightly to comfort and convenience, so weighed down by conventionality and social expectations. Perhaps it was simply an admiration, tinged with a bit of envy, for individuals who could lead lives based on principle without wavering. Such a fierce dedication to an idea, the Kellams had!

YET, HOWEVER extreme the Kellams might seem, they are unique in neither their actions nor their thinking. They are, in fact, part of a small but tenacious tradition that has its roots far back in history. It's fair to say that every mechanical or technological innovation has been met with resistance by some element of the population.

My subject is technology resisters. It is not a mellifluous term. It seems as awkward and as alienating as technology itself can be, the grinding of verbal gears. But both the Kellams and the notorious Unabomber Ted Kaczynski fit in there somewhere, without apology, and it's not easy to find another word or phrase that stretches that far. The Amish and the Mennonites fit in there as well, but so do the protestors who are willing to risk arrest and injury to destroy genetically engineered test crops.

Thinking seriously about the social and economic implications of technology picked up steam with the quickening pace of technological development itself, with the engines of the industrial revolution. The roots of modern technology resistance are in the original Luddites, a loose-knit group of protestors who in a brief rebellion in the early 1800s smashed the factory machinery of growing industrialism. As a theme, resistance to technology appears in Romantic and Victorian literature, in transcendentalism, in the Arts and Crafts movement, the agrarian movement, the environmental movement. It is present today in the writers who cling to their typewriters; the fine cabinetmakers who cherish their old tools; the hand-weavers and basket-makers and potters and needlework enthusiasts who keep to their craft against all logic; the herbalists and organic growers who are convinced that what they do is important and brook no argument—all those who cling consciously in whatever manner or degree to the old ways. Although there are obvious exceptions, more often than not resisting comes down to individual decisions: whether to have a television or a cell phone or a microwave oven; whether to drive a car; whether to heat with wood instead of oil.

Today there are conscious resisters around the globe, sometimes aware of one another, sometimes not. Some consistent ways of thinking are embraced by all these individuals, and for all the difference between violence and non-violence, there are common, bedrock principles that link them to a venerable history. Most, wherever they are, carry out their resistance quietly, without public announcement, without any desire to be noticed. In our time, resisting technology—given its virtually unquestioned acceptance as an integral part of modern life, coupled with widespread appreciation of its benefits—is a profoundly radical act (often by normally very unradical people). Such resistance can generate open hostility for the simple reason that technophiles, or those who for whatever reason have cast their lot unwaveringly with technology, understand that the act of resisting is a quiet but determined rejection of the very principles that undergird Western culture: efficiency, industrialism, sometimes science, and usually capitalism or at least commercialism, and most certainly materialism. Resisters mock all that.

Resisters become living critics of the culture, their very presence and ways of life seen as an open expression of disapproval by those who have given their relationship to technology little thought at all—or if they have given it thought, have come up with no reason to reject it or even to question it. At best, resisters are considered cranks; at worst, threatening or even dangerous. And yet, as the sense grows that technology must no longer go unquestioned, the podium is taken by a new breed of enlightened technophiles, such as Bill Joy, whose now-famous article in *Wired* magazine in 1999 raised the specter of a future, no longer distant and imagined, in which the robots or the self-replicating nanotechnologies take over. At the other end of the political spectrum, Francis Fukuyama, in *Our Posthuman Future: Consequences of the Biotechnology Revolution,* braves the wrath of the scientific-industrial complex—which can be punishing—to ask whether we might be creating a future in which human personality has been standardized with psychotropic drugs and human reproduction has become industrialized and commodified. It is a future, he suggests, in which no one would actually wish to live. It can be avoided, he proposes, by evaluating new technologies using a new set of standards based on human values. Fukuyama acknowledges the paradoxical nature of human inventiveness—the belief that for all our cleverness, technological development is not within our power to stop; that somehow we are predestined to move unthinkingly into whatever world scientific innovation can devise. This would imply that we are not, in fact, in control, that something else is; that cleverness has a life of its own beyond consciousness—a troubling conclusion that few seem to care to consider. Fukuyama disagrees: "We do not have to regard ourselves as slaves to inevitable technological progress when that progress does not serve human ends." [1]

Technology resisters are convinced of that. Curiously, it is they, and not the technophiles, who retain their faith in human ability.

There are also those for whom resisting technology may not be overt; it may be thought of as secondary to the primary goal, and yet it lurks in the background. Loggers in northern Maine in late 1998 blocked border crossings with their trucks and skidders to keep out Canadian workers who were taking their jobs. But they were also protesting Canadian logging practices that favored the feller-bunchers, great machines that cut, strip, and bundle a tree as if it were as fragile as a stalk of hay. These machines not only allow one man to do the work of five but facilitate the wholesale destruction of the forests—which the American loggers recognized would eventually leave them with no jobs at all. The essence of their protest, then, was against the machine.

In a similar spirit, protestors in Great Britain lived for extended periods in tree houses or excavated tunnels, risking arrest and physical harm, to block the construction of a motorway near Winchester that would destroy an area of special beauty and cultural importance. Indigenous people of Canada and Chinese peasants alike have actively challenged the building of dams that will destroy their traditional lands, tear apart their history, and disrupt their lives. Villagers in India have wrapped themselves around trees to protect them from loggers; in America's northwestern forests, individuals —Julia Butterfly Hill is the best known—have lived for astonishingly long periods high in the trees to keep them from being downed. Japanese activists challenged the building of a new runway at the Narita airport. In Great Britain, fields of genetically engineered crops have been pulled again and again, the perpetrators risking jail. Virtually around the world, individuals are putting their bodies on the line, and at the bottom of each protest is an invading technology that puts at risk something considered of great importance.

Some protests are literary and quietly express a real longing for a beauty relinquished to modernization. In his essay "In Praise of Shadows," Junichiro Tanizaki, who died in 1965, wrote of his longing for the lost corners of darkness that were once characteristic of Japanese interiors, lost as Western technology abolished shadows with electric lights. Perhaps, he says wistfully, "we may be allowed at least one mansion where we can turn off the electric lights and see what it is like without them." Other writers reveal a yearning to recapture the sense of self as a physical and mental entity, lost or misplaced in the alienation of modern life. In his essay "An Entrance to the Woods," Wendell Berry writes of a growing sense of serenity as he becomes accustomed, on a foray into the forest, to the lack of human company and of technology. "I am alive in the world, this moment, without the help or the interference of any machine. I can move without reference to anything except the lay of the land and the capabilities of my own body. . . . I am reduced to my irreducible self." Common to both writers is a profound sense of loss and an awareness that technology has a way of coming between the individual and feelings that cannot be measured or charted or counted but are nevertheless treasured.

Modern technology clearly does threaten what people value, whether it is a way of life, or a way of thinking, or an ecosystem, or beauty—or even simply tranquility. It would seem that to live peacefully should be considered a basic right, yet we only rarely acknowledge the extent to which technology has usurped that right with confounding and deafening noise to which individuals are expected to adapt. Irritating, mechanical sound can simply, in and of itself, drive people mad. In the late 1990s, residents of the Minor Road Heights housing project near the end of the runway at the airport in Louisville, Kentucky, found the noise of constantly landing planes so unbearable that one man said publicly that he was "ready to take out guns and shoot them."

These are desperate people, says Chellis Glendinning, author of *When Technology Wounds*, "seeking to protect the livelihoods, communities, and families we love, which lie on the verge of destruction."[2] Their protests are rarely successful. Technology is a juggernaut: powerful, determined and seemingly unstoppable. The construction of the motorway in Great Britain eventually went forward. The residents of Minor Road were relocated and the airport expanded. The rare successes get attention—fleetingly. The removal of a dam in Maine to let the river flow unimpeded so that the fish might breed again received worldwide media coverage. But in general, the protests fail. Yet the failures have little deterrent effect on subsequent actions and may, in fact, raise the stakes.

A few hours before dawn in late autumn of 1998, fires lit the night sky over Vail, Colorado, a resort town and a winter playground for the superrich. An e-mail message to the press followed:

> On behalf of the lynx, five buildings and four ski lifts at Vail were reduced to ashes on the night of Sunday, October 18. . . . Putting profits ahead of Colorado's wildlife will not be tolerated. This action is just a warning. We will be back if this greedy corporation "Vail Resorts Inc" continues to trespass into wild and unroaded areas.

The signature: Earth Liberation Front (ELF).

The impetus for the attack? A week earlier the courts had rejected a legal challenge by local environmentalists, who had attempted to halt a planned expansion of development in the area. The environmentalists had argued that more development would undermine the planned reintroduction of the lynx, which it was felt needed wild, open land to survive and thrive.

The attack was an example of what the news media like to call ecoterrorism, although it is property, not people, against which the actions were directed, and the label seems intentionally designed to put such protests and actions, even when nonviolent, into a category that will inflame public opinion and arouse opposition. Today, when the word *terrorist* inspires both fear and hatred, its application is virtually a death sentence, although one could argue that an excessively liberal application of the label may tend to dilute its power.

Technology resisters can include, at one end of a spectrum, those who do more questioning than rejecting—and I put myself in that category—as well as, at the other end, those who go to violent extremes in their rage against the modern technological world and the degradation it has caused the planet. In between fall the traditional technology resisters: certain religious groups; the environmentalists who see technology and industrialism as responsible for impending ecological disaster; the "simple livers" who reject consumerism and materialism; the "back-to-the-landers" who attempt to recreate an agrarian relationship to nature that rejects the factory approach to farming as unsustainable and unsupportable; craftsmen and craftswomen, laborers, loggers, and fishermen who see technology and its corporate life-support system as threatening their way of working and their communities; and intellectual Luddites, who have studied the literature and history of technology and industrialism and find little to be optimistic about. Technology resistance can be expressed in ways that are negative and destructive, passive and separatist, or positive and creative.

There are overlaps throughout the tradition. Helen and Scott Nearing, whose *Good Life* series of books inspired several generations of back-to-the-landers, arrived at their approach to simple living through a complex mixture of religious belief (his rooted in a "muscular" Christianity, hers in Eastern mysticism); environmentalism; a political ideology that included socialist theory coupled with a strong support for working men, women, and children, a related rejection of capitalism and materialism; and all that undergirded by pacifism, vegetarianism, and a profound respect for the animal kingdom.

At the same time, the definition of technology resisters might well include groups on the far right who reject technology for entirely different reasons— usually because it breeds a kind of subservience to large systems controlled by government or corporate entities. But percolating beneath it all is a growing realization that we as a society are now completely dependent upon the hand on the electric switch, vulnerable to any whim and to anyone with reason to throw it. Some of us live comfortably with this notion; others find it positively threatening and struggle to protect themselves as best they can— thus the survivalist wing.

Some people, such as the Kellams, can withdraw and avoid the confrontation with technology, but for others, such as the dwellers at the end of the airport runway, technology has a curious ability to inspire rage. Whether it manifests itself in a repressed impulse, a momentary loss of control—perfectly sane friends tell me that other people's cell phone use, a balky piece of machinery, or an overly complex voice-mail system can push them dangerously close to the edge—or a planned attack depends entirely on the amount of alienation experienced by the individual. My own suspicion is that frustration with technology is a large part of what is collectively called "stress" and is responsible for far more violence in our society than we recognize.

If we look closely at the Kellams, the fact that technology played such a minor role in the way the they lived seems, at first, almost incidental—an accident or an afterthought. In fact, although spurning technology was not the primary goal, it was key. The Kellams understood that relying on machines—to the extent that they required a constant source of energy and demanded frequent attention—represented a loss of privacy, of independence, of simplicity, and of control; and, in creating noise, a loss of the silence they preferred. They understood that technologies come with hidden costs, and their apparent liberating effect, if the costs were properly tallied, can turn out to be an illusion. The automobile is liberating, for instance, but the cost of owning an automobile requires a servitude to what may be an unpleasant job that is anything but liberating. A gasoline-powered motor might have been nice, but there would have been the cost, the maintenance, the smell, the hideous sound—and, perhaps, the lure of too easy access. There was a price to be paid for convenience, and for this couple, it was too high.

What was truly odd about the Kellams—the aspect of their life that separates them from a good many of the rest of us—was that they lived so consciously. They looked closely at every object (or individual) that entered their territory and made judgments and decisions about whether each contributed to or distracted from a clearly defined way of living. This approach represents a conscious prioritizing of values and clear decisions about what was important, coupled with the discipline to resist.

To look at it in a slightly different way, the Kellams and others like them accord objects, mechanical or not, great power because they understand their potential to affect their lives. In a consumer society flooded with goods and technology, this is an unusual way of thinking. For most of us, the sole criterion for a new technology is "Is it useful?" or, perhaps more common today, "Does it enhance my image or my perception of myself in some way?" Seldom do we ask, "Precisely how will this thing, whatever it is, change my life and the lives of people around me, and will it be a good change in the long run?" And if we do consider these aspects of a technology, and find it wanting, how many of us have the will and the independence of spirit to resist, to make a conscious and positive choice to opt for an alternative that may be more demanding?

It would certainly be a mistake not to consider the appeal of new technologies. As humans, we are drawn to innovation, to cleverness, to novelty. Gadgetry fascinates, and the newest technologies are magical in their potential to amaze. There are technophiles for whom every new invention is a delightful toy; yet although true resisters are a minority, a great many ordinary people who would never think of themselves as radical have serious misgivings about the long-term benefit of this or that innovation. Some resist in small, symbolic ways: avoiding or rejecting one appliance or another, refusing some selected accoutrement of the plugged-in culture. Many more are simply resigned to what seems inevitable. "You can't stop progress," they say with a rueful shake of the head. Still others manage to put aside any concerns when the immediate benefits of a gadget or process seem to outweigh theoretical worries. For most people, it's not hard to accept the hum of the refrigerator and, with it, subservience to maintaining (at whatever cost) a steady supply of electricity, if the exchange means safer, more convenient, longer-lasting fresh food. A no-brainer, as they say. But not for the Kellams. They made do with a bucket in a well and turned it into a virtue.

On the trip out to the Kellams' island, I was very conscious of the GPS, the radar, and the powerful surge of the gasoline-driven engine of our boat. Yet Art and Nan rejected not simply the convenience but also the relative safety that technology could provide. As I looked down at their small rowboat now disintegrating high on the rocky beach, the contrast was sharply defined between the ease with which my group had reached the island and the laborious and dangerous trip it must have been for them. Their commitment to their chosen way of life hadn't simply meant abandoning ease and convenience; it also meant exposing themselves to serious risk. It was as if by accepting this risk they had moved a degree closer to the natural world, itself a place of no guarantees. They lived with a certain acceptance of danger as natural and inevitable; a danger that carried with it the ever-present and acceptable fact of death. And in accepting that certainty, they lived more freely.

To resist technology at whatever level and in whatever way represents a reality-based way of thinking that accords power and presence to objects. This way of thinking recognizes that the things we use are not merely benign but have the ability to shape those that use them and that far from being neutral, objects, tools, and machines reflect the society, the culture, the organizational structure, the politics, the economic ideology, and the sensibilities of those that create them. Thus, to turn on a computer is not the simple act it seems, but a gesture that accepts, either consciously or unconsciously, a particular view of reality and supports the particular economic, political, industrial, and commercial order that created the technology and finds it useful, whether one is aware of it or not. To say, as some environmentalists do as they delight in the convenience and communication potential of e-mail, that one is simply using the technology while rejecting the system behind it is to delude oneself. As they are using the e-mail and the computer, the computer is using them in ways that may be very subtle. It is positioning them at a desk, away from the world; reshaping their bodies and hands; refocusing their eyes; changing the way their minds work; adjusting their expectations; opening their communications to easy tracking and potential manipulation; exposing their computer to virus attacks; creating a history that may be unwelcome; allowing themselves to be inundated with commercial advertisements; and requiring that they earn enough to maintain the expensive equipment that requires constant maintenance and upgrades. The price of that instant, worldwide communication is very high indeed, and any thought that one is not, by using the computer, a full-fledged part of the system that produced the computer is an illusion. Less and less does it even remain an individual choice whether or not one cooperates with the increasingly computerized world. Almost daily the option not to participate becomes more of a struggle as expectations and demands are transformed. My telephone bill now says that no longer will the company respond to questions about my bill by mail. The only recourse is to contact them via the Internet. The degree to which this kind of action represents tyranny goes virtually unacknowledged and unquestioned.

There is an element of deconstruction in that thought process. And yet there is no one single political ideology associated with antitechnology groups. The movement, if anything so scattered and disorganized can be called that, is as anticommunist as it is anticapitalist, more libertarian than liberal—and still neither one nor the other. Scott Nearing, while remaining dedicated to the principle of simple living his entire life, early on rejected the Communist party—or, more likely, the Communist party rejected him as being too independent-minded. The World Socialist web site excoriated ELF for its arson in Vail, calling it a "reactionary political act." ELF, Earth

First!, and the Animal Liberation Front, wrote David Walsh for the online publication, are not left wing, but "are deeply misanthropic and view contemporary society itself with suspicion and hostility." Calling the group profoundly pessimistic and antisocial, Walsh writes:

> The anti-scientific, anti-rationalist core of this argument is clear. Support for these movements comes from a layer of the population that is repelled by the reality of modern capitalism, but sees no basis for transforming society in a progressive and humane fashion, and is generally hostile to the only social force capable of carrying through such a change, the working class . . .
>
> The targets of this hostility toward modern society are often those living in urban centers, who are viewed as a rapidly-multiplying mass, threatening to consume the earth's resources. The logic of this outlook pushes its proponents in the direction of extreme right-wing and even neo-fascist elements. There is an ideological link between the bleak pronouncements of Earth First!, Unabomber Theodore Kaczynski's rambling attacks on technology and the paranoid views of survivalist and Militia movements.

In a very real sense, Walsh is right. Sven Birkerts points out the same thing in *The Gutenberg Elegies*. The Luddite stance, he says, is out of favor among intellectually "progressive" people who "tend to equate technological primitivism, or recidivism, with conservatism of the N.R.A. stripe." Says Birkerts:

> The implication would seem to be that the new technology has a strictly liberal pedigree. But a moment's contemplation of the electronic ministries of the televangelists or resources of our Defense Department think tanks ought to disabuse of that notion. I don't think the technology question breaks down along conventional political lines.[3]

And, indeed, it doesn't. In fact, at this point it has rather open arms and no litmus tests.

And so who exactly is a technology resister? Most of us, if pressed, will admit to reservations about some product of modern science. Many of us have had the passing thought that for all its obvious advantages, technology has not lived up to its billing. Which one of us has not, at times, considered the role of technology in the declining quality of life; worried about the rising tide of chemical pollution and cancer; mourned a natural world that seems to be vanishing? Many of us wonder if the enthusiastic economic and political support for unimpeded technological advance is a wise thing; wonder if someone ought to be questioning more seriously and more loudly and to greater effect what might be undone, what might be forgotten, what might be lost in the process of unimpeded progress; and wonder whether those losses were truly what we had in mind. A general uneasiness arises today about the potential for loss of privacy and the possibilities of expanded government surveillance in the world of vast international databases and implanted microchips; about the Frankensteinian potential of uncontrolled biotechnology; about a robotic future in which the machine controls all. It is as if we have signed a progress contract without reading the fine print.

And what, after all, is technology? Is it a simple screw? Is it the wheel? Is it a printing press? Is it nuclear fission? Such questions and definitions have occupied writers and philosophers for a century now. No innovation is without impact, yet the effects are not equal. Some are more or less desirable than others. To think seriously about technology, it will be necessary to examine the nature of mechanical innovation, to look at which inventions have the potential to alleviate the unpleasant aspects of labor without damaging something important about human existence, to make some attempt to sort the good from the bad. Why, after all, does the Amish farmer choose the horse-drawn plow over the tractor? There is a reason. But there are different ideas about what constitutes "appropriate technology," and various groups have drawn the line in different places. Even within the Amish sects there are conflicting ideas. What is consistent is the thoughtfulness of approach. "Let us consider this innovation and what impact it will have on our lives," they say. "Let us ask, not simply what it will do, but what it will undo."

Technology resisters were once called Luddites. Today they—we, for in taking on this tale I admit my own concerns—are called neo-Luddites. We are united, writes Kirkpatrick Sale in his history of the Luddite uprising, by a simple set of beliefs.

> Luddism has meant a strain of opposition to the domination of industrial technology and to its values of mechanization, consumption, exploitation, growth, competition, novelty, and progress—a kind of solid indelible body of beliefs existing subaqueously as it were, refusing to be eroded by the sweeping tides of triumphant modernism. It is a strain of opposition, of naysaying, that has not been dispelled in all these decades by however many elaborate machines or more elaborate visions the technophiles have paraded.[4]

And yet Luddism turns out not simply to be against the machine but for something else: for that quality of humanness that the machine, in all its various manifestations, would overrule. To dig into the richness of literature following the Luddite uprising will be to discern the shape of protests against the machine and to find that they confirm those very qualities of being human. We will begin to discover that the machine and life are natural enemies and that to oppose the machine is, in fact, to opt for life in all its richness and variety.

Yet the word, the concept, the identity had its beginnings in a small band of men who refused to give in without a fight.

CHAPTER TWO

The Frame Breakers

THE WORD *Luddite* IS NEWLY TRENDY. IT FINDS ITS way into articles and essays at the elite edge of media consumption and is flung as a stylish insult at holdouts against this or that innovation or technology. It is usually meant as a lighthearted taunt of those who refuse or are unable to keep up with what is commonly referred to as progress. Applied to oneself, it is often a form of denial—as in, "I'm no Luddite," or, more often, faintly apologetic, as in "I'm no Luddite, but . . . " (a phrase that goes just before the admission that some technology or innovation is disliked or has been spurned). Although people who use and hear the word have clearly come to understand its general meaning—it connotes a misguided and hopeless attempt to resist technological innovation—it's a fair bet that few know precisely where the term came from.

Those who swore allegiance to Ned Ludd (or King Ludd) earned themselves the name, although precisely who he was remains a mystery. But whatever its origins, between 1811 and 1816, in the five central manufacturing counties of England—a triangle that included parts of Lancashire, Yorkshire, Cheshire, Derbyshire, Nottinghamshire, and Leicester—organized groups of men, under the Luddite banner, raised whatever weapons they could muster, from muskets and revolvers to hatchets and blacksmith hammers, and in furious reaction to the installation of new technology that was taking their jobs and disrupting their lives, smashed certain types of mechanical looms.

It was an uprising that frightened the establishment of the day. Government and business leaders in the stately halls of London who were drawing up the blueprints for a new industrialism could envision quite another future for the country: one of efficient mass production of cheaper goods, enhanced trade, and greater profit. The wants and needs of working families in the Midlands played only a small role in that vision. These workers were to be, as perhaps they had begun to suspect, merely cogs in the machinery of the industrial revolution. It was a role they chose to resist.

Here is what the Luddite reaction was not. It was not a mindless gesture of uncontrolled rage at the new. The stockingers, croppers, and shearers had first attempted to ameliorate the effects of the new machines in other, peaceful ways, with failed attempts at negotiating and bargaining. Their attacks were selective; they chose their targets for clearly defined reasons. And they were not simply reacting to the loss of jobs, but to something more: the loss of a way of life. They had good reason to be frustrated and angry.

Nevertheless, the government's suppression of the movement with troops was swift and brutal. The most intense period of the Luddite Rebellion, with its secret meetings and midnight machine-smashing and factory-torching raids, was brief and apparently futile. Yet sympathy for both the workers' plight and the principle behind their actions has endured for nearly two hundred years—in literature and thinking, but also in the popular imagination, as evidenced by the bumper strip seen not long ago that said, simply, "Ned Ludd Lives."

IN 1996, author Kirkpatrick Sale stood before a public forum and performed a similarly iconoclastic, seemingly irrational, and apparently quixotic act: he smashed a computer. It might have been designed to draw attention to his new book, *Rebels Against the Future: The Luddites and Their War on the Industrial Revolution*. It was also intended to make the connection between resisting technology then and resisting it now. Sale's computer smashing was a gesture that resonated with historical meaning, harking back to a time when such a challenge to the introduction of a powerful technology had been taken very seriously indeed. But few reporters who covered the smashing had likely read his book or fully appreciated the connections he was trying to make. Reactions in the press tended to see the gesture as amusing and quaintly eccentric. The computer is a device that every major enterprise now depends upon absolutely. The personal computer has, within a generation, moved from clever novelty to a position of indisputable dominance at both work and home. Computer technology is behind everything, and is now too embedded in our society to be questioned lightly. We are wedded to the computer, dependent upon it as if it were a respirator tube, the removal of which now has potentially severe and unpleasant—perhaps life-threatening—consequences. And that is understood if not consciously, then at some level. Abolishing the computer now seems, to the working world, inconceivable, and so with his computer-smashing gesture, Sale became a curiosity—a crank.

But the revolt of that long-ago rebellious English lot, and Sale's sympathetic gesture today, has resonance and meaning still. Technology should not go unquestioned, Sale was saying. It should not be complacently accepted without a thorough evaluation of its potential impact on ordinary lives, on human communities, and on the natural world. At the very least, the consequences of introducing a technology should be thoroughly understood so that trade-offs can be consciously considered. And it may well turn out that from time to time a technology needs to be protested, resisted, or rejected if its effects are found to be unacceptable or its costs too high. That is what Sale was trying to say, and that is what the Luddites did, with an anguished howl that echoes down the corridors of time.

THE ORIGINAL rebellion began in the same area of England as the long-vanished Sherwood Forest, that deep and mysterious grove that had served as backdrop and source of the mythical Robin Hood tales. The locally popular tradition, a familiar story repeated generation after generation, gave inspiration and encouragement to the impulse of the region's inhabitants to violate the law for the sake of the common good. The Luddites were fully conscious that they were venturing down a road "trod by an earlier set of courageous troublemakers," says Sale; they even identified letters as being posted from "Robin Hood's Cave" or "Ned Ludd's office, Sherwood Forest." [1] They were not true revolutionaries, not born and bred activists, but skilled workingmen—artisans rather than factory workers—who had become the victims of a process that was beginning to be called progress. The industrial revolution was not yet a concept; it was instead a radical and ongoing transformation, a taking-over of essential functions by machines, with all that implies, and it was affecting people's lives. Although many clearly saw the benefits of more efficient production and the appeal of transferring backbreaking work to inanimate gears and wheels, there were others who saw equally clearly that the order of things, an order that was not altogether unpleasant, would be forever changed. The energy and the pace of change allowed about as much tolerance for anyone who stood in the way as the new locomotives that accompanied industrialism would have for a duck on the tracks.

It was a time not unlike our own, when change was coming at a frantic pace; when the scent of cataclysm could be caught in the hiss and grease and grinding gears of impending modernism. Nothing—nothing—would be as it had been, and the rebellion was a desperate cry amid the clanging and crashing of metal on metal that heralded a new age. There seemed to be no precedent for the steam-driven mills and the factories and ironworks that were appearing so rapidly and creating a presence as nothing before them had. It was as if they had sprung fully formed, suddenly and without warning, steaming and blazing forth from some mysterious and godlike source, so powerful did they seem.

Anne Seward, a poet known as the "Swan of Lichfield," where she spent most of her life, had written earlier, in the late eighteenth century, of the ironworks at Coalbrookdale on the River Severn, a landscape she remembered in her poem of that name for "thy grassy lanes, thy woodwild glens, / Thy knolls and bubbling wells, thy rocks, and streams," now invaded by a belching monster—a Cyclops, she called it—that could not be ignored. Yet even within this description of a scene of violation there is a certain begrudging acknowledgment of awe at this instrument of utter transformation that could paint hills red and change the very nature of the sky.

> . . . hear, in mingled tones,
> Shout their throng'e barge, their pond'rous engines clang
> Through thy coy dales; while red the countless fires,
> With umber'd flames, flicker on all thy hills,
> Dark'ning the Summer's sun with columns large,
> Of thick, sulphureous smoke, which spread, like palls,
> That screen the dead, upon thy sylvan robe
> Of thy aspiring rocks; pollute thy gales,
> And stain thy glassy waters.

The second decade of the nineteenth century was also a time of political and economic tension in England. The country was still at war with Napoleon. Trade blockades and embargoes limited the export of fabric and apparel, which in turn hurt the areas of England where these goods were produced. And a series of laws meant to contain and control any sympathetic Jacobin impulses or other subversive ideas created further resentment.

These were turbulent times. It didn't take much, in the eighteenth and early nineteenth centuries in England, to bring on a riot. Tom Paine's *Common Sense* had been printed in America in 1776 to give support for American independence, but it was well known in England. Paine's *Rights of Man,* written in 1791 and 1792, was a blueprint for an egalitarian society. In it he emphasized that most of the order that prevails in a country is not the result of government but of a complex interdependency and trust, a kind of natural order, that exists among its people. Government had been heavy-handed: "Instead of consolidating the society, it divided it; it deprived it of its natural cohesion."[2] And in 1794 and 1795, Paine's *Age of Reason,* by challenging the authority of the Bible, did for theology what his earlier writings had done for government. Paine seriously undermined any inclination on the part of the people to feel a particular obligation to authority from whatever source, political or religious.

It is hard today to envision how radical these books were. Ordinary individuals felt empowered by Paine's words both to think for themselves and to stand up for rights they'd hardly known they had. Although banned, copies had always been available—a common method of obtaining it was to select a book from a bookseller's cart, then give the vendor twice the price, whereupon he would slip a copy of one of Paine's books into the parcel. Paine's writing had helped crystallize concepts of liberty, representative government, and human rights in the minds of a good portion of the population—even as the ruling class wished him in jail or worse. Even twenty years later, as the new machines began to appear, a perceptible residue of Paineite radicalism remained.

At the same time, grievances against enclosures, press-gangs, bread prices, tolls, excise taxes, and new machinery all could be "reason enough" to take to the streets in protest. "The British people were noted throughout Europe for their turbulence, and the people of London astonished foreign visitors by their lack of deference," notes the historian E. P. Thompson in *The Making of the English Working Class.*[3] Some of these uprisings were organized by outsiders and were deliberate attempts to rouse the mob to create political pressure for reform, but others were spontaneous direct actions by frustrated individuals. Of this latter type, bread and food riots were most common, and the protests, sometimes culminating in the looting of shops, were "legitimized," says Thompson, "by the assumptions of an older moral economy, which taught the immorality of any unfair method of forcing up the price of provisions by profiteering upon the necessities of the people."[4] Workers expected that wages set and agreed upon would be suffi-cient to cover basic necessities—this was only right and just, part of the unwritten contract between master and worker—and the idea that prices would rise and fall according to supply and demand, a bedrock assumption of a developing market economy, was not a concept that had yet taken hold in the minds of ordinary working folk. Any sudden increase in prices was thus a reason to riot.

But whatever the cause of the unrest, the government was nevertheless relentless in its attempt to control and isolate expressions of disaffection whenever and wherever they arose. Not every effort demanded soldiers, however. Individuals or groups could be tarnished by mere accusations of treasonous conspiracy or by exaggerating the threat of insurrection with wild allegations—some generated by infiltrators from within the dissident movements themselves. "In a sense," says Thompson, "the government *needed* conspirators to justify the continuation of the repressive legislation which prevented nation-wide popular organization."[5]

It was in this atmosphere that the Luddite Rebellion had its beginnings. The government's oppressive surveillance and infiltration led to such in-creases in secrecy within the dissident groups that it was sometimes diffi-cult for them to operate at all. Suspicion ran riot; many were suspected of double-dealing. Thus there are no personal reminiscences, no periodicals, no meeting minutes—unfortunately for us. With government spies every-where, looking for evidence, watching the post, the risk was simply too great and remained so. When Luddism became a hanging offense, secrets were kept for forty years or more. To have announced oneself a Luddite, even after the rebellion had ended, would certainly have attracted unwanted attention from the law. Thus the stories, the songs, the memories of the rebellion were not committed to paper but "were handed down as a secret tradition," Thompson tells us, sung or told to grandchildren.[6] What is known of the actual rebellion, therefore, is mainly from secondary sources or from its

opposition or from the occasional anonymous letter to the newspaper claim-
ing (and likely) to be from the followers of Ned Ludd.

And who was this King Ludd? There is no definitive answer but any number of competing ideas. Various individuals in the uprising seemed to have
used the name as a pseudonym, applying "General" or "King" in front of it
with ironic humor. In 1811, the *Nottingham Review* had itself offered an
explanation, saying that a reluctant weaving apprentice named Ned Ludd
had been beaten for refusing to work and, in retaliation, had taken a hammer and smashed his knitting machine. He was given credit, thereafter, for
any smashed machinery: "Ned Ludd must have done it," was probably said
with a wink and a nudge. This story has variations, and there are other expla-
nations besides: attempts to link Ludd to a real King Lud reputed to be
fierce in battle, or even to an early King Ludeca, about whom little is known
but whose kingdom of Mercia was in the Midlands region. There is also a
Cumbrian phrase using the word *lud* to mean heap. None of these explana-
tions seems entirely satisfactory. Perhaps all are true in the way meanings
and associations have of blending. But Luddite, with its onomatopoetic resonance, seems a good name for a machine smasher, in any case.

Those who organized the Luddite Rebellion were for the most part among
the aristocracy of the weaving industry: men who were called croppers and
shearers and those who operated the knitting frames. The first two classes,
highly skilled artisans, were facing the inevitable introduction of two
machines—the gig mill and the shearing frame—that could essentially eliminate the need for their work. No one supposed that these machines could
do the job as well—but they could do it. And inevitably the decision would
be made that the higher quality cloth produced by the craftsmen was simply
not worth paying for if an acceptable substitute could be produced by
mechanical means at far less cost.

It was not as if, at the first sign of the new machines, the croppers and
shearers simply took to the streets. They had attempted to negotiate compromises with the factory owners over a long period. They had proposed a
more gradual introduction of the machines, with alternative work found for
the displaced men. A tax per yard was proposed that could raise money for
a fund to help those made redundant who were trying to find work. The
workers had raised between ten thousand and twelve thousand pounds—an
astonishing amount for the times and coming from people of such modest
means. This was used to hire solicitors to put their case before Parliament

and to represent them before the committees charged with regulating the industry. It was to no avail. The factory owners, their hand strengthened by new laws restricting worker "combination" or unionization and collective bargaining (which was seen as another form of seditious activity), forced the issue, pressing their advantage. Thompson describes the farce that they and their representatives met with when they presented their case to the newly formed committee appointed to inquire into the woolen trade:

> It would be a sad understatement to say that the men's witnesses before the 1806 Committee met with a frosty reception. They and their counsel were browbeaten and threatened by the advocates of *laissez faire* and the anti-Jacobin tribunes of order. Petitions were seen as evidence of conspiracy. Witnesses whom the croppers had sent to London and maintained at such expense were interrogated like criminals. . . . It was held to be an outrageous offence that they had collected money from outside their own ranks and had been in contact with the woolen workers of the west. They were forced to reveal the names of their fellow officers. Their books were seized. Their accounts were scrutinized. The Committee dropped all pretence of judicial impartiality, and constituted itself into an investigative tribunal.[7]

The very effort and efficiency the men had put into presenting their case was used against them. Clearly the ability to organize to that degree and to that level of efficiency made them dangerous to the factory owners and the government. Pitt's Two Acts, which had suspended habeas corpus and banned seditious meetings, had expired in 1795, then been reinstated for another year. Any form of organized activity among groups remained illegal, although meetings could be called. Oaths and secret societies were illegal as well. The workers were squeezed on the one side by economics and on the other by an oppressive government. The middle was an uncomfortable place to be. To the government, the group of weavers—although they had taken pains to operate in the open and, they thought, within the law—represented a potential force that could be called into action. In response, the smart thing was instead to operate quietly and out of sight. One more petition was presented and rejected. In 1809 all the protective laws, weak as they had been, were repealed, and with that, hopes were dashed. It was clear that there would be nothing to stop the gig mill or the shearing frame, or the employment of children and unskilled workers in the jobs—now in factories—that these men had once held.[8]

The cloth workers now understood precisely what they were up against.

It was little wonder that the idea of violent recourse began to form out of this frustration. But it was not an entirely new idea. There was, in fact, a long tradition of machine-breaking, although usually the rationale had been to express resentment at some unresolved grievance rather than to direct anger against the machines themselves. As Thompson points out, it had included not only the destruction of looms and materials but the filling of pits, the damaging of pit-head gear, even the burning of houses of unpopular employers. Now the focus changed.

In the end, the charge was first led not by the woolen workers, who had carried their grievances to London, but by the framework knitters, or stockingers. And it was not just a reaction to the machines. The Luddite effort grew out of events that were transforming and challenging individual lives, certainly. But the rebellion is better understood as an armed resistance against the force these men saw threatening their collective way of life; a force that, in their own words, was "hurtful to commonality." As historian Malcolm Thomis has said, "If workmen disliked certain machines, it was because of the use to which they were being put, not because they were machines or because they were new,"9 an observation that puts the machines in a larger context.

These men had worked with machines before. But their trade had been a cottage industry, or at least local and modest. Many of the stockingers worked by themselves or in small village workshops—aligned with the small masters, as they were called, with only three or four looms, in control of their time and requiring, perhaps, the help of a child. Their raw materials had often come from nearby. Their lives during previous years of prosperity, have been described as pleasant, their houses and small gardens well tended, the families well dressed, their sitting rooms pleasantly furnished.

But conditions were changing rapidly. It was not so much a particular machine that raised the stockingers' ire but new patterns of labor forced upon them by unscrupulous middle men and the least principled hosiers who were substituting poor quality work, which could be sold more cheaply and so drove out the good. The men felt underpaid and ill-used. Cut-ups, or stockings sown together from knitted material woven on a wide loom, were being substituted for the fine seamless stockings that had once been the standard. But cheap stockings could be made efficiently and sold cheaply, and the less discerning customer hardly knew the difference or didn't care.

So the frames weren't attacked because they were new, but because they produced inferior goods that were undercutting those the stockingers produced. And just like the croppers, they felt that every law that had protected them was being ignored or repealed, and every attempt to redress the matter peacefully was being challenged.

In addition to the new machines, the centralization of work would become a matter of concern as well, clearly adding to the difficulty of the workers' situation. Call it the mindless application of the rule of efficiency demanded by the new machines, for they required a constant source of power. And so the factories first rose, five and six stories of brick, along the streams in the valleys. Then, when steam provided the power, they could be grouped in what would become larger centers of production near transportation. Because the new plants and machines were costly, they needed to be run continuously, and labor had to be found for that perpetual work, lit in the long winter evenings by the flicker of gaslight. But the new machines were easier to operate. Less strength and less skill were required. Each machine could do the work of six or seven men. Women and children could keep many of them going, although under brutal conditions and with lower wages. Family life was being destroyed. Skilled craftsmen were reduced to selling cheap goods on the street or accepting support from wives and children who labored within a pitiless system.

Economic circumstances contributed to the frustrations of the cloth workers. It had been a bad summer, first cold enough in June of 1811 to kill young plants with a heavy frost. Then it had turned hot and dry. It was the third year in a row of bad harvests, and to add to the troubles, much of the food produced went to feed the soldiers fighting—endlessly, it seemed— Napoleon, now in Portugal. To make matters worse, laws prevented the export of cotton stockings and handkerchiefs, and they were accumulating in the warehouses. Also, the fickle dictates of fashion had changed, requiring that knee-breeches and stockings be replaced with long trousers, thus reducing demand further. Work was thus scarce to begin with; then, to top it off, the owners of the new machines could employ a woman and a child to do what six men had done—and for less pay. The consequences: a week's wages could no longer—in the face of rising food prices—begin to feed a family properly. Oatmeal cooked in water, boiled potatoes: there was little else for the working poor. Desperation was in the air. There were other causes of woe, but the machines were identifiable symbols of what had gone wrong. The workers' once moderately comfortable lives seemed a vanishing dream without possibility of being recreated short of drastic action.

It is hard now to know what happened on those dark nights, in the huddled clandestine meetings in the hollows or the woods, but it is known that the first "frame-breaking" took place in the village of Burwell, not far from Nottingham. A band of men with blackened faces, assigned numbers instead of names, mustered, shouldered their weapons, and set off for the weaving shop of a man named Hollingsworth. They broke in and destroyed a half-dozen of what were probably lace-making machines. A few nights later they returned to finish the job, but Hollingsworth and his men were waiting. A young man, John Westley, was shot and killed trying to get in through a shutter, and—incensed that their "justifiable" violence would be met with "unjustifiable" violence—the workers broke into the factory and house and, after destroying furniture (the family and workers had slipped out the back), set the buildings alight.

As uncontrolled as these attacks appear, it is important to note that they were not entirely random. When frames began to be smashed, a very selective process was employed, says Thompson. The Luddites destroyed only those that produced inferior goods. Those on which stockings were properly made were left intact.

In the weeks that followed, there were other attacks on shops where the mechanical frames had been installed—as well as attacks on frames that were being transported out of the district for safe storage. A few days later, a thousand armed men marched into Sutton and broke between thirty and seventy frames. The factory owners felt besieged. The local magistrates called for help in restoring order from a militia unit quartered nearby. But sympathy for the weavers was growing. When Westley's body was carried through the town of Arnold later that same week, it was accompanied by a crowd of nearly a thousand defiant men, says Sale.[10] The infamous Riot Act was then read, threatening the arrest of anyone who did not disperse at once. It was too late to calm this crowd. They dispersed, but only to regroup. Anger and frustration now ran deep in the population, and justifications in the form of anonymous letters and flyers making the Luddite case began to appear in the newspapers or nailed to boards. Perhaps it was now, at this intense moment, with supporters around them, that this Luddite song was composed and sung:

And night by night when all is still
And the moon is hid behind the hill,
We forward march to do our will
With hatchet, pike and gun!
O, the cropper lads for me,
The gallant lads for me,
Who with lusty stroke
The shear frames broke,
The cropper lads for me! [11]

The emotions generated would be hard to contain. Within months the uprising had spread to Yorkshire and Lancashire, and the stakes were raised with raids on factories, burglaries, and arson. But the government had mounted a response as well, and it was equally determined to stop the violence and stamp out the insurrection with a resolute ferocity.

It was in Yorkshire that the raids seemed most organized. One in particular, against the hated William Cartwright, is widely recalled. Cartwright was a prominent mill owner in Yorkshire, successful but not well loved. One of the new breed of mill owner, his factory at Rawfolds housed fifty shearing frames running smoothly and endlessly using water power from the nearby stream. The raid was led by George Mellor, a cropper (a finisher of wool), but not just weavers were involved. Among the men were blacksmiths and other workers who understood what the machines had in store for them. The machines would, for one thing, eliminate any illusion of control they had over their lives.

The raid was well organized, but Cartwright was prepared that night. He was waiting with four workmen and five men from a nearby militia. When the Luddites broke windows and began firing into the building, his men fired back. The raiders tried to batter down the reinforced door, but they failed, and Cartwright began ringing a bell to alert military reinforcements stationed nearby. The firing continued, and three of the raiders were wounded, two badly. As the troops arrived and the Luddites retreated, Mellor himself told the wounded—with tears in his eyes, said observers—that they must be left behind but must never reveal the names of their comrades.

Cartwright found the wounded men and interrogated them before getting medical help, until he sensed the growing anger from bystanders. After minimal care and more interrogation, the men died without revealing names.

The less severely wounded, who had been helped from the scene by their comrades, were cared for outside the district or in secret until they were healed, a sign of the widespread sympathy and support the rebellion had in the district. Two others apparently died later and were buried in secret by the Reverend Patrick Brontë, father of Charlotte Brontë, who would later write in *Shirley*:

> Certain inventions in machinery were introduced into the staple manufac-
> turers of the north, which, greatly reducing the number of hands necessary
> to be employed, threw thousands out of work, and left them without legiti-
> mate means of sustaining life. A bad harvest supervened. Distress reached
> its climax, Endurance, over-goaded, stretched the hand of fraternity to sedi-
> tion; the throes of a sort of moral earthquake were felt heaving under the
> hills of the northern counties.[12]

Sale denies that Brontë had Luddite sympathies, but it is mysterious that anyone without them could write, as she does next: "Misery generates hate: these sufferers hated the machines which they believed took their bread from them; they hated the buildings which contained those machines; they hated the manufacturers who owned those buildings."[13]

In the early months of 1812, in the Midland triangle of Luddite activity, there was a new sense of unease. The frame-breaking continued, and fear of becoming entangled in the ongoing violence kept those who were not involved at home behind closed doors and shuttered windows. Now the attacks were openly described as an insurrection. Troops were dispatched, between three and four thousand of them. More frequent arrests were made, rewards were offered, spies were paid, townspeople were interviewed and reinterviewed by magistrates, and by February a bill had been intro-duced calling for the death penalty for those destroying or injuring frames. In March, the bill was passed, and machine-breaking became a capital crime.

In the two years the frame breakers were active, the damage they inflicted amounted to more than £100,000, an amount that factory owners and gov-ernment officials considered a serious threat to the economic order of the countryside. The threat was not simply to order, however, but "in ways not always articulated, to industrial progress itself." Says Sale:

> They were . . . rebels against the future that was being assigned to them by
> the new political economy then taking hold in Britain, in which it was

argued that those who controlled capital were able to do almost anything they wished, encouraged and protected by government and king, without much in the way of laws or ethics or customs to restrain them.[14]

And this future was in the interests of the industrialists and the British government. From their perspective, it was a revolt that needed to be put down quickly, smartly, and permanently. The government felt it necessary to demonstrate that quality, still valued today, of being willing to establish the appropriate climate for business by whatever means at hand. And if that meant repressing and controlling an unruly labor force, that was what must be done. There was no attempt to alleviate the social disruption the machines created, which governments today might consider a wise idea. Instead, London eventually quartered as many as 14,400 troops in an area of about 2,100 square miles with a population of a million or so. To illustrate how forcible a response this was, Sale notes that had you been in the area at the time, one of every seventy people you saw would have been a soldier. And that was not the limit of the response. The voluntary militia was called in as well—numbering probably 20,000 in the area. The magistrates, constables, and agents were enlisted in the cause. The Luddites were infiltrated. Informers were paid. Even though little evidence could be pried from the close-knit and sympathetic communities from which the rebels came, the Luddite effort had little chance against such measures. Individuals were arrested and tried. After the first trials, eight were hanged, seventeen transported, thirteen imprisoned, and twenty acquitted. The trials would continue, with similar results. In January of 1813, fourteen more were hanged. There were sporadic episodes of machine-smashing in the next few years, but as Sale puts it, "The neck of Luddism was broken" on the gallows of York Castle on that dark January Saturday.[15] The cost of quashing the rebellion has been calculated by various historians at around £1.5 million, but what was at stake was far more important to Great Britain in the eyes of the government and industrialists: it was, in a word, the industrial revolution.

The rebellion, then, was not merely against the new machines but against something even larger and more ominous. What these workers were seeing, says Sale, was "their ordered society of craft and custom and community begin to give way."[16] In its place was a new system that would change the previous ways, not simply of making goods but of marketing them. A new order was to be imposed that would reshape both the physical and cultural landscape, disturbing every aspect of lives that had been lived in way that had seen little real change for hundreds of years. Industrialization would change it all, and seldom for the better—at least not from the perspective of these men and their families. They had been proud and independent artisans; they would become little more than servants—if they could secure new jobs. In truth, they were battling the idea of laissez faire: the theory that wages, prices, and supply could best find an appropriate balance without government playing a role, a system that took no account of the individual cost of radical change. The needs of the workers and their families had not been factored into the equation except as the impersonal force called demand. Or as David Noble puts it, "they were struggling against the efforts of capital to restructure social relations and the patterns of production at their expense using technology as a vehicle.[17]

The process was turning proud men into paupers; the sense of having lost social status was acute; and constitutional rights—for it seemed they had none. At the same time, they had virtually the full support of their communities; public opinion was on their side. "The large employers, and the factory system generally, stirred up profound hostility among small masters," says Thompson. When the first steam mill had been built in Bradford in 1797, it had been to the "accompaniment of menacing and hooting crowds," he says.[18]

> It is easy to forget how evil a reputation the new cotton mills had acquired. They were centres of exploitation, monstrous prisons in which children were confined, centres of immorality and of industrial conflict; above all, they reduced the industrial artisan to "a dependant State." A way of life was at stake for the community, and, hence, we must see the croppers' opposition to particular machines as being very much more than a particular group of skilled workers defending their own livelihood. These machines symbolized the encroachment of the factory *system*.[19]

This intense dislike of the factory system was not limited to the workers. For some manufacturers it became a moral issue. One sold a prosperous business rather than use machinery that he felt to be "a means of oppression on the part of the rich and of corresponding degradation and misery to the poor."[20] There was sympathy among the public for the plight of the cloth workers that lent sanction to the activities of the Luddites. There were few indeed who liked the factory system, who supported the use of the machines, or who felt no compassion for the misplaced workers or regret for the losses incurred as both manufacturing and community were transformed. Says Thompson:

> What was at issue was the "freedom" of the capitalist to destroy the customs of the trade, whether by new machinery, by the factory-system, or by unrestricted competition, beating-down wages, undercutting his rivals, and undermining standards of craftsmanship. We are so accustomed to the notion that it was both inevitable and "progressive" that trade should have been freed in the early 19th century from "restrictive practices", that it requires an effort of imagination to understand that the "free" factory owner or large hosier, or cotton-manufacturer, who built his fortune by these means, was regarded not only with jealousy but as a man engaging in *immoral* and *illegal* practices. . . . They could see no "natural law" by which one man, or a few men, could engage in practices which brought manifest injury to their fellows.[21]

Despite the widespread local support, the Luddite Rebellion was a failure. The machines, except in a few isolated instances, remained. New ones appeared. Owners were able to hold down wages. More factories were built, and economic conditions improved only erratically. Although Sale points out that historians have juggled the figures to make the effects of the industrial revolution look less painful to contemporary students of labor, the life of the workers in the English Midlands remained miserable.[22] And one cause of that misery was the blackness of the soot-filled air from the coal-fired, engine-driven machinery, a nasty blackness that permeated homes and coated everything it touched. Along with it came the fouling of the rivers with industrial waste and untreated sewage. Truly, it would seem from the perspective of the inhabitants of a miserable hole on some backstreet of Manchester, the world had ended.

"Luddism at its core," says Sale, "was a heterogeneous howl of protest and defiance, but once that cry was heard in the land and the only response of officialdom and merchantry was indifference, indignation or inhibition, it hardly knew what to do, how to continue, where to move."[23] If their howl could not be heard over the roar of the machines, what was left to do? The hearts of the Luddites and their sympathizers had been broken as effectively as the necks of the hanged. The way that people worked would be forever transformed by the machine, which required tending, knew no morning or night, and demanded a division of labor in the industrial setting that separated the worker from the product. Handwork—individual, creative, satisfying—was on the way out except as an exercise of determined principle.

That might have been the end of it. And yet, the name sticks. The Luddites and their rebellion against the machine cannot, it seems, be forgotten. We find meaning and relevance in that protest still, a tantalizing glimpse of possibility, an echo of thoughts each of us has surely had at one time or another as we struggle to adapt to some balky piece of demanding technology. Differences of class and time dissolve as we detect a commonality with these protestors.

What is not as clear from the standard histories is that the concerns of the Luddites were not limited to a handful of rough workmen roused to violence. Nor did those concerns end with the hangings. The Luddites had supporters, some of them well placed, such as Lord Byron. The Luddites had sympathizers, some of them respected thinkers and writers and artists of the day, such as William Wordsworth and Percy Bysshe Shelley; individuals who knew that something other than jobs was at stake in the relentless pressure of industrialization. There were those—such as Thomas Carlyle, John Ruskin, Charles Dickens, Mary Shelley, and William Morris—who saw that the machine had the potential to damage the very essence of what it means to be human in all those ways that humanness is expressed. And there were those who understood clearly, as did Henry David Thoreau, that the damage could well extend beyond humans, affecting our relationship with the world around us in ways that were likely to be undesirable, coming between humans and the natural world, destroying pride in work, dehumanizing daily activities, reorienting allegiances, and reshaping lives.

Although it has roots far back in history, there is, in fact, a consistent thread of thinking about humans and technology that begins around the time of the Luddite Rebellion and continues without a break up to the present. Resistance to the domination of the machine has branched into the arts, nature, agriculture, labor, politics, and spirituality. Follow those connections, and a continuing tradition of thought and art and action begins to emerge. And with it comes the revelation that those who are concerned about technology are not alone; have never been alone.

CHAPTER THREE

ℛomantic Inclinations

HERE IS AN INTRIGUING GAP IN THE LIFE OF POET, painter, mystic, and eccentric William Blake. No one is quite certain what he was doing between the years 1811 and 1817. No major works were published during that time, and mentions of him are rare. It is almost as if he had vanished. There was gossipy speculation that he had been committed to an asylum for madness, but there is no evidence for that either. Eventually he reappeared, but the absence remains an enduring puzzle.

To someone interested in the Luddite uprising, those particular dates leap from the page. The first frame-breaking forays began in 1811, and although the organized rebellion lasted no more than 18 months, effectively ending with the deaths of those fourteen men on the gallows at York Castle in 1813, sporadic attacks continued until 1816 when, to all appearances, the movement was moribund. To suppose that the overly anxious and high-strung Blake was involved in these very physical and risky undertakings; to imagine that he donned a cap and raised a hammer against the cogs and wheels of industrialization, or even that he recited verse to spur on the rebels, is a stretch of the imagination springing from nothing more than the superficial coincidence of digits.

In all probability, Blake was neatly tucked up in his two-room flat at 17 South Moulton Street, being served cups of tea by his patient and adoring wife, Catherine, as he worked and reworked his painting of *The Last Judgment* or his epic poem, "Jerusalem." To imagine this genius of delicate sensibility on Luddite forays seems a reckless flight of fancy. But it is tempting —and not as big a stretch as it might seem at first.

Blake; William Wordsworth; Samuel Taylor Coleridge; Percy Bysshe Shelley; George Gordon, Lord Byron; and John Keats are considered the chief poets of the Romantic period. All can be linked in one way or another to what was taking place in the Midlands in 1811. Only three, to my knowledge, expressed their sympathies for the Luddite Rebellion in explicit ways; within their writings, however, can be found support for the values the frame breakers were defending—values they clearly shared.

Both the Luddites and the Romantic poets (at least during certain periods in their lives) were rebels with political views that were radical enough to draw the attention of a government on the lookout for subversives. Both were defending what they cared about from a powerful force they recognized as threatening. By itself, that would be a tenuous link; of course there is more. In the work of the Romantic poets, there is a lament over what the machine is doing to workers, to the cities, and to the landscape, but there is also an affirmation of those things that the machine is not; of all those qualities of animation, intuition, emotion, and sensibility—of humanness and of human needs—that are beyond the capabilities of the machine. In the Romantic age, then, we begin to see the sensibility that inspired the Luddite Rebellion take on a positive form. Scattered throughout their poetry, prose, and letters is a dawning acknowledgment of what the industrial age has done and will do, as well as an appealing articulation of precisely what it is that is too important to be lost in the process.

These were unsettled times. Old orders, old ways of living, old assumptions were all under attack. Only thirty-five years before, a British colony had revolted and established an idealistic democratic experiment; a monarch and his entourage had lost their heads to a rabble with notions of freedom, equality, and self-rule; an upstart had seized the crown of France, placed it upon his own head and set about waging war; and everywhere scientific and religious assumptions were being questioned, as were means of governing and the very workings of society that then prevailed. Life was still physically perilous. If nobility everywhere, in the small of night, sensed on their necks an itch where the guillotine might bite, free thinkers could also imagine the roughness of rope: hangings were common events. Nor did anyone think himself immune to the common ailments, from cholera to consumption, that could and did strike with democratic fairness at any moment. This very fragility of life supported in some — especially the young — a certain recklessness. Shelley, who thought himself suffering from a physical condition likely to mean an early demise, and Keats, who did suffer from tuberculosis and died early of the disease, clearly felt some urgency to make their mark at a time in their lives when caution had not yet extended its frozen grip.

The innovation of movable type had inevitably led to movable ideas, with unsettling effects, from religious dissent to political and social reform. Thomas Paine's *Rights of Man,* which proposed the novel idea that ordinary people possessed them, had been followed shortly by Mary Wollstonecraft's *A Vindication of the Rights of Woman,* which dared to question institutions, such as marriage, that had previously been taken for granted. Strong feelings and a keen sense of justice everywhere filled public lecture halls. An assumption shared by workers and intellectuals alike underlay all these protests: that certain things — the right to reasonably priced bread, for instance — were moral issues worth defending. There was, on the other hand, a vast reservoir of Tory sentiment that did not see things in this light at all. These new ways of thinking were a threat to an order that had worked well enough for them, and the ongoing economic restructuring presaged by the new factory system promised even better times. That opposition unwittingly served to unite the weavers and the thinkers and the writers further.

In this combustible atmosphere, the machine was making its presence felt in new and powerful ways, and some of the changes were welcomed. The steam-driven engine held out a promise of speeding transportation and improving manufacturing so appealing, so irresistible, even, that its obviously less desirable effects were mostly overlooked. Changes were incremental, and so much of the population not directly affected became conditioned to them. One factory in a valley produced unpleasant fumes, but no one yet imagined the sooty, sky-blackening pall that fifty in close proximity would eventually create. One new mill might displace a few workers and rearrange the workers' community in ways that were neither pleasant nor anticipated. But as growth continued, its social effects were becoming too obvious to overlook. Thus, in an atmosphere predisposed to riot and protest, the rebellion of the Luddites should have been anticipated. It was unique in the context of other uprisings only in its length, the long-term commitment of its participants, its level of violence, and the fact that the violence was directed against the machine.

In France, a violent uprising had changed everything. But the French Revolution of twenty-plus years earlier that had initially so impressed had turned first sour, then terrifying. Relations with French citizens for those in England who wanted to maintain a connection had become complex and tense; then risky; and finally, with the Revolutionary and Napoleonic wars, impossible. The seemingly endless conflict had taxed the English both figuratively and literally, sapping both economic and psychic resources.

William Wordsworth would later famously say of this earlier, revolutionary time, "Bliss was it in that dawn to be alive, But to be young was very heaven."[1] The air crackled with both excitement and danger. Nevertheless, England had been divided, in the years just after the fall of the Bastille, into those who wanted to maintain what was for them a comfortable political status quo and those who were willing to risk upheaval and change for the prospect of something that might be better. The wealthy remained mostly insulated from the economic consequences of war, but for the poor simply surviving remained a genuine challenge. By the dates of the Luddite uprising, the country had actually calmed a bit politically.

Some writers have tried to separate what had been taking place among the working classes, where there were strong urges to improve conditions by whatever means, from what was going on in cultural circles, but there was, at least initially, a strong connection between them. Fearing precisely that spirit of revolution and reform, Parliament had passed—though not without opposition—repressive acts that defined large gatherings where inflammatory ideas were exchanged or promoted as treasonous activity and that made not just "combination" or unionization, but political activism itself, a very risky business. Talk of republics and reformation during the war with France was dangerous and unwise. Spies were dispatched to the countryside to monitor, report on, and actively harass those whose thinking, speaking, and writing hinted at dissent. That included, without doubt, Coleridge, Words-worth, Shelley, and Blake—who more than hinted.

The evidence is strong that these four in particular drew the attention of the government for their sympathy with ideas of political reform, and yet certainly the sympathies of all these writers extended to the oppressed workers in England, who were struggling under the new factory system. Coleridge was generally for reform. Wordsworth was concerned for the workers well before the Luddite Rebellion itself. Keats wrote scathingly of government oppression in cleverly disguised phrases that did not escape his readers but were not blatant enough to challenge the law. Byron and Shelley would be open in their support for the weavers, not just in their poetry but in other, more public, ways as well.

Blake had worn the red hat of the Jacobin proudly when the French Revolution was fresh and promising, but after the days of terror in the streets in 1792 he is said to have taken it off. It may have been jammed into a bottom drawer, but it retained its symbolic presence in his life. He did not abandon his republican ideas. As government tightened the screws, however, caution seemed wise. The French Revolution, ironically, was having an effect opposite the one intended. Booksellers and printers were fined or imprisoned for selling or printing seditious materials. Tom Paine, who had stirred the populace with his provocative words, which not only pointed the way to reform but called into question conventional religious views, was driven into exile. William Godwin, of whom Shelley was an adoring disciple, rather quickly modified the radical views he had promoted in *Political Justice* into a system for "benevolence," in which he replaced a taste for revolution with a preference for politeness. Godwin responded to the repressive Two Acts by noting that they might be needed to inhibit radicals such as John Thelwall but were so overly broad that they might be used to stifle philosophers such as himself. Thelwall, a vocal reformer with a strong, incautious debating style, was forced to disguise his speeches as lectures on Roman history. Still, he carried a pistol for defense, sometimes actually drawing it as he barely escaped mob violence clearly organized by the government. He was harassed and pressured and eventually would be tried and ultimately silenced. For one brief period he had been a genuine link between the world of the Romantic poets and that of the weavers, but in the end he transformed himself into an instructor in elocution.

In the early years of the nineteenth century, then, the British government systematically and effectively silenced the voices of dissent in one way or another: usually intimidation was sufficient, but some dissenters were actually imprisoned, and many of the Luddites, of course, felt that final tightening of the noose. (The number of capital crimes increased significantly between 1760 and 1810, and many were crimes against property.)

The popular brew may have been capped by these repressive measures, but the fermentation of ideas continued. They flowed freely, if sometimes disguised by complexity and obfuscation, in the writings of Blake. When he was clearer, his courage failed. His poem, "The French Revolution," was to have filled seven books. Only the first was set and printed, and it was never published. Joseph Johnson, the printer who was well known to the reformers, probably warned Blake of the possible unpleasant political consequences.

Blake came from a family of religious Dissenters, a broad term that could apply to any of several alternatives to the Church of England, from Presbyterian to Quaker congregations. It was a tradition that carried with it a predisposition for the support of civil and religious liberties. He was steeped in antinomianism, the view that religious laws do not apply to and are unnecessary for believers, who, by sincerely believing, can do no wrong. This sentiment against biblical laws carried over naturally to viewing civil laws as having little authority. Dissenters were not lawbreakers, but at least those in the antinomian tradition did not accord the laws of man automatic respect. The volatile mixture of Dissenting tradition and the inspiration of the French Revolution had produced a subtle but significant change in the mood and nature of unrest. Suddenly ordinary workingmen from villages and towns around the country exhibited a new democratic consciousness and wanted rights for themselves. But equally, the final convulsive days of the eighteenth century represented a desperate effort by these same workers to maintain, if not the old political order, then the traditional economic and social order against the forces that were attempting to impose the new, under which—it was already becoming all too clear—they would have even fewer rights than before. When the pressures of industrialization met the forces of government repression, the workers were squeezed in between. More than once the poets became their voices.

Shelley, in his early work "Queen Mab," written just at the time of the Luddite Rebellion, looks unflinchingly at the source of the trouble, the power behind the machine:

Power, like a desolating pestilence,
Pollutes whate'ver it touches; and obedience,
Bane of all genius, virtue, freedom, truth,
Makes slaves of men, and of the human frame
A mechanized automaton.[2]

A few years later, following the Peterloo Massacre, Shelley's sympathies with the struggle of workers, and its link to political reform, are clearly delineated in "The Mask of Anarchy":

"What is Freedom?—ye can tell
That which slavery is, too well—
For its very name has grown
To an echo of our own.
"'Tis to work, and have such pay
As just keeps life from day to day
In your limbs as in a cell
For the tyrants' use to dwell:
"So that ye for them are made
Loom, and plough, and sword, and spade,
With or without your own will bent
To their defence and nourishment.
"'Tis to see your children weak
With their mothers pine and peak,
When the winter winds are bleak,—
They are dying whilst I speak.[3]

In a similar vein, Blake wrote: "A machine is not a man nor a work of art." Instead, "It is destructive of humanity and art." His verses acknowledge the harsh consequences of these tireless, mindless, mechanical bullies. In "Jerusalem" his vision of hell reverberates with images of the factory, mill, and pit, the crashing, clanging, grinding, pounding sounds of industrialism. The machine becomes the metaphor for repression.

. . . .Cruel works
Of many wheels I view; wheel without wheel,
With cogs tyrannic,
Moving by compulsion each other.[4]

Although Blake's radicalism was perhaps instinctive and did not carry him so far as to join any reform societies, he not only worked for the publisher Joseph Johnson but dined with him and his circle, which included many of the most notable radicals and thinkers of the day. In this heady intellectual atmosphere, libertarian banners were designed and poems were composed in praise of revolutionary heroes. The not-so-distant war with America had drawn together in its unpopularity much of London, uniting in common cause the merchants and Dissenters. Blake's family included both: he knew firsthand both the rewards and the costs of unconventional thinking and acting. Blake had, in fact, two brushes with repression, one of them quite serious, in which he was tried for seditious remarks against the king. Supported by influential patrons, he won the case.

The somewhat fragile link between the working classes and intellectuals that the French Revolution engendered waned as the executions in France continued, but Blake was hardly the only Romantic poet whose sympathies lay, at least initially, with France and with ideas of reform. Wordsworth and Coleridge would take pains in later years to downplay publicly what they seemed to look back on as youthful enthusiasm, but there are strong indications that both were seriously involved with groups that felt a connection with the Revolution. The source of this support was a deep well of idealism that took in every aspect of life from the intimacy of individual relationships to the public arena of politics. Coleridge was associated with radical Unitarians such as William Frend and George Dyer, and he was inspired by their ideas. He had planned, along with Robert Southey, the Fricker sisters (Sara Fricker became his wife), and others of their friends, to start a utopian community called Pantisocracy along the Susquehanna. Eventually the plan was abandoned, but Coleridge would remain linked to the idea in the minds of many. Utopian plans, then as now, speak loudly of dissatisfaction with things as they are, implying an unspoken disloyalty that rankles and threatens those who adapt rather than complain, and the plans for this ideal community made him an object of ridicule to some and a suspicious figure to others.

The Wordsworths, for William and his sister Dorothy had set up housekeeping together by then in a comfortable rented house, were joined by Coleridge in the summer of 1797, and one can almost feel the energy created as these three personalities came together. Here were brilliant and passionate individuals who could not only share ideas but liked the same things: endless treks in the countryside with sensitivities sharpened to every stimulation from the extraordinary natural world around them in the Lake District. Miraculously for such strong personalities, they liked one another as well. It was a blending as successful as the addition of yeast to flour and water.

Nothing would do when the visit ended but that William and Dorothy join Coleridge in Nether Stowey, where he and his wife Sara lived. A rental was found, and the three—now four—resumed their fruitful association. It was here, too, that Coleridge and Wordsworth had their own run-in with a government spy. Again, the story is often dismissed as a silly error on the part of an ignorant informer—Coleridge himself later painted it that way—but there was more to it that that. Wordsworth and Coleridge were suspected by their neighbors, with some justification, of holding Jacobinite views. They had been observed entertaining the infamous John Thelwall, who was searching for a safe haven from political harassment (and, not finding it, moved on), and apparently there had been joking references to "talk of treason," which were overheard and dutifully dispatched to government offices. But the spy seems to have been satisfied that the nest of subversives was nothing more than a clutch of disgruntled poets who, if not entirely blameless, were essentially harmless. In any event, intimidation did its nasty work, and the poets took more care to watch their tongues. These Romantic poets then, were not only inclined to sympathize with the Luddite cause, they knew first hand the price of original thinking and likely felt some kinship with the urge to rebel.

The stimulating brew of radical politics and rusticity that characterized the Wordsworth-Coleridge experience could have come from the recipe handed down by the hugely influential Jean-Jacques Rousseau thirty-five years before. In three books, beginning with his *Discourse on the Arts and Sciences,* followed by his *Discourse on Inequality* and then by *The Social Contract,* he outlined a philosophy that would question the notion of human advancement—have we or haven't we progressed?—then set the stage for revolution. His first book was written during a period heavily influenced by the English philosopher Francis Bacon, when science and rationalism were seen as holding the potential to greatly improve the human condition. The organization of information, according to Bacon, would be key to progress: this need to organize and classify characterized the science of the times. But first it was necessary to banish religion, superstition, and tradition, replacing them with the systematic organization of empirical knowledge. Denis Diderot was the editor of a project to do just that, a massive *Encyclopédie* that would bring together the talents and expertise of France's intellectuals. Rousseau had contributed first pieces on music, then on other subjects, until he realized that he strongly disagreed with the entire premise.

Rousseau's awakening came when he was told of an essay competition on the question, "Has the revival of the arts and sciences done more to corrupt or purify morals?" and the answer came to him in a powerful and overwhelming rush of emotions that caused him to sit down under a tree and weep. The result was an essay on the corruption of morals by art that, in its unfashionable position, won the competition. From this iconoclastic awakening, it was only a short step to the realization that the notion of progress was an illusion. Far from being our savior, he decided, science was encouraging an ever-spiraling descent that began with the development of civilized society. Humans were now neither better off, happier, nor more virtuous, Rousseau concluded, than they had been in their natural, or "savage," state. In austere simplicity, without property or the longing for it, humans had satisfied their needs without envy or greed. Agriculture meant land disputes. Greed had predicated the need for arithmetic (trade, which required numbers and counting, was all about ownership), property had created crime, crime the need for laws. Every invention of a tool, from the hoe to the plow, had served only to make humans weaker; every modern condition had further debilitated society. The abundance that was the Baconian promise of progress therefore led only to corruption and decline, he observed.

His essay on inequality, in which the accumulation of wealth by some led to the enslavement of others, would be followed by *The Social Contract,* which introduced the great themes of liberty and virtue, synonymous with freedom. The dilemma is how to be both organized by a social contract and at the same time free. The answer is that the contract must be freely entered into by those who are enforced by it, a voluntary submission of wills for the corporate good, a recipe for revolution—or totalitarianism.

Entranced by the larger points of his radical treatises, the public of his day —which extended throughout Europe and far beyond—was unconcerned with such complexities. They heard the call of the natural, the appeal of simplicity, the possibility of government organized by its citizens and reshaped to *their* desires and needs; they heard an echo of the freedoms and virtues that had been lost in civilization, urbanization, and materialism. Three decades later, Rousseau's ideas, when they were reexamined in the new Romantic mood, simply reinforced what these poets already felt to be true.

THE VILLAGE of Maulds Meaburn is not on the tourist route, the trade route, or any other route I can think of. But if you are coming over the hill on the back road from Appleby, you can just glimpse it down in the valley. So well does the scattering of stone buildings fit into the landscape that, at first glimpse, it might be a geological feature and not a man-made cluster. The road is narrow and twisting along here, and there is no good place for a car to stop for a better look. But if you are walking, you can pick a spot, lean on one of the stone walls for which Cumbria is famous, and gaze down at a scene that must have changed very little in several hundred years.

As English villages go, Maulds Meaburn is not particularly distinguished architecturally, historically, or even in charm. Its houses are simple and unpretentious, snugged up to the river, gardens walled against the ubiquitous sheep. The hills protect it and catch what sun there is; "Sunny Valley," some of the locals call it. It is a place geological forces might have shaped with human habitation in mind: sheltered, fertile, and well-supplied with fresh water. There are at least six pre-Roman settlements—now little more than mounds in the pastures, but still distinguishable—within easy walking distance of the village. That tells you this was always a good place to live; good before electricity and central heating and thermopane windows, a good place to live when site selection was a matter of survival.

The stone houses circle a piece of common land, and under the grand trees there are sheep. They graze, sleep on the grass, nurse their young, or, oblivious to the distinctions humans make, wander in the road—or anywhere else they please, if not prevented from it. Thus the stone walls. The human inhabitants have walled themselves in; sheep rule, it seems. They stand on the stone bridge that crosses the Lyvennet, the small river that flows through the valley and the town, and from there they gaze either stupidly or stubbornly, take your pick, at the cars that want to cross, scattering only at the last minute, and begrudgingly at that.

"Mint sauce," a friend of mine always mutters, as if the threat of becoming roast lamb will move them along more quickly.

The sheep leave a mess on what could be pleasant green, which demands the wearing of the tall rubber boots that are part of the Cumbrian uniform and they are with doubt responsible for the generally treeless character of the Lake District. Still, there is no doubt that they add to the charm of the place. Humans and animals are living in close proximity, and dung notwithstanding, there is a pleasant, appropriate sort of feeling to the arrangement. Humans relax when there are animals around—just seeing them lowers the blood pressure—and this mix of human and animal has an ancient, primitive feel to it in a world where separation of man and beast, coupled with a kind of enforced sterility, is the order of the day.

This section of Cumbria is to the east of the official Lake District where Wordsworth; his contemporaries; and a succession of poets, writers, and painters found, and continue to find', inspiration. The landscape is calmer here; the shapes of the hills and mountains less dramatic; and the lakes, and thus the tourists, missing altogether. It is, nevertheless, a place where people and landscape are closely connected—the landscape dominates the vision, the psyche, and the purse, as many people depend upon it for their livelihood.

Maulds Meaburn, in all its quaintness, is the kind of anomaly people are drawn to today, seemingly a step back in time to a slower paced existence in which human activity and the natural world have struck an agreeable balance. Living in the village for six months as I did some years ago, there evolved, almost at once, a change in the pace of my activities. I slowed, predictably, but the order of the day began to be shaped not simply by the clock but by the sky, the color of the day, the rhythms of dawn and dusk, with the sheep as silent witness.

And yet today Maulds Meaburn is a fraud. It is real enough in a physical sense, not some artificial reconstruction. But it now has the feeling of a shell. Its inhabitants are increasingly from somewhere else: retirees or people who commute to work in another, larger town. There are certainly working farms in the neighborhood, but just as many have been converted into pleasant country residences. There is no village store, no post office, no pub; it no longer functions as a village. The inhabitants are not united by work, and only a few are bound to the place by inheritance or dependent upon one another for support as they once were. Community ties remain, but they are weak; something to be worked at. Only isolation and building regulations maintain the illusion of something that economic, social, and technological forces have elsewhere left behind. And yet there are those who work at maintaining the illusion of Maulds Meaburn or the thousand villages like it scattered across the English countryside. It is the kind of bucolic scene that appears in travel brochures precisely because it is where a large number of people imagine they would like to be. There is a small voice within us that some still listen to; a voice that tells us we need what is there and that even the illusion of community and balance, bound up with the world around, is better than nothing.

This feeling that some nurture, this need for nature and human activity to be in harmony, this impulse to reinforce and preserve particular conditions and connections from the past—a vision of ourselves that persists, without utility poles and satellite dishes, where certain values are implied in the simple arrangement of things—is called romantic.

To call something romantic today is, in the prevailing sense of the word, to remove it from serious consideration. Whatever is being so described may be interesting, charming, entertaining, even desirable from the perspective of organized seduction, but it will not be important. It will not be something that will make things run faster or more smoothly, or operate with more efficiency, or turn a larger profit. It is apt to be considered, in at least one part of our minds, as peripheral and of small consequence. Seldom do we stop to think how that pejorative interpretation got there, when humans incline so naturally to all that romantic is.

Blake, Wordsworth, Coleridge, Byron, and Keats are known today as the chief poets of the British Romantic period—hardly of small consequence—and yet, from the contemporary perspective, their work is tainted by the label. We approach them with preconceptions and dismiss the flowing and "flowery" language as unsuitable and anachronistic, their feelings toward nature as overwrought; the excess of emotion and imagination seems out of place in a stainless-steel world. But I wonder if it is. Behind the superficialities of an unfamiliar style lie principles that need a second look. The Romantic period begins before and extends beyond the time of the Luddite Rebellion, and even beyond its political sympathies, yet there are strong echoes in Romantic verse and prose of the principles and values the Luddites were fighting for, the right to the simple pleasures and satisfactions that human life might be expected to provide.

Today Romantic drags behind it the dead weight of what are considered negative associations. It represents an opting for the emotional over the logical, the subjective over the objective. Romanticism, in our terms, is the opposite of control, conjuring a certain wildness and unpredictability. It is about soft light, shades of pink, sweet scents, warm tears, fading music, flowing silk, rustling leaves, eddies in quiet brooks, dramatic vistas, and birdsong. It is, in most people's minds, about the world of the senses.

When applied to these writers, one can see the logic and appropriateness, if not the justice. And in truth, it was not some petulant critic but Wordsworth and his sister Dorothy who began to describe their own poetical responses to the natural world around them in such terms—and they did so knowing that "romantic" referred in common parlance, even then, to tales of passion and exotic locales. Dorothy, in a letter, talked about the romantic country-side and the villages of Somerset while she and William were visiting Cole-ridge, and gradually they bandied the word among themselves to describe not just the scenery but their own lives and the world around them.

"Romantic" was a way of seeing, a certain cast of light that could trans-form anything. In this new illumination, the imagination could play with the unfamiliarity of familiar things, accentuating the strangeness of the half-vis-ible. This sensation of newness, of possibility, of transformation defined the word. This was the mind at playful work, allowed to range and create and interact with the ever-changing nature of reality. The Romantics' priorities were with the exercise of imagination, with excess, with the mystical and, at times, the irrational. The natural world was a powerful and important place where God dwelt; human emotions, intuitions and yearnings were not sim-ply valid, but vital, and could be trusted. "Born as the Renaissance world was coming to an end," says Malcolm Muggeridge of Blake, he was pro-foundly distrustful of the intellect as a means of finding truth and of science as a means of exploring it.[5] The direct experience of the individual alone—without the intervention of the scientific method—could be trusted as Blake's first lines of "Auguries of Innocence" so eloquently express:

> *To see a World in a grain of sand*
> *And a Heaven in a wild flower*
> *Hold Infinity in the palm of your hand*
> *And Eternity in an hour.*

The Wordsworths and Coleridge, then others in their set—Robert Southey, Charles and Mary Lamb, John Thelwall—set out to redefine romantic—not as a word; they never used it to describe their poetry—but as a way of experiencing reality. In the end they were defined by it. Wordsworth's early poems only hint at these goals. The introduction to "Lyrical Ballads" may have overstated the originality of these works, but the aim of echoing natural speech and elevating the ordinary to the extraordi-nary successfully challenged existing conventions. These poets, and those who caught the mood, would echo the churning natural world in their choice of form and language, playing with variety within unity, randomness and spontaneity within a loosely defined form, showing a willingness to tolerate the unexpected, the odd, the organic; abjuring control and premeditation.

And yet, as antimodernist as this approach seems, within the writings of this period—the poetry, especially—are found those verses, lines, and ideas that continue to ring with familiarity precisely because they resonate with meaning even today, a time wedded to the rational and the scientific; the objective and the unemotional. "Nature never did betray the heart that loved her," Wordsworth tells us and we believe. "The world is too much with us, late and soon/Getting and spending, we lay waste our powers,"[6] he writes, and we know precisely what he means.

We remember from history and literature not simply what is taught but what is personally meaningful, what seems true to that part of us that was present before the machines began to shape our thinking and our judgments. That our expectations have been shaped by technology is obvious from our reaction to the term *romantic,* for it is everything that the machine is not. Today, without giving it a conscious thought, our allegiance is to a stern standard shaped by the demands of a scientific and industrial paradigm that, having established a model of quantifiable objectivity and cultivated detachment, colors our perception of emotion, intuition, imagination, and the sensual, dragging them down to second-class status. Just as the sleepless machines of industrialization took no account of the tired limbs and bleary eyes of the humans who operated them or of the communities they disrupted or of the landscape they destroyed, so the texture of individual human experience, with all its passion and unpredictability, is lost in the machine-made smoothness of our commitment to modernism.

And yet, as Jacques Barzun points out about the Romantic period in *From Dawn to Decadence,* "It is obvious that an age that left scores of masterpieces in every art and original ideas still current cannot have been populated exclusively by men and women weak in judgment and continually lovelorn and subject to illusion."[7]

Clearly there is something important in Romanticism that, at least on the visible surface of our current cultural thinking, is no longer highly valued and yet that we still respond to. How do we resolve that contradiction? What, one might ask, is the modern mind missing? What have we unwit-

tingly left behind in the rush to mechanize, and what have we deluded ourselves into presuming that we can do without? Isn't the persistent resonance
of ideas and images from the work of the Romantics evidence of its importance at an almost physical level; don't we have a gut sense of what we need?
"Little we see in Nature that is ours; / We have given our hearts away, a sordid boon!" Wordsworth reminds us, and we need no convincing.

The obvious answer is that there is a cavernous space today between what
people are asked to think, expected to think, taught to think by those in
whose interest it is that they think that way, and what, in inclination and
unguarded moments, they actually think. We are not the people we are supposed to be. We have not fit as cleanly and smoothly as we sometimes like
to think into the world of reason and efficiency and practicality. The advertising world knows this, the entertainment world knows this, the publishing
world knows this: All play at one time or another to these unmentionable
needs for romance and fantasy and a yearning for simpler times. And we
know this. Our attempts to live bifurcated lives, adjusting ourselves to the
demands of the mechanical-technological world, feel uncomfortable precisely because the marriage between human and machine is an awkward
union.

Blake knew in the early 1800s what the machine would do. It is repeatedly linked in his verse with visions of hell. In writing about Blake and his
work, Malcolm Muggeridge notes:

> So beginning with Bacon, a great transformation was taking place in the
> human condition. The machine, first seemingly a servant, would infallibly
> become a demonic master, poisoning our air, polluting our rivers and lakes,
> flattening our landscape, destroying our handicrafts and our art, and
> smothering the imagination whereby man's creativity could relate itself to
> God.[8]

With the shock of this change before them, the Romantic poets saw literature as a way of coping with the reverberations of the machine, if not as a
way of understanding them fully. They may well have considered their work
as a means of reshaping the new machine-reality, however unlikely that
was to occur. Nevertheless, Romanticism was the safety value of the new
order.

What do these writers of the Romantic period have to tell us about the sensual impoverishment of modern life? What is the cost of depravation? The answers are suggested by looking more closely at their lives and work.

HERE WERE poets who were strong individuals with intensely personal standards for what they created. They were certainly not all alike. Wordsworth put strong emphasis on the natural world and his personal response to it, yet Blake seems to have cared less for nature. But if the Romantic poets had one thing in common, it was that they chafed against the confines of eighteenth-century ways of thinking, especially the preoccupation with order and form that was characteristic of Bacon, Newton, and Locke. Neoclassicism had reduced nature to a set of scientific rules. The world was being sorted, ordered, prioritized, and planned in a way that began to define progress but was really about control.

Looking back on the eighteenth century, we have come to see and accept it as the Age of Enlightenment, a time when the forces of reason triumphed and rightly so, we smugly assume. And so it comes as something of a surprise to realize that what now seems obvious, because it eventually won, would not seem as obvious then. There existed, especially in the Dissident religions that blossomed with the greater availability of copies of the Bible in the vernacular and of other spiritual reading material, a strain of anti-Enlightenment sentiment that opposed reason, that frowned upon the application of law.

If this strain of thinking was more prevalent in the working and merchant classes, the scent of anti-Enlightenment thinking and feeling—at times verging dangerously on anti-intellectualism—was carried on the shoulders of the reform movement into the intellectual circles where the Romantic poets were to be found. Said Wordsworth in the poem "The Tables Turned,"

> Enough of science and of art;
> Close up these barren leaves;
> Come forth, and bring with you a heart
> That watches and receives.

These poets assumed that there were other ways of knowing. Intuition, emotional response, mysticism: each had its place. Wordsworth's reference to art is to self-conscious artfulness, not creative expression, which was found in abundance. Lockean empiricism, with its skepticism and its reliance on appearance alone as the basis for human knowledge, was, to the Romantics, suspect. Under this regimentation of thought, every aspect of life is subjected to the application of reason, which has the effect of mechanizing and demeaning it.

Today Western society accepts almost without question the notion that we can know a thing by careful observation; our allegiance to the idea of objectivity and verifiable information is strong. Validation comes from measuring and counting, and status is accorded to those who measure and count with confidence. As psychologist Fran Stettner says, "Today the white coat has replaced the white collar as the symbol of authority."[9] But Blake observed, "We are led to Believe a Lie when we see not Thro the Eye."[10] The surface was not to be trusted. Knowledge lay at another level, where the alchemic mix of sensibility and intuition—combined with simple yet careful observation—produced a knowing deeper and more profound. Among the Romantics there were some, such as Shelley, who expressed an intense interest in new inventions and experimentation. Shelley seemed intrigued not so much with the cool rationality of science as with the "magic" of it: he was interested in experiments with electricity. But in general, these writers and painters opposed the imposition of reason and logic as the premier standard by which human activity is judged. In "Milton," Blake wrote:

> *Who publishes doubt & calls it knowledge; whose Science is Despair*
> *Whose pretence to knowledge is Envy, whose whole Science is*
> *To destroy the wisdom of ages to gratify ravenous Envy;*[11]

Just as Rousseau's original ideas of rights and liberty and rusticity had supported the thinking of the Romantics, this mistrust of science owed something to Pascal, who despite his brilliance as a scientist, at the very moment of the birth of science denounced its pretensions and foretold its downfall. That "incomparable intellect," says Malcolm Muggeridge, "devoted itself to showing how very little the intellect can do."[12] "There is nothing," said Pascal, nearly a century and a half before Blake, "which is so much in conformity with reason as the rejection of reason . . ."

For the Romantic poets, Newton and Locke became the enemy, a thought Blake put into the mind of Milton in the poem of that name:

> *To bathe in the Waters of Life; to wash off the Not Human*
> *I come in Self-annihilation & the grandeur of Inspiration*

To cast off Rational Demonstration by Faith in the Saviour
To cast of the rotten rags of Memory by Inspiration
To cast off Bacon, Locke & Newton from Albions covering
To take off his filthy garments, & clothe him with Imagination [13]

What was Romanticism if not a rejection of those aspects of contemporary thinking that denied what it meant to be human and reduced both man and the natural world to mere moving parts? "Reason is, and ought only to be, the slave of the passions,"[14] David Hume had written in 1739, and this the Romantics translated into a natural mistrust of science and technology. Romanticism, Barzun says, validated both passion and risk.[15]

When Romanticism and science met, as they did in Johann Wolfgang van Goethe, it was a very different sort of science based on the assumption that only through an intense and contemplative relationship with nature can we comprehend its phenomena. It involved vigorous observation and thinking but allowed for the possibility of a mystical union with the observed that the new science would have discounted. Wordsworth agreed:

> *Our meddling intellect*
> *Mis-shapes the beauteous forms of things; —*
> *We murder to dissect* [16]

Turn instead to living nature, he suggests, open fully to what it teaches, validating simple powers of observation and experience over cold, mechanistic scientific investigation.

In fact, mistrust of science, as it was then developing, was a common and popular sentiment. Mary Shelley's horror story, *Frankenstein*, took up the theme, a popular one yet today, of science out of control; of the creation of a monster that has a life of its own. It touched on the pervasive fear that a relentless and unthinking commitment to the scientific could create mechanical monsters that would cause untold misery. Like Rousseau's natural man, Shelley's monster is naturally good until he is corrupted by contact with human society and learning. Frankenstein's fictional creator is condemned to spend his life attempting to undo what he has done. First published in 1818, a scant few years after the Luddite Rebellion was so firmly put down, *Frankenstein* exuded the fear of what technology might do and, in doing so, captured the public consciousness. Today's movie versions have put the original meaning aside, focusing instead on the evil of the monster rather than on the hubris of its creator.

If there was an aversion to applied reason in the thinking of the Romantic poets, it did not mean, however, that there was a serious rejection of intelligence or contemplation, or even any opposition to the diligent application of thought in the creation of poetry and critical prose, or indeed in the forming of political and philosophical opinions. Writing was worthy of serious and applied mental effort. Antirationalism is not the same as anti-intellectualism.

Neither was this antirationalism simply a sophisticated way of expressing what the Luddites felt about the industrial machines. But in both cases it was an acknowledgment of where reason can lead, where it can take society, if it is not carefully monitored and balanced with other aspects of perception and understanding. There were things worth protecting and preserving —nature, community, conviviality—and they had little to do with regimentation and mechanization either of ways of working and living or of thinking.

These poets and thinkers said something new, not just about the human relationship to nature but about our relationships to one another within a community and a society. There were aspects of the past that needed changing: political structures and religious orthodoxies, for instance. And yet there were aspects of the past that were worth preserving as well. Crudely defining conservatives as those who cling to the past and the old and liberals as those wedded to the future and the new is revealed, in looking at this period, as simplistic and unhelpful. The new industrialists were politically conservative, scientific adventurers operating out of dedicated self-interest. The backward glance of the Romantics, on the other hand, was not reactionary but a desire to defend what contributed to the harmonious functioning of the whole.

Wordsworth, for instance, who had been born into a respected upper-middle-class family, broke with the paternalistic class attitudes of his own upbringing toward people who worked with their hands or on the land or in the marketplace and genuinely respected their stories, customs, and ways of life. There was validity in the old ways, he pointed out, in the ancient tales, in the habits and speech and customs of country folk, and that value had the same appeal to William and Dorothy Wordsworth as it has today. The country cottage and the simple, bucolic life still hold the promise of restoration for many jaded urbanites, just as they did for Wordsworth when he needed to retreat.

In 1801, a decade before the Luddite Rebellion, Wordsworth wrote to the

English reformer Charles James Fox (to whom he had earlier sent a copy of "Lyrical Ballads") and asked him to consider the matter of the condition of working people:

> But recently by the spreading of manufactures through every part of the country, by the heavy taxes upon postage, by workhouses, Houses of Industry, and the invention of Soup-shops &c. &c. superadded to the encreasing disproportion between the price of labour and that of the necessaries of life, the bonds of domestic feeling among the poor, as far as the influence of these things has extended, have been weakened, and in innumerable instances entirely destroyed.[17]

Wordsworth saw that an entire class of people, who had held rural society together, was suffering under the new manufacturing conditions. He complained that small, poor but proud landowners were literally disappearing; families were being divided and, in the end, driven from their holdings. "This effect the present Rulers of this country are not conscious of, or they disregard it."[18] He sent Fox two poems, "The Brothers" and "Michael," to illustrate his point.

Blake, too, was not only sympathetic to revolution and political reform but aligned himself, at least in words, with those who recognized the tyranny of the new technologies as they began to dominate industrial production and then to change society. It was the lines from Blake's preface to his poem, "Milton," with its unforgettable image of "dark Satanic Mills," that would become the anthem of Britain's Labour party, and throughout his poetry, woven in among the fantastic visions for which he is better known, are his sympathies, always with the working men, women, and children struggling under the burdens of war, machinery, and social injustice; servants to a system of commerce with an "insatiable maw that must be fed." His poetry is littered with references that would resonate with the workers: smoke, darkness, wheels, bellowing flames, ringing hammers, "the dread Forge, trembling & shuddering along the Valleys," hungry children sacrificed to industry, "the slave groans in the dungeon of stone."

In Blake's disturbing vision, man, instead of being one with God, has separated himself, and "Down from the hills of Surrey/A black water accumulates," "The banks of the Thames are clouded!" He anticipates the wastage of the industrial landscape:

His Children exil'd from his breast pass to and fro before him
His birds are silent on his hills, flocks die beneath his branches
His tents are fall'n! his trumpets, and the sweet sound of his harp
Are silent on his clouded hills, that belch forth storms & fire
His milk of Cows and honey of Bees, & fruit of golden harvest,
Is gather'd in the scorching heat, & in the driving rain:
Where once he sat he weary walks in misery and pain:
His Giant beauty and perfection fallen into dust:
Till from within his witherd breast grown narrow with his woes:
The corn is turn'd to thistles & the apples into poison:
The birds of song to murderous crows, his joys to bitter groans!
The voices of children in his tents, to cries of helpless infants! [19]

Bʟᴀᴋᴇ ɢʀᴇᴡ up in London in a world of merchants and tradesmen—his father was a hosier—and from that association, perhaps, came his frequent use of images of weavers and looms and cloth. The family business was modest but successful. Blake was an artistically talented and imaginative child who was encouraged to follow his artistic inclinations. He apprenticed as an engraver and studied at the Royal Academy. His early work was light-hearted, but the mood faded quickly before the reality of London streets that as an adult he could not avoid seeing; streets crowded with prostitutes, many of them children; with boys sold by their families to work as chimney sweeps, who sometimes failed to survive the experience; surrounded by the crowds, the filth, the poverty, the cruelty and oppression of the city, observations summed up in the poem "London."

I wander thro' each charter'd street,
Near where the charter'd Thames does flow.
And mark in every face I meet
Marks of weakness, marks of woe.

In every cry of every Man,
In every Infants cry of fear,
In every voice: in every ban,
The mind-forg'd manacles I hear

How the Chimney-sweepers cry
Every blackning Church appalls,

And the hapless Soldiers sigh,
Runs in blood down Palace walls

But most thro' midnight streets I hear
How the youthful Harlots curse
Blasts the new-born Infants tear
And blights with plagues the Marriage hearse

"London" is one of his most directly accessible poems, the sense of urban alienation obvious, but it helps to know that "charter'd" refers to the ubiquity of commerce, also to the chartered companies that dominated London commerce at the time. As historian E. P. Thompson says of the poem, and who could put it better, "In a series of literal, unified images of great power Blake compresses an indictment of the acquisitive ethic, endorsed by the institutions of State, which divides man from man, brings him into mental and moral bondage, destroys the sources of joy, and brings, as its consequence, blindness and death."[20] The haberdasher's son, raised behind the tinkle of a shop bell, the rustle of silks, and the soft clatter of coins, saw as an adult a fuller vision of the human cost of such goods.

The captive in the mill of the stranger, sold for scanty hire.
They view their former life, they number moments over and over,
Stringing them on their remembrance as on a thread of sorrow.[21]

Whereas the link between the poets Blake, Wordsworth, and Coleridge and the Luddites was in sympathy and shared values, Byron and Shelley took a more active role. Newstead Abbey, the ancestral estate of George Gordon, Lord Byron, is less than ten miles north of Nottingham and not far to the south of what remains of that notorious source of rebellious attitudes, Sherwood Forest. In London, in 1811, working on the autobiographical poem he would call "Childe Harold," Byron heard news of the uprisings of workers in the area, which had in recent years become increasingly industrialized. He wrote to a friend in mid-December, taking a lighthearted tone: "I presume ye papers have told of ye Riots in Notts, breaking of frames & heads & outmaneuvering the military." He went on, "All my affairs are going on very badly, & I must rebel too if they don't amend."[22]

Byron took the matter more seriously than his tone implied. However much enormous differences in wealth and culture separated the aristocracy from working people in nineteenth-century England—it was a flamboyant and excessive age—there nevertheless remained a link, created by the land itself, among those who lived on or from it. He had not been raised rich, as his title might imply, but in real poverty in Aberdeen by his mother, and he remembered well the humiliation and genuine need of that time, an experience that sharpened sympathies others of his class were often lacking. However consistent his sympathies, he may have had other reasons for siding firmly with the workers. The leader of the militia at Nottingham, who had responded to the rebellion with brutality, was Captain Jack Masters. Byron's life was one "romantic," usually scandalous, episode after another, but above all others, the woman he could not forget was his neighbor, Mary Ann Chaworth, who had gone on to marry Masters.

But it was typical of Byron to present a misleading face to the world. (He maintained a pose that he was not a serious poet until a Scottish reviewer took him at his word, or perhaps accepted his challenge, and dismissed his work as irrelevant and amateurish.) After spending time at home over that Christmas, when surely the activities of the frame breakers in the area were a constant topic of conversation, their plight prompted him to take up their cause as the topic of his maiden speech in the House of Lords. His first address to the body—although he had been sitting since 1809—would be in opposition to a bill that authorized the death penalty for "destroying any stocking or lace frames." The bill was specifically aimed at the followers of Ned Ludd.

In his speech, Byron spoke passionately against the "absolute want" and "unparalleled distress" that had driven these men to "excesses so hazardous." He pointed out that however deplorable their means, the wretchedness of their state and their inability to support themselves on meager incomes led them to take desperate action. He objected to the excessive use of soldiers to control them and asked if "executioners must be let loose against your fellow citizens,"[23] rather than restoring peacefulness to the countryside and the workers to their livelihoods by other means. He lost the vote, but followed up his speech with a poem, ironic and bitter, railing against values that set machines above men. It appeared anonymously in the *London Morning Chronicle;* two verses of it read:

> *The rascals, perhaps, may betake them to robbing,*
> *The dogs to be sure have got nothing to eat—*
> *So if we can hang them for breaking a bobbin,*
> *'Twill save all the Government's money and meat:*

Men are more easily made than machinery—
Stockings fetch better prices than lives—
Gibbets on Sherwood will heighten the scenery,
Showing how Commerce, how Liberty thrives![24]

At about the same time, Percy Shelley, freshly returned from a trip to Scotland and the North Country where he had seen for himself the poverty and despair in the area, wrote to Elizabeth Hitchener:

> I have been led into reasonings which make me hate more and more the existing establishment of every kind . . . have beheld scenes of misery. . . . [The workers] are reduced to starvation. My friend, the military are gone to Nott'm   Curses light on them for their motives if they destroy one of its famine[-]wasted inhabitants. . . . The groans of the wretched may pass unheeded til the latest moment of this infamous revelry [of the rich], till the story burst upon them and the oppressed take furious vengeance on the oppressors.[25]

At the same time he was writing "Queen Mab," a poem he knew to be— with its unflinching and unflattering portraits of royalty, commerce, and exploitation—radical, perhaps unpublishable, and certainly dangerous. He published it himself and gave it to his friends. It is seldom included in anthologies, but when read in the spirit in which it was written, it is compelling and unapologetically revolutionary, blending politics with mysticism and fantasy. There is no need to ask why workers were Shelley's most devoted readers and why the volume eventually became virtually a textbook for radicalism, for it is a catalogue of injustice.

Red glows the tyrant's stamp-mark on its bloom,
Withering and cankering deep its passive prime.
He has invented lying words and modes,
Empty and vain as his own coreless heart;
Evasive meanings, nothings of much sound,
To lure the heedless victim to the toils
Spread round the valley of its paradise.

. . . .These puppets of his schemes he moves at will
Even as the slaves by force or famine driven
Beneath a vulgar master, to perform
A task of cold and brutal drudgery;

Hardened to hope, insensible to fear,
Scarce living pulleys of a dead machine,
Mere wheels of work and articles of trade,
That grace the proud and noisy pump of wealth![26]

As did Blake, he draws special attention to the children who emerge in infancy "from its new tenement" and see nothing but desolation and hopelessness:

No shade, no shelter from the sweeping storms of pitiless power . . .
On its wretched frame,
Poisoned, perchance, by the disease and woe
Heaped on the wretched parent, whence it sprung . . .
May breathe not. The untainting light of day
May visit not its longings. It is bound
Ere it has life: yea, all the chains are forged
Long ere its being; all liberty and love
And peace is torn from its defencelessness;
Cursed from its birth, even from its cradle doomed
To abjectness and bondage![27]

It is hardly surprising that after leaving the Lake District for Wales, he began a fund for the children of the Luddite rebels.[28]

These poets understood the factory system—as it then was almost always applied—as the product of reason taken to extremes without regard for consequences. Their empathy was also, in part, an outgrowth of their confidence in and respect for the individual experience, ultimately unshareable but no less valuable for that. In poetry, the individual experience allows for individual interpretation. For weavers, it's translated into individual rights.

"He is the rock of defence for human nature; an upholder and preserver, carrying everywhere with him relationship and love," wrote Wordsworth of the poet in his preface to "Lyrical Ballads," and a poet so described could not easily turn from the plight of the worker.

But what good can a poet actually do? John Keats had wondered. Confronting "the agonies, the strife / Of human hearts" had been his aim in 1816, but by 1819—by which time he had composed most of his extant works—Keats was discouraged, says Romantic scholar David Pirie, seeing himself and his fellow intellectual set as "dreamers weak" and wondering, in "The

Fall of Hyperion," "What benefit canst thou do, or all thy tribe / To the great world."

Today critics and scholars tend to paint Keats as an eloquent aesthete, concerned primarily with sound, emotion, sensuality, and imagination—all of which is true—and to dismiss any deeper, more serious aspects of his work. They often overlook the clear political content in his work, says Pirie. Readers and reviewers of his own time, however, knew very well what he was about, recognizing in his use of certain evocative words and subtle references a "lisped sedition," as one critic phrased it.

Following the Luddite Rebellion and other citizen uprisings, the government, and along with it the ruling and manufacturing classes, remained edgy and defensive. Sympathy for the demands of protestors and rebels was certainly enough to arouse the vitriol of the conservative critics—and anything perceived to encourage unrest, however subtly, was dangerous. Keats was cautious and censored himself—there were laws against seditious writing—and he withheld from publication some of his most radical poetry, convinced that it would be seen as politically subversive and a violation of the laws of the time. His political jabs, when they came, were sly and cloaked in various disguises. Nevertheless, a close reading of his work, looking for the references he planted, reveals a different Keats, one who clearly sympathized—even identified—with working-class goals and struggles.

He was not as far from the working class as one might suppose. His father had owned stables, and he himself had trained as a doctor—a profession whose status was not then what it is today. Critics referred to him as "not a gentleman" in social status, and he could count himself among the disenfranchised as well: he was never wealthy enough to vote. He could identify with hardship, with struggle, and with unfairness. Instead of siding with the merchant class, which appreciated the activities of the government in quelling uprisings, Keats—in a letter written around the time of the Luddite Rebellion, when the countryside was filled with soldiers empowered to keep order—found himself "disgusted" by the "extensive barracks" the government had established in the Midlands and said that the "worst thing" that "Napoleon has done," is to teach the British government "how to organize their monstrous armies."[29] Did he in fact support the frame breakers? Pirie does not feel Keats's sentiments allowed him to go quite that far, but certainly he was interested in and sympathetic to their plight and angered by the excessive government repression.

The Luddite Rebellion was over by 1817, but the movement by ordinary citizens to secure minimal rights to bargain and to express grievances continued, and when the war with France had ended in 1815, the government could devote even more time and resources to dealing with this "threat." Again Keats made clear in his letters his sentiments for rights and against attempts to suppress "our freedom."

Despite his low social status and relative lack of income, there is evidence in these letters that Keats, who lived in comfort and security among the intellectual elite in London, worried that he might forget or lose his sense of unity with "the people"; their poverty; and their struggles for freedom of the press and the right to vote, to meet, to organize, and to express their grievances.

This sense of guilt might have had its origins, in 1819, when government soldiers—joined by merchants, shopkeepers, and publicans—advanced with drawn swords on thousands of unarmed men, women, and children at a political rally for constitutional reforms: election ballots and extended suffrage, among others. It was not just the numbers of these marchers—eighty thousand of them, each committee bearing its own flag—but their discipline that aroused so much fear. The rabble, says E. P. Thompson, had been transformed into "a disciplined *class*." The Manchester yeomen and magistrates responded savagely, and when it was over, 11 were dead and more than 400 injured, 161 by saber wounds. It has come to be called the Peterloo Massacre—the government, without France as an enemy, was apparently willing to wage war against its own citizens—but the participation by the yeomanry made it "class warfare" as well, says E. P. Thompson. It was not a "panic of horsemen," as others have suggested, that prompted the violence, says Thompson, but "the panic of class hatred."[30] It was an event that galvanized the public and solidified liberal leanings in many citizens. Keats did not remain unaffected. It was not a contest between Whig and Tory, he wrote, but "between right and wrong."[31]

In poem after poem, too hastily dismissed as mere paeans to nature and solitude, there are the unnoticed revolutionary phrases, the ones, Pirie says, that "pay their compliments to a modern patriot who defies tyranny."[32] In "To Charles Cowden Clark," for instance, Keats describes the wild poppies in a field of oats, then notes how they "show their scarlet coats, / So pert and useless that they bring to mind / the scarlet coats that pester human kind." There was nothing even vaguely subtle about his poem "To Leigh Hunt, Esq.," which defends Hunt, who had been forced to spend two years in prison for violating censorship laws. And critics of his own time did indeed point to Keats's association with notorious liberals and did see his poetry as politically defiant. But it was his apparent inability to "know his place" in society as much as his sympathy for the working class that critics found so annoying. His irritating revolutionary insight was apparently his view, says Pirie, that the opinions of the laboring classes mattered. Other works, including such well-known examples as "Ode to a Grecian Urn" and "Endymion," reveal, when decoded, their rebellious sides as well.

The real wonder is that Keats's hostility to the government could be so easily missed by critics today. Pirie makes a good case that this radicalism of Keats has been intentionally ignored—he uses the word "censored." In some cases, the record has been distorted in the effort to imply that Keats had no politics. But why? The degree to which such activism remains inconvenient, even today, is plain enough. The idea that art, populism, and activism can find common ground continues to create discomfort for those in power, or for those who are happy supporting power, and how convenient to the status quo, whatever it might be, if the poets of the Romantic period can be dismissed as politically inconsequential.

Perhaps it was indeed the brutal suppression of the Luddite Rebellion that first raised Keats's sympathies, but afterward, as the focus of public uprisings shifted to more general demands for rights and freedoms, he remained supportive, and he expressed his solidarity in words that were clear enough to his readers then. And the emphasis in his work was always on the individual, the human, on sensibility, intellect, creativity, and will.

IF NEW THINKING about order and rationalism had influenced eighteenth-century writing, it was now, in the nineteenth century, having more influence on daily life as these modes of thinking actually began to be applied to manufacturing and to living. The potential to produce goods more cheaply with mechanization, even if it diminished quality, or to reduce labor costs, even if it meant hardship for the community, was compellingly attractive. It was then—as the smoke from factories began to darken the skies over industrial areas; as the rivers became sewers; as traditional ways of life, closely connected to nature, were disturbed; and as ugliness blotted the landscape—that the best poets of the day came to the defense of what they held most dear and saw on the verge of vanishing. Industrialization—or its impact—was offensive.

Blake was not the only one to respond to the horrors of urban congestion. Coleridge had a similar reaction after his visit to Cologne in the poem of that name:

> *In Köhln, a town of monks and bones,*
> *And pavements fanged with murderous stones,*
> *And rags, and hags, and hideous wenches;*
> *I counted two and seventy stenches,*
> *All well defined, and several stinks!*
> *Ye Nymphs that reign o'er sewers and sinks,*
> *The river Rhine, it is well known,*
> *Doth wash your city of Cologne;*
> *But tell me Nymphs, what power devine*
> *Shall henceforth wash the river Rhine?*

The natural world, free and clean and uncongested, was, by implication, much preferred. For Rousseau, the natural state of man was the one in which he would, if left to his own devices, make decisions that were ethically sound; hence it was morally superior. Critics have pointed as well to the characteristic Romantic emphasis on the subjective nature of the mind, which represented a conscious turning from the exterior world to that center of the self. In short, Romanticism was a reaffirmation of the natural and the human and the subjective as opposed to the mechanical and all those things that were undermining man's relationship with nature and with other human beings. If the substance of Wordsworth's verse were overlooked, the titles of his shorter works alone are evidence enough of his intense preoccupation with nature: "To The Cuckoo," "The Rainbow," " To a Butterfly," "The Glow-worm," "To the Small Celandine," "To the Same Flower," "The Sparrow's Nest."

Wordsworth's fears that his chosen landscape would be invaded by the mechanical are expressed directly in his "Sonnet on the projected Kendal and Windermere Railway":

> *Is then no nook of English ground secure*
> *from rash assault? Schemes of retirement sown*
> *In youth, and 'mid the busy world kept pure*
> *As when their earliest flowers of hope were blown,*
> *Must perish;—how can they this blight endure?*

And must he too the ruthless change bemoan
Who scorns a false utilitarian lure
'Mid his paternal fields at random thrown?

But the trains would come. The mechanical looms would come. The peace of the countryside would be shattered by the grinding sound of motors and metal on metal. For writers so conscious and appreciative of beauty, it was especially distressing to see it held in increasingly small regard. In a time that would see a revolution in the production and distribution of goods, there would be an infusion into the marketplace of cheap products that were shoddy and artless. It wouldn't be long before that prompted a rebellion of sorts as well.

There is recognition among these poets, even in the excitement of a time of extraordinary change, that important—perhaps vital—things were being lost and replaced by inferior standards that would come to be regretted. With the new economic order came the imposition of a value system that actually denied value to those things that made life worth living: family, community, relationships, solitude, thoughtfulness. And finally, in an age dedicated to reason, there was a turning away, on the part of leading philosophers and thinkers, from the spiritual and the imaginative aspects of human life— modes of thinking that were inconvenient for the new economics. Efficiency was cold-blooded. Romantics were hot-blooded, inward-turning in protest, seeking to make a point about the appropriateness of human observation and interpretation; of wild, unconstrained thought that went where it went, unrestrained by artificially imposed boundaries of rationalism. Throughout the work of these poets is a deep sense of mystery. For some, God is present in nature in a way that America's transcendentalists would echo several decades later. Even Shelley, who early on had championed atheism, echoed in "Queen Mab" the Quaker belief that something of God was present in every being, and this too would emerge later in transcendentalism.

The protests of the Romantics were as desperate in their way as the protests of the Luddites. There would be no troops, but there would be critics. The Romantic period would be called, by some critics of the following century, a dangerous break with humanist principles and traditional Christian beliefs, suspicious on grounds of nature worship and politics, preoccupied with love and passion and unsettling theories of genius. And happily, all of these criticisms were true.

The industrial revolution triumphed. Economists say, correctly, that each change brought by industrialization produces new jobs. And that is true. But the old worker seldom gets the new job. Workers lost. Nature lost. The machines won. There would be other "Luddite" uprisings in Germany and elsewhere against the mechanization that was undoing the social order and destroying lives, and many of these same sentiments are to be found in German Romanticism as well. Everywhere, as the machine began to dominate, there was awareness among the thoughtful of what was at stake and what stood to be lost, and it would not be lost without a fight.

Clearly, to the extent that they elevated an irrational, unruly world of sensual delight, tied to nature and to human preferences, the Romantics were also undermining the bricks and mortar of a new economic reality that would prove most efficient and most profitable. To the extent that they resented the intrusion of the mechanical into the pristine natural world that provided inspiration, they were standing in the way of progress. And the link between progress and capitalism was already being made. Wrote Shelley in "Queen Mab":

> Commerce has set the mark of selfishness,
> The signet of its all-enslaving power,
> Upon a shining ore, and called it gold;
> Before whose image bow the vulgar great,
> The vainly rich, the miserable proud,
> The mob of peasants, nobles, priests, and kings,
> And with blind feelings reverence the power
> That grinds them to the dust of misery;
> But in the temple of their hireling hearts
> Gold is a living god, and rules in scorn
> All earthly things but virtue. . . .
>
> Even as the slaves by force or famine driven
> Beneath a vulgar master, to perform
> A task of cold and brutal drudgery;
> Hardened to hope, insensible to fear,
> Scarce living pulleys of a dead machine,
> Mere wheels of work, and articles of trade,
> That grace the proud and noisy pomp of wealth?

And so they must be put down. I do not suggest that this process was reasoned out or intentional, but merely that as the demands of the new order were fully accepted and understood at an unconscious level, what was necessary became what felt natural. Notwithstanding their huge popularity with the reading public, the Romantics must be subtly dismissed as irrelevant and even dangerous.

This tactic remains as useful as ever. To object to some technological innovation today is equally likely to invite name-calling. "Luddite" first, and then "Romantic," became and are used still as terms of derision, applied to anyone who values aspects of human life that don't translate easily into efficiency or who rejects, resists, challenges, or even questions the stampede of modernism.

CHAPTER FOUR

The Mechanized Hand

I N THE SITTING-ROOM OF A COMFORTABLE SUBURBAN house just south of London, a prosperous sherry merchant took up the first segment of a newly serialized novel and began reading it to his wife and teenage son. The year was 1836 and the work was *The Pickwick Papers*, written by a 24-year-old journalist named Charles Dickens, who would, under the appealing guise of compelling fiction, provide astute social commentary for the next thirty years. The attentive teenager was the seventeen-year-old John Ruskin, a man who was to become England's most famous art critic. Ruskin's ideas, first about art and architecture and later about economics and the nature of work, would penetrate the consciousness of one age and have an impact on the next. Each of these men, in very different yet curiously complementary ways, would become an outstanding voice of his time. They were both articulating concerns raised by a growing acceptance of utilitarianism, which was separating individuals not only from nature but from their own natures—from the creative, imaginative, and spiritual aspects of human existence—while at the same time imposing a new and ill-fitting mechanical model on every sort of human activity from education to architecture. In his essay, "Signs of the Times," historian Thomas Carlyle had pointed out "how the mechanical genius of our time has diffused itself into quite other provinces. Not the external and the physical alone is now managed by machinery, but the internal and spiritual also."[1]

In the Luddite spirit, Dickens would dramatize in some of his novels what the machine was doing to society, while Ruskin would mine the medieval past for a model of what art, architecture, and society could be if skilled craftsmen had the freedom to exercise individual creativity instead of working under factory conditions. And Carlyle would be a mentor for both.

In the third decade of the nineteenth century, society was deeply divided between the rich and the poor, the powerful and the powerless. The new wealth was different from old wealth. The economic power held by new industrialists and merchants had little to do with ownership of land and agricultural production, as it once had. This was a new mercantile class that wanted, not surprisingly, to exercise the power it had so recently earned and, on the positive side, that led to an extension of the franchise and to some reform.

Economic theory struggled to keep pace with the rapid rate of change. In 1776 Adam Smith had written *Wealth of Nations,* in which he had laid out a blueprint for economic advancement. His theory held that prosperity, which he defined as the accumulation of wealth, was most likely to be achieved by individuals pursuing their own interests without the interference of government. The role of the state, other than arbitrating when those interests conflicted, was simply to stay out of the way. This pursuit of individual well-being would, by increasing the nation's wealth, ultimately benefit the entire community. This is the "rising tide lifts all boats" theory (which would be echoed by Reaganomics in the 1980s). It was not yet the nineteenth-century doctrine of *laissez faire* but laid a credible foundation for it.

Inherent in Smith's theory was the notion that greater efficiency translates into greater profit. One way to produce this efficiency was to create divisions of labor in the manufacturing process. An individual need not be responsible for making one product from start to finish but only for one part of the process, which he or she would repeat again and again, undoubtedly becoming more skilled and faster at that single task. This was not an entirely new idea, but now it became linked to a particular theory. The result would be greater production for less expenditure of time (wages) and energy. Efficiency would be the key to economic success.

The faults of this theory were obvious even to Smith. There would be little pride of work under such a system, and the worker would be distanced and alienated from what he produced, but Smith didn't feel his task was to involve himself in such matters. He was not looking at what was good or bad for the individual but at what, in abstraction, he presumed would be good for the economy as a whole. He was, in effect, looking at the workers with detachment, as if they were merely pieces of equipment, emotionless and soulless. Smith was doing for economics what Descartes and his followers had proposed for science: breaking the problem into pieces with the idea that studying the way these pieces operated could help an understanding of the whole. These particular pieces just happened to be human.

The British economist David Ricardo took Smith's theory and attempted, in *The Principles of Political Economy and Taxation,* published in 1817, to make it more scientific by systematizing laws of cause and effect. His most memorable contribution was to propose that the amount of labor going into a product and its distribution determined its value, which he called the "Labor Theory of Value." Now the laborer had become little more than a unit in the production process to be measured and valued according to his output and nothing more. Ricardo understood and admitted the implications:

> The opinion entertained by the labouring class, that the employment of machinery is frequently detrimental to their interests, is not founded on prejudice and error, but is conformable to the correct principles of political economy.[2]

T. R. Malthus extended this line of thinking further into the icy realm of economic theory by coolly proposing that the growth of population would be regulated by the agency of starvation, because population tended to grow faster than its means of subsistence. This idea, which Smith had hinted at and Ricardo developed, resulted in what came to be called the "Iron Law of Wages," which held that wages would find a natural level when the threat of starvation was serious enough to discourage population increases.

There are people who can think in these sorts of abstract terms—and there are others, like Dickens, who cannot; who see all too clearly how such ideas translate into human reality. But this sort of mechanistic materialism served as support and comfort for the factory owners, who could, with such encouragement, ignore the realities of fear- and hunger-induced population and wage control.

Jeremy Bentham, founder of the philosophy of utilitarianism, envisioned human conduct as ordered simply by pain and pleasure. Reduced simplistically to the credo, "The greatest good for the greatest number," the theory relies heavily on the definition and quantification of pleasure and happiness to achieve this state. Self-interest was the primary motivator of human affairs, in Bentham's view, and laws and other regulatory institutions were necessary simply to see that the individual, in attempting to please himself, didn't harm the larger community. Out of this concept of utility, the government bureaucracy—with its penchant for measuring and counting and ordering—quickly evolved.

Although father and son would come to see the world differently, especially as the son aged, James Mill and John Stuart Mill would bring the ideas of the classical economists together with utilitarianism in a theory proposing that economic laws were natural, inevitable, and as little subject to influence as the laws of physics. Poverty was inevitable, and any attempt to alleviate it was doomed. Attempts to correct it, in fact, would unsettle the economy and thus the well-being of the community and the nation as a whole. Echoing Malthus, the theory assumed that the plight of the poor would be improved when they saw their condition clearly and honestly and sensibly took action to reduce their numbers. This might take a miserable generation or two and would involve, in the days before reliable birth control, considerable restraint, but it sounded good in theory. Government's role was simply to create the conditions under which the law of supply and demand and enlightened self-interest could work naturally without impediment. But theories are one thing; the real-world effects are quite another.

J. S. Mill had not yet written his *Principles of Political Economy* (published in 1848) when Dickens was writing *The Pickwick Papers*, but the effects of classical economic theory and utilitarianism were already becoming all too apparent. Eventually Dickens would become a more sensitive observer of class and economic differences and of human misery, but this is what the young Ruskin would have heard his father read as Mr. Pickwick's coach approached Birmingham:

> It was quite dark when Mr. Pickwick roused himself sufficiently to look out of the window. The straggling cottages by the road-side, the dingy hue of every object visible, the murky atmosphere, the paths of cinders and brick-dust, the deep-red glow of furnace fires in the distance, the volumes of dense smoke issuing heavily forth from high toppling chimneys, blackening

and obscuring everything around; the glare of distant lights, the ponderous waggons which toiled along the road, laden with clashing rods of iron, or piled with heavy goods—all betokened their rapid approach to the great working town of Birmingham.

As they rattled through the narrow thoroughfares leading to the heart of the turmoil, the sights and sounds of earnest occupation struck more forcibly on the senses. The streets were thronged with working-people. The hum of labour resounded from every house, lights gleamed from the long casement windows in the attic stories, and the whirl of wheels and noise of machinery shook the trembling walls. The fires, whose lurid sullen light had been visible for miles, blazed fiercely up, in the great works and factories of the town. The din of hammers, the rushing of steam, and the dead heavy clanking of engines, was the harsh music which arose from every quarter.[3]

This was a new vision of hell, shaped not by Dante's imagination but by the machine. Nothing quite like it would ever have been seen before in the natural world, unless it was a volcano or an uncontrolled conflagration. It was not something Ruskin would have seen or heard in his neighborhood, where he awoke to the sounds of birds in the suburban garden his mother had carefully designed. Nor would he have experienced it on his trips with his family to the Continent, where he was introduced to the best the art world had to offer; nor was he likely to have seen such sights on excursions with his parents to the Lake District, where he walked the hills with Wordsworth's *Guide to the District of the Lakes* in his hand. He would eventually see such scenes from his own coach windows as he traveled to Manchester, but that would come much later. Ruskin, as a young and even as a middle-aged man, was protected from such realities, but through Dickens these images were not unknown to him.

Dickens, in turn, may have benefited from what he came to know of Ruskin's views. In every age there is a cross-pollination of ideas. In *Hard Times*, published in 1854, five years after Ruskin's *The Seven Lamps of Architecture* and three years after the first volume of *Stones of Venice*. Dickens sounds very much like Ruskin when he notes the sameness not just of industrial architecture but of architecture inspired by industry: the monotonous repetition of square, featureless structures designed not for humans, it would seem, but for workers who were thought of only as "Hands," as if Cartesian thinking had extended to isolating that sole piece of the body that was useful to industry, to the neglect of every other. The implication of this architecture was that the "Heads" might benefit in some way from decoration and design, but what need did the "Hands" have for such things?

Both men drew support for their ideas about the mechanizing aspects of utilitarianism from Thomas Carlyle, the irascible historian, biographer, and social critic who, then as now, inspired as much controversy as he did admiration. All three of these men, along with novelists such as Mrs. Gaskell and Charlotte Brontë, saw with painful clarity the problems of the age, but they were up against human nature, a countervailing force of great strength, which they all acknowledged.

There is within every human the perpetual pull of opposites. Fear taunts courage; willpower struggles with appetite; order with disorder. Caution tugs at curiosity as impulse teases aversion. For all the stimulation of the new, there remains the powerful comfort and security of the known. We are, like Dr. Doolittle's famous Pushme-Pullyou, conflicted creatures. Individuality is defined by these differences, by where the balance is finally struck.

But one impulse in particular seems to have weak competition or none at all. The appeal of ease, or the less-taxing option, is unquestioned. Only the obstinate, the perverse, the eccentric, or the mad, the conventional wisdom goes, intentionally choose the more difficult over the easier method of reaching a goal. The hatchet or the ax over the chain saw? "I like the feel of the ax in my hand, the resistance, the thud of impact. I like to feel I am linked to what I am doing. I like the quiet in the forest, the smell of rosin, even the living shudder of the tree as the ax bites," says the old woodsman. The logger smiles, pulls the starter on his chain saw, and has seven trees down in the time the woodsman spends on one. And then the logger's boss brings in the feller-buncher, the giant machine that grasps each tree in a steel embrace, then cuts it and stacks it with its downed companions as if it were kindling; and the logger smiles no more as the new machine does the work of seven chain-saw-bearing men and he finds himself reading want ads. Seldom, however, is the original impulse to make things easier questioned.

The religious have always known that ease is a dangerous road to travel. One reason for caution is that it's sometimes hard to tell who the real beneficiary is. Or whether something is really as easy as it at first seems. Or whether ease costs more than it appears to. Or whether something is being lost in the transition that hasn't been mentioned, or foreseen, or accounted for. Machines, in the time of Carlyle, Dickens, and Ruskin, were making production easier. The matter of "at what cost" had just begun to be considered, and then only by a very few.

Close on the heels of ease is cheap, and the combination, especially in goods, is virtually irresistible. Low cost and convenience: the machine made it possible. Manufacturing saw the advantages of cheaper, faster production at once, and consumption and materialism followed, the words taking on new meaning. The materialist philosophy of the eighteenth century—knowledge literally based on what one could see or feel, an objectification of reality that dismissed other ways of knowing—evolved to represent an approach to living based on what one could buy. Under materialism, the philosophy, reality was only what could be measured; under materialism, the way of life, reality was defined by what could be bought and sold. The Victorian era was defined by a new abundance of "things." Even in America, which lagged a bit behind in industrializing, Emerson would observe, "Things are in the saddle and ride mankind."[4] Suddenly people of relatively modest means could aspire to a proliferation of goods—or facsimiles—once reserved for the rich. The possessor of one sturdy pair of hose might now aspire to half a dozen—less sturdy, perhaps, and prone to weakness here and there, but discernment is no match for delight. The girl trudging to the factory could now envision a bright ribbon for her hair, some compensation for physical misery. There is a human penchant for luxury, abundance, and decoration, and the machine—or what it produced—could satisfy, if not perfectly, then adequately. We are—most of us—easily pleased.

The people who protested the machines were those whose lives and work were tied to the machine's repetitive and relentless demands; those who lived in the soot-covered pall of industrial exhalations; or those who had empathy, rare as it was, for the individuals who did. The working conditions had troubled Wordsworth in "Excursion":

> *A little-one, subjected to the arts*
> *Of modern ingenuity, and made*
> *The senseless member of a vast machine,*
> *Serving as doth a spindle or a wheel*[5]

Now, in the 1840s, the murky, industrial violation of the landscape that Anna Seward had written about in 1785 and the desolate approach to a major industrial town that Dickens described in *The Pickwick Papers* were at their worst. Even the wings of moths, scientists now can see in looking at collections made over time, darkened over the years as they adapted to the darkening of the skies.

Yet it is also a human characteristic that even as we give in to seduction we are conscious, at some level, of having been seduced; of having abandoned common sense for pleasure. And even if the costs of abandoned reason are ignored or, in the pleasure of the moment, have yet to be counted, we suspect they might be more than we bargained for. Thus a certain uneasiness pervaded the Victorian age. The pace of change was dramatic and unsettling. The influence of the machine, now running at full bore, was transforming everything, undermining conventions and comfortable assumptions. The shudder of a shifting paradigm could be felt under even a well-shod heel.

Thomas Carlyle grappled with that confusion. A Scotsman from Dumphreeshire, he was an imposing man with red hair and beard and a forceful manner both in person and in prose. Today his affection for authority, which felt alarmingly like a recipe for totalitarianism and subsequently fed an era of fascism; his toying with notions of racial superiority; and the challenging nature of his sometimes almost impenetrable prose style, have rendered him out of favor if not entirely forgotten. Yet his appeal was not limited to the established intellectuals of his day but extended to the self-educated, that new breed who, with greater access to books, was growing in importance and influence. His insights into the effects of mechanization, industrialization, and science greatly influenced Ruskin, Dickens, Emerson, Thoreau, and William Morris.

Carlyle is best known today for his satire, *Sartor Resartus,* a none too subtle attack on the superficial nature of a society that uses artificial indicators of class and distinction. Through the voice of a fictitious German philosopher whom he calls Drogenes Teufelsdröckh, he projects his own transcendentalist opinions, borrowed from the German Romantic movement and Goethe. Using this device, he is able both to project his ideas and to distance himself from them—a practical approach when so much of what he said might be found unpleasant by those who would feel most sharply the sting of his critical views.

"What is there that we cannot love, since all was created by God," he writes, an idea that seems appealing and almost conventional but that has the potential to lead to "dangerous" thoughts if followed logically—which is

precisely what Carlyle did. Nature—all of it— is suddenly on an equal footing with humankind. His view is really a version of Romantic pantheism
that goes far beyond Wordsworth's idea of being at one with nature on an
intellectual level. "Despise not the rag from which man makes paper or the
litter from which the earth makes Corn. Rightly viewed no meanest object
is insignificant; all objects are as windows through which the philosophic
eye looks into Infinitude itself," he writes.[6]

It was one thing to admire nature; quite another to assign equal "created
by God" status to the ordinary, as he does in that passage, a notion that bothered those of a more establishment or fundamentalist or capitalistic bent
then—and now. The idea that everything has intrinsic value could compete
with, if not challenge, the understanding of humans as the supreme beings
in the theological and worldly hierarchy, and it could even undermine the
view of nature that is essential to capitalism: that the earth's resources are
there for humans to use as they wish. What might happen if everything—
the earth, plants, animals—became sacred? How would that change the
prevailing economic worldview? The origin of the twentieth-century philosophy of deep ecology, seen as profoundly radical to many, is based on a similar idea, minus God. Carlyle was a man with unsettling ideas for the status
quo then and now, and he was and is admired or hated depending upon
one's point of view. There is no middle ground because Carlyle leaves no
room in the middle.

Carlyle's prose style is bombastic, repetitive, and digressive—and yet,
says historian E. P. Thompson, "His writings are among the greatest quarries
of ideas in the first half of the nineteenth century, shot through with occasional gleams of the profoundest revolutionary insight."[7]

Carlyle called the prevailing economic philosophies of the day "the
Dismal Science," and in the 1830s and 1840s he was one of very few who
condemned the industrial age these ideas supported. What put Carlyle at
complete odds with the prevailing theories was that, although no longer a
Christian, he believed in God and saw man as a spiritual being whose greatest happiness would be found not in the acquisition of material goods but in
following the moral dictates of his heart. This heart that dictated moral
imperatives could not be located by the anatomists or the scientists and had
no place in the world as it was rapidly being reordered, but the creed of "The
greatest happiness for the greatest number," with its materialistic implications, was morally repugnant to Carlyle. Man found satisfaction in work.

Laissez faire, an economic philosophy that seemed to deny people the all-important *right* to work—jobs, under this hands-off economic model, were linked to supply and demand and were not guaranteed   was unacceptable.

Carlyle leaped ahead to predict the effects of science (whether economic theory, physics, biology, or geology) on religion, repercussions that were not so obvious then, and he was concerned that scientific and utilitarian thought, if broadly applied, might have an unexpected impact on human relations as well. Science, he says, seems intent on substituting measuring and counting for more human and qualitative means of perception. Teufelsdröckh echoes Mary Shelley's *Frankenstein* fantasy of science out of control with a vision of an apparition of his own creation: a bodiless "Head," preserved alive, all rationality and no heart. (C.S. Lewis would repeat this idea a century later in his science fiction fantasy *That Hideous Strength*.)

> "Shall your Science," exclaims [Teufelsdröckh], "proceed in the small chink-lighted, or even oil-lighted, underground workshop of Logic alone; and man's mind become an Arithmetical Mill, whereof Memory is in the Hopper, and mere Tables of Sines and Tangents, Codification and Treatises of what you call Political Economy, are the Meal? And what is that Science, which the scientific head alone, were it screwed off, and (like the Doctor's in the Arabian Tale) set in a basin to keep it alive, could prosecute without shadow of a heart,—but one other of the mechanical and menial handicrafts for which the Scientific Head (having a Soul in it) is too noble an organ? I mean that Thought without Reverence is barren, perhaps poisonous; at best, dies like cookery with the day that called it forth; does not live, like sowing, in successive tilths and wider-spreading harvests, bringing food and plenteous increase to all Time."[8]

It was science and numbers that drove the new machines, and in this changing and dangerous world, Carlyle's sympathies lay, as did those of Blake and Byron before him, with the factory workers.

His call for reform in his 1839 essay "Chartism"—that midcentury movement for broader suffrage, the secret ballot, and other political reforms—was bold but no more radical than the ideas of other reformers. It was, however, profoundly felt, with a powerful empathy that made it compelling. Carlyle was deeply pained by injustice, as Dickens would be a few years later. But he was also very conscious that it wasn't simply the economic system that was at fault but the ideas behind it, the very thinking that made it possible. A fist-thumping anger against the machine and all that is mechanical thunders through his prose. He saw that a reliance on counting and measuring, as benign and even important as they might appear to be, could lead to the regrettable domination of statistics and tables. He had already, in 1839, taken the measure of the weaknesses of numbers, pinpointing their potential to distort and misrepresent and their ability to be misused—but also noting their power. The tyranny of numbers could bring just as abrupt an end to a discussion then as it can now. "With what serene conclusiveness a member of some Useful-Knowledge Society stops your mouth with a fig-ure of arithmetic. To him it seems he has there extracted the elixir of the matter, on which now nothing more can be said."[9]

But it was "Sign of the Times," his very first essay on social themes, pub-lished anonymously (but widely recognized as his), that in 1829 unleashed the full force of his rhetoric against the machine:

> Were we required to characterise this age of ours by any single epithet, we should be tempted to call it, not an Heroical, Devotional, Philosophical, or Moral Age, but, above all others, the Mechanical Age. It is the Age of Machinery, in every outward and inward sense of that word; the age which, with its whole undivided might, forwards, teaches and practises the great art of adapting means to ends.[10]

Everything, even the simplest operation, he noted, seemed to require the intervention of some sort of "contrivance":

> On every hand, the living artisan is driven from his workshop, to make room for a speedier, inanimate one. The shuttle drops from the fingers of the weaver, and falls into iron fingers that ply it faster. The sailor furls his sail and lays down his oar; and bids a strong, unwearied servant, on vaporous wings, bear him through the waters. . . . There is no end to machinery. Even the horse is stripped of his harness, and finds a fleet fire-horse yoked in his stead. Nay, we have an artist that hatches chickens by steam; the very brood-hen is to be superseded? For all earthly, and for some unearthly pur-poses, we have machines and mechanic furtherances; for mincing our cab-bages; for casting us into magnetic sleep. We move mountains, and make seas our smooth highway; nothing can resist us. We war with rude Nature; and by our resistless engines, come off always victorious, and loaded with spoils.[11]

Those who stood to benefit from the changing economic order could dis-miss Carlyle as someone who wanted to stop progress or who failed to see the ultimate benefit of cheaper consumer goods, or simply as a crank. But what Carlyle saw clearly was that employing the machine so extensively had begun to make people feel inadequate, if not useless. Carefully cultivated skills and pride in craftsmanship became worthless as commodities, point-less luxuries in a marketplace where the machine standard was "good enough" because it was cheap. Working life—which, whatever its attendant hardships, had been varied and interesting as people participated in the making of goods from raw material to finished product—was now a parade of endless sameness, of boring repetition that dulled and stunted the human mind.

The machine *has* accomplished many things, he admitted. That was obvious to anyone. People are better "fed, clothed, lodged." More *things* are available. But the abundance of things was only a small part of the transfor-mation that was under way as the industrial age picked up steam. People had begun to think and act differently, and he identified the impact of the machine at the heart of the shift. Machines are not human. There is a rigid-ity, a uniformity, a predictability, a ruthlessness, a thoughtlessness, a com-plete absence of emotion in their operation. And yet they get things done. How clear it was becoming to many that people could accomplish more if only they could be more like machines and less like themselves. It was a simple but stunning idea. It opened a world of related ideas. Institutions could be redesigned using the mechanical-industrial model. Humans should adapt—and would be the better for it—assumed those infatuated with the notion of perfectibility.

Carlyle saw the fallacy of the argument at once. Just as machines were not humans, it was equally true that humans were not machines. People did not operate effectively in the same ways as machines; their talents lay else-where. And yet, step by incautious step, society was being reordered as if they were machines. The attempts to effect this transformation—beyond the factory, the prison, or the school, where individuals had little or no con-trol over their lives—were generally failures. People were difficult to order outside controlled situations. Yet with the efficient mechanical model before them, those in whose interests it was to see it applied to humans would keep on trying—then and now.

But to look at the disadvantages of mechanization is to see only half the picture. Doubtless the age was advancing, admitted Carlyle. "Its very unrest, its ceaseless activity, its discontent contains matter of promise." He acknowledged, even as he bemoaned the increasing distance, social and economic, between the classes, the rich and the poor, that education had increased the level of "thinking minds." But he was most prescient in discerning that the nature of the mechanical model had begun to spread its influence over institutions in a way that was harmful. Education, politics, even religion were being reorganized along regimented lines, he observed. "Men are grown mechanical in head and in heart, as well as in hand. They have lost faith in individual endeavor, and in natural force of any kind." The same held true for philosophy. Locke's "whole doctrine is mechanical," he noted. Civil government was commonly referred to as the Machine of Society,

> and [we] talk of it as the grand working wheel from which all private machines must derive, or to which they must adapt their movements. Considered merely as a metaphor, all this is well enough; but here, as in so many other cases, the "foam hardens itself into a shell," and the shadow we have wantonly evoked stands terrible before us and will not depart at our bidding.[12]

When the metaphor becomes reality, Carlyle understood, when the standards of industrial efficiency replicate themselves throughout society, clothed in other garb, until our institutions and even our thoughts are mechanized, expect trouble.

Dickens seized upon the mechanization of thinking in education in his novel *Hard Times* (1854). Yet it was really the third of three novels by Dickens that had dealt with the worst effects of the prevailing social and economic system, coming after *Bleak House* (1852–53)and *Domby and Son* (1846). Although published some 15 years after "Sign of the Times," it is dedicated to Carlyle. *Hard Times* is often described as a novel about industrialization. Indeed, it begins with a memorable description of industrialized fictional Coketown (assumed to be Preston):

> It was a town of red brick, or of brick that would have been red if the smoke and ashes had allowed it; but, as matters stood it was a town of unnatural red and black like the painted face of a savage. It was a town of machinery and tall chimneys, out of which interminable serpents of smoke trailed themselves for ever and ever, and never got uncoiled. It had a black canal in it, and a river that ran purple with ill-smelling dye, and vast piles of building full of windows where there was a rattling and a trembling all day long, and

where the piston of the steam-engine worked monotonously up and down, like the head of an elephant in a state of melancholy madness. It contained several large streets all very like one another, and many small streets still more like one another, inhabited by people equally like one another, who all went in and out at the same hours, with the same sound upon the same pavements, to do the same work, and to whom every day was the same as yesterday and tomorrow, and every year the counterpart of the last and the next.[13]

There is, in *Hard Times,* a relentless attack on the polluting effects of industrialization—and on the denying posture of the industrialists. Mr. Bounderby, the town's leading success story, is pleased to point out the virtues of the city's foul air in a way that reminds us rather forcefully that in public relations, nothing has changed.

"First of all, you see our smoke," he tells a newcomer. "That's meat and drink to us. It's the healthiest thing in the world in all respects, and particularly for the lungs." And Mr. Bounderby is no less pleased to talk about the conditions in the factories themselves. "It's the pleasantest work there is, and it's the lightest work there is, and it's the best paid work there is."[14]

And the demands of his workers are unreasonable, a matter of their weak character or constitution. "There's not a Hand in this town, sir, man, woman, or child, but has one ultimate object in life. That object is, to be fed on turtle soup and venison with a gold spoon."[15]

Actually, it was a work environment where a "Hand" could be fined for talking, singing. or whistling and most assuredly for daring to bargain for his labor. Someone who complained about conditions or pay was not only out of a job but branded a troublemaker and unlikely to find one elsewhere.

But for all the vivid descriptions of miserable living and working conditions found throughout, *Hard Times* is less about industrialization per se than it is about the mechanization that was beginning to have an iron grip on the way individual lives were lived out—not only those of factory workers but those of middle-class people who were being taught to think in new ways. It is not the worker who is the chief character of Dickens's tale, but Louisa, a young woman raised to think in a rigid and scientific manner; carefully trained to reject anything but the rational and the logical; taught to ignore anything that could not be proven by statistics and, above all, never to "wonder."

"Now, what I want is Facts. Teach these boys and girls nothing but Facts.

Facts alone are wanted in life. Plant nothing else, and root out everything else. You can only form the minds of reasoning animals upon Facts: nothing else will ever be of any service to them," Mr. M'Choakumchild tells the local schoolteacher, Mr. Gradgrind, as the book opens.

"He and some one hundred and forty other schoolmasters," writes Dickens, "had been lately turned at the same time, in the same factory, on the same principles, like so many pianoforte legs." Poor Louisa, who thinks that she might "fancy" flowers on her carpet, if she were to install one, is told, "But that's it! You are never to fancy":

> "You are to be in all things regulated and governed," said the gentleman, "by fact. We hope to have, before long, a board of fact composed of commissioners of fact, who will force the people to be a people of fact, and of nothing but fact. You must discard the word Fancy altogether."[16]

Predictably, this approach leads to a blighted and unfulfilled life, until her heart is touched and she acts out of "irrational" sympathy. At the crisis point of her life, she returns home, reminded that

> first coming upon Reason through the tender light of Fancy, she had seen it a beneficent god, deferring to gods as great as itself: not a grim Idol, cruel and cold, with its victims bound hand to foot, and its big dumb shape set up with a sightless stare, never to be moved by anything but so many calculated tons of leverage—what had she to do with these? Her remembrances of home and childhood, were remembrances of the drying up of every spring and fountain in her young heart as it gushed out.[17]

There were some who were disappointed in Dickens for not attacking the working conditions more strongly and for talking about education when he could have been telling of striking workers. Even Ruskin was critical. It was one of Dickens's most important books, which he felt "should be studied with close and earnest care by persons interested in social questions," but the character of Bounderby had been exaggerated into a "dramatic monster, instead of a characteristic example of a worldly master."[18]

But Dickens understood the climate of his times well enough; he seemed to know how far he could go and still retain his audience. Charlotte Brontë's *Jane Eyre* had been attacked for being too sympathetic toward the poor and not sympathetic enough to the rich. Mrs. Gaskell's *Mary Barton,* and other novels—Disraeli's, *Sybil* for example—that looked too closely at the "condition of England" question, the sharp divisions between rich and poor, came in for similar criticism. *Hard Times,* which was published in the second half of Dickens's career, notwithstanding complaints by those of a reforming nature that it did not go far enough, would be described by Macauley as "sullen socialism," and such criticisms were beginning to damage his reputation. But Dickens saw clearly that industrialism and utilitarianism depended upon each other in ways he hoped to make transparent to others.

It is difficult today—when a network of social and welfare programs, however imperfect, takes the edge off poverty; when the right to a free pub- lic education is assumed; when children are, at least in most Western coun- tries, protected by child labor laws—to imagine the terrible conditions in nineteenth-century England. It is too easy to think of Dickens's stories as *merely* caricatures and exaggerations, when, in fact, they were based firmly on the parliamentary reports he read as a journalist and his own careful observations. Before the Poor Laws were passed in 1834, farm wages had been fixed but rents and the prices of other necessities allowed to rise natu- rally. The gap left farm workers destitute. The dole, administered by local parishes, prevented outright starvation: Malthus was not taken literally, and the English were not entirely without sympathy when the consequences of poverty were brought to their attention. Parish handouts were based on the number of mouths to feed, and, as stingy as they were, they did in fact have the effect of encouraging—or at least not discouraging—the production of another mouth. As the growing population failed to find work in the fields, people gravitated to the new industrial areas where the overabundance of workers kept wages low. During the forty years prior to the passage of the Poor Laws, the number of paupers doubled. The rural poor had become ragged, malnourished, and hopeless; condemned to a life term of poverty with no possibility of parole.

The poorest families were broken up and sent to grim workhouses where conditions were designed to discourage lingering. The best hope for the children of these families was to find work in one of the dangerous occupa- tions available to them, such as sweeping chimneys. But they were equally likely, says Edgar Johnson in his biography of Dickens, to descend into the dark streets of crime. The picture Dickens painted of this system in *Oliver Twist* is as vivid and compelling as it is bleak and dispiriting. Dickens knew too well the damp, the grime, the stench, the squalor, the desperation— and the misery and sickness—of the workhouse, because not only had he observed these conditions, he had actually lived them.

Dickens had been born to "gentlemanly" status, but after a few years of comfort and pleasure, he had experienced a desperate poverty when his impractical father, through mismanagement and bad luck, bankrupted his family. His father was sent to debtor's prison, his mother reduced to pawning or selling everything but a few essential pieces of furniture; and Dickens himself, at the age of twelve, went out to work tying labels on pots of blacking. His education, when his father reestablished himself, was spotty, but when he turned to journalism, his eye for detail, ability to understand character, ear for speech, well-trained powers of recall, and wisdom to see where it all fit in a compelling narrative could not be matched. The public loved him.

From our perspective, what is interesting is his transformation from a boy who thought rebellious radicals deserved hanging to a man who, by 1840, could not ignore the desperate social inequalities and an institutionalized system of unfairness. Daily, on his walks through London, he saw filth and congestion and the crime and disease these conditions fostered. He read in the parliamentary reports the hideous conditions under which children worked, half-dressed in rags, pulling coal-laden carts through calf-high water deep within the dark mines. In 1841 he contributed to a newspaper a series of verses chiding the Tories and others who opposed labor reforms and later that year wrote to a friend, "How radical I am getting!" But this radicalism was based on a simple sense of what was just and what was not. He knew from personal experience how unfair life could be and saw in society what others found expedient to ignore.

He shared Carlyle's contempt for a government that—controlled by industrial interests, the aristocracy, and rich merchants—was ignoring and failing its people, and he saw little prospect of reform coming from a middle class that identified with and aspired to the standard of the upper classes. Change was unlikely to come from that quarter unless people of the middle class could be enlightened while they were being entertained. After his early successes, he saw his own abilities and popularity as a means of penetrating this middle-class myopia. Although injustice is always an underlying theme, direct social criticism is only one of many subcurrents in most of his books. Yet in *Oliver Twist, Bleak House, Domby and Son,* and finally *Hard Times,* he directly attacked materialism, greed, and the obtuseness of the moneyed classes, along with the industrial system that fed these evils.

Dickens's England in *Bleak House* is one in which right principles have been obscured. People see only what they want to see. The tale opens with a fog that is both literal and allegorical. It is London's fog, but it is also England's; a fog that blurs the reality of a society that is blind to the failure of its own institutions, the effects of rapid industrialization, and the high cost of selfish interests and greed. "The key institution in *Bleak House* is the Court of Chancery," says Edgar Johnson, and "both Law and fog are fundamentally symbols of all the murky forces that suffocate the creative energies of mankind."[19] Krooks' death from spontaneous human combustion is finally the only fitting symbolic solution, an explosive end to human corruption.

Dickens had, by now, become a literary revolutionary, pointing out a host of social ills badly needing reform. And yet he was writing in a period that has come to be called the counterrevolution. Fifty years before, the possibilities of change had felt exciting. Then, as society began to shudder and crack under the weight of rapid industrialization, the ominous rumblings underfoot began to feel dangerous. Strikes meant violence, and the revolutionary spirit with which many had sympathized was now checked and subdued. Dickens's popularity allowed some leeway in bringing up these subjects, especially when they were laid out in the context of a compelling tale, but as Tory critics turned up their noses at his social criticism, even he had to watch his step.

A SOCIETY UNDER this much pressure needed a safety valve. In *Hard Times*, nature is an outlet for the frustrations brought on by the arduous, regimented, and exhausting demands of the factories and industrialization. The factory workers—ironically—take the train until it passes the last smokestack and has traveled beyond the clank and clamor of the town to meadows and woods, where they can walk in solitude and pleasure, restoring themselves. Nature is where the train and the factory have not yet reached, and healing is found here.

In Mrs. Gaskell's *Mary Barton*, nature plays a similar role. The book opens on Green Heys Fields, where the workers have gathered to relax and play games. In describing this as yet unspoiled spot, Mrs. Gaskell allows herself that nostalgic backward glance to the rural life that had once been common: the close relationship with animals and plants, the day shaped by light and weather instead of by the demands of commerce, industry, and the clock. This bucolic beginning stands in contrast to the harshness of the urban and industrial life that follows.

Dickens read *Mary Barton* and admired it, and he asked Mrs. Gaskell to write for his magazine, *Household Words,* which she happily agreed to do. Elizabeth Cleghorn Gaskell was born in London in 1810 but grew up farther north. She married the Rev. William Gaskell when she was twenty-two, and her life as a minister's wife was spent raising her children and working among the poor. Her writing was sporadic until *Mary Barton* made her a celebrity, but afterward she wrote and published steadily.

In writing about the world of Manchester that Gaskell saw in her minis-terial work, she was attempting to correct, for her middle-class readers, what she perceived as the chief cause of England's distress: not just the growing economic divisions between rich and poor but the great chasm that pre-vented those whose feet rested on Turkish carpets from having any idea what was happening in the mean streets of this industrial city. This chasm, she felt, grew chiefly out of ignorance. Individuals—whether workers, house servants, merchants, factory owners, or aristocrats—were so separated that they knew little or nothing about one another's lives, and the effects of this ignorance could be and were both dangerous and tragic.

The workers in *Mary Barton* saw their "lottery-like" existence, their sud-den shifts from relative comfort to dire straits, against a passing parade of the rich gowns, carriages, and shopping trips of their masters and their fam-ilies. In *Mary Barton,* anger against the condition of the workers is direct, as personal conflict and tragedy are laid out against a backdrop of the factory town. This is Gaskell's topic, as she spells out quite clearly in her preface to the book:

> I had always felt a deep sympathy with the care-worn men, who looked as if doomed to struggle their lives in strange alternatings between work and want; forced to and fro by circumstances. I saw that they were sore and irritable against the rich, the even tenor of whose seemingly happy lives appeared to increase the anguish caused by the lottery-like nature of their own.

They were bound to each other by common interests, she says, and yet "the woes, which come with ever-returning tide-like flood to overwhelm the workmen in our manufacturing towns pass unregarded by all but the sufferers."

Gaskell invents nostalgia, that longing and need for the simpler life away from the noise and stress of the town. Old Alice, who is forced to make her living in the city, is a transitional figure who has never made her peace with the urban life she must lead and still yearns for what she has left behind. She returns to the countryside of her youth to pick her healing herbs and remains, in the book, a link between the life-giving past and the death-dealing present in and around the factories.

Gaskell's sympathies did not change, and yet her next novel, *North and South,* was more subtle, perhaps because *Mary Barton* had been criticized for being too sympathetic to the workers. Her approach is more even-handed, allowing discussions of the advantages and disadvantages of collective bargaining. One factory owner is portrayed sympathetically as sincerely concerned about his workers' well-being, and indeed, there were some who were. The central concern is the issue of duty and how much the individual is entitled to risk for the sake of some principle. What are his or her obligations and responsibilities to a larger community or, indeed, to a higher authority in the conduct of life and in the making of decisions? The manner is which this conflict is resolved has the potential to affect society in a powerful way. But in both novels, she captures the misery of the dispirited workers who, as victims of the machines, have lost any reasonable expectation of satisfaction or any sense of personal worth.

These writers had not chosen their topics on whim. The industrial cities were growing at an astounding rate. The population of Liverpool had increased in the fifty years between 1801 and 1851 from 78,000 to 376,000. Similar numbers were reported in Manchester-Salford and Birmingham and, to a lesser extent, in Leeds and Sheffield. These cities were swelled by workers who had come looking for jobs and who had to be housed as cheaply as possible, and the slums grew with the numbers. Back-to-back row houses with inadequate sanitation created the conditions that Frederick Engels recorded in his classic 1845 work, *The Conditions of the Working Class in England.*

It seems important to note that the twenty-four-year-old Engels, who had come from Germany only a few years before as a representative of his father's business, wrote this book in German for a German audience. It was translated into English by an American woman in 1885 and was not published in England until 1892, nearly a half-century after it had first been written. And by then, some of the worst abuses had been corrected.

But in 1845 Engels noted how neatly Manchester was divided so that a visitor need never see the slums; need never even know they were there. But they were there, nevertheless—with little or no public transportation, it was obvious that workers had to live near the factories. The factories had to be located beside the river, both for a source of water and for a place to send waste water, and however easily one might divert one's eyes from living conditions, it was impossible to ignore what flowed through the city, a "narrow, coal black, stinking river full of rubbish."

Alongside the river were several tanneries, "and they fill[ed] the neighborhood with the stench of animal putrefication," and "above them were dye works, bone mills, and gas works; work and workers tied to each other; prisoners of circumstance." When the river at the bottom of this slope dried up in summer, it left "a long string of the most disgusting blackish-green slime pools . . . from the depths of which miasmatic gas constantly arouse."[20]

To document the appalling conditions under which men, women, and children worked and lived, Engels used not only his own observations but, as Dickens had, official parliamentary reports that documented the sixty-four-hour work week; the rates of death and maiming; the lack of education for the children; the filthy, damp, and miserable lodgings; the hardship suffered by young mothers and the babies they were forced to leave in the care of barely older children as they returned to work; the malnutrition; the illness; the grinding fatigue.

This, then, was the real cost of cheap hosiery, and between those who wore stockings and those who made them no conversation was possible. The gap was too great. England was, as Disraeli wrote in his novel *Sybil,* two nations; "between whom there is no intercourse and sympathy, who are as ignorant of each others habits, thoughts, and feeling as if they were dwellers in different zones, or inhabitants of different planets; who are formed by a different breeding, are fed by a different food, are ordered by different manners, and are not governed by the same laws." And what were these two nations? "THE RICH AND THE POOR" came the reply.[21]

Charlotte Brontë's *Shirley,* on the other hand, boldly raised the additional issue of the position of women in society and examined a conflict of the recent past that many would have preferred to forget: she took on the Luddite Rebellion itself. Brontë's first novel, *Jane Eyre,* published under the name of Currer Bell, was a triumph. It was a hard act to follow, particularly because in *Shirley* she was attempting something different, a novel in which both history and social concerns would play an important role. *Shirley* is not about the individual in society so much as it is about the individual shaped by society.

Certainly the subject was a dramatic departure from the romance of *Jane Eyre*, and in writing a book that neatly fits into the "condition of England" category of novels Charlotte was taking a risk with an audience she had so recently created. She opens the book with a raid by the frame breakers. If Brontë is no Luddite, clearly she is sympathetic to the cause. Brontë soon interjects, in her own voice as the omniscient author, an accurate description of the times. She notes the war with France, the stresses and fatigue it created, the trade embargoes, the overstock of goods that stocked warehouses.

The story has two heroines: Carolyn Haseltine and Shirley Keeldar. The first is the ward of her clergyman uncle, the second the heir to an estate. Carolyn, who has a gentle, compliant personality, is in love with her cousin, Robert Moore, owner of a mill. Brontë understood the economic forces pushing the new machinery, and yet she saw the dilemma:

> At this crisis, certain inventions in machinery were introduced into the staple manufactures of the north, which greatly reducing the number of hands necessary to be employed, threw thousands out of work, and left them without legitimate means of sustaining life. A bad harvest supervened. Distress reached its climax. Endurance, overgoaded, stretched the hand of fraternity to sedition. The throes of a sort of moral earthquake were felt heaving under the hills of the northern counties. But, as is usual in such cases, nobody took much notice. When a food-riot broke out in a manufacturing town, when a gig-mill was burnt to the ground, or a manufacturer's house was attacked, the furniture thrown into the streets, and the family forced to flee for their lives, some locals were or were not taken by the local magistracy; a ringleader was detected, or more frequently suffered to elude detection; newspaper paragraphs were written on the subject, and the thing stopped.[22]

Her sympathies were with those whom the machines had put out of work, and her recitation of the excuses for why conditions could not be ameliorated has a very clear ironic tone. Of course Progress could not be stopped nor Science held back nor blamed:

> As to the sufferers, whose sole inheritance was labour, and who had lost that inheritance — who could not get work, and consequently could not get

wages, and consequently could not get bread — they were left to suffer on; perhaps inevitably left: it would not do to stop the progress of invention, to damage science by discouraging its improvements; the war could not be terminated, efficient relief could not be raised: there was no help then; so the unemployed underwent their destiny — ate the bread and drank the waters of affliction.[23]

Brontë understood the thinking of the workers and appreciated how their rage could be directed at a visible symbol of their misery, and there is passion in her voice as she says:

Misery generates hate: these sufferers hated the machines which they believed took their bread from them; they hated the buildings which contained those machines; they hated the manufacturers who owned those buildings.[24]

Robert is nevertheless determined, despite the attacks, to install new machinery that he hopes will save his business. Because of the embargoes, his warehouse is filled to the top with unsold cloth; and, as he explains to a pleading worker, it will do that worker no good if he goes out of business and there is no mill at all. He is pressured by the installation of the frames elsewhere, he says.

The workers themselves seem to face the inevitability of the new machines, asking only that they be phased in gradually. One worker pleads with Moore:

"We're thrown out o'work wi' these frames: we can get nought to do: we can earn nought. What is to be done? Mun we say, wisht! And lig us down and dee? . . . Will n't ye gie us a bit o' time? . . . Will n't ye consent to mak' your changes rather more slowly?" asks a worker.[25]

Shirley endeavors to set up a fund that will help the starving families. There is a direct attack on the mill, which Robert and men he has called upon to help him fend off, and Shirley is as concerned for the wounded attackers as she is for Robert Moore's plight.

Brontë's book is still a romance, albeit with a social theme, and it is the resolution of affections that takes a higher priority at the end than the resolution of social ills. Although one senses in her writing a feeling of inevitability about the industrial era, it is not without strong misgivings. Carolyn listens, with some alarm, as Robert outlines his plans for a prosperous future:

As for me, if I succeed as I intend to do, my success will add to his [Robert's brother's, who will marry Shirley] and Shirley's income: I can double the value of their mill-property: I can line yonder barren Hollow with lines of cottages, and rows of cottage-gardens—

Robert! And root up the copse?

The copse shall be firewood ere five years elapse; the beautiful wild ravine shall be a smooth descent; the green natural terrace shall be a paved street: there shall be cottages in the dark ravine, and cottages on the lonely slopes: the rough pebbled track shall be an even, firm, broad, black, sooty road, bedded with the sinders from my mill: and my mill, Caroline—my mill shall fill its present yard.

Horrible! You will change our blue hill-country air into the Stilbro' smoke atmosphere.

I will pour the waters of Pactolus through the valley of Briarfield.

I like the beck a thousand times better.

I will get an act for enclosing Nunnely Common, and parceling it out into farms.

Stilbro' Moor, however, defies you, thank Heaven. What can you grow in Bilberry Moss.[26]

The copse is a lovely wood where Caroline had spent contemplative time. Pactolus is a river in Asia Minor traditionally believed to be rich in gold. The beck is a pleasant stream. Robert's plan for getting an act in order to divide up commonly held land into private ownership is part of the "enclosure" process that undermined the sense of community and that was strongly resisted by local people. Only "worthless" Stilbro' Moor, which could not support agriculture and was apparently useless to humans, would remain untouched.

Brontë ends the book as the omniscient author, and the valley is now nearly as Robert had planned it would be:

The other day I passed up the Hollow, which tradition says was once green, and lone, and wild; and there I saw the manufacturer's day-dreams embodied in substantial stone and brick and ashes—the cinder-black highway, the cottages, and the cottage-gardens; there I saw a mighty mill, and a chimney, ambitious as the tower of Babel.[27]

Her housekeeper tells her how it once was and describes how her own mother, on a summer evening some fifty years earlier, had come running in "just at the edge of dark," describing a farish (fairy) she had seen in Fieldhead Hollow: "And that was the last fairish that was seen in this countryside . . . a lonesome spot it was—and a bonnie spot—full of oak trees and nut trees. It is altered now."[28]

Brontë now turns sly as she ends the book. "The story is told. I think I now see the judicious reader putting on his spectacles to look for the moral. It would be an insult to his sagacity to offer directions. I only say, God speed him in the quest!"[29]

In one after another character in *Shirley,* the conflict Brontë presents involves denial of the right to feel. The social and economic system did not allow it. Feelings did not translate into anything of material value in this narrow and constrained scheme. Feelings were worse than useless: they were dangerous.

The Romantic poets had understood intuitively the importance of feelings, but in the period they were writing, at the very start of the industrial revolution, they had not, perhaps, understood how devastating the denial of feeling would become in a society increasingly dedicated to the needs of the machines. *Shirley* confirmed the role of feeling, even ending with a lament for the loss of a world of imaginative fantasy—a world inhabited by fairies.

Although *Shirley* offered no program for eliminating the divisions and discriminations within society other than charity, compassion, and "job-opportunities," it was this utilitarian and machinelike denial of feeling that allowed one segment of society, the privileged, to wall itself off from the rest. In essence, the right to feel is the right to be, to have one's existence, one's needs, and even one's preferences acknowledged as valid. The reuniting of a divided country depended upon the restoration of this right. Brontë wasn't the only one who understood that discounting the immeasurable qualities and needs of the human experience was a dangerous trend.

John Ruskin, art critic, essayist, and popular lecturer, has almost been forgotten outside of Victorian studies. And "forgotten" would hardly need a qualifier if it were not for the recent release of the second volume of Tim Hilton's biography, *John Ruskin: The Later Years,* the reviews of which predictably bypassed Ruskin's extraordinary work and influence to focus, with the infantile prurient preoccupation of most of today's media, on Ruskin's relationship with Rosa LaTouche, whom he adored from the time she was eleven years old. It's worth noting that he remained both entranced by and devoted to LaTouche well into her adulthood, until her death at twenty-seven, which surely contradicts the impression that it was only children who interested him. Nevertheless, it is also clear that Ruskin was attracted to sexually innocent and unworldly young women; perhaps he was repelled by mature sexual reality, but equally likely he hoped to shape their unformed minds as his parents had shaped his own. He was an only child of devoted older parents who had the means and intelligence to design and carry out an elaborate strategy for educating their son to become the man they felt he had the potential to be.

Rosa LaTouche's parents forbade their association—and their marriage when she was older—when his intentions became clear and when the circumstances of his first failed marriage were revealed. He had allowed his marriage to Effie Gray to be dissolved on the grounds that it had never been consummated, although he would later deny that he was incapable of consummating it. Yet though there is little doubt that his frustrating relationship with LaTouche affected his concentration and perhaps influenced the content of his work on occasion—how could it not?—it is really a sidebar of the sort snatched upon by publicists, and thrilling to reviewers, that in no way diminishes the quality or impact of Ruskin's life's work.

John Ruskin was a genius of the first order, without exaggeration one of the greatest writers and thinkers of the nineteenth century. In addition to his vast correspondence—literally tens of thousands of letters—his many public lectures, and his diaries, Ruskin published 250 titles. Today, when art critics occupy a highly specialized and elitist niche and have little or no impact on what artists either think or produce (and I can say that, having been one)—or even on what the art-buying public accepts as the criteria for excellence (if, indeed, the concept of excellence is even considered relevant today)—it is difficult to reconstruct in the imagination a time in which the voice of an art critic reverberated with authority throughout the English-speaking world and beyond or to believe that such a man might have his ideas on economic and social matters taken seriously—even if they were *seriously* rejected by many.

I first learned of Ruskin in college art history courses. Looking back at the texts we used, it is astonishing to see that he is not mentioned in them at all. But his influence was duly noted by my professors, although his ideas were then, in the 1960s, thoroughly out of favor. We read Nikolaus Pevsner instead, among others, and I, at least, accepted without much question Pevsner's admiration for the cool detachment of modern architecture; his confidence that, as he said of Walter Gropius, his design "represented the creative energy of this world in which we work and which we want to master, a world of science and technology, of speed and danger, of hard struggles and no personal security."[30] What in any other age would have been a condition to avoid, Pevsner made into a virtue a necessary accommodation to the realities of the modern, industrialized world. There was a certain utopian thrill in that comfortless vision: the challenging possibility of human perfectibility, an unflinching rejection of romance and nostalgia, seasoned with a faintly unhealthy whiff of conscious self-denial. One must sacrifice for the cause of Progress, and with the sacrifice of nooks and crannies, molding and decoration, chintz and down-filled pillows, and the gleam of polished mahogany, there came a certain moral superiority.

More than a teacher's words, it is often a raised eyebrow or the shrug of a shoulder that projects opinion, and there was in those classrooms a grudging admiration for Ruskin—who could deny his impact?—although it was accompanied by what looked very much like a sneer. Ruskin had spurned Progress for a backward glance, a glance into the past that had come to be seen as a cold, dark place, filled with ignorance and superstition, out of which came nothing that had not been improved upon. And those improvements had, in turn, greatly benefited the health, welfare, and state of mind of everyone. There was no point at all in looking back for inspiration; certainly not, as Ruskin suggested, to the Gothic. The past, it sometimes seemed, was interesting only for the possibility of discovering signs of progress. The only individuals truly worth remembering, it was implied, were those who were on the cusp of what eventually became some dominant trend. Ruskin's ideas—though interesting; even inspiring—had gone nowhere and thus did not justify serious consideration. And yet Ruskin had presciently warned against that cold modernist vision, speaking to an audience of young architects: "You shall draw out your plates of glass, and beat out your bars of iron till you have encompassed us all . . . with endless perspective of black skeleton and blinding square."[31]

The sixties were a period still dominated by the critical writing and thoughts of Clement Greenburg, perhaps the last authoritarian voice of the visual arts, who would have preferred that a painting show as little sign as possible of having been produced by a human rather than a machine. In this atmosphere, Ruskin, for whom the human errors and idiosyncratic approaches of Gothic carvers were highly desirable, was anathema.

On my undergraduate walls were the predictable reproductions of Russian constructivists and the cubists, but the aesthetic preferences I felt obliged to apologize for were like Ruskin's for the work of J. M. W. Turner. In fact, it was at this hesitant admission that a professor said, "Read Ruskin," for it was in defense of Turner that Ruskin began writing. His critical attention and sympathy would soon turn toward the Pre-Raphaelite Brotherhood, a group of painters who looked for inspiration and direction to what they knew of painting before Raphael.

Ruskin was only seventeen when he first challenged an unfavorable review of Turner's work that had appeared in *Blackwoods Magazine.* This response was never published, but he incorporated the ideas into *Modern Painters,* the first volume of which—written at the age of twenty-four, his having (after a break for illness) only just earned his degree from Christ Church, Oxford—established him as a voice of authority on landscape painting, and, for a time, as a literary celebrity. He would soon retreat to his study from the stylishly social world to begin the second volume.

Ruskin had not consulted other authorities or asked for advice before publishing *Modern Painters,* which might well explain its originality. It burst forth, a creative gesture from a fresh mind. It is an unusual book; in the words of Ruskin biographer Tim Hilton:

> It is philosophy and aesthetics, and much more than that. It is poetry. It is prose. It is a treatise. It is a great pamphlet. It is a defence or rather a vindication. It is a sermon. It is art criticism, art history, a commentary on recent exhibitions, or an introduction to certain collections. It is a meditation on landscape, or an exercise in how the eye may examine nature.[32]

It is even more. Ruskin was laying the groundwork for a line of thinking that would ultimately take him in a very different direction. He would begin to question not only the factory system but the underlying economic principles that fostered it, and he would question what the dedication to these principles had undermined. He would look not just simply at the rapid demise of craftsmanship and tradition but at the fouling of the air and the destruction of the countryside. At the very beginning of his career, Ruskin had established and embraced his subject—painting, and later, architecture—with passion and brilliance. And yet his subject was in fact to be nothing less than life itself, whatever that encompassed. He would not confine himself, nor let art confine itself, and it was this very characteristic that would delight and endear, and eventually endanger. In the end, I believe, he would push too far; try too hard; he would try to grasp the whole and would suffer gravely for it. Like Icarus, he would fly too close to the sun.

Ruskin's life was a search for integrity or wholeness. He used the word *truth*, which in our relativistic age presents difficulties. But for Ruskin, truth was not about dogma or creed but about unity and integration, and at its core was a dedication to honesty. The truth of art began with a seeing that went beyond superficial impressions to the essence of the subject. This way of seeing entailed more than simply careful observation or empathy. To draw a tree required one to know how a tree grows and to grow with the tree. And here integration is the key, for although the insistence on feeling was inherited from Wordsworth and the Romantics, there was a growing emphasis, as Ruskin developed, on a new scientific perspective.

Ruskin was a man balanced precariously between two ages. When he climbed about the Lake District hills with Wordsworth's guide in his hands, he nevertheless had a contemporary interest in science that went beyond the poet's view of the appropriate relationship with nature. It was a time of frenzied collecting, classifying, and naming; a time when nature must be ordered and reordered with a kind of Victorian tidiness; and Ruskin was a serious amateur botanist and geologist, a great collector of specimens of all sorts.

Ruskin had been raised in a theological atmosphere of evangelical Protestantism. (Indeed, most churchgoers of the time accepted a more or less literal reading of the Bible.) His parents hoped he would become a clergyman, and his mother directed his religious education with that in mind. For Ruskin, nature was God's handiwork; evidence of a supreme presence and a sign of a benevolent master. And yet the new sciences of geology and then of evolution, both of which interested him, undermined that sort of literalism For someone with a natural sensitivity that had been finely honed in a protected atmosphere where the inclination for poetry and art had been given full exposure and encouragement, nature, theology, art, and science merged neatly with intense feelings. If his focus was art, it was only important because it could lead beyond the material to the spiritual. A new science that brought God into question was thus deeply disturbing. When this view of nature was pitted against a growing industrial culture, the tensions increased. As one looks at the periods of depression Ruskin experienced later in life, it is not difficult to imagine that his growing inability to integrate these ideas was partly responsible.

But in his first volume of *Modern Painters,* there were few such concerns. In it he laid a groundwork for his thinking that, while it would mature and be increasingly filled out, would not change substantially. The artist must actually look closely at nature. There was no substitute for that. And the world must be represented not in idealized form but as it is. One must look at particulars of nature, because the eventual goal is unification. The smallest part influences the whole.

> The more we know and the more we feel, the more we separate; we separate to obtain a more perfect unity. The geologist distinguishes [each rock], and in distinguishing connects them. Each becomes different from his fellow, but in differing from, assumes a relation to, his fellow; they are no more each the repetition of the other, they are parts of a system; and each implies and is connected with the existence of the rest. The generalization then is right, true and noble, which is based on the knowledge of the distinctions and observance of the relations of individual kinds. That generalization is wrong, false, and contemptible, which is based on ignorance of the one, and disturbance of the other.[33]

Ruskin is demonstrating that close observation and analysis are not incompatible with a holistic goal. In the first volume of *Modern Painters,* he lays down the fundamental principles of a vision of the world that is unified and infinite—but a world that is at the same time infused with the spiritual presence of the divine. He comes to this understanding by looking at landscape painting, and in particular the works of Turner, and his instructions are directed to both the observers and creators of art. But Ruskin's style, for the modern reader, can be at best bewildering and at worst infuriating simply because we have become so accustomed to specialization: The physician must stick to medicine, the botanist to plants, the art critic to art. Ruskin instead uses art as a jumping-off point, writing as he thinks, seeing no separation between the world as it is represented in art and as it is lived. Divisions between topics are artificial constructs; one thought naturally leads to another, and it may or may not be the topic he began with. The reader must follow and put aside impatience for the pleasures of digression. I suspect his readers and many admirers were conscious at some level that what applied to the making and appreciation of art had meaning beyond art.

The human view of the natural world has varied with the amount of control we have been able to exert over it. Our perspective has shifted away from the human as near-passive observer in an awe-filled natural world that could, in kaleidoscopic mood swings, smile warmly or, seemingly on a whim, turn violent and destructive—a view that led naturally to the deification of these powerful forces. Nature began to seem more benign and could be more easily admired when humans learned to manage it better. This change in viewpoint led to the great era of nature poetry and landscape painting. But these were subtle shifts of the eye over time: from the view of nature as backdrop; to one that idealized landscape for its capacity to inspire; to Wordsworth's approach, which advised a deeper, more intense, empathetic involvement with the natural world. For the full measure of appreciation, one must not simply see and admire nature but feel and become a part of it.

The next major shift, a direct result of the new industrialization, was to see nature as a resource for human well-being. This position was reinforced by a growing scientific perspective that abandoned feeling for a mechanical view of nature in which the changes that were continually occurring, whether in the growth of a flower or of a child, became a mindless process based solely on the organism's drive to survive.

Ruskin fell between these two camps, both chronologically and by inclination. Reared as he was on Wordsworth and the other Romantic poets, he understood and appreciated the sensual and direct relationship with the natural world. Nature must be looked at as she was, worthy in her own right, not idealized as through a picture frame of our own ideas and desires. The truth that Ruskin sought is not the generalized view of nature in which one mountain is like another; nor is it simply the scientist's perspective in which the particular is examined and classified and analyzed, divorced from context. It lies somewhere in between. Generalization would be appropriate, in Ruskin's view, if it saw a particular rock in relation to all other rocks, to trees, to insects and plants; if it saw the rock as an integral part of the system, a part of the unified whole. It is no stretch to see that Ruskin's approach need not be limited to art. He was an ecologist—whether, at that point, he understood it in our terms or not. His appreciation of the world around him was holistic and unified, and he urged others to think as he did.

As he began to tackle the subject of architecture in *The Seven Lamps of Architecture* and *The Stones of Venice,* another aspect of wholeness was revealed: a strengthening link between the craftsman, his impulse and effort, and what he produces. How satisfactory and pleasurable the final effect of a building might be upon the viewer is related directly to circumstances of its creation; to facts about the builder himself, said Ruskin. What he discovered in the architecture that he found most pleasing and satisfying is variety, an effective use of light and shade, a respect for the intrinsic nature of the material.

Ruskin understood and agreed with Wordsworth's appreciation of buildings that fit neatly, and not intrusively, into the landscape; buildings constructed of local materials whose colors blended with the natural world around them; and Ruskin took this idea even further. It wasn't just that the colors blended and the materials were sympathetic but that there was a deeper sense of right and wrong involved. Wood and stone each possess certain unique qualities that can produce particular effects. Thus it is unwise to try to make a delicate screen of stone, a material better suited to more massive, weightier, and rougher purposes, when wood is more appropriate for that purpose. Using the materials of the region and doing so with a regard for their inherent qualities represents an ethical and moral approach to building, in that the very nature of a material deserves respect, and using local materials represents a link to the natural world that can improve not just appearance but perception, sensation, and emotion.

The pleasures of the eye are, in fact, tied to this feeling of appropriateness, Ruskin pointed out. We feel happier about what we see when there is variety, imperfection, the dancing of light and shade, materials that seem to be used in ways that represent what they are. And the reason we feel happier is that the best buildings are representations, to a greater or lesser extent, of nature. Ruskin understood and appreciated the concept of "Biophilia," the idea that humans are drawn to nature, a century before biologist E.O. Wilson would define it as a theory. He saw in architecture the compulsion of humans to recreate the natural world. The towering spires of Gothic cathedrals echo the jagged silhouettes of the towering conifers of the forest even as they reach upward to the heavens as a visual metaphor for spiritual aspirations.

A drive for unnatural perfection, on the other hand, is to be avoided. It is seldom found in nature; it is a product of the machine. What Ruskin was seeing in Gothic architecture were signs of life—in the nature of the design, in the use of materials, in the work of those who had built the structures— and it was that which provided excitement and pleasure. But these signs were not sufficient in themselves. It was not a style or a means of construction that could be merely copied—which was what he later disliked about the buildings of the Gothic revival—simply because the effect was pleasing to the eye. The architecture must be a genuine expression of the people and the times. It had to emerge from the real feelings of its creators, the craftsmen who by individuating their work revealed a sincere love of nature, a true appreciation and understanding of the materials, and a deep love for the ultimate creator. This is the essence, the integrity Ruskin responded to and searched for.

If the best architecture is that which honestly reflects its time, Ruskin was presented with a dilemma when looking at construction in his own. All around him Gothic buildings began to appear, but usually as churches and schools, not as homes and factories and railway stations. He pointed out to a group of businessmen the implications of this fact; how odd it was that people should want to live under one school of architecture and worship under another. If it meant that the Gothic was sacred, what did that say about the architecture reserved for homes and workplaces—that these were places where profane activities took place? He was not trying to deny the sacredness of their churches, he hastily assured his probably irritated audience, nor trying to prove the sacredness of their homes, but to demonstrate "that the whole earth is" sacred. There should be no divisions between work, play, worship, and life—or indeed nature.

This is a rather odd view for a nineteenth-century thinker. It has elements of transcendentalism, Quakerism, and Buddhism, none of which Ruskin showed any particular interest in. And so it seems that this is really pure Ruskin, with overtones of Carlyle, who had earlier implied as much. And it is an idea that finds increasing expression today in environmentalism.

As Ruskin matured, the early rigidity of his religiosity disappeared. He had an "unconversion" experience before writing the third volume of *Modern Painters* which separated him abruptly from his early fundamentalist upbringing and caused him to regret what he felt were some of the narrow and priggish pronouncements of volume one. Later, he gradually returned to a more universal theology. God remained, but as a creator who now transcended narrow arguments over dogma or creed to preside over life in all its various forms.

And yet his view of the necessity for integrity between the times and temper of a people and its architecture presented difficulty when he confronted his own time, for clearly there was not only a difference in the architecture used for one function or another, but it was easy enough to see where the money was applied in creating grand structures and just what that meant. In addressing a group of businessmen—and one wonders why this hectoring, opinionated speaker was so popular—he told them:

> It is long since you built a great cathedral; and how you would laugh at me if I proposed building a cathedral on the top of one of those hills of yours, to make it an Acropolis! But your railroad mounds, vaster than the walls of Babylon; your railroad stations, vaster than the temple of Ephesus, and innumerable; your chimneys, how much more mighty and costly than cathedral spires! Your harbour-piers; your warehouses; your exchanges!—all these are built to your great Goddess of "Getting-on"; and she has formed, and will continue to form, your architecture, as long as you worship her; and it is quite vain to ask me to tell you how to build to her; you know far better than I.[34]

If the great Gothic architecture he so admired had emerged from a way of thinking about religion and society and commerce and nature that he could respect, then he could only look with disdain on his own time because it was obvious that what was being built reflected values with which he had little sympathy. And it was at this point that he began to get into serious trouble with some of his earlier admirers, because it was at this point that his critical eye focused more sharply on just what was causing society to go so wrong. And it is no surprise that he concluded the causes were ethical and moral. When he realized that what was responsible for things going so wrong was the very thing that was making the wheels of Victorian society turn so rapidly and profitably, there was bound to be trouble.

His father urged him to complete *Modern Painters*. Instead he would interrupt the series with *The Seven Lamps of Architecture* and *The Stones of Venice*. Eventually he would complete *Modern Painters*, but his mind was already on other things. The truth to nature that Ruskin had found essential to the best art and to beauty had always, he had to conclude, possessed moral overtones. Ruskin knew that both good and evil were present in nature, and he praised those who had the courage to take nature on. When he shifted his attention to architecture, he disdained the classical and the Palladian others admired, seeing in Renaissance thinking a turning away from God and nature to focus on man. Whereas the gaze of the Gothic had been out-ward (away from man to the world around him) and upward (toward the spiritual and the infinite), the Renaissance had placed the physical reality of the human as an example of perfection at the center of thought. Leonardo da Vinci's famous drawing of man, with arms outstretched to the edges of the world, is the icon for this way of thinking. Ruskin understood the emphasis on proportion and mathematical perfection, so admired by classicism, as a revival of un-Christian, Roman thinking. There was nothing natural about it. It was an idealism created out of intellect, essentially arrogant and self-serving, that separated man from the God-created world around him.

But Ruskin's most important contribution was to understand that art and architecture reflect the moral temper of the time, an idea Marx and Marxist art and literary critics would later expand upon. Art and architecture grew out of whatever went into them, whether it was materials, current ideas, or the laboring conditions of the workers or artisans actually doing the construction. What he had seen before him in Venice, as he observed and wrote, was a past on the verge of destruction; a past he felt compelled to analyze, record, and write about in an effort to stay that destruction. It was not simply one style of building being replaced by another, but a way of life and thinking being overlaid with one he thought very much inferior. It is ironic that the ideas of this profoundly conservative thinker, whose ideals were based on medieval social patterns, could have had such an impact on the British socialist movement, and yet it has often been the case that the far right and the far left find common ground in the idealistic nature, if not means of implementation, of their goals. Although his sense of impending loss might appear to be nothing more than the backward glance of a conservative thinker, Ruskin's critique had social implications, and they were radical. If the quality of ornament on a cathedral—varied, lively, individualistic, and creative—directly reflected the conditions of labor that created them, then the conditions of his own time must be improved if one wanted better design. Because in classicism design is reduced to a stylistic convention, Ruskin thought, it is servile, subjecting the worker to boring, unimaginative repetition, demeaning his intellect and creativity and turning what could be the joy of production into a dreary, soul-destroying activity. It was a short leap from that conclusion to seeing that this servility had been grossly multiplied by industrial production, which employed a division of labor, with the worker performing only one repetitive action in a series of actions, never being allowed the satisfaction of accomplishment. Classicism might have put man at the center of things as a theoretical symbol of perfection, but it also allowed the individual to be conceptually reduced to a crude piece of machinery used to carry out some worthy production goal, and it was this sort of inconsistency that Ruskin could not tolerate. If God had been present in the process of creating Gothic cathedrals, it was because both nature and man were seen as important, each valued for its unique qualities. The richness of the creative process reflects more than the direct action of the hand: it is a sign of life, a reflection of the human spirit; in the soullessness of machines and factories lived death and injustice.

Having once made this connection, Ruskin grew increasingly uncomfortable as the parlor prize of wealthy, upper-class art lovers. He saw and heard around him, in the well-appointed drawing rooms of the affluent, an arrogance, a lack of understanding of the real cost of that comfort. The contrast between the abundance of the Victorian parlor and the soulless drudgery that made it possible was more than he could endure silently. He felt obliged to speak out. Ruskin was aware of his own popularity and the power of words. Perhaps he actually thought he might be able to reorder society. Or perhaps he only knew he must try.

When he had finished the last volume of *Modern Painters* and, exhausted, returned to his favorite haunts in Switzerland to recover, Ruskin began writing the essays that would eventually become *Unto This Last*. His feelings about the nature of work and its manifestation in design were well resolved. He had been teaching drawing free of charge at the new Working Men's College, an outgrowth of the Christian Socialist movement and an effort to provide educational opportunity for those who would otherwise be unlikely to find cultural enrichment. Ruskin, whose old-fashioned conservatism did not incline him to participate in group social experiments, was nevertheless delighted to do his part for this good cause, and his students found him a wonderful teacher. Perhaps he hoped to find there—or recreate—that kind of energetic and genuine artistic expression he had so often observed in Gothic ornament, where ordinary stonecutters had created designs of such originality and liveliness.

His economic writing comes as something of a shock. It is an apparent diversion from art and architecture, and because of its radical nature, it would bring him the first serious censure of his career. And yet one can look at his other work and see the seeds of his thinking firmly planted in that soil. The connecting link is what he would call truth and I would call integrity. There should be a lack of distance between what you are and what you say;

between what you think and what you do; between the materials you use and how you use them; between the culture and its art and architecture; between the reality of the natural world in which you reside and how you respect it; between the religion you profess and the social structure you shape with your actions; between the product you create and the means you use to create it. Integrity is honesty; honesty is truth.

The essays of *Unto This Last* were first written for the new *Cornhill Magazine,* edited by the novelist William Thackeray, who could be counted among Ruskin's friends. They were to appear in monthly installments. The first, "The Roots of Honour," on the subject of fair wage, begins with a chastisement of economists who separate theory from reality, treating the worker as if he were nothing more than a production unit. The economists, Ruskin wrote, would say that "the social affections" are only

> accidental and disturbing elements in human nature; but avarice and the desire of progress are constant elements. Let us eliminate the inconsistents, and, considering the human being merely as a covetous machine, examine by what laws of labour, purchase, and sale, the greatest accumulative result in wealth is obtainable.[35]

Patiently he explained why this cannot be so; how human feelings and sensibilities and values enter into the equation; how treating the worker as if he or she had no soul is not only cruel but counterproductive. The manufacturer should treat all his workers with the same respect he would his own son. It might sound strange, said Ruskin, but "the only real strangeness in the matter being, nevertheless, that it should so sound."[36] It was, after all, only common sense.

In the case of both Dickens and Ruskin, it was the fact of their popularity that gave them the freedom to speak. They both spoke plainly. But in the upholstered nests of Victorian complacency, the meaning of their words was muffled. Those who could hear, who understood the radical nature of the message, didn't like what they heard; and as people will do when they sense the principles that support their own comfort being challenged, they attacked. "Windy hysterics," and "Intolerable twaddle," the *Saturday Review* responded after the first installment. It was the case then, as now, that any hint of the truth that has the potential to cause people to take a closer look at the economic system must be stopped at once, and then as now the most common tactic was to cast aspersions on the credibility of the critique and the critic. Yet even his publisher considered that the opinions of this "con-servative" were too socialistic to be accepted. But Ruskin continued . . . at least for a while. He responded to his critics in his next installment and attacked them with the same vigor they had applied to him. The economist of the day would say, he wrote, that social concerns had never been part of their economic equation. "Our science is simply the science of getting rich. . . . Persons who follow its precepts do actually become rich, and persons who disobey them become poor. Every capitalist of Europe has acquired his fortune by following the known laws of our science, and increases his capi-tal daily by an adherence to them."[37]

What Ruskin was doing in this mockery of economic theory was stripping it of all its niceties. This "getting rich" was really what economic theory was about, and the conditions of the workers or the environment or anything else that got in the way be damned. Manufacturers acted as if it were per-fectly possible for everyone to be rich, when clearly it wasn't. To begin with, wealth was limited. Thus, "The force of the guinea you have in your pocket depends wholly on the default of a guinea in your neighbor's pocket." The real economy, he said,

> consists simply in the production, preservation, and distribution, at the fittest time and place, of useful or pleasurable things. The farmer who cuts his hay at the right time; the shipwright who drives his bolts well home in sound wood; the builder who lays good bricks in well-tempered morter; the housewife who takes care of her furniture in the parlour, and gaurds against all waste in her kitchen; and the singer who rightly disciplines, and never overstrains her voice, are all political economists in the true and final sense: adding continually to the riches and well-being of the nation to which they belong.
>
> But merchantile economy . . . signified the accumulation, in the hands of individuals, of legal or moral claim upon, or power over, the labour of others; every such claim implying precisely as much poverty or debt on one side, as it implies riches or right on the other. It does not, therefore, neces-sirily involve an addition to the actual property, or well-being of the state.[38]

In this second essay, Ruskin showed how economic principles applied in some situations result in less benefit to the nation rather than more, partic-ularly when merchants take advantage of a shortage to make an excessive profit. You cannot separate the accumulation of wealth from issues of moral-ity, he said. Money is not wealth:

That which seems to be wealth may in verity be only the gilded index of far-reaching ruin; a wrecker's handful of coin gleaned from the beach to which he has beguiled an argosy; a camp-follower's bundle of rags unwrapped from the breasts of goodly soldiers dead. . . . And therefore, the idea that directions can be given for the gaining of wealth, irrespectively of the consideration of its moral sources, or that any general and technical law of purchase and gain can be set down for national practice, is perhaps the most insolently futile of all that ever beguiled men through their vices.[39]

Real wealth, he suggested, would be better defined as "producing as many as possible full-breathed, bright-eyed, and happy-hearted human creatures." He turned the clichéd assumptions of economics upside down and shook them vigorously to see what they were made of, demonstrating that the most basic business principle may or may not represent morality and may not even accrue to the national benefit:

So far as I know, there is not in history record of anything so disgraceful to the human intellect as the modern idea that the commercial text, "Buy in the cheapest market and sell in the dearest," represents, or under any circumstances could represent, an available principle of national economy. Buy in the cheapest market?—yes; but what made your market cheap? Charcoal may be cheap among your roof timbers after a fire, and bricks may be cheap in your streets after an earthquake; but fire and earthquake may not therefore be national benefits. Sell in the dearest?—yes, truly; but what made your market dear? You sold your bread well to-day: was it to a dying man who gave his last coin for it, and will never need bread more; or to a rich man who to-morrow will buy your farm over your head; or to a soldier on his way to pillage the bank in which you have put your fortune?[40]

It's quite easy to see how this sort of thinking would alarm virtually all those whose prosperity depended upon blocking these thoughts from their minds or rationalizing their practice in some quite different way. As the protests to this disruptive thinking continued to pour into the magazine, Thackeray and Gibson, the publisher, became increasingly alarmed. The series must end. Ruskin had only gotten started. The third essay , "Qui Judicatis Terram," quoted many a passage from a wise "Jew merchant," who is, in fact, King Solomon of the Bible. "The getting of treasures by a lying tongue is a vanity tossed to and fro of them that seek death," he quotes. And "Treasurers of wickedness profit nothing: but justice delivers from death." There is no let-up. Again, the merchant says, "He that oppreseth the poor to increase his riches, shall surely come to want." His tone is ironic and mocking of the businessmen who follow the economic theory of the day with little regard for the words of the religion they profess. It is disgraceful to think of the common doctrines of political economy as a science, he says, and chief among the reasons is that "I know of no previous instance in history of a nation's establishing a systematic disobedience to the first principles of its professed religion."[41]

Ruskin was now unveiling and attacking the hypocrisy of a nation that adhered to one idea on Sunday and quite another on Monday morning. It was intolerable. He must be stopped. And he was. He was allowed one final essay. It would be a long one, he said. And with that he would compose "Ad Valorem," the final piece of what would be brought together as *Unto This Last*.

In this final essay, Ruskin the conservationist began to appear, and in his view of nature we can hear something of the modern ecologist. The real science of political economy, as opposed to the bastard science, teaches the nation "to desire and labour for the things that lead to life: and . . . to scorn and destroy the things that lead to destruction."[42] In Ruskin, one senses the man for whom the link between himself and the world around him is no longer something observed but something intensely felt. He knows that separation and alienation are death:

> No air is sweet that is silent; it is only sweet when full of low currents of under sound—triplets of birds, and murmur and chirp of insects, and deep-toned words of men, and wayward trebles of childhood. As the art of life is learned, it will be found at last that all lovely things are also necessary;—the wild flower by the wayside, as well as the tended corn; and the wild birds and creatures of the forest, as well as the tended cattle.[43]

As one senses the urgency in this essay of getting it all in and coming to a conclusion, Ruskin exhibits the common-sensical wisdom of a Benjamin Franklin:

> True economy is the law of the house. Strive to make that law strict, simple, generous: waste nothing, and grudge nothing. Care in nowise to make more of money, but care to make much of it, remembering always the great, palpable, inevitable fact—the rule and root of all economy—that what one person has, another cannot have; and that every atom of substance, of whatever kind, used or consumed, is so much human life spent.[44]

Luxury was being bought at great cost, he reminded his readers—as if they still needed more reminding. It can "only be enjoyed by the ignorant; the cruelest man living could not sit at his feast unless blindfolded." The reality of the economy could no longer be ignored, he said. "Raise the veil boldly"; look around. Perhaps he forgot how few people actually want to see. But here also he injects his most famous observation, the phrase that best sums up his personal philosophy: "There is no Wealth but Life."[45]

Ruskin was not a man to be put off by the kind of reaction he had received. If anything, the hysteria of the opposition felt like confirmation. Didn't it prove his point? He spent little time brooding over the termination of the series and began a sequel, *Munera Pulveris,* that would begin where *Unto This Last* left off and be more positive in tone; it would look for ways to reorder the economic system. And he wanted *Unto This Last* to be in print when *Munera Pulveris* came out.

This new book, too, would appear as a series of essays, this time in *Fraser's Magazine.* Again the series was cut short because of criticism. And *Unto This Last* would sell fitfully at first—some copies of the first edition of one thousand remained unsold a decade after its publication—but when it was reprinted in 1877, it began selling at the rate of around two thousand copies a year and continued to do so for the next twenty years or so. By 1910, more than a hundred thousand copies had been sold, and a survey of the first twenty-nine Labour members of Parliament in 1906 revealed that they considered *Unto This Last* to be the book that had most influenced them. It is certainly possible to see Ruskin's writing as influencing some of the social legislation that was subsequently passed. But by then the mood had changed, and even economists were seeing, for a time, the dreadful flaws in the old theories.

It was never Ruskin's intention simply to talk about the economy and the nature of work. He put his ideas into action in various ways. The projects he organized for his Oxford students, such as restoring a country lane and salvaging a spring from pollution and debris, have been mocked by critics as impractical, utopian, pointless. And yet it is just such small projects that are praised today. The difficulty of changing an entire economic order with a grand plan should not be underestimated. The effectiveness of small gestures and the nature of incremental change are now better understood, and the idea of small-scale projects is well established and appreciated. In that light, Ruskin's support and encouragement of efforts to maintain hand-weaving and embroidery, to establish the Guild of St. George to replicate the laws and methods of life as they had been known and carried out at Venice, Florence, and other cities at the period of their greatest achievements, seem entirely appropriate.

In light of what we know today about the limited nature of resources, it comes as a surprise to realize that Ruskin encouraged consumption. But it was a kind of consumption that was not to be undertaken lightly. He realized that it was not what was manufactured so much as what was being consumed that was creating a problem and that what one chose to consume was vital to the shaping of society—a very modern idea. Thus he encouraged the spending of money—he attempted to spend all of his own—on goods that supported activities he considered helpful to society. Buying silverware was not an indulgence if it supported skilled sliversmiths, for instance, or beautiful fabric if it supported a fine weaver. What was not appropriate was simply to sit back and live off of earned interest. Everyone should engage in some sort of useful labor, even if it was spending what one had to support what one truly cared about.

As Ruskin grew older, he began to experience periods of mental instability. One essay in particular is seen as a sign of his increasing irrationality. It is called *Storm-Cloud of the Nineteenth Century,* and it was delivered as a lecture in 1884 when he had already suffered one nervous breakdown. In it, Ruskin talked about observations he had made over a number of years, during which he recorded changes in the pattern of weather and, in particular, the shape and nature of cloud formations. The bright, high, billowy cumulus clouds of earlier years, the wonderful weather he remembered, the clear skies of his youth, were disappearing. In their place was something he called a "plague wind" that was surely bringing death and devastation.

It is perfectly clear that Ruskin was depressed by the changes he saw around him. Pristine landscapes he remembered were being destroyed by construction and destruction; manufacturing and pollution. He could no longer find joy in the things that had previously delighted him, in both art and nature. It is also true that weather patterns had changed, which his biographers later document, and even his critics admit that other observers noted the miserable weather. Frederick Engels wrote in 1883 of the terrible conditions that had made the last months of Karl Marx's life unpleasant, the bad weather, the cold and the damp that had seemed to follow him from Africa to England and then to the Isle of Wight and that kept him from shaking off the cough and colds they had brought on. But, of course, Ruskin's essay is about more than simply weather. He was discouraged over the Franco-Prussian War as well as by the growing industrialization around him. There were two hundred smokestacks within two miles of his house, which no doubt contributed to the gloomy sky. But clearly he is looking into a future that is bleak, and the vision has unnerved him. He summed up what there is to look forward to in a few terrible words: "Blanched sun,—blighted grass,—blinded man."[46]

It is important to remember that Ruskin had been carefully observing nature for his entire life. His powers of observation are not to be doubted. And he had observed these plague clouds, driven by plague winds, since the 1870s. But it was in 1884 that he delivered his lecture, and it could well be that he was impelled to take up the topic when the weather turned especially bad. Today we know that volcanic eruptions can have worldwide impact on the weather, and in fact, in the 1990s two cool, damp summers were attributed to the eruption of Mount Pinatubo in the Philippines. What has not been noted is that two eruptions of Krakatoa took place in 1883, the first in May and the second, a massive eruption, in September. This eruption, four and a half times larger than the eruption of Mount St. Helens in 1980, had a profound effect not only on the atmosphere but on climate. The temperature for the next two years was, on average, 1.5°F cooler because of soot in the air. Sunsets took on a strange and ominous reddish glow. It was a phenomenon noticed around the world, although it was not directly associated with the eruption in people's minds, as it likely would be today. And so, adding to the gloom of growing pollution was the trigger of an unusual occurrence. Even Ruskin's description of a "plague cloud" was perhaps more accurate than he realized. In 1999, author David Keys proposed that an eruption of Krakatoa in the sixth century was responsible for a dramatic change in climate in Ireland that had an impact on health. First came crop failure, then famine, and then a series of plague outbreaks. War followed.

But Ruskin's vision was more than climate-related, more than a mere observation of the effects of pollution. It was a warning. As the late art critic Peter Fuller wrote in his book *Theoria*,

> For Ruskin . . . there was something terrible in the process of industrial-ization itself, something deprived men and women of that which made labour meaningful, and ultimately, seemed to upset the unity between man and the natural world. . . . Even if we cannot accept the technological

premises of Ruskin's argument, we who live in the shadow of the mushroom cloud of the twentieth century, and in the era of Chernobyl, acid rain, and clouds of poisonous gas, ought, perhaps, to be able to recognise the prophetic realism of his imagination. Development of the forces of production did not lead, in the 1950s, or at any other time, anywhere, to the creation of societies which resembled bucholic, richly ornamented, garden cities.[47]

A generation earlier, Carlyle's vision had been of hope:

If Mechanism, like some glass bell, encircles and imprisons us; if the soul looks forth on a fair heavenly country where it cannot reach, and pines, and in its scanty atmosphere is ready to perish,—yet the bell is but of glass; one bold stroke to break the bell in pieces, and thou are delivered![48]

Ruskin could no longer sustain that optimism. As his mind became increasingly strained, he first worked on his autobiography. Then he became silent. During the last ten years of his life, he wrote nothing at all. The glass bell seemed made of stone.

CHAPTER FIVE

Golden Bees, Plain Cottages, and Apple Trees

I F YOU TOOK *The Lackawanna Valley,* A PAINTING BY George Inness, and drew a curtain over the right half, you would see a typical American scene of the mid-nineteenth century: bucolic, rural, pastoral in mood. A young boy beside a tall, mature tree—a chestnut, likely—gazes out over open fields to a wood. Beyond that there are signs of a town—a steeple, a puff of smoke—and then mountains. If you looked very closely, you might see that the small, dark shapes in the field just beyond the boy are, in fact, stumps, and the realization might be a little unsettling. But they are not intrusive, and America—this pleasant rural scene of fields and distant town—was, after all, carved from the wilderness.

Uncover the entire painting, and the mood changes. What seemed a hedge dividing fields turns out to be an embankment and railway track, and coming up to the middle of the painting, charging into and out of that potent center—the sense of movement is strong—is a locomotive pouring steam. Today, when there is real nostalgia for the romance of steam, the scene might still feel bucolic, but Inness made the contrast clear enough. Just behind the engine is a prominent roundhouse where the trains are maintained and stored, a technological centerpiece.

This painting, completed in 1856, was commissioned to pay homage to the machine. It was ordered up by the proud owners of the Delaware, Lackawanna, and Western Railroad. (Its subject matter is profoundly different from Inness's usual work in which a mystical—he was a Swedenborgian—and usually Romantic view of nature prevails.) The size of the roundhouse is slightly exaggerated, but otherwise the painting captures the scene accurately. But its meaning is ambiguous. Is it truly a paean to progress, as the railway barons intended it to be, or is it a lament for what has been lost in the process? Seen in the context of the entire picture, the stumps become more obviously symbolic: nature amputated. The raw earth around the roundhouse and the streets of the distant town (Scranton, Pennsylvania) begin to look like scars. The path leading from the foreground to where the boy sits in contemplation is another abrasion, the soil bare, worn by countless footsteps.

And yet, the broad vista that includes these small flaws invites the viewer to make mental repairs, to blot out the spindly brick chimneys from which the smoke curls. One could wait a few minutes and the train would be gone. The trees might, if left alone, grow again. The haze that already obscures the mountains could lift. The message of the painting is complex. But fittingly so.

The United States in 1856 was at a critical juncture. An image persisted of the country both as a pastoral retreat and as a wilderness full of opportunity and wanting only to be reordered. Yet expansion and advancement, the spirit of the times, demanded ruthless transformation of the unspoiled landscape and a shift of control from natural to human forces. The landscape was to be conquered.

The very pace of the country was quickening, from foot and horse to locomotive speed. The ownership of time was about to shift from individual to corporate. The windup alarm clock would not be invented for twenty more years, but the whistle of the morning train could serve as a wake-up call. Soon there would be no excuse for being late to work. The gazing boy reclines in a relaxed way that technological advancement will discourage. Who now sprawls on the grass simply to gaze? Perhaps Inness meant to suggest as much. Still, he seems to say, there is time to change our minds; it has gone this far, but the change is not yet irrevocable. It is not yet too late.

Pastoral America was a state of mind, Leo Marx points out in *The Machine in the Garden*. It was a stage set for the classic tale from Virgil; created, it seemed, for withdrawing from the world at large (Europe) to "begin a new life in a fresh, green landscape."[1] It was a prospect that excited the European mind as its vast promise was contemplated. Spread before the new citizens lay the chance of realizing what had been a poetic dream vision. On this verdant and unblemished slate might be written a new history. The past dragged at the trouser leg of opportunity and optimism in the Old World. Here there was no past, only promise and possibility.

Rousseau had proposed that one might shed the bankrupt institutions of civilization, the stale culture and enervating history, to begin again in innocence, and that spirit was in the air. The Indian was Rousseau's natural man, and the pioneer, setting out for life in the woods or on the empty plain, was only a step behind him. Romanticism, with its yearnings to reunite with nature, could find full expression in the American wilderness and on the American frontier. Or could it?

As played out in the Romantic movement, the restorative role of nature is best seen in the context of a settled community, an established culture, from which one retreats to be revitalized and to which one returns with a new understanding. The reality for the American settler was quite different. It was not romantics who undertook the expansion—or, it might have been, but they weren't likely to last long. The successful individuals were of a more practical, utilitarian spirit. When this "can-do" spirit encountered the rigors of the experience, the reality was brutal. Challenges were to be met; animals were to be killed; trees were to be cut; Indians were to be conquered, driven off, or simply slain; anything that stood in the way was fair game. There was very little romance involved.

The coastal skirts of the New World had been shaped much as the communities that had been left behind in the Old. New England towns were not much different in organization from European towns, and the inhabitants continued for many years to turn toward Europe for the culture of books and music and art. But that focus ended at the edge of the clearing. The trek to the west, which reduced life to the bare necessities, all but eliminated culture. The Bible might have traveled with a pioneer family, but as a conveyor of culture, it is limited. Thus the new experience was without context, and the pioneer, instead of being healed by the experience of nature—as Rousseau and the Romantics had envisioned—was instead coarsened by the very act of hacking a path through it. "Instead of seeking Nature in a wise passiveness, as Wordsworth urged, he raped his new mistress in a blind fury of obstreperous passion," writes Lewis Mumford in *The Golden Day*. In the old barbarian invasions of Europe, the Goths and Vandals were transformed into Romans, they were "civilized." But this time, says Mumford, "The movement into backwoods America turned the European into a barbarian."[2]

The reality for the pioneer was that he wasn't confronting nature as much as he was evading the complications of the society left behind without really creating a new one. The experience was not as refreshing as it was numbing, and without the culture to relate to, it tended to extremes.

Domesticating the landscape demanded a practical, goal-oriented efficiency. There was work to be done and little time for dreaming. utilitarianism triumphed and then translated, as the years wore on, into expediency. The prized attributes were inventiveness and the entrepreneurial spirit. There were few opportunities on the frontier for the leisurely contemplation of nature that Romanticism required, and the innocence of rusticity that Rousseau had imagined in the France of cultivated fields, cleared meadows, and tidy groves confronted the New World realities of simple survival. But in New England, where a European tidiness prevailed, there were opportunities for the leisure that appreciating nature required. It seems an almost perfect moment, when the balance between human and nature, from the European perspective, was as healthy as it is ever likely to be.

A dozen years before Inness finished his enigmatic painting, in 1844, Nathaniel Hawthorne sat quietly in a clearing in the woods near Concord, Massachusetts, and waited. His plan was to write directly and simply about the experience with all the accuracy and art he could muster. He notes the plants with the attention to detail of a Pre-Raphaelite painter, he dips into the shadows, he refuses to ignore the litter of the forest floor. He records the animal sounds and the human ones as well: a village clock, a cowbell. And the mood holds. He creates a sense of tranquil repose. "Much of this harmonious effect is evoked by the delicate interlacing of sounds that seem to unify society, landscape, and mind," says Leo Marx.[3]

And then, the mood changes sharply.

> But, hark! there is the whistle of the locomotive—the long shriek, harsh, above all other harshness, for the space of a mile cannot mollify it into harmony. It tells a story of busy men, citizens, from the hot street, who have come to spend a day in a country village, men of business; in short of all unquietness; and no wonder that it gives such a startling shriek, since it brings the noisy world into the midst of our slumberous peace. As our

thoughts repose again, after this interruption, we find ourselves gazing up at the leaves, and comparing their different aspects, the beautiful diversity of green.[4]

Into the tranquility of the natural landscape another world has intruded. Hawthorne returns to his meditation, but something has changed. He watches an anthill and aimlessly fills one of its holes with sand, then observes the frantic effort by the ants to repair the damage. He wonders what they think of this sudden, inexplicable event, and as he rises to leave he notes the clouds scattered across the sky. His peace destroyed, he has destroyed the peace of other creatures, and before him the omens are not good.

The intrusion of the train would become a common theme in the literature of this period. Thoreau, by Walden Pond, would be interrupted by the shrieking sounds of the locomotive:

> The whistle of the locomotive penetrates my woods summer and winter, sounding like the scream of a hawk sailing over some farmer's yard, informing me that many restless city merchants are arriving within the circle of the town, or adventurous country traders from the other side. As they come under one horizon, they shout their warning to get off the track to the other, heard sometimes through the circles of two towns.[5]

Emerson would write in his journal:

> I hear the whistle of the locomotive in the woods. Wherever that music comes it has its sequel. It is the voice of the civility of the Nineteenth Century saying, "Here I am." It is interrogative: it is prophetic: and this Cassandra is believer: Whew! Whew! Whew! How is real estate here in the swamp and wilderness? Ho for Boston! Whew! Whew![6]

Emerson saw that the train would bring change at an enhanced pace; more business-minded than Thoreau, he envisioned the buildings that would cluster about the stops and the access that would encourage development wherever the tracks led. Although there is irony in his tone, a hint of doubt, he cannot help being caught up in the excitement of the moment.

The link between these writers and European Romanticism—Wordsworth, remember, protested the coming of the train to Kendal—is direct, although Romanticism had become such an insult by the 1960s, so tempting to mock and ridicule, that Leo Marx avoids making the connection. He points out that the attitude both toward technology and toward nature goes deeper than the Romantic connection, and surely he is right about that. There has always been a strain of thinking that found in wild nature not only a source of satisfaction but a cure for the disease of too much civilization and sophistication. "We need the tonic of wilderness,"[7] Thoreau said, but he was only the most recent at the time to make that observation. Its value in restoring health had been observed by Hippocrates; Lao-tse, the Chinese philosopher of the sixth century B.C., had advised the court to find relief from the artificiality of its experience in the bamboo groves. The refrain echoes throughout the classics.

America the wild garden was, even in 1705 when Robert Beverley wrote his *History and Present State of Virginia*, envisioned as the antidote to what ailed England. Beverley saw the Indians in a healthy state of primitive innocence, full of enthusiasm, with plenty of leisure and yet a comfortable existence—which contrasted with what he called the debauched, corrupted, vain society that "had depraved and inslaved the Rest of Mankind."[8] This native America satisfied utopian yearnings. Here was a garden of earthly delights inhabited by a happy and satisfied people. And yet, for all that Beverley admired the Indians, he never suggested that the Europeans adopt their life. What he seemed to expect was that those for whom he was writing might, with their advanced knowledge, be improved nevertheless by appreciating Indian ways. Perhaps the intuitive and spontaneous nature of the Indians' life might be blended with the industry and refinement of European civilization. He wanted, says Marx, "nothing less than the ideal reconciliation of nature and art which had been depicted by writers of pastoral since Virgil's time."[9]

There had seemed room enough in the United States to effect this reconciliation. In the great emptiness, the train was a way of coping with the space. There was no thought that in this vast landscape industry or the factory could ever dominate as it had in England. Steam was power; it seemed quite natural and appropriate, a useful harnessing of a natural force—at least that's the way Emerson saw it at first. And thus, for a while at least, the concerns of Americans about the potential undesirable effects of industrialization were not as pronounced as they were in England, where the transformation was well advanced. There were misgivings, but they could and would be stilled.

Tʜᴇ ᴛʀᴀɪɴ was far more than a simple interruption, however. The town and the country had been separate places, both metaphorically and actually; the rural life had nothing to do with urban life. The train would eradicate that separation. It would penetrate as nothing else could, entering the sacred landscape with aggressive force, pushing its way into virgin territory that would never again be the same.

At the same time, it could disguise its brutishness with charm. It could drape its inconveniences with the cloak of practicality and efficiency and seduce its way into any community. People knew, in raw terms, what they were giving up and what they were getting; it was a fair and open trade in that regard. But only a few understood the more subtle effects of the exchange. As Thoreau, and Carlyle before him, saw, the presence of the machine would begin to change the way individuals thought and acted. Thoreau notes in ironic tones how it has altered the behavior of his neighbors in Concord:

> The departings and arrivals of the cars are now the epoch in the village day. They go and come with such regularity and precision, and their whistle can be heard so far, that farmers set their clocks by them, and thus one well conducted institution regulates the whole country. Have not men improved somewhat in punctuality since the railroad was invented? Do they not talk and think faster in the depot than they did in the stage-office? There is something electrifying in the atmosphere of the former place. I have been astonished at the miracles it has wrought; that some of my neighbors, who, I should have prophesied, once for all, would never get to Boston by so prompt a conveyance, are on hand when the bell rings. To do things "railroad fashion" is now the byword.[10]

Here is observed and recorded the subtle shifting from natural time—set by the sun, the seasons, the tides, the demands of domestic husbandry—to mechanical time, set by the comings and goings of the train. The train would wait for no one. The schedule set the new pace. This was the new discipline, more demanding than anything seen before. There was no room to maneuver against either technology or those who set its tempo. The machine did not conform itself to people; people conformed themselves to the machine. "But lo! men have become the tools of their tools,"[11] Thoreau notes. And as he points out, the machine standard began to be admired. The train set the pace, both actually and fashionably.

Nevertheless, the train *was* "progress" and, as such, demanded due respect; for people might discuss the nuances of established religion in their parlors, but beyond the talk of traditional theology lay a more recent truth: that progress was the new faith and science the creed of the priesthood. America was still caught up in the excitement of possibility. Thus, the feelings even of poets and artists with regard to the new technologies were complex. Even those wise enough to note and count the disadvantages of the huffing, heaving machines had to keep an honest score and tote up the rewards as well. Thoreau and Emerson, especially, seem impressed at times by the power and strength of this emblem of progress. Wrote Thoreau, with perhaps a touch of irony:

> When I hear the iron horse make the hills echo with his snort like thunder, shaking the earth with his feet, and breathing fire and smoke from his nostrils (what kind of winged horse or fiery dragon they will put into the new Mythology I don't know), it seems as if the earth had got a race now worthy to inhabit it. If all were as it seems, and men made the elements their servants for noble ends.[12]

In *The Birth of Neurosis: Myth, Malady, and the Victorians,* George Frederick Drinka notes the potential for the train, when it first appeared, to induce powerful and unanticipated responses. The railway neurosis—"hysteria, anxiety, or nervous exhaustion"—was, according to Drinka, a common phenomenon in the medical literature during the 1880s and 1890s (which, since the train had been around for quite some time by then, may indicate either that the medical profession was late in identifying it or that cases only began to be noticeable when train travel became more common). And why not? Nothing in the human experience had prepared the psyche for such a violent sensual assault—the charging, hissing, fire-belching dragon of the nightmare—and instinctive fearfulness was bolstered by the not-infrequent accidents that occurred.

Alongside the more exotic manifestations of train phobia—a ringing in the ears, stabbing pains, terrifying dreams, dizziness, a pounding heart, sweating, flushing, and blushing—were the fears of the ordinary, non-train-traveling folk who, from the time of the first line between Liverpool and Manchester in 1830, had worried that the thundering beasts would make the fields barren; dry up the milk cows; poison the fields; and, in general, cast a blight on the countryside. Of course, in a general way, they were right. Diseases were—and are—more easily carried from one place to another by modern transportation, as even Thoreau noticed. And the mass transportation of food animals, whether by train or by truck, is being credited today for bringing on and perpetuating England's foot-and-mouth epidemic.

But medicine documented the new disorder and knew where to lay the blame. The train was the embodiment of the stress-provoking nature of technological progress. "By the turn of the century," says Drinka, "the symptom pictures outlined by Charcot and others seemed to be well established by science, and the progressive symbols of society, such as the railways, to be responsible for the breakdown of the human nervous system." [13]

And so, like Inness, the writers of the day were conflicted. Perhaps it is the role of the poet to find and explore the middle ground between apprehension and adaptation and to map the path toward the latter. The task before these writers was to discover an acceptable reconciliation between man's animal nature and his rational nature, and each shriek of the whistle made the task more urgent. Their mission was to consider what man's place might be on what Emerson called in his essay "Nature," "this green ball which floats him through the heavens." Emerson, himself, would certainly try.

In December of 1832 (when Thoreau was only fifteen), Ralph Waldo Emerson heard there was a ship preparing to leave Boston Harbor for southern Europe, and he impulsively decided to book passage. The 236-ton *Jasper*, cleared for Malta, headed out on Christmas Day. The gray and cheerless seas, the sullen swells of a coming storm: all seemed fitting. Emerson was only twenty-eight, a bright, successful, and sometimes difficult young man, as yet mostly unknown outside his own community. But in the past year he had lost his beloved young wife, Ellen, to tuberculosis; two of his brothers were ill, likely with the same disease; he had resigned his ministry at the Second Church in Boston over the issue of Holy Communion; and he himself was suffering with a prolonged attack of diarrheal disease. The captain took him on with misgivings, not really certain he could survive the trip.

Before leaving, Emerson cut all material ties. He gave up his house; sent his furniture to be auctioned; and found another residence for his mother, who had been living with him. He was searching for warmth, literally and perhaps psychologically. The New England winter had begun, and he scarcely felt up to facing it physically in his debilitated state. Perhaps the sun could effect a cure.

Today we would say he was a young man in crisis. He had lost his wife, and if not his faith, at least the comfortable assumptions of a familiar theological form. He had severed the ties and obligations of position and property and was in intellectual turmoil. He had given only one part of the story to his congregation as the reason for his resignation. There was more. His ideas about the very nature of a relationship with God were in flux. He was already a man for whom ideas were vital. His life was to be based on principle, and those principles must be carefully considered. The concept that within each individual is the spark of the divine, a Quaker teaching that already rang true, was incompatible with the notion that one needed a certified mediator between oneself and God's word. His faith was strong, but unorthodox. In the Boston world where church attendance was virtually obligatory for "respectable" people, to question the need for ministers was unsettling, perhaps even disturbing.

The flip side of loss is freedom. Emerson was suddenly unencumbered. He could pursue health and ideas at the same time. Although his concepts of the divine and of the human relationship to the natural world were not yet fully formed, the groundwork had been laid for what would be a radical revisionist view that would contribute significantly to American letters and thought. But Emerson's stature has a curious aspect. Does anyone today actually read him carefully? To do so would be to discover an American cultural icon who was opposed to virtually everything America was in the process of becoming. Commercialism, conspicuous consumption, the neglect of and alienation from nature: all were to be avoided by those who were a part of the loose community of thoughtful people he would surround himself with. Instead, his values would find agreement today with those of neo-Luddites; his was an antimaterial, antimechanical, antireductionist voice pleading for unity in a material, mechanical, reductionist, dualistic world.

A retired high school teacher of my acquaintance scoffs at the mention of Emerson's name. "We laughed at him in my class," she says. Idealism and enthusiasm are easy to make fun of in a culture in the throes of a lurid affair with getting and spending, in thrall to novelty and sensationalism, and addicted to hype. But the current mocking of idealism and utopian visions can be one of two things: either a sad admission that advancement in society is simply unrealistic and doomed to fail, or the wisdom to see that visions of human perfection can all too quickly evolve into authoritarianism. There is no inevitability here; one can be an idealist without being an authoritarian, and this was Emerson. His appreciation was for the natural evolution of community; the organic development of ideas; and if he considered that a simpler life was appropriate, it was advice, not a dictate.

We know a great deal today about what Emerson was thinking because he left careful records. He began writing in his journals early and clearly saw them as a reservoir of material for future writing projects. He recorded the books he read, the passages he felt important; he recorded bits of his Aunt Mary Moody Emerson's amazing letters, and his journal reflected the thinking they provoked. As these journals accumulated, he made careful indexes so that he could find the material quickly. Eventually there would be 230 of them. He and his friends and family also wrote numerous letters, many of which, like the journals, have been carefully preserved. And they passed these journals and these letters back and forth among themselves, sharing the news and thoughts within their extended circle. His mind was an organ to be exercised and developed, and he charted a map of that progression.

Today, as people communicate by the ether of e-mail and records are translated into fragile digital form—news comes that it will cost $20 million to convert the video record that CNN has accumulated over its short life to digitization, which may itself be outmoded in a decade or two—we may be lost to the future; becoming, despite our compulsive recording, the mysterious generation of which there is no record. But Emerson's mind we can follow; he made sure of that. And there is something about his confidence that is significant as well. Emerson knew that what he thought, read, and wrote was important, not because he had clear intimations of his own place in history and letters but because of his confidence in the individual and in that spark of originality and creativity that lies within—views he clearly formed early that would be echoed in his later essays.

Before he boarded the *Jasper,* his thinking had been strongly influenced by his reading of James Marsh's lengthy 1829 introduction to Coleridge's *Aids to Reflection.* Marsh—interpreting Coleridge—emphasized that the ultimate sources of philosophy, morals, and religion must be found within "our own being or they are not found at all." This assumed, said Marsh, that humans were endowed with a peculiar power called reason. Reason could be variously defined (Kant had one idea; Coleridge another), but for Emerson it meant a power higher than the senses. It went beyond "understanding," which was nothing more than calculation based on information gleaned from what one observed from the material world. Mere thinking was simply a compiling of facts; reason referred to something deeper, a well of intuitive information against which experience could be measured, checked, and tested. Inspiration could be found in this reservoir as well.

Marsh described this reasoning ability, as it pertained to language, as "a living power consubstantial with the power of thought that gave birth to it, and answering and calling into action a corresponding energy in our minds."[14] Writers and composers know what this means: those moments when the words or notations seem to flow with an energy of their own; when they seem to come from somewhere else as if they were being dictated. Far from being rare, this is a rather common phenomenon, and so the experience can make one comfortable with the idea.

Emerson, for whom this notion certainly rang true, had, by his openness to this idea, entered into mystical territory now, with all that adventure implied. He was an admirer of Wordsworth, and he responded warmly to the views of the Romantic poets for whom this concept was essential. He was already well acquainted with Quaker thinking, which considered that revelation had not ended with the Bible and could be present to individuals as what they called the "light," within and was available to anyone through silent waiting. He had been profoundly moved by an oration of Sampson Reed's on the nature of genius and then by Reed's ideas that would become his book, *Observations on the Growth of the Mind*. Reed, who was a Swedenborgian, proposed a correspondence between the visible and invisible worlds.

A synthesis of his personal reading and listening was beginning to take shape in Emerson's mind. He was concluding, as had the Romantic poets, that there were other ways of knowing, that there was something unique about the individual, that the material world and information accumulated solely through the senses had its limitations.

His early readings—the classic teachings of Plato and Plutarch; the insight, individualism, and directness of Montaigne's personal essays, filled with everyday observations that elevated the ordinary—were merging with these newer influences, mingling as well as with what he was learning about natural systems. He had read the latest "scientific" nature studies. He had studied carefully the three-volume *Histoire Comparée des systèmes de philosophie* of Joseph de Gerando and found support for his own sense of the interdependence of human society. But Gerando also introduced Emerson to ideas from Eastern philosophy, some of which, at a younger age, he had disdained. Now he was ready to consider them. He had read and admired Thomas Carlyle's early anonymous magazine articles on Goethe and Jean-Paul Richter, an experimental German author of whose writing Carlyle said, "One only observation we shall make: it is not mechanical or skeptical; it springs not from the forum of the laboratory, but from the depths of the human spirit . . . from amid the vortices of life he looks up to a heavenly lodestar; the solution of what is visible and transient, he finds in what is invisible and eternal."[15]

This was the goal. This synthesis of possibility, of spirit, and of reason; this rejection of the formulaic, the rigid, and the material; this new understanding of natural systems, when coupled with his growing appreciation of individuality stirred that tingling sense of genius Emerson had begun to feel emerging within himself. All these ideas were being absorbed, sorted, interpreted, and tested through the medium of his own experience and feeling of rightness. He had a growing sense of being able to rely on himself and his judgments. From Coleridge he had learned to trust that intuitive burst of insight, and Gerando had prompted him to look throughout history to find examples of moments when the use of what he now called "reason" had manifested itself. If chance favors the prepared mind, it was time for it to make an appearance.

EMERSON HAD not planned for his European trip far in advance, but he was nevertheless ready. There were people he knew he wanted to meet, things he wanted to see. However ill-advised from the practical standpoint the venture seemed in his physical and mental state, it was the right trip and the right time. The change of scenery and climate would, in fact, do wonders for him as he made his way northward through Europe. It was in Paris that, reenergized, he would have his own Gerando moment, a creative burst of insight that would shape his future thinking. It took place not on his visit to any of the luminaries he admired, but in a garden, the Jardins des Plantes. This was not a pleasure garden, but more of what we might think of today as a research facility. Here were growing plants laid out according to a system of classification laid out by Antoine Laurent de Jussieu. The collection also included specimens of fish, insects, and shells, all of them organized so that one could see and understand their interrelationships. In this panorama of life-forms, Emerson saw at once the connections among them—the repetition of certain characteristics.

It is striking to me that he records how moved he was by this insight. It was, indeed, as if he had recognized something familiar, and the reassurance was profound.

These similarities among living things, Herschel had written in his *Discourse*, "cross and intersect one another, as it were, in every possible way, and have for their very aim to interweave all the objects of nature together in a close and compact web of mutual relations and dependency."[16] Now these words became real. The evidence was before him. Robert D. Richardson, Jr., in his biography, *Emerson: The Mind on Fire*, writes of this experience: "Perhaps for the first time since Ellen's death, Emerson felt an agitated, sympathetic—almost physical—connection with the natural world. He was powerfully affected." Emerson himself expressed it unforgettably: "I feel the centipede in me—cayman, carp, eagle, and fox. I am moved by strange sympathies."[17]

Emerson was, at this time, powerfully attracted to science—but to biology, not technology. Later he would grow dissatisfied and impatient with rigid classifications, but for now he was enthralled. Could he have succeeded as the naturalist that he felt, in this burst of enthusiasm, he wanted to be? His profoundly emotional response to his new sense of oneness with the natural world is the antithesis of the cool detachment and objectivity demanded by the world of science. It was, instead, entirely intuitive; he grasped the implications of this connectedness as a powerful insight of precisely the sort he had noted in Gerando's work. This is transcendentalism, rising above the material and the limited information provided by the senses to discover through insight and intuition a sense of oneness with an organic, living universe.

He had moved beyond—far beyond—the biblical confines of creation theory. Now, says Richardson, he was more interested in the relationship between the natural world and the human mind than he was in the natural world as proof of a designing deity. He shares this interest with Kant; the German philosopher Friedrich Schelling; and, of course, the English Romantic poets.

Before returning home, Emerson went to England and there visited with the aging Wordsworth and Coleridge—but, more important, with Carlyle. They hit it off famously, and Emerson stayed over to walk and talk with the irascible Scot. An association had formed: both would be moved by their meeting, and a correspondence that would fill two large volumes would begin. Emerson would return to Boston filled, as every traveler is, with the stimulation of new experiences. He had been exhilarated by the art he had seen in Italy, the insights he had gained in France, and the links he had formed in England. And his health was restored. (Thus reversing the dictate to find renewal in nature. He had found it in variety and cultural stimulation, the message being that we need both nature and culture.) He would begin to lecture, and the ideas that had been both stimulated and reinforced would soon be incorporated into what he wrote and said. The groundwork for the American experience of transcendentalism, as we have come to think of it, was being plowed and raked and sown.

WHAT IS it in the soil of Concord, Massachusetts, that might have inspired what has been called the American Renaissance, the stirring of a nascent intellectual culture that would address not just religious thinking but literature, philosophy, feminism, and a view of the natural world that resembles what today we call ecology? In truth, the magnetic quality was not some native mineral substance but Emerson himself. His roots were in the town and it was there, in 1836, that he brought his second wife, Lydia, whom he called Lydian, to live in a large house—soon made larger—that sat conveniently by the main road so that the coach could let off his many visitors. Emerson wanted to create not a utopian community, as some of his friends later did at Brook Farm and Fruitlands, but a neighborhood. He invited virtually everyone he admired—from Margaret Fuller to Bronson Alcott to Henry David Thoreau, all serious writers and thinkers—to establish a residence there. He helped sponsor some and opened his own house to others. When he hoped to attract the poet William Ellery Channing, he wrote to Fuller, "I comfort myself with the hope that he will find Concord habitable and we shall have poets and friends of poets and see the golden bees of Pindus swarming on our plain cottages and apple trees."[18] It would be only a week later that Fuller herself would come for a lengthy stay, Thoreau was already living in the Emerson house, and Hawthorne and his bride had just moved into the nearby old manse that Emerson's grandfather had built before the Revolutionary War.

What was the appeal of Concord? It was familiar: Emerson had spent summers there beside the famous battlefield and the languid Concord River, which flowed quietly past the orchard behind the house. Concord was convenient to both Cambridge, where he had studied at Harvard, and Boston, where he had grown up. It was a pleasant town in an appealing, bucolic setting. And it was already peopled with the sort of residents who considered, and were disposed to take up, the burning issues of the day. As Emerson and Lydian were settling into their new house in 1835, several of the women of Concord, among them Emerson's aunt and Thoreau's mother —Thoreau, too, was from Concord—were organizing an antislavery society. Emerson was firmly against slavery but gave only passive support because he distrusted organized movements. His role was to be that of thinker and not doer, and he made no apology for it. But his sympathies meant offering hospitality to noted abolitionists and defending Harriet Martineau, a visiting author from Scotland who was writing a candid appraisal of American society and who had been strongly criticized for speaking out against slavery while visiting in the South. For some, insulting one's hosts was apparently a greater crime than owning people. In Concord, probably just as many opposed abolition as supported it, but the town was nevertheless peopled with a base of thinking, concerned citizens. And having chosen it as a good place to live, Emerson was set on attracting as many of his interesting and stimulating friends as he could.

The word *transcendental* did not originate with Emerson or anyone in his circle. It is found in the writings of the German philosopher Immanuel Kant, who responded to Locke's material and empirical world with a vision of one that was, instead, intuitive, moral, idealistic, and individual. What was in the mind, Locke had proposed, was only what had been experienced by the senses. Kant answered by demonstrating that not all important ideas came from experience; some came from within the mind itself. Experience could be acquired through these intuitions. Emerson's moment of awareness in the Jardins des Plantes had been just such an experience

These Germanic ideas were often discussed in the circles in which Emerson lectured. Lydia Jackson was, in fact, described as a "soaring Transcendentalist" even before she and Emerson were married. It was only in 1836 that the first meeting of the Transcendental Club occurred; and when George Putnam, Henry Hedge, George Ripley, and Emerson met at Willard's Hotel in Cambridge, it was not to found a club but to organize occasional gatherings of people who found the state of American thought "very unsatisfactory." What they really meant was that they considered Harvard thinking stale and outdated. As an institution they feared it had become rigid, cautious, and closed to new ideas.

Religion wasn't the only concern. There were other issues at stake: slavery, the treatment of Indians, feminism—all were beginning to be talked about in thoughtful circles. The Transcendental Club set out to share and disseminate ideas. One serious question was whether theology was a help or a hindrance in the development of the mind. If it remained mired in convention, rigid, and closed, it seemed more of a hindrance. Transcendentalism was an opening up to possibility, a way of thinking that allowed religion to play a more vital role in the rapidly changing world in which it existed; to consider the individual, the society, the economy, nature, and technology in the same breath. The old New England Protestantism might have a hard time with Darwin, but transcendentalism would later be able to sit down with Evolution and have a nice cup of tea.

The notion that intuition counted for something—an idea that validated individual thinking, especially when linked with the Quaker concept of divinity within each individual—weakened support for any institution that depended upon a hierarchy of authority, the Church included. Not only the clergy but even such an authority as the Bible could be questioned. And if that spark of divinity were present throughout the natural world—transcendentalists were often accused of pantheism, although that wasn't precisely what they had in mind—then the logical conclusion was that the natural world must be respected. Carlyle had implied as much, and transcendentalism bolstered the idea.

The group expanded. Soon it would include sympathizers such as Alcott, James Clarke, Orestes Brownson, and Convers Francis; and before long Emerson, who well appreciated that women had much to offer, would make certain that Margaret Fuller and other women were included. (And that was a practical idea, since Fuller took on the editorship of *The Dial,* the group's publication, willingly assuming major responsibility until eventually she tired of her unpaid servitude and moved on to a salaried position elsewhere.)

It would be a mistake, however tempting, to see in transcendentalism any sort of fully developed environmentalism. In some of his speeches, Emerson spoke with what seemed almost enthusiasm for some of the technological developments of his time (although his enthusiasms were most pronounced in lectures he chose not to print until late in life when he felt forced into it but no longer had the capacity to edit the material.) But then, the factory smoke had not yet filled the valleys around Concord, and although Emerson and Thoreau might remark on the changes the train had brought about, their way of life in what was still rural Massachusetts did not seem particularly threatened by technological advancement. And yet the transcendental vision of nature as a unified whole laid the groundwork for much later thinking and writing.

What is the connection between transcendentalism and Luddism? Certainly there were no overt machine breakers in this group, although Thoreau can be counted a genuine "machine resister." But what needed to be broken, many transcendentalists believed, was the tyranny of mechanical thinking. In the end, like the Luddite Rebellion itself, the effect would hardly be noticed. As Leo Marx says, while there were "sporadic and ineffectual" impulses to resist the occasional gesture of defiance, there was no organized resistance to industrialization in America because there was no "alternative theory of society" strong enough to create political support.

Even before Emerson had given his first lecture in 1834, the idea, says Marx, that the "the aims of the Republic would be realized through the power of machine production was evolving into what can only be called the official American ideology of industrialism."

Emerson responded to that machine reality in his address on "The Transcendentalist."

> Amidst the downward tendency and proneness of things. When every voice is raised for a new road or another statue or a subscription of stock; for an improvement in dress, or in dentistry; for a new house or a larger business; for a political party, or the division of an estate;—will you not tolerate one or two solitary voices in the land speaking for thoughts and principles not marketable or perishable?

It is a plaintive cry; one that might well be heard today. In crude terms, industrialism "won" and transcendentalism "lost." That is the way Emerson felt then and how the issue is often viewed today. Yet if one looks closely, it is easy to see how the ideas of Emerson and his friends are still being played out today in attitudes about the environment, about simplicity, and about community that still may be in the minority but nevertheless have an impact on society as a whole.

Scholars always seem to struggle to define transcendentalism, and many don't even try. It is too murky, seemingly too diverse for easy analysis. What definition could include both Emerson's very civilized town life and at the same time the Fruitlands experiment, where the residents were strictly vegans, used no horses to plow the fields, and spent a great deal of time—the men, at least; the women seemed never to rest—just thinking. (Louisa May Alcott, daughter of the difficult Bronson Alcott, wrote a very funny story about life at Fruitlands that is well worth searching out.) When the fullness of the transcendental experience is closely observed, however, certain characteristics and commonalties emerge. If there was no Luddite movement of resistance in America with which to sympathize, if the chief factory towns were somewhere else, what is revealed in the writings of Emerson, Thoreau, and other transcendentalists is a more positive association with the enduring resistance to technology. They preferred and promoted what the factory was not: freedom, individuality, a close link to nature and natural ways, the solitary effort as opposed to the corporate (whether it was corporate worship or the industrial model of division of labor). They valued what the machine could never produce: creativity, originality, leaps of thought, the synthesis of divergent ideas, a sense of the divine. Within Emerson's writing, definite links with Luddite thinking can be found. He questions the assumption that progress is inevitable. "Society never advances," he writes in "Self-Reliance." "It recedes as fast on one side as it gains on the other." He doubts the guarantee of benefits from technology. "The harm of the improved machinery may compensate its good." And he wonders whether the advances of science have not, in fact, left us weaker.

> The civilized man has built a coach, but has lost the use of his feet. He is supported on crutches, but lacks so much support of muscle. He has got a fine Geneva watch, but he has lost the skill to tell the hour by the sun. . . . His note-books impair his memory; his libraries overload his wit; the insurance office increases the number of accidents; and it may be a question whether machinery does not encumber; whether we have not lost by refinement some energy, by a Christianity entrenched in establishment and form, some vigor of wild virtue.

In his essay "Nature," he notes, as Thoreau would later, how vital the natural world is to our well being: "These enchantments are medicinal, they sober and heal us." Nature offers relief from the alienation inherent in the mechanistic age.

> Critics who complain of the sickly separation of the beauty of nature from the thing to be done, must consider that our hunting of the picturesque is

inseparable from our protest against false society. Man is fallen; nature is erect, and serves as a differential thermometer, detecting the presence or absence of the divine sentiment in man.

In this essay Emerson reveals his appreciation for the sensitivity and fragile nature of the planet and the potential for its critical balance to be upset: "A little heat, that is, a little motion, is all that differences the bald, dazzling white, and deadly cold poles of the earth from the prolific tropical climates." He understands the constantly changing movement that is inherent in nature, and its complex interconnectedness: "The whirling bubble on the surface of a brook, admits us to the secret of the mechanics of the sky. Every shell on the beach is a key to it." And he quells our expectations for managing nature almost as if he foresaw the age of biotechnology.

> They say that by electro-magnetism, your salad shall be grown from the seed, whilst your fowl is roasting for dinner: it is a symbol of our modern aims and endeavors,—of our condensation and acceleration of objects: but nothing is gained: nature cannot be cheated: man's life is but seventy salads long, grow they swift or grow they slow. In these checks and impossibilities, however, we find our advantage, not less than in the impulses.

The beliefs that we have come to call transcendentalism are clear in the near-final lines of this essay, words that transcend the notion of separation. "Every moment instructs, and every object, for wisdom is infused into every form."

The contrast between Emerson and Thoreau is significant and instructive. Their ideas and principles are similar, and they were friends, but their personal style could hardly have been more different. Emerson was, in a sense, the prisoner of his social position and the expectations that others had for him. For Thoreau, the expectations and pressures of society were fewer and less compelling. He could take to the woods; Emerson with his family could not. And he didn't have to. Emerson's financial situation was sufficient to support his life and his work. Thoreau had to figure out how to do what he wanted to do.

Nor could Emerson get beyond his basic optimistic assumption that natural systems—and humankind was surely one—operated under some sort of divine plan that would, like a child's tippy toy, right itself. The idea that we might outwit the natural order to our own misfortune may have occurred to him—there is evidence for that in the passage above on the electromagnetic salad—but it did not dominate his thinking. And he understood well enough that inconsistency is also an essential aspect of our natures. "A foolish consistency is the hobgoblin of little minds," he said in "Self-Reliance," and this too seems a perfect Luddite thought, antimechanistic and yet very human and ultimately very wise, for it is because of change and variation that evolution is successful and it is in adaptability that strength lies.

Emerson was not oblivious to the effects of rapid mechanization. The stupefying nature of industrialization is one of the first things Emerson questioned in his address "The American Scholar," presented in 1837. "Perhaps the time is already come," he said, "when the sluggard intellect of this continent will look from under its iron lids and fill the postponed expectation of the world with something better than the exertions of mechanical skill." He challenged the influence of industrialism and Cartesian thinking that was leading to increasing specialization. "Man is not a farmer, or a professor, or an engineer, but he is all. Man is priest, and scholar, and statesman, and producer, and soldier. In the *divided* or social state, these functions are parceled out to individuals, each of whom aims to do his stint of the joint work, whilst each other performs his." This specialization is enervating to society, Emerson believed, and deprives it of the talents and capacities of its members.

The very richness of Emerson's thinking, touching as it does on so many topics, makes him difficult to reduce to a formula. Lewis Mumford points insightfully to his unique contribution, which is his "affirmation of both physics and dialectic, of both science and myth,"[19] which justified the artist, the poet, and the saint without disdaining the order and power that science had achieved. The balance was critical: science was helpful—in its place. For Emerson, says Mumford,

> Matter and spirit were not enemies in conflict: they were phases of man's experience: matter passed into spirit and became a symbol: spirit passed into matter and gave it a form; and symbols and forms were the essences through which man lived and fulfilled his proper being. Who was there among Emerson's contemporaries in the Nineteenth Century that was gifted with such a complete vision?[20]

If by Mumford's standard the vision of Thoreau—that complex and solitary figure whose particular blend of genius and eccentricity left such a mark on American letters—was not as complete as Emerson's, there was nevertheless a quality that people could relate to, an awkward but perceptible humanity that contrasted agreeably with Emerson's icy stillness. Thoreau was brought to Emerson's attention as a bright and interesting young man while he was still at Harvard. Thoreau, in turn, would be profoundly impressed by Emerson's "Nature" and other essays. Here was a disciple, but that solid, glacial presence that was Emerson became, says Mumford, "the white mountain torrent of Thoreau."[21]

Thoreau's sojourn by Walden Pond was, in many ways, a carrying out of what Emerson had suggested for the young American scholar in his essay of that name: a period of solitude and contemplation. The translation of that experience into the prose of *Walden* has, like any other article of faith, believers and disbelievers, but it is the broadness of its appeal that is striking. Who would doubt that reclusive malcontents carry it in their backpacks when they take to the woods, but it cannot be lightly dismissed on that account. Such is its appeal that stockbrokers and film producers, presumably living lives of what Thoreau described as "quiet desperation," are said to listen to it in their cars as they fight L.A. freeway traffic.

A few years ago, the distinguished poet and critic Hayden Carruth attacked Thoreau in an essay called "The Man in the Box at Walden."[22] His reason for writing this cantankerous bit of bear-baiting was ostensibly to explain himself. In an earlier poem he had described Thoreau as an "idiot," and some critics had gone to great lengths, he says, to explain that he didn't mean it in the literal sense. Carruth is at pains to assure the world that, in fact, he did. Not that Thoreau wasn't perfectly intelligent—he didn't mean it in that sense. "It was a putdown, an expression of annoyance," says Carruth. "But it was taken, officially, as heresy, and a peculiar heresy at that. I had spat on the sacred cow and no one even wanted to admit I had done it."

His attack is visceral and heartfelt. I have met others who attack *Walden* on principle, and their reaction seems to be against the whole idea of living alone in simplicity in the woods. Rather than say that, however, the critical approach is usually to quibble: "Well, it really wasn't in the woods—it was only a mile from town," or "He only lived there two years," or "It wasn't even his land." Their reaction, as I see it, is actually against any gesture that has the capacity to undermine the social structure in which they have invested and committed themselves. Thoreau certainly does that.

Carruth describes Walden as "a work conceived in rancor and composed in scorn." It is, he says, "an elitist manifesto, a cranky, crabby diatribe. Its victims are its readers, and none escapes. Its author was sanctimonious, self-righteous, and ungenerous to the point of cruelty."

For someone who loved *Walden,* these words came as a shock. They were so different from my memory of the book and my sense of the nature of its author as to be incomprehensible. The only thing to do was to go back and read *Walden* again—carefully. Somewhat to my relief, my opinions stayed the same. So where had Carruth and I parted company? What, precisely, was he seeing that I had not? Or what was I seeing that he had not?

Carruth sees Thoreau as a selfish and unpleasant loner and loafer who not only shirked his responsibility to his community but criticized responsible, hard-working people, society, education, the economy, fashion, and art even as he did so, and he did so in a preaching tone. Oddly, Carruth sees *Walden* not as art itself but as a how-to manual for "failed artists." He apparently views Thoreau as a second-rate naturalist who incidentally wrote, rather than a serious writer for whom nature was one of many subjects. He quite misses the point that Thoreau set out to write a lengthy personal essay, conscious that he was using an unusual form for the time. And from that basic misconception, others follow.

"To escape, to be on one's own, without the anxiety of sex or the clutter of human responsibility: it is the dream of the failed man," Carruth writes of Thoreau. Thoreau had one compelling idea in building the Walden cottage, and that was to find time to work. He had been living in his family's boardinghouse, and the distractions of life had become too much. What he needed was to devise a way of supporting himself that still allowed him the time to think and write. The solution was to reorder his life to reduce the amount of money he needed to live and thus the time it took to earn that money. This meant, from a practical standpoint, taking simplicity as far as he could.

Life by the pond was an experiment; Thoreau says so himself. He left after two years because the experiment was over and because he was offered the opportunity to live in Emerson's house while Emerson was on an extended trip to Europe. *Walden* was never a recipe for what people *should* do but rather what they *could* do if they needed to. The message was that one might, if it were necessary or desirable, live not only simply but also pleasantly and, above all, cheaply. And in that simple state, books, nature, and one's own company were almost sufficient entertainment. *Almost,* because Thoreau was no loner. Not only did he have many visitors at Walden Pond, he walked into Concord every other day at least; and while there he saw friends, and not infrequently, in the eternal manner of hungry artists, stayed for dinner. He loved his solitude, but he was, by accounts of his friends and family, not reclusive or antisocial but affectionate, helpful, kind, and generous with his time.

For his view of society and economics, no excuse can be made. He was exceedingly critical. As had Emerson, he had read Carlyle's *Sartor Resartus*, and if one wants to find fault, there are passages in *Walden* in which he discusses the superficiality of fashion that owe that book a great deal. Thoreau is not critical of his neighbors as individual personalities but of their willingness to knuckle under to the questionable demands of society and the hard work that capitulation requires. The blame lies with the seductive nature of materialism and consumption and with that state of mind that becomes willing to sacrifice so much of life for what he sees as the dubious goal of collecting trifles. He discovers for himself, hoeing in his own bean field—an attempt at "income generation"—the poor economics of farming, and he laments the system that has left area farmers tied to the land and to debt from which they are unlikely ever to escape. He is sorry to see that most working people have no time to enjoy leisure. "He has no time to be any thing but a machine," Thoreau writes of the laborer. And there is the supreme irony of working hard enough to make oneself sick in order to "lay up something against a sick day."[23]

Thoreau was a practical man and saw that people could be seduced by the novelty and excitement of new technologies without considering whether they lived up to their promises or whether they were actually needed.

> Our inventions are wont to be pretty toys, which distract our attention from serious things. They are but improved means to an unimproved end, an end which it was already but too easy to arrive at; as railroads lead to Boston or New York. We are in great haste to construct a magnetic telegraph from Maine to Texas; but Maine and Texas, it may be, have nothing important to communicate.[24]

He criticized the general decline of education (and who has not?) In fact, all his complaints seem pretty valid and none of them particularly original. What is original is the intense focus and consistency of Thoreau's common-sense philosophy, the appealing glimpse he gives the reader of his personal life, and his unforgettable phrasing. And there is that undercurrent of humor that surfaces now and then: Maine may have even less to say to Texas today than it did in 1845.

But to return to Carruth's criticism: When, exactly, did it become bad taste to criticize society? Or is it Thoreau's assumption that there is a right and a wrong way to live that rankles so? It is perhaps this moralistic tone, this assumption that one way of living is better than another, that bothers Carruth. And yet, what Thoreau is suggesting is that the really vital thing is to find time for life itself.

> I went to the woods because I wished to live deliberately, to front only the essential facts of life, and see if I could not learn what it had to teach, and not, when I came to die, discover that I had not lived. I did not wish to live what was not life, living is so dear; nor did I wish to practise resignation, unless it was quite necessary. I wanted to live deep and suck out all the marrow of life, to live so sturdily and Spartan-like as to put to rout all that was not life, to cut a broad swath and shave close, to drive life into a corner, and reduce it to its lowest terms, and, if it proved to be mean, why then to get the whole and genuine meanness of it, and publish its meanness to the world; or if it were sublime, to know it by experience, and be able to give a true account of it in my next excursion.[25]

Which of us, overwhelmed by the trivialities of daily existence, cannot wish, with Thoreau, to experience life with that intensity? He would die at forty-five of tuberculosis, as did far too many at that time. The disease was pandemic, vicious, impartial, and impatient. Perhaps, when he wrote those words, he already understood his own fragility.

The appeal of *Walden,* then, is not in its litany of complaints but in the positive chapters that follow, in its hopefulness. The hope of *Walden* is not that one will build a house in the woods but that an individual might actually exert more control over his or her life. Freedom is the unsettling message of *Walden,* independence its underlying theme. *Walden* is a message of positive action; it is not all talk. A man with ideas carried them out. He envisioned a life, created it, and lived it, and for that reason it has the ring of authenticity and the pleasant smell of integrity. He did not rent a cabin for the summer; he built it and survived the winter—not one winter, but two. And then, having done what he set out to do, he returned to his community, having refreshed not only himself but most of his readers. There is nothing sacred about *Walden,* but it has become myth; it is now, and for the foreseeable future, synonymous with the revitalizing potential of solitude and simplicity, the soft, round sound of the word itself conjuring an image of independent tranquility that will be hard to erase from the collective mind.

In this intentionally narrowed sphere of existence Thoreau, who had eliminated as many distractions as possible, had time to consider seriously the most basic aspects of life, which most of us carry out unthinkingly, and he was willing to share these insights. "In proportion as he simplifies his life, the laws of the universe will appear less complex, and solitude will not be solitude, nor poverty poverty, nor weakness weakness,"[26] he tells us, and those of us tangled in the wires and buttons of modern civilization can only hope it is true.

Carruth can be forgiven his own dislike of this sort of prose, or even his dislike of its author. What is unforgivable is his distortion by selective editing of Thoreau's meaning. The title, "The Man in the Box at Walden," comes from a passage that describes how, when walking down the railroad track, Thoreau saw a large wooden toolbox, and "it suggested to me that every man who was hard pushed might get such a one for a dollar, and, having bored a few auger holes in it, to admit the air at least, get into it when it rained and at night, and hook down the lid, and so have freedom in his love."[27]

Or at least this is what Carruth has quoted from the passage. Here Carruth reminds me of my Labrador retriever, Millie. We can be walking by the most magnificent seashore, the air fresh, the sun shining, the waves crashing splendidly against the shore, and yet she is oblivious to all this wonder. Instead she will go racing off and find the only dead herring on the beach and rub herself in it, and the scent of that dead fish will taint the car on the way home, and then the house and then me, when I try to wash it off. Carruth has that talent. He has attempted to taint *Walden* and its author with a quotation he has taken out of context.

Thoreau, in this passage, is once again struggling with the perplexing and eternal question of how to get by as a writer whose work has yet to sell. His concern is to discover "how slight a shelter is absolutely necessary." He notes how well the Indians survive in their tents of cotton while the snow lies deep around their circumference. And he begins that passage by saying, "Formerly, when how to get my living honestly, with freedom left for my proper pursuits, was a question which vexed me even more than it does now, for unfortunately I am become somewhat callous, I used to see a large box by the railroad. . . . " The passage ends, not with "have freedom in his love"

(Carruth takes this to mean masturbation and, in his eagerness to make the point, has neglected to include the final phrase) but with "have freedom in his love and in his soul be free."[28] Far from a reference to masturbation, this is a partial line from Richard Lovelace's poem, "To Althea from Prison," the one whose last stanza reads familiarly:

> *Stone walls do not a prison make,*
> *Nor iron bars a cage;*
> *Minds innocent and quiet take*
> *That for an hermitage;*
> *If I have freedom in my love*
> *And in my soul am free,*
> *Angels alone, that soar above*
> *Enjoy such liberty.*

Transforming this tribute to human dignity and adaptability into a treatise on masturbation is a peculiarly modern trick, and yet once on this theme Carruth repeats it, rubbing this dead herring over the work when serious critical analysis fails him. The difference between my dog Millie and Carruth is that Millie thinks she smells lovely, whereas Carruth seems to know precisely what he is doing. And, of course, it is immaterial. If he meant to imply that Thoreau was a failed person because his love life was unsuccessful and because he valued solitude, then Carruth is condemning to failure a large proportion of the world's inhabitants. And if the assumption is therefore that works cannot stand on their own but must be evaluated on the basis of their authors' lifestyles, then we are in dangerous territory that the critic would be wise to steer clear of. Not many of us can bear that sort of scrutiny.

When Carruth's essay gets beyond dead herrings, we come to what may be his deepest concern. Thoreau, he says, is a utopian—even if his is a utopian society of one—and we all know where that can lead. "We know today," says Carruth, with a misplaced confidence, "what to think of that nineteenth-century current, the utopian spirit. We know how it spread and joined with other notions of determinism and ultimacy, until in our own century it issued into many totalitarianisms, not political merely but in every phase of life. We know in America where it has brought us, politically, economically, socially, and all in the name of freedom."

This is rather like discarding every religious impulse because of the

Crusades or the Catholic Church's history of creating martyrs. The utopian impulse is a hopeful notion, based on the premise that societies are capable of improvement or, in our dreams, of perfectibility. Thoreau had that encouraging sense of human potential, but his approach was practical. He knew of the nearby Shaker community, and some of his most respected friends—who helped raise the beams of his Walden cottage—had just come from two failed utopian communities, Fruitlands and Brook Farm, and he had rejected these alternatives. His approach was different: build the house, plant the beans, see what happens. The beans were a failure; the life was a success. "A success? He left after two years," Carruth might well say. But where is it written that change must be permanent? Or that a good thing will be better if it lasts forever.

To work well, a society must be organic and elastic in its organization. Its collective premise must have evolved out of common need. Its common purpose must be honestly felt. It must be open to change as life around it changes. Utopian societies inevitably go sour and fail when a mechanistic model is applied. When the Brook Farm experiment of Thoreau's day linked itself with Charles Fourier, the French utopian, and took on that reformed but still rigid Fouristic structure, it was doomed. (In fact, both Thoreau and Emerson had flatly turned down invitations to join.) Its inflexible organization could not adapt to everyday realities. A community that wishes to survive will resemble a living organism, successful when it is firmly undergirded with a commonly held and valid principle (one that does not violate the natural order of things) and able to find that perfect balance between organization and adaptability. Therein lies the difference between the Shakers, who have disappeared, and the Quakers, who have not. It goes without saying that such a community will be healthy within itself and therefore of no danger to the rest of the world. The distinguishing mark of the ugly side of utopianism is its reliance on a mechanical model. Resistance to the machine is such a strong theme in *Walden* that Carruth need have nothing to fear on that front.

The threat of mindless mechanization is illustrated repeatedly in *Walden* by the railroad. Thoreau understood its significance. The old order was changing and the new was not necessarily an improvement. Often the mention of the railroad is a vehicle for an observation about what particular thing might be lost in a particular change. The promise of the railroad is easy transportation, for instance, but Thoreau points out that if he began walking when someone else began working to earn the money to take the train, he would be likely to get there first.

How much time we spend—or waste—working is a constant theme in *Walden*. The legacy of Puritanism, with its persistent message of work as demonstration of moral superiority, lingers in our society. Conversely, avoiding work smacks of immorality. Thoreau's perspective is thus unsettling. Time spent working is time taken from living, which should be our real goal, he says.

"This spending of the best part of one's life earning money in order to enjoy a questionable liberty during the least valuable part of it [old age] reminds me of the Englishman who went to India to make a fortune first, in order that he might return to England and live the life of a poet. He should have gone up garret at once." Thoreau thinks of the railroad in terms of the people who have built it, the workers who have sacrificed much to lay the rails. "We do not ride on the railroad; it rides upon us. Did you ever think what those sleepers are that underlie the railroad? Each one is a man, an Irishman, or a Yankee man. The rails are laid on them, and they are covered with sand, and the cars run smoothly over them."[29]

Thoreau imagines the train as a live and powerful animal that needs nourishing and stabling like some impressive beast—and he is impressed—but his reservations are there as well. "If the enterprise were as innocent as it is early!"[30] he says of the morning train. At the same time, he cannot ignore the amazing trade and commerce that the trains convey, and he confesses that no one is so independent that they can do without the goods trains transport.

With a sympathy for the displaced workers that has overtones of Luddism, he watches the cattle cars and notices the drovers, no longer herding, "their vocation gone, but still clinging to their useless sticks as their badge of office." Now missing, a casualty of progress, are their dogs. "They are quite thrown out; they have lost the scent. . . . Their vocation, too, is gone. They will slink back to their kennels in disgrace or perchance run wild and strike a league with the wolf and the fox. So is your pastoral life whirled past and away. But the bell rings, and I must get off the track and let the cars go by. . . . I will not have my eyes put out and my ears spoiled by its smoke and steam and hissing."[31]

And here is the essence of Thoreau, the technology resister. The train and all it symbolizes has its advantages, but it has undone a way of life that also had value, and for Thoreau personally, it will interfere with what he sees and hears and thus with what he can do. He must get off the track and let the cars go by. This stepping aside is not without its challenges. "Now that the cars are gone by and all the restless world with them, and the fishes in the pond no longer feel their rumbling, I am more alone than ever."[32]

Thoreau was not a recluse—there is ample evidence for that. The traffic to and from Walden Pond, to glean from his journals and letters, was frequent. Thoreau's loneliness is that of the man who feels compelled to take a different path—in this case, of rejecting not society but the increasingly complex and distracting technological world that was so insistently entering his own and demanding a part of it—and perhaps inevitably his feelings turn fiercer as he sees what the train has done to nature. In the chapter "The Ponds," Thoreau laments the cutting of the woods around the pond and the plan, then under consideration, of tapping it for Concord's water supply. Walden Pond has been affected by the railroad as well:

> That devilish Iron Horse, whose ear-rending neigh is heard throughout the town, has muddied the Boiling Spring with his foot, and he it is that has browsed off all the woods on Walden shore; that Trojan horse, with a thousand men in his belly, introduced by mercenary Greeks. Where is the country's champion, the Moore of Moore Hall, to meet him at the Deep Cut and thrust an avenging lance between the ribs of the bloated pest?[33]

The Moore of Moore Hall was the dragon slayer in Thomas Percy's *Reliques of Ancient English Poetry* (1765), and clearly Thoreau did not see himself capable of taking on this task alone. He could only wonder that we have become tied to mechanical taskmasters, and it is this servitude that he wished to avoid. The factory smoke had not yet begun to darken the skies around Concord—the mills were mostly in Lowell, Manchester, Fall River, and Clifton—but he had seen them, had visited the mill in Clifton, and had no illusions: they were not operated for mankind to be "well and honestly clad, but unquestionably that the corporations may be enriched."[34] The way they were run was anathema to what he believed to be right. "We belong to the community. It is not the tailor alone who is the ninth part of a man; it is as much the preacher, and the merchant and the farmer. Where is this division of labor to end? and what object does it finally serve."[35]

Industrialization fostered an increase of wants, in order to, as Mumford puts it, "provide the machine with an outlet for its ever-too-plentiful supply.

Thoreau simply asked: 'Shall we always study to obtain more of these things, and not sometimes be content with less?'"[36]

But Thoreau's contribution is not limited to his model for coexistence with nature or his advice for living or even his good example. When he chose to be arrested and go to jail rather than pay a tax that supported the Mexican War, the Fugitive Slave Law, and slavery itself, his influence would echo around the globe. It might not have if his friend and fellow transcendentalist, Elizabeth Peabody, had not asked permission to reprint a lecture he had given explaining why he had done so. It appeared in a very short-lived journal she published, but the essay died with the journal, only to be republished posthumously when *A Yankee in Canada with Anti-Slavery and Reform Papers* appeared. It was discovered by Tolstoy, who wrote to *The North American Review* asking why Americans paid so much attention to their moneyed people while ignoring Thoreau. It was discovered by Gandhi, in 1907, who reprinted it as "Civil Disobedience," and, on the advice of former U.S. Senator Harris Wofford, who had been to India and studied Gandhi's teachings, it was read by Martin Luther King. The rest, as they say, is history. What one makes of that remarkable sequence of events, I leave to the reader.

The premise of "Civil Disobedience" is frighteningly simple: that unjust laws may, with good conscience, be disobeyed. This was so unsettling that Senator Joseph McCarthy had the essay removed from some local libraries and eliminated from the offerings of the always political U.S. Information Service libraries, which operated abroad. During the civil rights movement and the protests against the war in Vietnam, it took on new significance and became widely read.

The Luddites smashed weaving machines; Thoreau smashed assumptions and raised the question of just and unjust laws and of "a higher authority." The whole notion of democracy is thrown into question when the majority is viewed as a tyrant:

> But a government in which the majority rule in all cases cannot be based on justice, even as far as men understand it. Can there not be a government in which majorities do not virtually decide right and wrong, but conscience? Must the citizen ever for a moment, or in the least degree, resign his conscience to the legislator? Why has every man a conscience then? I think that we should be men first, and subjects afterward. It is not desirable to cultivate a respect for the law, so much as for the right. The only obligation which I have a right to assume, is to do at any time what I think right.[37]

Surely it is not coincidence that "Civil Disobedience" is littered with allusions and references to machines and the effects on society of thinking mechanically. On armies: "The mass of men serve the state thus, not as men mainly, but as machines, with their bodies." On government's support of—and his opposition to—slavery: "All machines have their friction; and possibly this does enough good to counterbalance the evil. . . . But when the friction comes to have its machine, and oppression and robbery are organized, I say, let us not have such a machine any longer." On justice:

> If the injustice is part of the necessary friction of the machine of government, let it go, let it go: perchance it will wear smooth,—certainly the machine will wear out. If the injustice has a spring, or a pulley, or a rope, or a crank, exclusively for itself, then perhaps you may consider whether the remedy will not be worse than the evil; but if it is of such a nature that it requires you to be the agent of injustice to another, then, I say, break the law. Let your life be a counter friction to stop the machine.

Stop the machine. But it would not be stopped. It could not be stopped, then, whether it had entered into the nature of our government or our thinking or into our nature. It had, by now, gained momentum and assumed a life of its own.

In Edward Manet's painting *The Railway*, begun in 1872 and completed a year later, a child, hair tightly confined, stands holding the railings of an iron fence, looking out onto a cloud of steam from an unseen train. Her gesture is the essence of curiosity. The appeal of the machine is a given. A young woman, who might be her mother, sits, her loose hair flowing, her back to this scene. She holds in her lap a young, sleeping puppy and a book, metaphors for nature and culture, her loose hair the essence of life. The unasked question is which will triumph. By the end of the century, the answer seemed all too clear.

CHAPTER SIX

Signs of Life

IF THE NAME WILLIAM MORRIS IS FAMILIAR TODAY, it is likely because of the famous Morris chair his decorating company produced—copies of which still linger in front of the fireplaces of musty summer cottages. Or because of his wallpaper and fabric designs, which still find their way onto gift wrap, greeting cards, and book covers as well as walls and sofas. No single person had more influence on the decorative arts in the nineteenth century than William Morris, and his influence resounds today. But he was far more than simply a designer. In his time—he lived from 1834 to 1896—he was one of England's most widely read authors, a translator of Norse sagas, and the creator of both long narrative poems and short pieces; medieval tales as well as essays on the decorative arts, economics, politics, and life in general. He was a man of astonishing productivity and influence who changed the way people thought about the decoration of their homes— and thus how they lived their lives. It has been remarked that during his lifetime the look of every house in England revealed his influence, which is probably an exaggeration, but not much of one.

He fits into our niche—indeed, takes a preeminent position—because his life and work and enduring legacy epitomize the tradition that emerged in protest against the factory system. He promoted a way of thinking that extols the vibrant energy of life processes in all their various manifestations while rejecting the numbing influence of the machine. Together, the ideas of John Ruskin and William Morris would inspire the Arts and Crafts movement, which would reverberate for a generation or two, especially in the United Kingdom and the United States but on the Continent as well. At a time when the factory process was rapidly undermining tradition, quality, craftsmanship, and creativity, the movement would restore confidence in the work of individual hands.

As an art student in the 1960s, I was indoctrinated into modernism. It was not something that came naturally. A sincere appreciation eventually developed, but it was an arranged marriage, not a passion—just an enduring domestic arrangement fostered by the resigned conviction that there really wasn't much choice if art was to be a serious pursuit. Progress, as it applied to painting, had led us from Giotto (anything earlier was more or less ignored) through the centuries (always improving, it was implied) to the present and any number of distinct modern idioms. The payoff for the artist was to be Ultimate Freedom. There were now no rules for making art. And yet, in reality, there were at least three. There was to be no talk of beauty, no narrative content, and no emulation of the past. In a pre-postmodern era, there was to be no looking back.

Modernism had a tyrannical aspect. The past wasn't just a foreign country, it was forbidden territory. But there was a niggling worry that if the pure white canvas loomed as a kind of ultimate modernist triumph—a negation of nature, the sensual, the romantic, the human, and just about everything else in the bargain—it had a certain finality. What next? Where precisely was one to go? Attempts to find a way out of this dilemma all felt like ways of avoiding the obvious. Art was dead; modernism had killed it. It was perhaps not a premeditated crime, but it was inevitable. And the fact that so many of us kept on making art in the face of such obvious discouragement was evidence of some primitive impulse toward mark-making that had no place in the cool intellectualism one was meant to assume. (Some found a way out. Jackson Pollack was the ultimate Romantic, posing as a Modern.)

Still, there was an inevitable gap between theory and reality. It was possible to admire, both intellectually and aesthetically, the glass house of Philip Johnson and still fail to imagine oneself actually living there. As art critic

Suzi Gablik noted in *Has Modernism Failed?* "From the start the mystique of modern art has always been that it is not generally popular, or even comprehended, except by an elite few. The art dealer and critic John Bernard Myers once asked Marcel Duchamp how many people he thought *really* liked avant-garde art and Duchamp replied, 'Oh, maybe ten in New York and one or two in New Jersey.'"[1]

Yet modernism dominated intellectually. Its triumph—at least architecturally—was aided and abetted by economic forces. The plain, square rooms, devoid of molding and optimally functional (yet no fun at all), were, in fact, cheaper to build. Aesthetics and efficiency had merged. The truth—that almost no one wanted to live in the sterile coolness of a modernist interior—was not to be uttered.

Then I discovered the designs of William Morris, and all that carefully cultivated indifference to the past evaporated. He is one of ours, this William Morris; this painter, poet, essayist, lecturer; this designer of stained glass and tapestry, of furniture, of wallpaper and fabric, and of the most beautiful books in the world. His response to life is simple: Yes. We shall have it. As much as we want and more. Everywhere, in all its manifestations. We shall have it in our bedchambers and in our gardens. His oft-quoted directive is simple: "Have nothing in your house which you do not know to be useful or believe to be beautiful." And that about sums it up. If diligently applied, it is transforming.

There is a vastness to Morris's work that is reflected in the breadth of his production as well as his thinking. When he died, one of his physicians attributed his demise to "just having been William Morris," since he had maintained a level of activity throughout his life that would have been difficult for ten New Yorkers to equal. Yet there is a solid consistency to all that he undertook, perhaps best described as a passionate search for integration. Morris wanted to bring together art and life; art and nature; work and life; the craftsman and the object; architecture, community, and a life of art; the past and the present; the real and the imaginary; fantasy and fact. Not one of these should lose sight of the other. The craftsman should know the material; understand its history; use it in a way that is best suited to its nature; appreciate, and optimally create, the design; take pleasure in his or her work; and feel that life and work are not separate activities but one satisfying pursuit. This integration (a word with the same Latin root as *integrity*) would produce something that was, by its nature, superior and beautiful. Morris's vision of domesticity was central to his work. The life he valued, and strove to achieve, was one surrounded by beauty, nature, good food and wine, friends, and family enjoying each other and life itself. His domestic life was complicated—his wife formed intense relationships, assumed to be physical, with two other men, including Morris's good friend Dante Gabriel Rossetti—but his broad-minded indulgence preserved what was most important to him, which was the warm and lively domestic scene.

In Morris there lay a huge natural energy that wanted to spread out and take in the far reaches of experience, and yet whatever he absorbed and whatever it was transformed into had, in the end, a peculiarly British character. A preference for northern Europe was in his blood and character; a love for piles of gray stones and misty landscapes, for flower meadows and tumbling streams. The fields and meadows and flora of his youthful explorations were part of his being, and his memory and knowledge of those things became his work. In his fabric and wallpaper, flowers and vines and other natural forms intertwine in complex patterns that allow the eye to move in and out of the created space, never resting, never entirely satisfied, yet never fatigued.

His was a search for the skills of the human hand that he felt had been, or were on the verge of being, lost. How had the old tapestries and embroideries been produced? He and his wife and friends picked apart old specimens, thread by thread, to see how it was done. How had the best colors been achieved in dyeing? To find out meant rejecting the new chemical dyes and reinventing the old, plant-based colors—an effort that took years of study and experimentation and angry insistence that second-best would not do. The highest standards, in fact, were vital to everything he did, and yet he resented and resisted temptations to focus too narrowly if it meant losing the vision of the whole. He would always be suspicious of perfectionism, identifying it correctly as being more characteristic of the machine than of the human hand.

He is remembered not only for his prodigious output, his ideas about gardens and architecture, his topography and book design, his research into forgotten techniques and his revival of forgotten skills, but also for his support of egalitarian principles and ideas of workplace reform. His was a revolutionary mind, challenging conventional ideas at every turn. The seeds of resistance to technology that had been planted by Romanticism, by Carlyle, by Dickens, and by Ruskin, were now swelling to vibrant expression in Morris.

William Morris was born into a family—eventually, a large one—that had profited from speculation and investment in the very era of rapid industrialization that he would come to deplore. Throughout his life there would be a conflict between his principles and the business that had provided him his capital, as well as the "industry" he created to support himself and his family.

His preferences were clear from an early age. Morris was drawn to the landscapes he had grown up with, the fields and marshes around his home where he had roamed on his pony. Not far away was Epping Forest, a shadowy and mysterious world of massive hornbeams. There his imagination could range freely, and he would come to know that forest "yard by yard." He was fascinated with birds and equally with plants; even as a young boy he had his own gardens. He was drawn to water. He loved its mutating quality, the excitement as it transformed itself from marsh and stream to river. Water in any form was an avenue of adventure offering possibilities for escape. A river could take one away, whether mentally or actually, and perhaps for that reason, he preferred to live near one. As a child, the places where he could play out the plots and fantasies of his favorite stories became his favorite landscapes. The imagination and playfulness of the child would remain in the serious and hard-working man he would become.

Morris was equally drawn to antiquities, to mounds and earthworks, to ancient sites of any kind, and he became fascinated with medieval manuscripts. He was a romantic child, who "responded to the drama of the isolated building: the cottage in the clearing; the tower on the hillside,"[2] writes Fiona MacCarthy in her wonderful biography, *William Morris*. She describes how the discovery and exploration of Queen Elizabeth's Hunting Lodge at Chingford gave him a feeling for special kinds of places, "solid structure, quirky detail; the sense of the organic, the accretion of past history; and a certain loneliness."[3] His sense of place, she says, was so intense as to be almost a disability. Beloved houses, churches, and landscapes mattered terribly to him, and their potential destruction, misguided "improvement," or abandonment caused a pain that might as well have been physical.

Morris spent his school years at Marlborough, then "a new and very rough school." Its library was its redeeming quality, and like so many bright youngsters, he educated himself when formal education failed. Within exploring distance were numerous Neolithic and Bronze Age remains. Avebury, Silbury Hill, the Kennet Long Barrows, and the Ridgeway were not far off—close enough to give his fascination with the past something to feed upon. Old things: that is what he loved.

When Morris reached Oxford in 1853, one of the first people he met was the young Edward Burne-Jones. They soon formed a friendship that was to last the rest of their lives. Oxford, the city as well as the institution, would affect them both profoundly. Morris was conscious, I believe, of being at a critical historical juncture, a moment when a valuable past was on the verge of extinction. It is clear from his letters, the observations of others, and his later reflections on the time that Morris was acutely sensitive to the need to defend what was personally relevant before it was swept away by enthusiasm for the new. Burne-Jones had similar feelings.

The city was at a point of transition. The railway had only recently arrived, and already its influence was reshaping whatever it touched. Nevertheless, by shifting his glance at crucial moments, says MacCarthy, Morris could avoid seeing the worst effects of the onrushing development and imagine the city as it had been. In his mind it became an ideal—what a city should be.

Oxford, in fact, still retained much of its medieval quality: narrow, winding streets busy with life; the sounds of bells; gray-roofed houses on a human scale; a sense of enclosure. He and Burne-Jones, who had come from King Edward's Grammar School in Birmingham, were, because of crowded conditions, assigned a day-room together outside the college. Soon they would draw around them a group of friends they called The Set, all interesting; talented; and, perhaps most of all, enthusiastic. Morris had read Carlyle—his copy of *Past and Present* is still kept with a collection of his belongings at Exeter, his Oxford college—and was lastingly affected by what historian E. P. Thompson called that "blustering Old Testament attack on the morality of industrial capitalism, contrasted with an idealized picture of life in the monastery of St. Edmundsbury in the 12th century."[4] Carlyle's politics, like Ruskin's, could be described as a curious blend of the reactionary and the progressive—peculiarly suited to, or at least tolerated by, their age—a kind of "feudal socialism," as Marx and Engels would call it.

The flood of reason that characterized eighteenth-century philosophies had swept away the past—or had tried to. The focus for the nineteenth century was a future that could be consciously reshaped and ordered to suit. It was about possibility. There was a palpable enthusiasm in the air of industrialism and the new sciences that envisioned nothing that applied reason could not eventually achieve or transform or explain. The past was a cold and dreary place that needed to be wiped away—or at least forgotten. There was another choice: it could be romanticized as a diversion.

Romanticism, in its triumph, had salvaged the past and in the process became, if not actually antireason, at least highly suspicious of its applications. But Romanticism had found its inspiration not only in metaphorical revolt but in actual revolution, and that was over. Even the uprisings of 1839 and 1848 were over. The French Revolution had kicked off, in a sense, our "contemporary present," as John McHale puts it in *The Future of the Future*. It was a "dividing line after which our major social movement and ideas are colored by its rhetoric or polarized within its major issues."[5] The European world had been truly transformed in terms of the way individuals thought about liberty and social, political, and economic relationships. Now, as Morris took up his place at Oxford, Romanticism was winding down.

"The great aspirations at the source of the Romantic Revolt—for the freeing of mankind from a corrupt oppression, for the liberation of man's senses, affections, and reason, for equality between men and between the sexes— were being destroyed by each new advance of industrial capitalism,"[6] observes E. P. Thompson. He notes that even at the time of Keats, thirty years before, "all values were becoming . . . tainted with the property values of the market, all life being bought and sold."[7] No realistic revolt against the oppressive materialism of the Victorian age seemed feasible. One could only retreat—or perhaps, hide.

Without that potential for revolution, Romanticism could now simply console within the sheltered interior world of the retreating individual. Wordsworth had encouraged a direct communication with nature and urged that the speech of ordinary individuals be listened to. Such simple remedies for the increasing alienation people felt no longer seemed up to the challenge. They had been superseded by a preference for escapist fantasy and an admiration for style. It was a Romanticism of limited vision; a palliative.

The mood that these young Oxford men felt around them was shaped by a number of elements. England was in the midst of an Arthurian revival that had begun in the late eighteenth century with Sir Walter Scott's rediscovery of Sir Thomas Malory's *Morte d'Arthur*. From 1830 until he became poet laureate in 1850, Tennyson had written first "The Lady of Shalott," then "Sir Launcelot and Queen Guinevere," "Morte d' Arthur," and "Sir Galahad," and all were popular. The fantasy past was a diversion, but it was also a hideaway for those who failed—or simply refused—to adapt to the new industrial age. Not only the industrial workers but the industrialists themselves, it seemed, needed what this fantasy past had to offer. The Pre-Raphaelite painters and William Morris and his friends would turn to these stories and legends with an intellectual approach that went beyond the easy temptation of amusing diversion and sought to find within them a recipe for improving their present. For Morris, change would come with "evolution, not revolution."

Romanticism, says Thompson, has often been seen as a symptom of decadence within a culture. But why decadence? Why not simply failure of the culture itself? Morris recognized the failed and destructive elements of his time, including a pace of change that in its momentum, when it was not actually running over, was hurtling past and leaving behind aspects of culture and tradition that were important to a healthy society. His response was to delve into the legacy of a more successful period to preserve those things that needed preserving and to establish standards for art and design—standards for living—that might endure.

The house is on fire; what must we save? The train was bearing down on Oxford, the cathedral towns of France—indeed, most of the world. Quick, what must be gotten out of its way? There was that sort of urgency to his efforts. (Morris would later form, in 1877, the Society for the Preservation of Antiquities, or Anti-Scrape, as he called it and by which it is still known, with the objective not only of preserving the country's architectural heritage but of protecting it from thoughtless and ignorant "restoration" and "improvement.")

Burne-Jones, Morris, and friends fell upon Arthurianism not simply as an intellectual exercise but "as an extension of religion, adopting the chivalric as a rule of life,"[8] observes MacCarthy. It was romantic, principled, mystical, and spiritual; and it wasn't so much that it shaped their lives as that it provided a framework for what they were already feeling and for their personal taste. And it *was* personal. It is obvious that other people reacted quite differently to the same set of circumstances; Oxford produced men who would become scientists, engineers, and industrialists. That fact makes it clear that it was what Morris and Burne-Jones and their friends brought to Oxford that made the difference. They knew quite well what moved them. It was the powerful energy of a past when myth and imagination and the delights of the senses were not separated from ordinary life. They suspected, rightly or wrongly, that the medieval past had blended these elements in a more satisfactory way, and they longed to recreate that atmosphere to whatever degree was now possible. Thus, their relationship was one not just of friendship but of shared idealism and commitment to principles; of fraternity.

Several of The Set, including Morris and Burne-Jones, came to Oxford seeing their future in the Anglican Church and planning to be ordained. The Oxford movement, which favored a restoration of the Church of England to its Catholic origins, had been controversial and divisive, but after two decades, its influence was now on the wane. The self-discipline of the converted John Henry Newman, as well as the idealism of the Christian Socialist Charles Kingsley, combined with the liturgical elaboration of Anglo Catholicism—the "smells and bells" wing of the church—still had its appeal, however. Elaborate vestments, artful liturgy, complex ceremony, Latin choirs: the medieval quality of the ecclesiastical movement, with its monastic overtones, could not help but seem attractive.

The town itself, in its cloistered splendor, created a feeling of being shut away from the world. Later Burne-Jones would describe its collegiality as "all friends living in the same street, and the street long and narrow and ending in the south wall, and the wall opening with a gate on to corn fields in the south, and the wild wood on the north—and no railways anywhere—all friends and all one's world tied up in the little city—and no news to come— only rumours and gossips at the city gate, telling things a month old, and all wrong."9

It was Morris who one day rushed into the room with a copy of John Ruskin's latest book and read it aloud to his friends. When Morris and Burne-Jones were at Oxford, Ruskin was in his mid-thirties, already the acclaimed author of the first two volumes of *Modern Painters*. The second volume of *The Stones of Venice,* in particular the seminal chapter, "On the Nature of Gothic Architecture," proved a profound influence. Here was an articulation, a confirmation, of what Morris already believed. Here was someone who not only connected the temper of the times—in this case the Gothic—to the art produced, but linked art and morality in a fresh way. The craftsmen of the Middle Ages, claimed Ruskin, lived and worked under a social structure that allowed them freedom of expression in the performance of their craft—unlike the workmen of the Victorian age, whose work and lives were shaped by the machine in a repressively uncreative way.

Ruskin's argument against the dehumanization of workers by the industrial division of labor made a strong impression on Morris. The very sameness of factory work meant that hours of boredom were followed by leisure activity, such as it was, that was completely unrelated. Life and work should be a whole. Why should one person do the designing and another do the work to carry out the design? The distinction between manual and intellectual labor was arbitrary and counterproductive, Ruskin would argue. This was a startling observation to make in the rigidly class-conscious Victorian world:

> We are always in these days endeavouring to separate the two; we want one man to be always thinking, and another to be always working, and we call one a gentleman, and the other an operative; whereas the workman ought often to be thinking, and the thinker often to be working, and both should be gentlemen, in the best sense.[10]

It was Ruskin, too, who introduced Morris and his friends to the work of the Pre-Raphaelite Brotherhood, which had preceded them at Oxford by only a few years. The Brotherhood—the original members were Holman Hunt, John Millais, and Dante Gabriel Rossetti, and they drew in others—was founded in 1848, and one of its objectives was integration of the arts, ideas, and life. These painters began with the assumption that poetry, painting, and design emerged from a common creative source. The painting was from nature, but the themes were often from legend, religion, and literature or in reaction to the political events of the day. It was this explicit narrative quality that made the modernist critic squirm, because this quality inevitably involves emotion. This was not art for art's sake, an idea that would eventually dominate. The purpose of these works was far more complex. Sometimes the subject was intentionally provocative, but always these were sensual works that assumed an emotional response. Pre-Raphaelite paintings, if they are mentioned at all, now typically get no more than offhand reference in art history surveys. Their objective was to recapture a certain directness of observation they had found, or imagined existed, in painting prior to the Renaissance. In the painting by John Everett Millais, Ophelia drowns amid the irises and the wild pink roses, a flower herself, returning quietly, painlessly, and above all, beautifully, to Mother Earth. Its beauty is otherworldly, the rendering precisely realistic, yet the effect utterly fantastic. As a group, these painters are considered too sentimental, too mystical, too everything. The fact that these were protest paintings—against not only the academy, with its brown, boring, and cautious renderings, but against industrialism, materialism, classicism, reductionism, scientism, and urbanism—either is not understood or is forgotten or ignored. The theme is hard to miss in the painting "Mariana" by Millais. A young woman stands at an open window either stretching or in ecstasy—one assumes the ambiguity is intentional. Her dress and the interior show the influence of medieval design, as do the stained glass panels in the windows. The cloth in front of her repeats the leafy pattern of the exterior seen through the window and to make the point that the distance between man and nature should be slight, leaves have blown in to land on the table and floor. There is a lush, sensuality and a sense of mystery to this painting that defies the industrial age.

The nature represented throughout the work of the Pre-Raphaelites bore little sign of the relentless advance of industrialization. Whether the natural world might lose the battle was a question that English painters had, by and large, failed to address, says Edward Mullins in *A Love Affair with Nature*. "The reaction of most artists to the upheaval around them was to pretend it was not actually happening. Their clients, after all, were still for the most part the landed gentry who also liked to pretend that it was not happening."[11]

Morris and his friends were drawn to these works, with their romantic detailing of nature blended with Arthurian fantasy, as Ruskin had been. Of course, at just about the time that Morris was discovering the Pre-Raphaelite Brotherhood (or PRB, as they signed themselves for a while), John Millais was busy seducing John Ruskin's unhappy wife. And Rossetti would seduce Morris's unhappy wife—but that was in the future. Morris hadn't yet even met Jane Burden, who would become not just his wife but one of Rossetti's most famous models and, in posing for his idealized pictures, a legend in her own time. Henry James, on a visit to Italy, would later write of meeting her: "I didn't fall in love with Mrs. William Morris, the strange, pale, livid, gaunt, silent, and yet in a manner graceful and picturesque, wife of the poet and paper-maker, who is spending the winter with the Howards, though doubtless she too has her merits. She has, for instance, wonderful aesthetic hair."[12] Eventually it would seem she became the paintings she posed for, an object of a distant and detached interest, unreal, a personality who remains today impossible to know.

Morris's first significant achievement, during his Oxford days, was in poetry; he produced it with an ease that startled even himself. Could it be this easy? he wondered. He shared with the Romantic poets (with Keats, in particular) the ability to paint pictures with words. But he had not yet settled on the arts as a profession. He still intended to be ordained—until a foray to Europe, armed with Ruskin, turned him toward architecture instead.

Morris and his friends traveled through France inspecting and falling in love with cathedrals (especially in Rouen), often on foot or by cart—a concession by his friends, in all probability, to avoid hearing Morris complain bitterly every time they took a train. (He would complain about trains more or less his entire life, even as he became an early commuter, using them extensively.) But he had a point. Foot or cart travel allowed him time to appreciate the flowers beside the road, the quiet countryside, and the most pleasing approaches to the great cathedral towns. Not long after his return to England, Morris told his widowed mother that he would not be the clergy-man she had expected, and he began to train as an architect. It was soon clear that his artistic skills—and interest—lay instead in the decorative arts.

I think it's fair to say that much that is wonderful from Morris emerged from sheer anger at the way things were, which he was able to translate into a demonstration of how they might be if people simply cared enough. We live in such utilitarian times, when relatively little importance is put on inte-rior design. Interior beauty is not the priority it once was; stylish, trendy, tra-ditional—these are understood, but beautiful no longer carries meaning. Design priorities have changed dramatically in recent centuries. When the famous houses of Williamsburg were constructed over four hundred years ago, more than half the cost was for interior decoration. Today that money goes into complex heating and cooling, elaborate mechanisms for creating physical rather than aesthetic comfort. When comparing these different sets of values, I often think of an old farmhouse I know in Virginia, an impres-sive brick structure that sits imposingly on a hill, up a dirt road, off the main road. When it was first occupied, it had no electricity, no real plumbing. And yet its parlor contains beautiful scenic wallpaper imported from France. These people lived lives more graceful and aesthetically cultured—without central heating—than most of us do today. Call it the triumph of the pipes, the wires, and the motors over art.

The lure of cheap industrial goods, and even the growing promises of mechanical labor-saving devices, had already begun to erode sensibilities when Morris became interested in design. There was intensity about his concern, a realization that came early in his life that what we have around us can shape our lives and can contribute or detract from our happiness.

I once called a friend, an artist, and realized she was distraught. "I've been lying on the floor pounding my fists in frustration," she said. "What on earth about?" I asked. "Bad design," was her wonderful reply. Morris likely felt that way. He was also a very physical person, prone to temper outbursts, and if he didn't end up pounding the floor over bad design, it's a wonder. He was very unhappy with the furniture then available, with both its poor quality and its careless, ill-considered form, and when he and Burne-Jones moved into a Red Lion Square flat together after finishing at Oxford, they began to create what they considered appropriate.

The lack of quality Morris saw around him was to plague him throughout his life. "It is a shoddy age," he declared. "Shoddy is king From the statesman to the shoemaker, all is shoddy."[13] He and Burne-Jones would put things right. Together they had made, and then decorated, huge pieces of furniture that characteristically served multiple functions: oversized tables and chairs and a settle with painted doors. These objects were both functional and a powerful presence in the room.

By 1857, both Morris and Burne-Jones were friends and protégés of Rossetti's. He had taken them under his wing, envisioning a second wave of Pre-Raphaelite painters. Morris would make a stab at it and would create a wonderfully majestic portrait of Jane Burden (usually denigrated by critics, perhaps out of sheer habit, for it seems to me one of the best of later Pre-Raphaelite works), but it was Burne-Jones who would finally settle on painting as a career and achieve, over the years, notable success.

One of Morris's great achievements was, in the end, one of his great disappointments. In 1858 he had his friend Phillip Webb design his perfect house, the place to which he would take his wife Jane not long after they were married. It was a wonderful red-brick re-creation (in mood) of a medieval manor set in an old orchard. This was his dream dwelling, the quintessential Pre-Raphaelite structure, with great, heavy doors; small, mullioned windows; and a massive, steep roof—yet filled with surprises at every turn. Built in an L shape around a courtyard, it gave a cloistered impression, enhanced by the turreted well-house in the center. Morris and his friends put tremendous energy into its decoration and then into living there. Jane had a strong influence on its character; she helped with the design and also created embroidery hangings. She, and the wives of his friends, wore loose, flowered gowns in its rooms in the spirit of progressive medievalism. Egalitarian principles thrived; the women studied craft and participated fully in the great rush of creativity, until the responsibilities of motherhood held them back.

But Red House proved to be too far away for Morris to run his new decorating business—Morris, Marshall, Faulkner & Co.—effectively; and already, perhaps, he had begun to sense the growing intensity of the friendship between Jane and Rossetti. His idyll was spoiled. He wanted, at first, to bring the company to Red House, to create there the workshop community he dreamed of, the integration of life and productivity. But the suicide of Rossetti's wife, Lizzy Sidal, from an overdose of laudanum after the death of her infant, followed by typhoid in the Burne-Jones family, which resulted in the death of their child; cast a cloud on new and enthusiastic enterprises. The timing was wrong; money was short; spirits were low. Morris abandoned the house, one of the great examples of a personal aesthetic translated into architecture and garden design, first hoping to sell it, then renting it, but never, in fact, returning. Instead, he moved his workshop and his family to Queen Square in London and got down to the serious business of being William Morris.

Later—with Rossetti—he would buy Kelmscott Manor, an Elizabethan house in Oxfordshire, as a summer and weekend retreat for his family (Perhaps this joint tenancy was to provide protection to Jane's reputation as the relationship with Rossetti developed. But for all Morris's broad-minded indulgence, he found the situation painful and took off on an expedition to Iceland in 1871.) This pile of gray stones, from which the delicious scents of history wafted, fulfilled his ideal of a dwelling that seemed to have grown naturally out of the soil. It had been built by local craftsmen from local materials, which gave it an intrinsic sense of place. The house had evolved imperfectly—yet perfectly—to the needs of the people who lived in it with the pure, organic quality that he sought, a feeling of natural harmony that he felt emerged from the synthesis of people and land, coupled with genuine need. It fit in with its surroundings, achieving a relationship to the structures around it, neither overpowering nor diminishing, but balanced.

Morris's chief inspiration had been the medieval, and what makes his nineteenth-century excursion into an even more distant past, if not entirely acceptable to the critical modern eye, at least tolerable as a design choice, is the total absence of sentimentality in his approach—something that could not be said for the Pre-Raphaelites. In Morris's hands, an admiration for the past was more than easy emotion. It was the essence of the medieval spirit he attempted to capture, not some lifeless copy, and his designs had a contemporary look for his time.

His relationship with the Gothic was certainly a yearning to recreate a way of life perceived as better, but it was not an infatuation; instead it was an overwhelming passion based on understanding and respect. Morris was an acknowledged expert on medieval manuscripts and tapestry. Following Ruskin's lead, he studied medieval craft and design and interpreted them with a keen eye and a sure hand to create something of his own time—and, surprisingly, of our own. His fabric and wallpaper designs, still commercially available today, have a compelling, unforgettable quality. The eye, once drawn, can escape only with effort; it is pulled in and around and back again and again in an elaborate dance with nature that is nevertheless about art and the human mind and hand. A Morris design is a harmonious blending of all these.

How were these textiles and papers actually made? How well was he able to adhere to his principles of labor? Morris despised all that the machine had produced, but could he reconcile this aversion with the practical needs of manufacturing?

In Carlyle's *Past and Present,* Morris found reflected his own sentiments about the dignity of labor. "All work, even cotton-spinning is noble; . . . ."[14] "All true work is sacred; in all true work, were it but true hand-labour, there is some divineness."[15] From Ruskin, Morris had confirmed the idea that the manner by which something was produced is important. As Thompson puts it, "At his best Ruskin sought to treat the arts as the expression of the whole *moral being* of the artist, and—through him—of the quality of life of the society in which the artist lived."[16]

The dangerous ideal of perfection is one to consider here. Both Morris and Ruskin understood the pitfall of attempting to achieve it in creating objects, but it is clear that the admonition against perfection can be extended to encompass much more. It does not imply any sort of carelessness or lack of skill but elevates the worthiness of the controlled creative impulse, the deviation, the happy accident. Tools can come close to creating perfection, but for humans, and for life itself, it is unnatural. Said Ruskin:

Observe, you are put to a stern choice in this matter. You must either make a tool of the creature, or a man of him. You cannot make both. Men were not intended to work with the accuracy of tools, to be precise and perfect in all their actions. If you will have that precision out of them, and make their fingers measure degrees like cog-wheels, and their arms strike curves like compasses, you must inhumanize them.[17]

To expect perfection, to uphold it as an ideal, is to establish an inappropriate mechanical standard. Therefore, the inherent imperfection of what human hands produce is something to treasure; and, by contrast, to aim for machinelike perfection is to demean and undermine that very humanness. In fact, the imperfection of life itself translates into adaptability. Perfection cannot be improved upon, so in a sense it represents death, for change and variation are essential to life.

But the central evil undermining the dignity of work and worker—for Ruskin and then for Morris—was the principle of the division of labor. This disassociation of the worker from both the design and the end product was what had transformed the craftsman into the laborer. Like the machine itself, division of labor was dehumanizing, a process that had made of the worker not the thoughtful creature he was by nature but little more than a machine himself, more useful only because more adaptable. Unlike mechanical equipment, the human laborer could be trained and retrained. Maintenance of this useful "machine" was left to the machine itself, which would, in the bargain, obligingly reproduce itself. What confounded the industrialist was that this machine could—and did, on occasion—think for itself and could decide that working conditions or pay were not to its liking, which inevitably caused trouble for factory owners. Thus, on the whole, unless prohibitively expensive, the genuine machine was preferred; if the machines couldn't do the job, or were too costly, then the workers who acted the most like machines—who were reliable and routinized in their actions and who put aside emotion, personal preferences, and creativity—were chosen. And it's easy enough to see how this industrial preference carried over into society in general. We are now at the point where for certain sorts of jobs it seems quite sensible to prefer in humans that working, producing, efficient ideal of nearly mechanical man.

(IBM would later become famous for carrying this concept into management, although as a model it lies at the heart of many common management principles. And, of course, it has always been the model in the military. Ironically, flexible, adaptable, creative individuals are highly desirable and in short supply at higher levels, precisely because these traits are discouraged at lower levels—a dilemma that training programs attempt to resolve; but once stifled, imagination and initiative are hard to revive. Creativity and individuality in the worker and the workplace enjoyed a brief—although distorted—revival in the dot-com boom of the late 1990s, but with the bust of 2000, they fell into disfavor once again.)

Morris struggled with the issue of producing goods, which he attempted to price competitively without resorting to the hated factory system. Ruskin had condemned the factory system in "The Nature of Gothic" for its focus on production over humanity. In fact, the concept of the factory system cannot be separated from the economic theory that finds it useful. Ruskin had plunged to the heart of the matter: the economic system has no interest in the well-being of human society itself but has essentially reduced humans to the role of either worker or consumer.

> The great cry that rises from all our manufacturing cities, louder than the furnace blast, is all in very deed for this—that we manufacture everything there except men; we blanch cotton and strengthen steel and refine sugar, and shape pottery, but to brighten, to strengthen, to refine, or to form a single living spirit, never enters into our estimate of advantages.[18]

The answer from the industrial capitalist was that human values are unimportant to the goal of the maximum production at the lowest cost. Efficiency was the premier value. It left no room for others. How could other values be considered in the production of goods that had to compete in the marketplace? This was Morris's challenge—urgent, because the idea of division of labor was seeping from the factory floor into the rest of society as well and reshaping the way people worked and thought and lived. In this new complex order, no one individual could be expected to comprehend the whole; each had a specific role, narrowly defined. The notion of the "Renaissance man" would seem foolish if not impossible in a world of experts. But the expert was, in a sense, an intellectual cripple, hobbled and tied to his or her field; incapable of participating fully or interacting with experts outside his or her precise area of specialization. This left the ultimate control, whether it was of the process or of the bureaucracy, in the hands of managers who did not need, and were not expected, to know anything except how to manage. The concern was taken up a few years after Ruskin by Karl Marx, who in *Capital* wrote:

> It is not the place, here to go on to show how division of labor seizes upon, not only the economical, but every other sphere of society, and everywhere lays the foundation of that all engrossing system of specialising and sorting men, that development in a man of one single faculty at the expense of all other faculties, which caused A. Ferguson, the master of Adam Smith, to exclaim: "We make a nation of Helots, and have no free citizens." [19]

But that the machine lightened labor was a given; it became dogma. And yet it too could be questioned. It was John Stuart Mill himself who said in his *Principles of Political Economy*, "It is questionable if all the mechanical inventions yet made have lightened the day's toil of any human being." [20] And some years later, Marx would point out that lessening the work of an individual, unless it happened to be the work of the factory owner himself, was not the purpose of introducing machinery; rather it was to increase output and cheapen the cost of the goods being manufactured, thereby increasing profits.

These ideas were very much on Morris's mind as he and his friends set about establishing the workrooms of their decorating company. At the core of their approach was the conviction that anyone could be trained to be a skilled craftsperson. It was an idea that sounded very much like the idea of Emerson—and before that, of the Quakers, the Swedenborgians, and Blake, among others—that everyone contained the spark of the divine, if creativity can be considered an aspect of the divine; and I believe Morris thought of it that way, although by now he had abandoned any pretense of religiosity. And so workers for the workshops were found anywhere—off the street, if need be, or the first to apply was hired—and then trained. And, indeed, many of them became exceptionally skilled.

There was certainly a more egalitarian feeling about the Morris workshops than about the traditional factory floor, even though the ideas and the impetus were clearly his. But he labored alongside his workers from time to time and applied more democratic principles of management. His was not the ideal workshop where the craftsmen were on an equal footing with management, nor did they often come up with their own designs. But they were better paid than the average, they were free to some degree to control their own time, and they could count on a fair hearing when they had a complaint.[21] That was innovative but not revolutionary. In his several locations, Morris either lived above the workrooms or installed workrooms in buildings connected to his residence. He was not the distant industrialist in the house on the hill or in another city; he generally maintained an intimate relationship with production and with his workers.

The closest Morris came to his vision of the peaceful working community was in the weaving workshops established at Merton Abbey. The setting was lovely, and the workers could take their lunch *en plein air* and even tend their individual gardens on the grounds during their free time. Freshly dyed goods were washed in the stream that ran through the property—a technique that would surely be frowned upon today from an environmental perspective—and laid to dry on the green lawns, a process that had a natural, wholesome feeling to it, whatever floods of blue and crimson floated down into the river.[22] After the company became fully his own, Morris instituted a profit-sharing arrangement. The workshop retained its comfortable size. The workforce seldom rose much above or fell much below a hundred, and less strenuous work was found for older employees who were no longer able to function well in their previous jobs.

In a sense, Morris made his individual peace with the machine. He hated the train yet became a commuter from his country home. He knew perfectly well that the very train that made it possible for him to spend the weekend in the country was cutting through the countryside he adored, bringing its noise and soot and crowds, reshaping towns and changing living patterns. Indeed, his own pattern of city and country living would have been impossible without it—an irony that should not be overlooked. But it is well to accept from the start that absolute purity on the issue of resistance to technology is not possible and that the actions of every person will be mediated by his or her individual resolution of needs with ideals. Perhaps Morris reasoned that he might conceivably be able to do something about the state of design and the quality of goods, but nothing about the train.

Morris also hated what the mechanical looms produced in the factories, and yet he hesitantly employed them in his own shops in ways he felt appropriate. He adhered to the philosophy many accept today, which is more problematic than generally realized, that it is not the machine, but how it is used, that matters.

Morris's company was a great success, but his clients were often the very moneyed, leisure class he despised. Was he ever able to implement fully the labor reforms to which he was committed? Morris struggled throughout his life with the challenge of maintaining both his principles and the domestic life he valued. His personal life was not an easy one. One of his daughters developed severe epilepsy, and Jane was often unwell, requiring treatment and attention. He was a generous man, with his family, with his friends, and with the causes and individuals he believed in. He never lived in a grand or extravagant manner, but he was determined to live a comfortable, harmonious, and aesthetic life. He admired beautiful things—books, rugs, tapestries—and bought them. Many of his purchases were for Morris & Co., as it later came to be called, but his was, at heart, an acquisitive nature. (His "simplified" interiors were not stark or austere by any means, but his principle of beautiful or useful was applied unsentimentally, nevertheless.)

If his dreams of creating a living and working community of artisans were only partially fulfilled, his compromises, on the whole, were in the interest of continuing his successful business while holding fast to his standards of quality and workmanship and avoiding the worst abuses of the factory system. It was a balancing act, but one in which he was generally successful. His workers were well trained and, on the whole, satisfied, and he created products of lasting significance.

As Morris grew older, he became frustrated with the "evolutionary" path to change that he had chosen. Morris quite suddenly became a socialist, and not simply of the parlor variety, dating his conversion experience to 1883. He took to the cause with a vigor that alarmed his friends and endangered some of his warmer relationships. He participated in protests, was present at riots, and eventually became for some an embarrassment and an outcast. At times he was intentionally challenging and provocative. When the Socialist League, to which he belonged, split off from the Social Democratic Federation, Morris left to form the Hammersmith Socialist Society, meetings of which were held in the converted Coach House—most recently the carpet workshop—of his Hammersmith home.

Many of Morris's later writings were for socialist publications or were presented as lectures. They contain some of his strongest opinions, not just on political and economic matters but on his disappointments and his aspirations for art. Here, for example, is a passage from his lecture "How I Became a Socialist," given in 1894:

The hope of the past times was gone, the struggles of mankind for many ages had produced nothing but this sordid, aimless, ugly confusion; the immediate future seemed to me likely to intensify all the present evils by sweeping away the last survivals of the days before the dull squalor of civilization had settled down on the world. This was a bad look-out indeed, and, if I may mention myself as a personality and not as a mere type, especially so to a man of my disposition, careless of metaphysics and religion, as well as of scientific analysis, but with a deep love of the earth and the life on it, and a passion for the history of the past of mankind. Think of it! Was it all to end in a counting-house on top of a cinder-heap, with . . . a Whig committee dealing out champagne to the rich and margarine to the poor in such convenient proportions as would make all men content together, though the pleasure of the eyes was gone from the world, and the place of Homer was to be taken by Huxley? Yet, believe me, in my heart, when I finally forced myself to look toward the future, that is what I saw in it, and, as far as I could tell, scarce anyone seemed to think it worth while to struggle against such a consummation of civilization.

The power of this sort of prose is that it is finally too heartfelt to mock. This is the plea of a man of vision and great passion who is simply beyond bearing what he sees before him—and sadly, in light of the numbing nature of consumerism that has developed, his vision was far-reaching and all too accurate.

With what we know today of the bleak and dreary nature of the repressive, class-divided, and bureaucratic communism of China and the former Soviet Union, how can we reconcile Morris's identification of himself as a socialist with what is known of him as a person? What Morris sought was an antidote to a capitalist system that was destructive to what he valued, and his particular social vision bore no resemblance to the eventual manifestation of state socialism in the Soviet Union, where it took on a depressing utilitarian and mechanical, not to mention harshly totalitarian, form. In fact, he was led to write his utopian novel, *News from Nowhere,* in direct response to Edward Bellamy's unappealing *Looking Backward,* a utopian novel featuring a centralized and drab society where work is sharply divided between intellectual and manual labor. Morris's vision is instead of a natural socialism where there is no greed, violence, or poverty; where peace reigns and harmony triumphs; and where there is a sincere respect for nature, art, love, and life.

The evidence for the Morris view is *News from Nowhere* itself. A member of the Socialist League (modeled, it would seem, on Morris himself) goes to sleep and on waking finds himself in a London transformed. Much of the city, he finds, has been cleared and reforested until there is less distinction between city and country. There are no poor people, it seems, no system of money, and everyone wears handcrafted medieval clothing.

Schools have been abolished, and learning has become a continual activity, available for those who want it. Nor is there any need for government, decisions being made among equals, and the Houses of Parliament have been transformed into vegetable stalls and a manure storage facility. Prisons have been abolished, and those who do commit crimes are sent off to a country retreat where they can recover from their feelings of guilt at their crime. There is no private property, land being held in common rather than by individuals or by the state, which has eliminated thievery as well as divorce courts. People move freely among relationships. Childbearing and domestic activities are respected, and men and women work together in harmony. Decisions are made in truly paticipatory ways within small groups. Yet the idea of pure independence for the individual has been rejected as impractical. Cooperation, it is recognized, is essential for the well-being of the entire community.

Work has become a healthy pleasure in the society of *News from Nowhere* because it incorporates individual creativity and earns the satisfying gratification of others. Production is geared to human need rather than growth, and quality thus triumphs over quantity. Handicraft has replaced mechanization. The only real concern is that there might be too little for people to do, but that problem is avoided by embellishing what is being made, a move that further develops artistic creativity.

This enormous change had come about following a period of civil war, after which people began to enjoy one another and to take pleasure in life. As the story begins to draw to a close, the narrator goes on a trip upriver to a beautiful house clearly modeled on Kelmscott Manor; but during a feast there he begins to disappear, and he wakes up once again in dingy Hammersmith.

News from Nowhere was not, of course, intended as a realistic picture of how life would be under socialism, E. P. Thompson point out. Rather, as its subtitle—*An Epic of Rest, Being Some Chapters from a Utopian Romance*—suggests, it provides an opportunity for repose, a rest from the constant competition of capitalism, and a point of departure for considering how things might be. Without a model of what society might be, real progress is impossible. And yet the best intention can go terribly wrong.

There is a poignant passage in Morris's other celebrated political book, *A Dream of John Ball*, that tackles this irony. Perhaps it takes a long life and a good memory of past campaigns to give this observation resonance, but as Morris writes:

> I . . . pondered how men fight and lose the battle, and the thing they fought for comes about in spite of their defeat, and when it comes turns out not to be what they meant, and other men have to fight for what they meant under another name.[23]

Whatever sympathies or antipathies one has to socialism, one would find it hard not to recognize the truth of the words about globalization and the free-market system that Morris speaks through Old Hammond, one of his characters in *News from Nowhere*:

> It is clear from all that we hear and read, that in the last age of civilization men got into a vicious circle in the matter of production, and in order to make the most of that facility they had gradually created (or allowed to grow, rather) a most elaborate system of buying and selling, which has been called the World-Market; and that World-Market, once set a-going, forced them to go on making more and more of these wares, whether they needed them or not. So that while (of course) they could not free themselves from the toil of making real necessaries, they created in a neverending series sham or artificial necessaries, which became, under the iron rule of the aforesaid World-Market, of equal importance to them with the real necessaries which supported life. By all this they burdened themselves with a prodigious mass of work merely for the sake of keeping their wretched system going. . . . Since they had forced themselves to stagger along under this horrible burden of unnecessary production, it became impossible for them to look upon labour and its results from any other point of view than one—to wit, the ceaseless endeavor to expend the least possible amount of labour on any article made, and yet at the same time to make as many articles as possible. To this "cheapening of production," as it was called, everything was sacrificed: the happiness of the workman at his work, nay, his most elementary comfort and bare health, his food, his clothes, his dwelling, his leisure, his amusement, his education—his life, in short—did not weigh a grain of sand in the balance against this dire necessity of "cheap produc-

tion" of things, a great part of which were not worth producing at all. . . .
The whole community, in fact, was cast into the jaws of this ravening monster, "the cheap production" forced upon it by the World-Market.[24]

Machines, in fact, are by no means eliminated entirely in Morris's vision for the future. They fit hesitantly into his concept of work as not only a healthy but a necessary element of the satisfying human life. He contemplates new forms of power that could aid work apparently without the effects of pollution. The machines here are not seen as alien. Old Hammond makes it clear that power, a word that in this context represents both machines and what drives them, should be available to accomplish what cannot be done, or done so well, by hand, or to take on tasks that are excessively laborious, tedious, repetitious, or very unpleasant. "What Morris is against is not the machines," Morris scholar Ray Watkinson says, "but the alienation, that under capitalism they produce."[25]

One aspect of this alienation is the toleration for inequality the machine produces. In *News from Nowhere*, the character Clair observes presciently that it results from a view of human life as separate from nature: "It was natural to people thinking in this way, that they should try to make nature their slave, since they thought 'nature' was something outside them."[26]

If nature is considered separate, Watkinson observes, the majority of humans can also be treated as objects to be exploited. "Morris not only hates the alienation between humans which comes from and gives rise to exploitation, but sees that the actual use of machinery, as well as its application, may itself be alienating."[27] There are certain aspects of weaving or woodwork, for instance, that are boring and repetitive. If that uninteresting and laborious aspect of creating something could be alleviated without damaging the end product in any way, then there was good argument for the use of a machine. Used freely in this way, in a craft setting, the machine could become an extension of the hand, in no way damaging to the process of creating. In actuality, under pressure of the economic system, without regard for the quality of the end product or the satisfaction of the worker, the use of the machines produced a different outcome:

Under the pressure of the market, in the pursuit of unlimited production, the implement itself is taken beyond that point to become a machine, severing the sensuous link, reducing the function of the intelligent hand, taking away the control of the worker's intuitive acts, reducing the workers, as the machine develops to its own perfection, to minders and servants—alienated in their work, and alienated in society by this degradation as they become less important than the machine they serve. And all this is not in the interest of making the object of use or beauty, but in making the commodity saleable on the widest market, and at the least but most profitable cost.[28]

Watkinson suggests that Morris began with a "romantic hostility" to the machine that he absorbed from Ruskin and that he was some time in discarding it. Eventually, however, he was able to put it into a social context, to see the machine either as a potential instrument for exploitation or, in the right hands and used appropriately, as potentially helpful. The question that remained unanswered was whether the economic system would allow it to be used in this way.

To read Morris, or to hear him—for what he wrote with the intention of delivering orally has a quality that can be *heard* in the mind—or to see what he accomplished, is to be offered a sense of possibility; a vision in a tired world of what might be achieved under the right circumstances. And it is this vision that has inspired so many. Writer Colin Ward, in his essay "An Essay Amongst New Folk: Making Nowhere Somewhere," tells of meeting the eighty-one-year-old Carl Feiss, who had been professor of architecture at Columbia University. Feiss told him how, in 1940, when the English architect Raymond Unwin (1863–1940) was dying, Unwin gave him three treasured objects. One was a tiny ruler, the next a pair of dividers, and the third a little vellum-bound copy of *News from Nowhere*. Unwin, who had been a friend of Morris's and a fellow utopian, told Feiss that the book was the key to every one of his architectural, social, and political opinions.

"How we loved our Morris when he came to us sharing our illusions, full of life and joy,"[29] Unwin had written in 1902. Morris was both inspiration and support for the people who became known as the Garden City architects, a movement spurred in 1898 by Sir Ebenezer Howard's *Tomorrow: A Peaceful Path to Real Reform*. What followed were planned communal living arrangements that incorporated natural light and fresh air into homes, "playing room and breathing room" and landscape in the design. Unwin and his partner, Barry Parker, implemented the Garden City concept at Letchworth in 1903.

In *News from Nowhere* there is a famous passage in which Morris describes his arrival at Kelmscott Manor, his first glimpse as he lifts the garden latch. The old house is surrounded by well-tended gardens in bloom, but Morris describes at length the flowers and the presence of different birds—the blackbirds singing, the doves cooing, the rooks and the swifts—and the perfect sense of rightness that the scene engenders. Ward identifies something he calls the NNQ, or the *News from Nowhere* Quotient, to describe the sense of wholeness, satisfaction, and sheer joy that individuals have expressed after finding themselves in settings similar to this. Lewis Mumford described in a letter to Frederic Osborn the same sensation upon visiting Welwyn Garden City, another of the early communities. He writes about the experience of breakfasts in the garden "mingling in my mind with the kind of morning fragrance that William Morris put into the opening pages of *News from Nowhere,* so that I feel I have actually had a foot in utopia in one moment in my life; a feeling that I never had as a mere visitor anywhere else before."[30] And I can apply the NNQ to the experience of tea on the lawn of friends' seventeenth-century house in Surrey, its leaning walls with their mullioned windows seemingly growing out of mellow cobbles; the ancient yew in the courtyard a benevolent presence; the garden, surrounded by high walls of old brick, supporting climbing roses. Birds sang, the scones were fresh, the honey pure from the Isle of Man, the friendships strong, and for one blessed instant all was right with the world. This is Morris's vision, and as Ward points out, it is an ecological one. It is not created simply by architectural design but by incorporating the natural world in a respectful way. There is, as Unwin says, joy here that is the essence of Morris and all he thought good and fine.

Ward defines the NNQ as several characteristics, the first being joy in the work of building itself. In an old building, this joy can only be conjectured in a kind of circuitous thought process: if one assumes that joy can only be felt where joy has been applied, one can suppose when joy is felt that it was, in fact, part of the building process. But in my friend's garden, it is certainly felt in the careful and loving tending of this property, and perhaps that is the stronger influence. One senses love and tenderness and respect in the air.

The second characteristic of the NNQ is the use of building materials that age in a natural and beautiful way. The way materials age is vital to our continuing appreciation of a building, and modern materials do not age well. In fact, they do not age at all, for aging is a process or organic transformation, a return to original materials. Synthetic materials do not decay, in that sense: they simply crumble, they give up.

The third characteristic is the incorporation and accommodation of the natural world. Morris's influence, Ward notes, can be seen not only in the Garden City movement but also more generally in the turning away from the overcrowded industrial cities that had sprung up. Said Morris:

> I want the town to be impregnated with the country, and the country with the intelligence and vivid life of the town. I want every homestead to be clean, orderly, and tidy; a lovely house surrounded by acres and acres of garden. On the other hand, I want the town to be clean, orderly, and tidy; in short, a garden with beautiful houses in it."[31]

As I was beginning this book, a contest of wills was going on in New York City. People in some of the most economically depressed areas of the city had recaptured vacant lots and in them created gardens. Here people grew vegetables and flowers, congregated to laugh and talk—raised their NNQ, if you will. But for the city's mayor, they had simply taken over city property that could be sold to developers. The protests were enduring, but the bulldozers were more powerful. The gardens were ripped out. It was an agonizing defeat: once again money and power triumphed over the human spirit. The gardens did more than bring joy; they acted as a safety valve for urban frustrations, but they were destroyed for short-term monetary gain and perhaps as a demonstration of cold authority.

MORRIS WAS a visionary in his linking of aesthetics, social relations, and environmental concerns. As Paddy O'Sullivan, a senior lecturer in environmental science at Polytechnic South West in England, points out:

> In fact Morris's potential contribution to "green" ideas and thought goes far beyond a mere aesthetic reaction to ecological disruption, and in *News from Nowhere,* extends to a detailed description of the social organization, economics, and government of a small-scale, decentralized society, as well as the likely appearance of its landscape. Morris achieved this by giving consideration to changes, which his political ideas, if put into practice, would bring about, first of all in human society, but also, and no less important, in the surrounding nature (or, in modern jargon, in "adjacent ecological systems").[32]

The kind of integration of view to which O'Sullivan is referring is evident in this excerpt from a lecture called "The Lesser Arts," written in 1877:

> I have a sort of faith . . . [t]hat art will make our streets as beautiful as the woods, as elevating as the mountain-sides: it will be a pleasure and a rest, and not a weight upon the spirits to come from the open country into town; every man's house will be fair and decent, soothing to his mind and helpful to his work: all the works of man that we live among and handle will be in harmony with nature, will be reasonable and beautiful: yet all will be simple and inspiriting, not childish and enervating; for as nothing of beauty and splendour that man's mind and hand may compass shall be wanted from our public buildings, so in no private dwelling will there be any signs of waste, pomp, or insolence, and every man will have his share of the best.[33]

O'Sullivan points out that the definition Morris gave to art was not a narrow one but encompassed all human enterprises. By 1877, Morris had not only recognized the links among community, art, and the environment but had seen the growing problems of pollution and considered how science might be useful in dealing with the concern if it were not already in thrall to industry and the military:

> And science—we have loved her well, and followed her diligently, what will she do? I fear she is so much in the pay of the counting-houses, the counting house and the drill sergeant, that she is too busy, and for the present will do nothing. Yet there are matters which I should have thought easy for her; say for example teaching Manchester how to consume its own smoke, or Leeds how to get rid of its superfluous black dye without turning it into the river, which would be as much worth her attention as the production of the heaviest black silks, or the biggest of useless guns. Anyhow, however it be done, unless people care about carrying on their business without making the world hideous, how can they care about Art? I know it will cost much both of time and money to better these things even a little; but I do not see how these can be better spent than in making life cheerful and honourable for others and for ourselves; and the gain of good life to the country at large that would result from men seriously setting about the bettering of decency of our big towns would be priceless, even if nothing specially good befell the arts in consequence.[34]

For Morris, a relationship with nature was vital to health and well-being. Nature must be cherished and respected just as were the ancient monuments, the old legends and sagas, and the disappearing craft techniques and skills he admired and preserved. There was no separation. These were signs of life; and life, in all its various manifestations, must always triumph for human society and the human spirit to thrive.

Mᴏʀʀɪs's ɢʀᴇᴀᴛᴇsᴛ impact may well have been on the development of what came to be known as the Arts and Crafts movement, that stirring of the spirit and the hands, lasting from 1875 to 1920, that would set folk—both elevated and ordinary, on both sides of the Atlantic and far beyond—to potting and painting and weaving and stitching. It is hardly surprising that it is so often described as "the art that is life."

The demand for a unification of all arts and crafts that Morris had so loudly proclaimed had, in fact, been achieved in his own workshops. His example would inspire the establishment of Arthur Mackmurdo's Century Guild in 1882 and, two years later, the Art Workers Guild, which Lewis Day and Walter Crane established. The movement was to "turn our artists into craftsmen and our craftsmen into artists,"[35] said Crane. (The use of the masculine term was irrelevant. Women were usually included in the movement.) In 1888, the Arts and Crafts Exhibition Society organized a series of exhibitions, demonstrations, and lectures that would further educate and involve the public in the aesthetic revolution. Morris was a socialist, but it was not so much his politics that shaped the communal aspect of the Arts and Crafts movement as the perception that the best work of the Middle Ages was produced by individuals working together. And that spirit, that unification of work and vision that had created objects both useful and beautiful, deserved recapturing. Art was a way of bringing people together, or, as Tolstoy said in *What Is Art?* it is "a means of union among men, joining them together in the same feelings, and indispensable for the life and progress towards well-being of individuals and of humanity."

The experience of Charles Robert (C. R.) Ashbee is typical of the manner in which this spirit would manifest itself. As a young activist and idealist from a prosperous family, he would direct his energies toward improving the conditions of the poor, and the decorative arts would provide a means of accomplishing that. In 1878 he formed the Guild of Handicraft in Whitechapel, one of London's most depressed areas, which began when he offered lectures on Ruskin to the workingmen there. The works were such an inspiration that a small, experimental group of workingmen began meeting to study design. Soon, says Fiona MacCarthy, who documented Ashbee's efforts in her book *The Simple Life,* "there were thirty men and boys involved in painting, modelling, plastercasting, gilding."[36]

Nineteenth-century England was astir with reform movements, of which Ashbee's was one. The plight of factory workers and the living conditions of the poor, both brought on by the factory system, were widely known by now. There were many young men—and some young women as well—who felt compelled to shed the trappings of wealth so that they could direct their energies and resources more effectively into attempts to transform society. Edward Carpenter, founder of the Fellowship of the New Life, noted in his journal the very day he gave away his dress clothes, an act of great symbolic importance, and shortly afterward headed north to participate in the hard labor of agriculture—likely to the amazement of his fellow laborers, who no doubt longed to escape it. But the founding of the fellowship had a broader aim: it was concerned not simply with the belief that manual labor was necessary for a healthy life but also with the need to reform diet and dress and to live out ideals of democracy within community. And Carpenter was not alone, MacCarthy points out. "As one of the main propagandists for the Simple Life, he had links with a great many of the groups of early Socialists and Anarchists, Feminists and Suffragists, Humanists and Naturalists, Sexologists, Theosophists and Psychical Researchers, which were burgeoning just then."[37]

In 1886, Ashbee had attended a meeting at the Hammersmith branch of the Socialist League in Morris's converted coach house, where he heard Carpenter lecture. Afterward he, Carpenter, and others, including Bernard Shaw, were invited to join Morris's long table for supper. MacCarthy quotes from Ashbee's memoirs:

> Old Morris was delightful, firing up with the warmth of his subject, all the enthusiasm of youth thrilling through veins and muscles; not a moment was he still, but ever sought to vent some of his immense energy. At length banging his hand upon the table: "No" said he, "the thing is this, if we had our Revolution tomorrow, what should we Socialists do the day after?" "Yes, what?" we all cried. And that the old man could not answer: "We should all be hanged because we are promising the people more than we can give them."[38]

They all walked home together, talking excitedly of the evening and the ideas they had exchanged. Ashbee became more and more caught up with

Carpenter's notion of forming a new civilization based on the concept of comradeship and built on the promise of the spirit, energy, and physical strength of England's young workingmen (and here he did mean men and not women).

Inspired by Carpenter, Ashbee, who had decided to become an architect, lived, while training, at Toynbee Hall, the East London settlement house that had been founded eleven years earlier by the Reverend Samuel Barnett, a famous social reformer. "The tide of fashionable philanthropy was then at its height,"[39] Ashbee would later recall. General interest in the reform effort was intense, observes MacCarthy:

> Toynbee Hall was thronging with titled people, politicians, cabinet ministers, eminent artists, university professors, bishops and relatively humble sightseers from the provinces, eager participants in the salvation of the poor. These visitors, many of whom would keep their carriages waiting in the slums outside, went home after dinner to more salubrious surroundings. But there was a nucleus of young university graduates in residence, which Ashbee was to join.[40]

The guild that Ashbee would form was one of many. They varied greatly in size and organization. But whether well thought out, as Ashbee's was, or small and "hopelessly inept," they were, says MacCarthy,

> very much the symptom of their time, the thinking person's protest in an age of increasing mass-production and a worsening environment. The Guilds looked back, with varying degrees of sense and eccentricity, to better days before industrialization when craftsmen took pride in their work and found joy from it. . . . There was then a feeling current—an idea which was to surface again and again, and is indeed still with us—that men were out of tune with their surroundings. Industrialization had destroyed all creativity. Division of labor took away responsibility. Capitalism, the tyrannical "cash nexus," had a terrible effect on the British workman's soul.[41]

The ideas of Carlyle and Ruskin had merged with those of Morris, and from his personal example, his lectures, his writing, and his work, the guilds and the Arts and Crafts movement had sprung. The idea that life in the city was unhealthy and unnatural had also been expressed by Carlyle and Ruskin. Soon three movements would merge and find unified expression in Ashbee: the Back-to-the-Land movement, which promised to restore individuals to a more natural and healthy existence in tune with the seasons and put them in touch with rural values (and, not incidentally, to help them reclaim lost rights); the Simple Life movement, which aimed to counter the excessive Victorian age; and the Arts and Craft movement. In 1902, Ashbee would move his now thriving Guild of Handicraft to the village of Chipping Camden in the Cotswolds, where he established a community.

The stylistically definable products of the guild remain a treasured part of the Arts and Crafts legacy. But it is Ashbee himself who is particularly interesting for our purposes, because he not only thought carefully about the machine but actually defined, in writing, precisely how it should and should not be used. To redefine his principles, he laid them out in his journal not long after moving the guild to Gloucestershire:

1. Machinery is necessary in modern production, so also is human individuality.
2. The recognition of Ethical principles in economics postulates a good and bad in the productions of machinery.
3. Machinery in so far as it destroys human individuality is bad, in so far as it develops it is good.[42]

Ashbee's idea in producing handmade objects was to effect a kind of transference of joy. The purchaser must feel it, and to do so was only possible if the craftsperson had experienced joy in creating the object. "Take away the producer's joy" Ashbee proposed, and you "destroy his interest, his care, his thought, turn him into a hack or a machine, in other words destroy his individuality and the work produced will not be so good."[43]

This idea that it was not the machine per se, but how it was used, that was damaging is one that has been repeated for generations and continues to be held today. Later writers would demonstrate that the machine could be damaging however it was used. But both Morris and Ashbee felt there were ways to employ technology that could actually enhance the experience of craftsmanship by alleviating some of the routine, taxing, and less interesting work. The key seems to have been whether the machine was in control of the worker or the worker in control of the machine. The latter had useful possibilities.

But the machine needed no encouragement. Its potential to lower production costs and increase profits, even if this was a contest that had no winner because someone else would inevitably find an even cheaper way to produce goods, gave it the clear advantage. It was the hand that needed protection—and the human being with the human spirit that it was attached to. This was not just a longing for a simpler past but an urgent effort to salvage something vital from the crushing effects of industrialization and then the impending domination of technology. And therein lies the real motivation behind the surging Arts and Crafts movement, which would leap the Atlantic Ocean to thrive in America between 1875 and 1920.

The cross-fertilization of ideas between England and the United States was constant. Just as Ruskin and Carlyle were widely read in America, so were Emerson and Thoreau popular on the Atlantic's opposite shore. Thoreau's _Walden,_ in particular, was further inspiration for the simple life.

Charles Eliot Norton is an intriguing figure in all this cross-fertilization. His name crops up again and again. He knew both Emerson and Ruskin; in fact, as a frequent traveler abroad from an influential Boston family, he collected famous acquaintances rather as a botanist collects specimens. His friendship and correspondence with Ruskin lasted forty-five years. As Harvard's first professor of art history, his name lives on in the Charles Eliot Norton Lectures, and he was the first president of the Boston Society of Arts and Crafts. He is credited with promoting the craftsman ideal through numerous projects. And yet he was an odd sort of friend for Ruskin: eagerly receptive but apparently not quite up to a full sharing of Ruskin's ideas. He seems—and this may well be unfair, but it is my strong impression— delighted to have been on such close terms with a celebrity figure, while not entirely sympathetic to Ruskin as a person, despite his attentiveness. If William Morris was one of ours, I'm not certain about Norton. In Norton's hands, Ruskin's ideas appear conservative and reactionary—perhaps because those words better describe Norton himself. But then, it is difficult for me to get beyond his acts of destruction on an afternoon in June of 1900 at Brant-wood on Lake Coniston. Norton, whom Ruskin had curiously and unwisely appointed as his literary executor, stood with Joan Severn, Ruskin's cousin, and with a stifling and exaggerated sense of Boston propriety consigned the entire correspondence between Ruskin and Rosa LaTouche—as well as photographs, drawings, and a lock of her hair—to a bonfire. He had already burned many of the letters he had received from Ruskin, and he would perhaps have burned Ruskin's journals as well if Ruskin had given them to him some years earlier, as Severn had suggested. Never mind that Ruskin had once said, "I never wrote a letter in my life that all the world is not free to read if they will."[44]

The destruction of Ruskin's correspondence with LaTouche reveals a prurient vandalism, a pathological narrow-mindedness that can hardly endear. It is difficult to get beyond that dreadful pyre. There is no doubt that Norton's bent was aesthetic, that he was a scholar; but there is an accidental quality to his enthusiasm. Earlier—along with Severn—he had urged Ruskin to call a halt to the production of pamphlets that were later published as *Fors Clavigera,* which many consider his best work. Ruskin's political and economic opinions simply embarrassed him.

He most assuredly did not feel, as Morris and Ashbee certainly did, that desperate and compelling need to transform the world at whatever personal cost. Nevertheless, he wrote books on medieval architecture and was involved in training programs to develop manual skills and in model housing for the poor. But as Richard Poirier observes in his review of James Turner's biography of Norton, there is no evidence that he had any feeling at all for the individual lives of the workingmen whose aesthetic sensibilities he was so interested in lifting. Despite Norton, the movement thrived in America.

Inevitably, the Arts and Crafts movement is described by art historians as a "nostalgia" or "longing" for a preindustrial age, and in a culture dedicated to the notion of progress, those words clearly diminish the principles and ideals upon which it is based. There is no doubt that the machine age was displacing traditional skills and techniques. Is it mere nostalgia to realize the value of these skills and to want to preserve them? Is it a simplistic longing for a preindustrial age that values what the talented and skilled human hand can produce; that cherishes the ideal of the working community; that honors qualities, principles, and ideas that have difficulty competing in a highly competitive marketplace? Or is that the judgment of the marketplace itself, which our society and culture has so internalized that we barely recognize it for what it is? There is no nostalgia in preserving what is worth preserving. Or perhaps we simply need to think again about nostalgia and recognize that the longing for better, more congenial times is normal, natural, and valuable. It is mocked only by those for whom it is convenient that we forget there were things about the past that are worth preserving, if the future is indeed to be better.

But wherever we place the unsympathetic Charles Eliot Norton in all this, there was a significant Anglo-American cultural exchange. The transcendentalists and the Brook Farm experience were important to Ashbee as models, and Walt Whitman was something of an inspiration. Ashbee made several trips to America to lecture, and he records in his journal meeting with, among others, Will Price, publisher of *The Artsman* and creator of the phrase "the art that is life," and Frank Lloyd Wright, who translated that spirit into residential architecture. May Morris, William's daughter, also visited America in 1909 to lecture on embroidery and jewelry design.

The exchange went both ways. Two of the best known figures in the American Arts and Crafts movement were profoundly moved by their visits to England and their exposure to the new designs. Elbert Hubbard, after visiting Morris's Kelmscott Press, returned to America to found the Roycroft press and community. Gustave Stickley, after seeing the designs of Ashbee and C. F. A. Voysey, introduced Craftsman furniture to America and devoted the first two issues of *The Craftsman* magazine, which he started in 1909, to Morris and Ruskin respectively.

America was also the location of perhaps the most successful blending of social work and the craft ideal. Hull House, established in 1889 by Jane Addams, was modeled on London's Toynbee Hall, where Ashbee had lived. Her cofounder, Ellen Gates Starr, had studied bookbinding with T. J. Cobden-Sanderson and would set up a hand-binding facility there. Basket-making, weaving, and other hand arts were very much a part of the program, which ultimately was designed to give the economically disadvantaged more control over their lives, more satisfaction, and more pleasure.

Classes in every kind of handwork thrived in both England and America, and the success of the movement became its failure. Eventually the professional standards of the founders declined as arts and crafts became a popular activity and then merely a hobby or leisure pastime rather than a way of life and a salary-generating work activity. With so many examples of handwork available for so little money from those for whom it was merely a recreational diversion, those producing work of the highest standard could hardly hope to survive in the marketplace. But the movement left its still-clear mark on both art and architecture, and in virtually every community in America of that vintage the discerning eye can find some example of this idealistic endeavor—let us not demean it by calling it simply a style, for it was more than that.

The Arts and Crafts movement was an extension of the spirit of the Luddite Rebellion. It began as an upper-class revolt, expressed not in the actual but in the metaphorical smashing of machines. In fact, there was a greater triumph over technology than mere smashing could achieve, because the movement represented a powerful turning point, however brief, when the machine was recognized for what it was and what it might destroy. William Morris and others chose to use the machine if it genuinely made life or work easier, but within a context that allowed the worker to remain in control. Consciousness of what the machine was doing and a keen awareness of the need to manage it effectively would soon fade. The Arts and Crafts movement didn't lose so much as the machine won. It was that simple. Soon those who could remember what it had all been about would dwindle to a precious few, and art historians Robert Judson Clark and Wendy Kaplan can gaze incredulously at the photograph of a woman in simple yet medievally inspired dress on the porch of a heavily timbered house with stained glass panels and write, with all seriousness, "The intended audience for such a curious image is uncertain."[45] The image was a weapon in a war with causalities of the spirit that ended in the defeat of the soul.

CHAPTER SEVEN

The Nature of Dissent

I N A LIFETIME THERE ARE SOME IMAGES THAT SEEM burned into the brain; visual memories that are lodged there as sharply and as permanently as a tattoo. Since September 11 there is almost no one who doesn't understand what that means. One of my most vivid visual memories implanted itself in 1990 in California. I was there to attend a conference, and I had rented a car to see something of the countryside. I headed straight for the hills outside Sacramento, not knowing exactly what to expect, but found myself increasingly disappointed, or perhaps frustrated is the better word. There were occasional glimpses of mountains in the far distance, but always there was an intrusion. No matter how potentially beautiful the scene, there was inevitably a house, or a commercial structure, or a utility pole, or a line of poles and strings of wires, the umbilical cords of modern human survival, spoiling everything. Finally, in one long view, otherwise pristine, the massive pylons marched across the valley and up the hills and into the distant mountains as if they were conquering giants. There seemed no glimpse of land where the footprint of humans had not been firmly planted, and these intrusions began to seem truly alien. I could not shake the feeling that they did not belong there; that some natural order had been violated, that the land had been invaded by a crude and insensitive lout. Was there no piece of the original California left? Nothing that had not been scarred?

A few days later, driving the interstate between Sacramento and San Francisco, now longing for a glimpse of California as it might have been, suddenly, there it was. The road ahead curved and climbed and for a moment was invisible, swallowed by the landscape, and on each side rose wonderful rolling hills, tawny and rich, accented with dark, irregular evergreen shapes. Against the sky the hills blotted out what might have been beyond, and the image remained for a moment, virgin and untainted. "That's it," I said to myself.

It lasted only a moment. As I reached the crest of the hill, an amazing sight came into view. Four bulldozers moved in ballet formation—I can see them now—climbing the other side of the hill, pushing the red soil in front of them, scraping the hills down to raw flesh, and behind them an enormous billboard announced proudly: "COMING SOON, Rolling Hills Estates." Had I been a moment earlier or later I would have missed the sequence entirely. I had the irrational sense that it was meant for me. I had glimpsed, in that moment, the end of the world, the last patch of wild beauty on that road as it died under the machine.

California is hardly unique in this regard; it just has so much to lose. All over America—all over the world, in fact—such scenes take place daily. Nor is this imprinting of the landscape unique to our time. It is the pace that has quickened, the degree of damage and the awful ease with which such transformations are accomplished—a single day and it's gone.

Not all signs of human presence are to be disparaged. There is such a thing as appropriate use. Some houses, some towns fit neatly and comfortably into the landscape, seem always to have been there, tucked into valleys, nestled under a copse of trees. But the degree of domination of the land now seems out of all proportion, as if there were a human compulsion to scent-mark and conquer every last square inch of the countryside; to claim it with metal and wires and pavement. This conquest is implemented with a crudeness and produces an ugliness that has become almost obscene and in any case deeply embarrassing. I felt then—and now—an impulse to apologize. But to whom? The spirit had withdrawn.

Not long afterward I picked up John Muir's *The Mountains of California* and read the first line, "Go where you may within the bounds of California, mountains are ever in sight, charming and glorifying every landscape," and then those pylons and those bulldozers reappeared in my mind, and I thought what a lucky thing it was for Muir that he was dead and how sad it is to have to think or say such a thing.

JOHN MUIR was one of the first to recognize that America's wilderness needed urgent protection from encroaching civilization. The American West had seemed vast and unspoiled, but by 1869, when Muir first began exploring the Sierra Nevada, human habitation and use were already leaving marks. Sheep were destroying vegetation where they grazed; great swaths of mountain were left bare by timber cutting. What he saw in valleys that seemed untouched was not as pristine as he supposed: periodic burning by Native Americans had kept the meadows he admired from being overtaken by new growth. But he appreciated early on the potential impact of heavier use.

It is not apparent that the original Luddites had made the link between advancing industrialism and the despoiling of the natural world. Their ire was focused fiercely on the disruption of their lives and values by the new machines. With their attention on the immediate economic and social impact of technology, the larger implications of the industrial revolution may have escaped them. The earliest effects of industrialization on the environment could sometimes, with a simple shift of gaze, be overlooked or ignored, or they were simply not understood. The plume of smoke from one factory, after all, was hardly distinguishable from the plumes of smoke from the weavers' own cottages, and the full implications of the fouled rivers lay downstream.

The Romantics, however, had seen clearly enough that industrialization was changing the natural world around them in undesirable ways, and they bemoaned the loss. Still, they could find solitude and tranquility in the countryside and were consoled. Yet even in the Lake District where John Ruskin lived, a growing cloud of pollution and his fertile imagination—especially when he ventured farther afield into the Midlands, where factories filled the valleys and the rivers had turned to sewers—could easily lead him to envision the true cost of progress. Despite his reputation, Ruskin's warnings about environmental degradation were dismissed—some considered them the ravings of an unbalanced mind.

Outside the industrial centers, the world was still, for the most part, a beautiful place; and well into the early nineteenth century, even in densely populated England, and certainly in less-populated America, there existed enough unblemished natural beauty and a sufficient reserve of suitable vistas to provide a balm for urban and industrial stresses.

Emerson enjoyed a nature that was manageable; indeed, his true preference was for the managed. He found great joy in his own well-tended garden. Thoreau, though regretful of the extensive cutting he saw in the Maine woods during his expedition there, could hardly feel, as he traversed the vastness of the forests that remained, any great concern or real sense of urgency about their ultimate disappearance. And yet within a generation or two, only isolated pockets of old-growth forests would remain. The impact of industrialism would be felt first by individuals in their private lives and in their communities; but inevitably, as the effect on the natural world could no longer be ignored or dismissed or avoided, resistance to the machine would take a new form. Eventually there would be direct links forged between the original Luddites and environmentalism. But for the environmental movement to begin, awareness of degradation had to reach what Malcolm Gladwell has famously established as the tipping point. And to raise awareness to that level would require individuals of special character and strong voice.

The link between environmental conservation and Luddism is both obvious and subtle. Obviously it is the bulldozer rampaging across the hillside, the massive feller-buncher in the forests, the internal combustion engine on wheels leaving its trail of pollutants, the great humming and breathing cities and the many motors that keep them running, the strip malls and the endless paving that have swallowed the natural environment. But in a more subtle way, industrialism compounded the damage caused by the well-established Judeo-Christian tradition that viewed nature as an object to be rightfully dominated. That is a viewpoint that has separated people from the land to the point that "land" has been transformed into "landscape," a mere stage set for human activity instead of the playing field of life. The Luddites had challenged what the machine was doing to human lives; the environmental movement would challenge what the machine was doing to the natural world. Among the earliest, most eloquent and influential individuals to recognize the dangers that advancing industrial civilization posed to nature was John Muir.

After emigrating with his family from Scotland in 1849 as a boy of eight,

Muir grew up on a farm in Wisconsin. At a time before the extensive use of farm machinery (the reaper had been invented in 1831), certainly before the engine-driven tractor, his contact with the earth was daily and intimate. It is no accident that many early naturalists were country dwellers—often farmers. Observation not just of plants but of birds, animals, and insects came naturally when ours was an agrarian culture. Muir loved what he saw and understood early on how fragile it all was. Yet he also loved the cleverness and the ingenuity of the mechanical.

Impoverished, he had gotten into college on the strength of the ingenious inventions he had displayed at the state agricultural fair in Madison, Wisconsin. His amazing early-rising machine would, at a preset hour and with a creaking of wheels and shifting of levers, fling the sleeper out of bed. This and other mechanical curiosities he had fabricated out of scrap metal and pieces of carved wood. They attracted great attention, some of which came from Jeanne Carr, the wife of Professor Ezra Slocum Carr. Not only would Muir be accepted into college—remarkable, given his meager schooling and lack of money—he would become a friend of the Carr family and be taken into that gracious literary environment, where his talent for writing was noted and encouraged.

Muir remained at the University of Wisconsin in Madison for three years. He left for what he would call the University of the Wilderness. For the next few years, he traveled through the Midwestern states and Canada, using his highly developed skills on the factory machines. At one factory job he lost an eye. Not finding the satisfaction he anticipated, he set out on a thousand-mile walk to the Gulf of Mexico. He became so ill from malaria that his plan to continue on to South America had to be abandoned. Tired and weak, he went instead to California and the mountains, and by 1869 he was working and hiking in the Sierra Nevada.

In 1871 Ralph Waldo Emerson had just completed an exhausting series of lectures at Harvard. They had not gone especially well. His memory was beginning to fail, and the enormous energy he had always relied upon was waning. He had struggled with his notes and found the editing a challenge he hardly felt up to. He should have a diversion, a holiday, his family decided. Perhaps, they thought, a last adventure.

The party of twelve set off, heading west in the luxury of a private railway car. Emerson stood on the rear platform of the last coach and watched the landscape change. Their primary destination was San Francisco, but it was on from there to Yosemite, where the party settled into a rustic hotel for a relaxed stay.

Emerson was by then hugely famous, a Great Man who everywhere attracted small crowds of admirers, generally too awed to do more than gawk. At the edge of one of those circles of admirers stood the young John Muir, almost as awed as the rest—but not quite.

Muir was only thirty-three, living in the valley, exploring, collecting plant specimens, writing in his journal. When he was not on the trail, he ran a small sawmill to support himself, and before that he had been a shepherd. Whatever his job, the point was simply to earn enough to support his real need, which was to be outside in the mountains, an experience he would recall when he looked back into his diaries to compose *My First Summer in the Sierra* some four decades later. Any typical passage reveals Muir's ability to describe with the sharp eye of the botanist and to convey at the same time his sense of exhilaration and wonder. It is this mixture of the scientific and the sensual that gives his writing such appeal.

But standing on the edge of the crowd that day, Muir was unpublished and virtually unknown, considered something of an eccentric, even—an impression enhanced, no doubt, by his neglected clothing; his wild, unkempt beard; and his perhaps even wilder scientific theories about the impact of glaciers on the geology of the region; opinions that were freely interwoven, for anyone who would listen (he often escorted visitors throughout the area), with lyrical descriptions of a spirit-filled nature. Many of these theories would prove, if not entirely correct—there had been several glaciers, not one—at least partially correct, but they were then widely criticized as the misguided conjectures of an amateur, and a strange amateur at that. He was intense and focused, almost alarmingly so; but if he was an eccentric, he was an eccentric with influential friends. As a protégé of the Carrs, he had been introduced to the humanities and to a way of life far different from the one he had lived as a boy. At the University of Wisconsin, Professor Carr had taught Muir to keep notebooks as Emerson did, "a Commonplace Book" containing not just observations but gleanings from other sources, and Mrs. Carr would help him make a smooth transition from the threadbare harshness of his boyhood to the widely respected man he would become.

Emerson's writing had made a strong impression on Muir. As Linnie Marsh Wolfe says of the atmosphere at the university in her 1945 biography, *Son of the Wilderness: The Life of John Muir:*

> Emerson's name and philosophy were in the very air one breathed at Madison. Here as throughout Eastern and Midwestern America the intellectuals banded into lyceums and literary societies, parroted his wise sayings, unconscious for the most part that in the phrases they so glibly mouthed lurked dynamite enough to blast into oblivion their pleasant little worlds of commerce and convention.[1]

But the Carrs were among the few who saw quite clearly what Emerson was getting at. Not only were they disciples, they were Emerson's friends. They understood his essays "Nature" and "The American Scholar" as invitations to free oneself from the ordinary and the conventional to embrace the creative and the original. Muir needed little encouragement. Just as Emerson had been, Muir was an original. He was hospitable to Emerson's ideas "because like cleavage planes in rocks, awaiting development, they were indigenous within himself."[2]

In the years in between Madison and Yosemite, Muir had corresponded with the Carrs, and Mrs. Carr maintained her nurturing friendship, sending individuals of like mind to look Muir up on their visits to Yosemite. It was she who alerted Muir to Emerson's arrival. She let Emerson know that Muir was one of those "spiritual children" who had translated his ideals into action. She imagined an electric meeting of minds, and so it was.

Muir, too shy to introduce himself, and thinking Emerson on the verge of leaving, sent Emerson a note so heavily scented with the essence of transcendentalism that the Sage of Concord would have found it difficult either to miss or to resist:

> Do not thus drift away with the mob while the spirits of these rocks and waters hail you after long waiting as their kinsman and persuade you closer to communion. . . . In the name of a hundred cascades that barbarous visitors never see . . . in the name of all the spirit creatures of these rocks and of this whole spiritual atmosphere, Do not leave us now.[3]

Muir invited Emerson to come to the mill to see his collection of specimens; and Emerson, to Muir's great delight, dropped by his cabin without warning. And he would come again, whenever he could sneak away from his group. Emerson had found in Muir his "Man Thinking," his "Poet, who looking upon Nature with unveiled eyes, could integrate the Parts into a mighty Whole," as Wolfe put it.[4]

The meeting of two such complementary minds was a great success and would be what Muir considered one of the two supreme moments of his life (the other being the discovery of a rare flower). Muir accompanied Emerson's group as it left the area, acting as a guide, identifying the trees as they passed. He hoped to persuade Emerson to experience the mountains and valleys and forests by camping out with him, but Emerson's friends were horrified and wouldn't hear of it. He might catch cold in the night air. It was not to be. After his death, John Burroughs found a list of Emerson's entitled "My Men." Among the nearly twenty names were those of Thoreau and Carlyle, of course, but the last entry was "John Muir."

In fact, Muir was not a scholar in the Emersonian mold—nor indeed much of a scholar at all. Although he would spend much of his later life writing books, he had a certain mistrust of them. Nature should be a direct experience, he thought. A close observation of nature was vital, and by gazing intently at a flower, trying to understand why it lived where it did, what challenges it experienced and overcame, Muir would experience a communion with the plant that he felt inevitably led to greater understanding than he could ever obtain from a book. His background had been sternly Protestant, but on the trip south his sense of the divine had manifested itself in something far closer to pantheism. Christianity taught that only man had a mortal soul. Surrounded by vegetation that seemed not just lively but alive, he questioned that assumption: "I think that this is something that we know exactly nothing about."[5] He was stepping out onto thin theological ice, suggesting that humans just might not hold God-given monopoly rights on the soul.

He did not stop there. An encounter with an ugly, dangerous alligator pushed him further. If Christianity had applied a value to the plants and animals based solely on how well they served human needs, relegating the unlovely or the dangerous to dispensable categories, he now questioned that valuation. "How narrow we selfish, conceited creatures are in our sympathies!" wrote Muir, "how blind to the rights of all the rest of creation."[6] This was not simply a shift in perspective; it was a questioning of the accepted religious orthodoxy that placed man solely in charge of the natural world, at the apex of a God-created order.

Whether his new insights into the relationship between humans and nature fit into any sort of religious orthodoxy no longer concerned Muir. He had moved beyond that. In *The Mountains of California,* he describes his experience on the aptly named Cathedral Peak:

> No feature, however, of all the noble landscape as seen from here seems more wonderful than the Cathedral itself, a temple displaying Nature's best masonry and sermons in stones. How often I have gazed at it from the tops of hills and ridges, and through openings in the forests on my many short excursions, devoutly wondering, admiring, longing? This I may say is the first time I have ever been at church in California, led here at last, every door graciously opened for the poor lonely worshiper. In our best times everything turns into religion, all the world seems a church and the mountains altars. And lo, here at last, in front of the Cathedral is blessed cassiope, ringing her thousands of sweet-toned bells, the sweetest church music I ever enjoyed.[7]

Presbyterianism had been discarded for something that suited him better, but this was no sudden conversion. His first glimpse of the rare white orchid *Calypso borealis* alone, next to a stream deep in the wood had driven him to tears. "I never before saw a plant so full of life; so perfectly spiritual," he later wrote. "It seemed pure enough for the throne of its Creator."[8] On an early foray to Canada, he had been asked to teach Sunday school and had instead taught the children botany as a way of telling them about Creation. He now felt keenly that the spirit of the Creator resided in and was demonstrated by every living thing, and that man held no particular birthright to dominion but was merely one of many, equal in the sight of God. There had been hints of such a philosophy in Carlyle, and Muir would read Carlyle, but he needed no encouragement in his newfound views. To Muir, the beauty of the natural world was the essence of holiness revealed.

However much Muir had delighted in Emerson's visit, in rereading Emerson's essays he was somewhat disappointed. He scribbled margin notes questioning some of Emerson's conclusions. Emerson had gone so far, and no further, in his understanding of the importance of nature. He was not really much of a naturalist, Muir decided. Nor was he much of an adventurer—even of ideas. In truth, Emerson had laid the foundation, and Muir was to set the next course.

Muir's life can be neatly divided into periods, each one giving him something he needed. He had thought he could never endure urban living, but when the time came to leave Yosemite, he found he not only could endure

but could come to enjoy some aspects of city life. But perhaps more important, he discovered that he could live by his writing, and the journals he had
so carefully kept became his resource.

Eventually this solitary figure, after several more wilderness adventures,
married and settled down to run the orchards belonging to his wife's family.
For some time, preoccupied with farm and family, he put down his pen. It
wasn't long before he had reason to pick it up again. The travel urge returned,
and on a trip to the Cascade Mountains in 1888, he stopped at Mount
Shasta, where he discovered not the forests he anticipated but great swaths
of destruction brought on by clear-cutting. He was heartsick. Increasingly,
he felt compelled to defend what remained of wilderness against encroaching industrialized civilization. By 1889, he had shrugged off some of his farm
responsibilities and resumed his writing.

Everywhere he turned, something else seemed in danger. On a return
visit to Yosemite, the vistas and the plant life stirred him as before, but pressures were growing and there was a painful awareness of how easily and
quickly conditions might change. The valley itself was under state control,
but it was exercised very loosely, and Muir was outraged by the crude commercialism he saw. There was little intrinsic respect for the geology of the
place: one man had gone so far as to redirect a side cascade of Nevada Falls
to make its flow more impressive to tourists. Muir wondered what would be
next: white-washing El Capitan? Climbing into the high country, he and
Robert Underwood Johnson of *Century* magazine—who had, over Muir's
years of creative silence, kept after him for articles—found damage from
sheep grazing and signs of illegal lumbering. Their interest in each other was
mutual: Johnson was eager for Muir to contribute to the magazine, and
Muir was after the prestige and readership of *Century.* A campaign to save
Yosemite was taking shape in his mind.

Muir wanted to avoid becoming embroiled in local politics. Instead his
approach would be to attempt to rally a larger, more far-flung constituency
through his writing. He submitted two articles to *Century,* and the battle
had begun. Eventually it would be won, if it is possible to consider the
streams of tourists that pass through the park a victory, but at least the trees
and high meadows and wildlife that Muir valued are protected. Not long
after his articles were published, a group met with Muir to organize a club
for mountain lovers in the West, and the Sierra Club was born. Muir was
president until he died. The campaign to preserve Yosemite, with nature-

loving amateurs and volunteers on one side and powerful economic interests on the other, would become a prototype for the environmental struggles
to follow. Of course, nothing was ever that simple. Motives for *saving* wilderness, concepts of what *saving* means, tactics for achieving goals: all of these
vary enormously from group to group and within groups, from individual to
individual. The nuances of a particular battle might put an individual on one
side in one skirmish and on the other side in the next.

It is worthwhile to stop for a moment and consider the word *conservation*
and what it implies. Muir is said never to have used it. His goal was protection or preservation. It began out of a passion—emotional, subjective,
unquantifiable, sensual, a soaring of that unlocatable body part called spirit
—for the trees and the wildlife he had discovered on his solitary treks into
the wilderness. He reveled in the beauty and the splendor of the places he
had seen. And he had come to have a profound respect for every element of
the landscape. Why should a creature such as a spider simply be crushed
without a second thought? The spider had a life; it didn't deserve to be killed
simply for existing—not even simply because it might pose a danger. Nature
was worthy of protection not just because it was useful in providing suste-
nance, or even simply for its aesthetic value; nor should it be destroyed
because it was in the way, or even necessarily because it presented some
danger. It had an inherent value. This was not a concept that many individuals, reared on the Judeo-Christian concept of "mankind's dominion over
the earth," appreciated. Value the spider, and the balance has shifted; on the
other side of the scale, human value diminishes. This idea was not just
unacceptable; it was blasphemy. Muir knew when to accommodate. He
learned to put into his arguments not simply the inherent values of protecting nature but the practical aspects. Says Stephen Fox, in his book *John
Muir and his Legacy: The American Conservation Movement,* "What really
piqued him was the wanton blasphemy of cutting down a Sequoia grove that
predated the Christian era," but he would phrase his defense of the grove in
terms of its usefulness, its ability to conserve rainfall and prevent erosion.[9]
He understood that moral grounds were insufficient in the culture for which
he was writing. The influence of the efficient, profit-oriented, technological,
and industrial approach was growing. The benefit of unspoiled nature simply because one loved it was not an idea that could compete with the argument of usefulness. The enemies of conservation demanded something
more than sentiment, and the only thing that could successfully challenge

the economic arguments they put forth were other economic arguments. Could Yosemite, as it was, provide some useful or practical benefit from the human perspective? This approach would become a standard way to frame preservation arguments. And so the word *conservation* represents a compromised way of thinking because it suggests "a more prudent, more efficient use by humans," rather than the "unjustifiable" goal of protection for its own sake. When conservation became the acceptable term, the memory of this shift in meaning was lost, Fox argues. And yet it represents a critical moment that would be defined in other ways.

The movement had its start among a group of thoughtful, progressive, and often wealthy individuals who were enthusiastic amateurs. When the battles became political, which happened almost at once, these amateurs had neither the time nor the expertise to take on the opposition under the new rules. If justification had to be shaped in terms of human needs, then credible experts were necessary to express that defense—with all the numbers, charts, and studies that implied—and "conservation professionalism" was born. Some of those new professionals continued the battle; others gravitated to the newly organized Forest Service, where the idea of the greatest good for the greatest number prevailed as a standard. If protection of the environment was to be lodged within government bureaucracies, passion had to be replaced with a new practicality that was based on science. Emotion was not a weapon that could be used successfully to combat corporate lobbies. If the defense of conservation couldn't be counted, measured, or mapped, it wasn't helpful. Fox quotes an early professional as saying, "There are just two things on this material earth—people and natural resources," or as Fox himself puts it, "the user and the used." Nature herself had no rights. This was, he says, "the triumph of the utilitarian approach," and the new professionals looked back in some embarrassment to the "sentimental" origins of conservationism.[10] Muir had inspired the battle, but his sort of emotional, sensual, spiritual approach was no longer considered helpful. But if the sentimental approach could not be used as a tactic for winning political battles, it was still useful for increasing membership, as the Sierra Club well appreciated. Individuals make their decisions using a very different set of criteria from those used by government.

Preserving America's wild land against the utilitarian view and its conjoined twin, economic reality, is the same battle the Luddites fought. What those smashers of technology had wanted to preserve was not so much nature—not then, not yet—but the traditional way of life they preferred; the one that felt more comfortable and more natural, that provided pleasure and satisfaction. They wanted to live and work in livable communities with their families around them. The link to nature was inherent in these traditional lives. These were not values that could be easily defended in terms of efficiency or usefulness or measurable output. Values have always had a hard time competing with commerce and efficiency, but the battle lines were defined with the industrial revolution, and with every year the utilitarian model grew in power and credibility until its predominance was no longer questioned. It had reshaped the argument. And yet it was still technology that was being fought—or rather, as Jacques Ellul calls it, "the technique," by which is meant far more than a mere machine or science, or even technology itself. It refers, rather, to a way of thinking that goes beyond any of its various components; think of a fog of utilitarianism that can penetrate unseen, undetected, into everything we do, shaping the culture in ways that are seldom considered. Think of the way that efficiency or division of labor or time-motion evaluations or even cost-benefit analysis began to sneak out of the factory and into parts of our lives where they had no business. Think of the way that *conservation,* with its overtones of utilitarianism, became the accepted term for what Muir wanted to do, when it was, in fact, nothing like what Muir wanted to do.

There would be victories for the preservation of the wild, because as industrialism thrived, as urbanism increased, as the separation between people and the natural world grew, so did the need for nature. If businesses limited themselves to thinking only in economic terms, individuals were free to act in ways that demonstrated other priorities. Teddy Roosevelt organized the Boone and Crockett Club with his friend George Bird Grinnell. What he wanted was to hunt big game, but he also wanted to preserve species and their habitat for their own sake. His feeling for the wilderness was part of a growing sense that there were great tracts of still unspoiled land in America that needed protection against the relentless human impulse to reorder, reshape, and control. And so these professionals would point out the practical: the genetic need for diversity in species; for wildlife in balance as a control; for birds as insect eaters; for plants as a potential source of human medicine —anything to avoid the simple argument that nature was worthy of protection simply because it existed. Even its potential to provide delight and wonder to future generations was a weak argument against its potential to be transformed into profit through resource extraction and commercial potential. The value placed on delight and wonder came down, in the end, to simply how much someone was willing to pay for it and who might get the concession.

The writings of John Muir fill many volumes. *The Mountains of California, The Yosemite, My First Summer in the Sierra, The Story of My Boyhood and Youth, Travels in Alaska,* and the story of his dog, *Stickeen,* are among the best known, but his journals are a tremendous resource for appreciating both his keen observations of nature and his ability to describe his experiences in ways that readers could relate to. In his autobiography he writes, "When I was a boy in Scotland I was fond of everything that was wild and all my life I've been growing fonder and fonder of wild places and wild creatures."[11] What he accomplished was the validation—for his readers, at least—that "fondness" needs no justification. The biologist E. O. Wilson would later call this fondness "biophilia" and make the case that it is part of what we are as human beings—but that is to get ahead of the story.

John Muir would not win all his battles, and the last, it is said, killed him. It was the fight to halt the damming of the Tuolumne River, which flowed into the Hetch Hetchy Valley in Yosemite. It had been included in the National Park Act of 1890 at Muir's request, but now San Francisco needed water. The plan was to plug the southern end of the valley to create a vast reservoir. Behind the simple goal of meeting demands for water was another plan: to generate hydroelectric power. What the generating facility might do to Yosemite could only be conjectured. Muir rallied all his resources and drew upon the reservoir of his influence. Complicating the matter was the unavoidable fact that the private water company supplying San Francisco provided poor and inefficient service, and the dam promised a government-run alternative that was appealing, whether one preferred that the valley remain unflooded or not. Even some in the conservation movement chose not to fight the project for that and other reasons. At the heart of the debate was that inevitable question of values. When pitted against the idea that protected lands must somehow pay for themselves in usefulness, the intrinsic worth of beauty and wilderness hardly had a chance. In a sense this was a pivotal fight, the implications of which went far beyond one dam. It would set a precedent for how these protected lands might be used.

Muir came in for personal attack during this battle, with an approach that would become a familiar one, as it is still used today. Before a Congressional hearing of the House Committee on Public Lands, San Francisco Mayor

James Phelan said of Muir, "I am sure he would sacrifice his own family for the preservation of beauty. He considers human life very cheap, and he considers the works of God superior."[12] The answer is that to value nature is to value human life, since the two cannot be separated. But that understanding would be some time coming.

Muir would carry the fight through to the end, telling his daughter, "I'll be relieved when it's settled, for it's killing me."[13] And it may well have, for he died a little over a year after the government's decision. Muir came face to face with the machine, and yet again, the machine won. The bill to flood Hetch Hetchy was passed in Congress late in 1913. Yet far from being a failure, the very process of challenging the dam was important, for it marked a critical juncture in the human relationship to nature, illustrating a new willingness to fight a prolonged battle against a change described as essential for progress.

John Muir was certainly not the first to write about nature with that particular blend of passion, close observation, and art. Before even Thoreau, in 1789, there had been Gilbert White's classic, *A Natural History of Selburne*, in which his careful observations of the flora and fauna of his quiet English village not only created a biological portrait but revealed the essence of what it means to have a sense of place. There was the correspondence of Thomas Gray; the journals of Dorothy Wordsworth; and the writings in the early 1800s of John Clare, a rural and unlettered naturalist, and of John Leonard Knapp, who was inspired by White. Phillip Henry Gosse's experiences as a naturalist in Canada and England found expression in books, published in the 1840s and 1850s, that equal Muir's in liveliness and charm. The writings of Richard Jefferies documented the English countryside in the 1870s in a manner that continues to inspire respect, yet that toward the end of his life "inclined increasingly to the feverish celebration of a kind of natural mysticism,"[14] as E. D. H. Johnson puts it in *The Poetry of Earth*.

In America, William Bartram explored what is now the southeastern part of the United States, where he collected plant specimens and made drawings of the area's flora and fauna. His record, *Travels,* published in 1791, has long been considered a major literary and scientific achievement. But Muir was arguably the first to write about the wilderness with protection from overuse, from commercialization, and from thoughtless exploitation as a primary motivating factor. Nor did he see nature as simply the playground of humankind.

In the early years of the twentieth century, as public interest in the remaining wilderness in America began to grow and more conservation groups were created—some by wealthy and remarkably "establishment" individuals—most of them assumed the utilitarian approach. The advertised goal of these organizations might be to save fish or fowl or habitat or mountaintop, but more often than not the ultimate objective was to ensure good fishing or duck shooting or a pristine wilderness in which to mountaineer. Even preserving wilderness for aesthetic value or as a safety valve for urban stress was primarily self-serving. The benefit to nature herself was usually a secondary consideration. The idea that the earth is here for the sole benefit of humankind was so firmly embedded in dominant religious tradition and the culture that the other view—that nature had intrinsic value, that it was entitled to existence and deserved respect—was seen as strange, radical, certainly threatening, definitely anti-Christian, and possibly pagan. And perhaps it was.

Muir's background was a strict Scottish Presbyterian one, but it is easy to see an acceptance of a spiritual presence or even animism in his writing. In *The Golden Bough,* Sir James George Frazier observes how many different ancient cultures consider one tree or another sacred or as inhabited by spirits, and he notes the remnants of this sense of sacredness that could still be detected in nineteenth-century Europe. There is a strong related tradition of the tree being animated, even of its giving a discernable shriek or cry at being cut, and it seems likely that some sense of the animation of nature lurks beneath the veneer of conventional religious thinking, the overlay being incomplete or more fragile than is assumed. Muir, alone in the wilderness for long stretches of time, reconsidered what he had been taught about the relationship of humans to the natural world. "The world we are told was made for man. A presumption that is totally unsupported by facts. . . . Nature's object in making animals and plants might possibly be first of all the happiness of each one of them, not the creation of all for the happiness of one. Why ought man to value himself as more than an infinitely small composing unit of the one great unit of creation?"[15] Muir asks. It was but a short step from there to questioning whether we humans had any real right to use nature beyond subsistence. And this question was profoundly inconvenient to economic and technological progress.

And yet, all along, despite that inconvenience, there were individuals who, if they did not go so far as this, began to ask the question Muir had asked. And if they did not hold this view intuitively, some came to it through experience. Will H. Dilg, an avid fly-fisherman who was to head the Izaak Walton League, felt keenly not only the joy of the sport but a basic incompatibility with urban life. "I am weary of civilization's madness," Fox quotes him as writing, "and I yearn for the harmonious gladness of the woods and the streams. I am so tired of your piles of buildings and I ache from your iron streets."[16]

In the stories of these early conservationists, many sound a similar lament, an actual physical need to be close to nature and away from the environment created by technology. Bernard DeVoto, a writer for *Harper's Magazine* who came to his environmental activism only in midlife, professed a dislike for Muir's approach. Yet his own words, shortly before his death, sounded a lot like Muir's philosophy.

> I have got to have the sight of clean water and the sound of running water. I have got to get to places where the sky-shine of cities does not dim the stars, where you can smell land and foliage, grasses and marshes, forest duff and aromatic plants and hot underbrush turning cool. Most of all, I have to learn again what quiet is. I believe that our culture is more likely to perish from noise than from radioactive fall out.[17]

If everyone felt this way, there would be no opposition to the preservation of wilderness. Clearly everyone does not. But after the Second World War, with its culmination in the dropping of the atomic bomb, there was the sudden awareness of just how far technology had gone; and for some this had a profound effect. Charles Lindbergh, while not a traditional conservationist, was one of those who became increasingly conscious of the dangers of the technology he had earlier embraced.

In his 1948 book, *Of Flight and Life*, Lindbergh wrote, "I grew up as a disciple of science. I know its fascination. I have felt the godlike power man derives from his machines." Flying over the countryside, he looked down on the roads and other human intrusions and felt something close to despair. "Somehow I feel every road and oil well is an imposition, an intruder on the solitude which once was mine as I flew over it. Looking down on them from the air, those marks seem like a disease—a rash spreading slowly over the earth's surface."[18] The remedy, he felt, was to rebuild a relationship between humans and the natural world.

Many of these amateurs, such as Lindbergh, made the connection, as

Thoreau had, between loving nature and living simply. Muir had gone on his weeklong treks into the mountains without so much as a blanket and with sparse provisions: a bit of tea, bread, and oatmeal. Lindbergh began to visit tribal groups in Asia and Africa, where he slept in the open and ate native fare. In Africa, aspects of civilization that had seemed so important in the developed world become immaterial. Measured time, the prime example of the influence of technique in ordinary lives, loses its significance in these surroundings.

But Lindbergh, a hero of early aviation, eventually reappraised its impact. In the early 1970s he opposed the supersonic transport (SST) plane because it wasted fuel and adversely impacted the environment with its exhaust and sonic boom. He questioned the conventional view of progress and the constant drive to increase speed. In battling the SST, he saw that need was not the driving factor in its development, but rather political and commercial interests. The question was whether these forces could be resisted and controlled; whether common sense could finally win out. In the end, the SST was one technology the United States did not opt for, although it was probably the unlikelihood of profit that tipped the balance in favor of rejection.

An archconservative in his early years and accused of Nazi sympathies, Lindbergh came to believe firmly in government protection of vulnerable natural resources and wild places. "There is nothing we can do anywhere in the world that is more important than protecting our natural environment,"[19] he told the Alaska legislature in 1968. Time was running out, he felt. An unconventional man, he was an unconventional conservationist, keeping his distance from an American movement that had been gaining ground from the time of the loss of the Hetch Hetchy Valley and working mainly through the international World Wildlife Fund.

At about the same time that Lindbergh was going through his own transformation after World War II, Aldo Leopold was already on his way to becoming recognized as one of the leading voices for the twentieth-century conservation-ecological movement. He began his professional life working for the Forest Service in the first decade of the new century. His degree was from the Yale School of Forestry, and his mind was set, by his training, in the utilitarian mode. But that would change, and in the end he would do more perhaps than Muir to change our view of nature, precisely because he had the credibility of the trained scientist in a culture that needed that reassurance.

Yet he was able to move well beyond the utilitarian position, typical of the Forest Service, to a broader ecological view. Nature had an intrinsic value that needed no justification, Leopold eventually understood. Additionally, he was able to translate the conservation ethic into practical plans for generational land restoration.

Having spent much of his boyhood, just before the turn of the century, in outdoor pursuits, camping, birding, and hunting, there was no sudden conversion to environmentalism; he had always loved the outdoors. But Leopold's contribution would be the gradual development over the course of a lifetime of the view that land and wildlife management approaches focusing on one aspect of a species's life, such as its habitat—or, indeed, focusing on one species to the exclusion of others in that habitat—were inadequate, doomed to fail, and in some cases destined to exacerbate the very problem that had inspired them in the first place. The approach to conserving the desirable deer—from the hunter's perspective—had led, with seeming logic, to the killing off of predators, namely the wolf. And yet that had soon resulted in a weak and unhealthy overpopulation of deer. Which in turn led to encouraging more hunters to cull the deer. Which required building a road into the wilderness so that they could reach the deer. Which divided the wilderness they had wanted to preserve. Leopold saw the complete folly of this approach, which had been planned with the short-term interests of humans in mind without considering the whole ecosystem. Taking part in the wolf cull, he had experienced his own moment of awakening. He had shot a mother wolf and had hurried down the slope in time to look into her wild eyes and see the dying of a green light. It was a moment he would never forget. He had seen something in those wild dying eyes that awakened him to the meaning of what he had just done. He could no longer distance and insulate himself with quite the same ease. His conservation utilitarianism had been supplanted with the beginnings of what would be a new science.

In 1928 Leopold left the Forestry Service to write a textbook on game management and then began teaching at the University of Wisconsin. There he bought an abandoned farm where he spent weekends with his family. Living in a modest structure he called "the shack," he worked at restoring habitat; composed hundreds of articles; and began writing *A Sand County Almanac*, which would be published posthumously. This rather modest book has become a classic. The appeal of Leopold's style may well be its humility; here is someone who knows a great deal, but clearly not everything. And it is that new sense of uncertainty that marks a shift of perspective. Man has stepped down from the apex of domination to gaze at the world in barely comprehending amazement. In an age in which conservation remained in the firm grip of specialization, Leopold was a generalist. He saw the complex interrelationships between the land and its resident creatures and understood that to dislodge one was to affect all in ways that could not be anticipated. And he was very aware that we have only the faintest inkling of what these creatures and plants require and what they do for one another.

The popularity of the book is due not simply to his powers of observation and his knowledge, or even to his humility, but to his fine nature writing. In describing the land he knows best, he can transport the reader from armchair to the place he describes.

> A dawn wind stirs on the great marsh. With almost imperceptible slowness it rolls a bank of fog across the wide morass. Like the white ghosts of a glacier the mists advance, riding over phalanxes of tamarack, sliding over bogmeadows heavy with dew. A single silence hangs from horizon to horizon.
>
> Out of some far recess of the sky a tinkling of little bells falls soft upon the listening land. Then again silence. Now comes a baying of some sweetthroated hound, soon the clamor of a responding pack. Then a far clear blast of hunting horns, out of the sky into the fog.
>
> High horns, low horns, silence and finally a pandemonium of trumpets, rattles, croaks and cries that almost shakes the bog with its nearness, but without yet disclosing whence it comes. At last a glint of sun reveals the approach of a great echelon of birds. On motionless wing they emerge from the lifting mists, sweep a final arc of sky, and settle in clangorous descending spirals to their feeding grounds. A new day has begun on the crane marsh.[20]

What Muir and Leopold had done with their writing was to help lay the groundwork for what would come to be called ecology, a vision of nature that assumed a complex interrelationship among every part of an ecosystem. To look at one species alone without considering its relationship to everything else in its environment was to distort the complexity of life. Gradually it would begin to dawn on us that we, too, are part of that ecosystem.

There would be a growing awareness that the notion of nature as simply a human resource to be dominated and managed by and for humans was not only short-sighted but, in the long-term, counterproductive. Although some "techno-optimists" envisioned a technological solution to every human-created problem, others doubted the likelihood of success of these high-tech fixes and simply preferred to avoid the necessity of repair in the first place. And yes, there was a growing realization that the human species is too clever and too destructive by half, apt to bring down, however unintentionally, not only other species but perhaps the entire delicate balance of the ecosystem.

THE GROWING disillusionment with progress itself, echoing throughout the conservation movement, inevitably welded the connection among politics, economics, and environmentalism. Just as one species in an ecosystem could not be eliminated without disturbing those that remained, so conservation could not be isolated from the other forces in society. Environmentalism began as an effort to protect wilderness, not as a liberal philosophy; but increasingly, those of a conservative political bent found it a challenge to reconcile protecting the environment with the demands of business expansion, growth, and "progress" without the authority of the government agencies. Gradually, many of those concerned with the environment gravitated to the political party that seemed less predisposed to take the side of business automatically and that demonstrated more inclination to consider the possibility of a federal solution to an environmental challenge. Thus, protecting the environment became associated with the Democratic party rather than the Republican party, despite the fact that a good many political conservatives are as passionately interested in the natural world as are liberals and progressives. With the accusation of "liberal" being flung at environmentalists, it is well to remember that Marxism, socialism, and communism are as committed to industrial progress as is capitalism. Love of nature has, in fact, no conventional politics.

As the environmental threats increased, more traditional forms of Christianity began to reinterpret Scripture in an attempt to revise or rethink what had clearly become a damaging paradigm. Could "dominion" not be reinterpreted to mean "stewardship" over the earth, for example? Surely this change signaled a more benign relationship with the natural world, yet the view remained essentially utilitarian. It was not, in fact, much of a change. The major Christian denominations were searching desperately for a way out of a theological blind alley, but many fundamentalist groups didn't bother to try. They held their ground. For those who envisioned an apocalyptic end sooner rather than later, the question was immaterial. What did it matter?

And yet the concepts of stewardship or even of dominion could be useful, despite their shortcomings, because the health of the planet did indeed now lie in our hands. It was becoming more and more difficult, as scientific information accumulated, for even congenital doubters to maintain that human activity wasn't playing a role in climate change. The ozone hole was growing, the rain forests were shrinking, the coral reefs were dying, and the songbirds were decreasing. Eventually, at one end of the spectrum would be those for whom every dying tree looked like a portent of the end of the world and, at the other, those who saw any expression of concern as evidence of a communist plot. The difficulty was that from one end of the spectrum to the other, everyone had something to lose.

I met David Brower for the first time when he was already an old man, robust and yet at the same time fragile. He died in 2000 at the age of eighty-eight, but that day he was speaking to a small, sympathetic crowd in Blue Hill, Maine. Afterward he signed books. Mine says "Persevere," as do probably ten thousand others, a perfect challenge for every individual, surely interpreted as an expression of Brower's personal confidence. He was, even then, a powerful and inspiring figure. One wanted to oblige.

Brower's biography—mountaineer, Yosemite dweller, president of the Sierra Club, defender of the wilderness—reads enough like John Muir's to prompt suspicions of direct reincarnation. His own wilderness experiences transformed him over time into an ardent preservationist of a then-new breed. The old Sierra Club had been founded with one of its aims "to render accessible" the mountains of the West. No encouragement was needed. By the 1950s they were far too accessible, and traditional expeditions by mule, the cutting of saplings for bed and shelter, and the building of campfires were taking their toll and leaving a damaged environment. The wilderness was being loved to death. The answer was to tread more lightly. Brower led the way in promoting this new awareness, but he was also instrumental in shifting the tone of the conservation movement from conciliatory to adversarial. The Sierra Club had been a social group of mainly well-heeled nature lovers. Under Brower, the gloves came off. The organization would be transformed into an aggressive weapon aimed at anything that encroached on the wilderness. There was too much at stake, Brower felt, to do otherwise. The cozy, mannerly relationship between the club and the Park and Forest Services was strained when Brower openly challenged their actions and questioned their motives. Brower was dedicated, impassioned, and very serious. Not a moment was to be wasted in protecting what remained and saving what was threatened.

Muir's battle against the Hetch Hetchy Dam had been lost, and environmentalists looking at the results some fifty years later—the ugly, muddy shores that were nothing like what the proponents' drawings had promised —now saw the crucial nature of every contest. Then came the Echo Park plan to construct a dam in Dinosaur National Monument in northwestern Colorado. This time it would be the canyons of the Green and Yampa rivers that would be flooded. The Sierra Club, in coalition with Howard Zahniser and the Wilderness Society, aimed to stop the project. Combating the Echo Park proposal evolved into a classic battle between the defenders of wilderness and the powerful commercial interests with their political and federal allies. It would resemble the Hetch Hetchy fight, but with a difference. There was a new sophistication to the conservation effort, with defenders of the canyons using both facts and figures, challenging the very science of the Bureau of Reclamation of the Department of Interior on the one hand and galvanizing public support on the other. DeVoto would write about the threatened land in *Saturday Evening Post;* and Alfred Knopf, newly attuned to preservation after publishing Wolfe's biography of Muir, leaped to the land's defense with *This Is Dinosaur,* with photographs and text edited by Wallace Stegner, which would introduce a broader public to the more or less hidden treasures that were under threat.

Stegner was by then the author of five novels and a professor at Stanford University where he taught creative writing and literature. The search for a sense of place and the compelling need to establish and maintain human connections were themes that repeated themselves in his fiction. Upon moving to California, he and his wife Mary had built a house in the peninsula foothills between the university and the Pacific Ocean. Preserving and protecting the green spaces as the developers eyed the land around them became an early preoccupation. There is something about California that breeds this intense love of nature, which manifests itself in those susceptible as a passion for defending the environment. Stegner, whose earlier forays into activism had been against racial prejudice, was no exception. He too made the ritual hikes into Yosemite with his wife and friends, but his work was also leading him in new directions.

In 1954, after a hard struggle with the research and uncharacteristic doubts about his ability to conquer the material, he published *Beyond the Hundredth Meridian: John Wesley Powell and the Second Opening of the West*. Powell had heroically and against great odds—he had lost an arm in the Civil War—surveyed the Colorado River by boat. The upper reaches of the Colorado race through narrow canyons overhung with high, sheer, and treacherous cliffs. They are, at places, virtually unclimbable under the best conditions. Powell's one-armed excursions up these cliffs to see the unexplored land above made for unforgettable passages in the book, but the process of writing the book changed Stegner as well. He emerged with a new consciousness that translated into a passion to protect wilderness lands.

He first expressed his fears that the incoming Republican administration would make a grab for public lands in an article entitled "One-Fourth of a Nation: Public Lands and Itching Fingers" (1953); then, concerned about plans to construct the Echo Park Dam in Dinosaur Monument, he published "Battle for Wilderness" in the *New Republic* in early 1954. What likely attracted Brower's attention was Stegner's fearless tone and his direct accusation in the text that the government agency involved, the Bureau of Reclamation, had specifically selected an area to flood that contained both scenic treasures and Indian artifacts and pictographs in order to "break down national park immunity," the idea that national parks were inviolate, and thus establish a precedent for land grabs. In 1955, Stegner published "We are Destroying Our National Parks" in the widely read *Sports Illustrated,* and Brower became convinced that here was the person to take on the editing of *This Is Dinosaur,* perhaps the first book specifically designed to change environmental politics where it really counted—in Washington. It would be distributed to every member of Congress, a move that Stegner remembered in 1985 as "an effective weapon in the first great conservation battle in recent times."[21] Says Stegner biographer Jackson J. Benson in his book *Wallace Stegner: His Life and Work,* "It was certainly the first time that all the major conservation organizations had come together in one cause to show their muscle in a matter of pending legislation."[22]

The photographs in *This Is Dinosaur* were compelling, but Stegner's introductory essay, "The Marks of Human Passage," was especially powerful. At its conclusion he said, "In the decades to come, it will not be only the buffalo and the trumpeter swan who will need sanctuaries. Our own species is going to need them too. . . . It needs them now."

In the end, of course, it became a political contest waged in the halls of

Capitol Hill. After a long, complex, and grueling battle, the protectors of the canyons won—perhaps to their surprise. There *have* been some successes in the ongoing challenge to the machine. Not surprisingly, when the tangled skein of the defense was unraveled, each thread seemed to lead back to Brower and his revitalized Sierra Club.

John McPhee has immortalized Brower in his 1971 book, *Encounters with the Archdruid.* In three encounters, Brower confronts, one by one, the geologist and mineral engineer, the developer, and the dam builder. In these sequences, all the arguments for and against development and use are aired as McPhee allows the dialogue to follow its own lead. Again and again Brower argues that nature doesn't need to prove herself useful, that she has intrinsic value. We've used so much of the planet. Just leave ten percent of wilderness as a kind of tithe, Brower pleads.

Writing, by itself, is a Luddite act. There is nothing inherently mechanical about creating a sentence or a string of sentences or a page or a book. Each sentence, whether felicitous or awkward, expresses a thought of some kind. Any combination of several words carries with it some indication of who wrote it. Because the choice of words is intuitive, it remains individual, a unique expression of character. Writing is a thoughtful process without being an entirely rational one. It is thinking illustrated—but even the most rigid structure allows room for individuality and creativity. It is, therefore, the antithesis of the machine. But in a mechanical age, credibility is linked to machinelike qualities of objectivity, detachment, and impersonality, none of which come naturally to humans.

For a number of years, this mechanical paradigm reigned, especially in journalism, although there has been a tendency recently to loosen up. Nevertheless, authority and credibility accrued to writing that was the most mechanical and the least human on the assumption that there was something—not just something, but *one* thing—that could be called the truth and that it could best be got at by the detached, uninvolved observer. The writer-reporter himself was required to disappear as a presence in the work.

McPhee is an interesting character himself, an illustrative example of what happens when a creative writer is obliged to submit himself to the dictates of the machine and yet is determined to find a way around it. McPhee, writing in one of the best journals of his time—the *New Yorker*—was bound and obliged to adhere to the prevailing standards. His approach, therefore, was to accompany people and record what he saw and heard. Of course, he could not record all he saw and heard—and wouldn't have wanted to, for selection is the essence of art, and McPhee is an artist. But in the interest of giving the appearance of objectivity, he recorded a great deal in meticulous detail. We have the sensation, reading McPhee, of looking at a fine photograph, a beautiful, detailed rendering of the real.

The intentionality of this attempt to relay objectivity is confirmed by the dust jacket of *Encounters with the Archdruid.* "This book," it says, "is not written from the point of view of any one of the four men." If that was true, then McPhee rigged the game, for it is a three-to-one contest: Brower against a triumvirate of articulate, reasonable utilitarians. And yet, we can still put McPhee on the side of the conservationists, with one foot tentatively in the neo Luddite camp, simply for bringing up the subject, for allowing the exchange of ideas to take place at all, for applying his own creative and artistic skills even while respecting the confines of the mechanical paradigm.

Despite being outgunned, it is Brower who triumphs in the book. McPhee's detachment is not simply an illusion but a subterfuge, and one that every reader understands and participates in. *Encounters,* because it is respectful enough of Brower's argument to allow it to compete openly and on an equal footing with the keenest and strongest arguments against it, takes its place with other environmental classics. And Brower, sometimes laconic and thoughtful, sometimes forceful, is equal to the task.

The environmental movement is peopled by "druids," says Charlie Fraser, one of Brower's antagonists who plans to develop Cumberland Island, Georgia, long held by a single family and thus as yet unspoiled. These, he says, are religious figures who sacrifice people and worship trees. And yet Brower seems at first so docile in this encounter that Fraser, writes McPhee, "wouldn't even call him a druid, and in a sense Fraser was right, for the rote behavior of an ordinary member of the priesthood should be simple to predict. This, however, was—as Fraser apparently did not grasp— no ordinary member of the priesthood. This was the inscrutable lord of the forest, the sacramentarian of *ecologia americana,* the Archdruid himself."[23]

And at once McPhee himself acknowledges and records that the transition from a Christian to a post-Christian world has been made. There is a new theology in the land, and it is an old one. D. H. Lawrence grasped something of its essence in his essay "New Mexico," when he observed a gathering of American Indians and saw a genuine expression of faith in their traditions and rituals. He caught a glimpse of something deeper, and his prose captures the essence of what McPhee sensed in Brower.

> It was a vast old religion, greater than anything we know: more starkly and nakedly religious. There is no God, no conception of a god. All is god. But it is not the pantheism we are accustomed to, which expresses itself as "God is everywhere, God is in everything." In the oldest religion, every thing was alive, not supernaturally but naturally alive. There were only deeper and deeper streams of life, vibrations of life more and more vast. So rocks were alive, but a mountain had a deeper, vaster life than a rock, and it was much harder for a man to bring his spirit, or his energy, into contact with the life of the mountain, and so he drew strength from the mountain, as from a great standing well of life, than it was to come into contact with the rock. And he had to put forth a great religious effort. For the whole life-effort of man was to get his life into contact with the elemental life of the cosmos, mountain-life, cloud-life, thunder-life, air-life, earth-life, sun-life. To come into immediate felt contact, and so derive energy, power, and a dark sort of joy. This effort into sheer naked contact, without an intermediary or mediator, is the root meaning of religion.[24]

And so Brower and Muir, who had first sought strength from the mountains, were understood, even by their enemies, to be seekers in this old/new religion, possessing a sense of sacredness that transcended all human concepts of time. And with that conceptualization of the vastness of the cosmos, the infinitesimally brief appearance of the man creature did, in fact, manifest itself in an unwritten yet felt theology that put immediate human needs into perspective. It was, for the utilitarians, easy to challenge: "You would put this tree, this mountain, this vista, this shore, as beautiful as it is, before the immediate needs of the human community?" The question is asked again and again in different ways, and the hesitant, "Well, yes," brings derision and condemnation.

Brower, and the Echo Park coalition that he and Zahniser had helped to build, knew their victory was in fact only a skirmish in a larger battle. The preservation of wild areas within the national parks was at the whim of the Park Service, which could, to satisfy a sudden need or change of thinking, build new roads, cabins—whatever seemed interesting at the time. The decision was theirs. The national forests, even those designated as roadless, were just as threatened. The scrawl of the presidential pen could undo wilderness protection. What was needed was a national policy—a system that would be a real challenge to attempts to violate the sanctity of wild places. This battle had Zahniser leading the charge. It would be prolonged and in the end required painful compromise. Zahniser saw the bill go through sixty-six rewritings. But as public support grew—the Sierra Club's membership had doubled during the Echo Park fight—the task became easier. Eventually, the legislation establishing wilderness areas that would not be subject to the whim of whatever administration was currently in office would sail through Congress in the summer of 1964 with only twelve "no" votes.

Stegner played a role here as well that was not vital, perhaps, but was memorable. In 1960, with Brower as his "cattleprod" as he described it later, he wrote a letter to the committee that had the task of reporting to Congress on the need for wilderness legislation. It has become something of a coda for wilderness protection and is known simply as Stegner's "Wilderness Letter." Reflecting on the letter some twenty years later, he said, "I was prepared to argue for the preservation of wilderness not simply as a scientific reserve, but as a spiritual resource . . . that could reassure us of our identity as a nation and a people."

It did that, certainly, but it also struck that place in the heart where we seem to recognize and store great truths. It has been republished in whole or in part countless times. It was antitechnological to its core: not just a plea for wilderness but a damning of the notion of Progress, of technological dependency, and of the religion of materialism; and it was as sharp and as pointed as an arrow.

> Something will have gone out of us as a people if we ever let the remaining wilderness be destroyed; if we permit the last virgin forests to be turned into comic books and plastic cigarette cases; if we drive the few remaining members of the wild species into zoos or to extinction; if we pollute the last clear air and dirty the last clean streams and push our paved roads through the last of the silence, so that never again will Americans be free in their own country from the noise, the exhausts, the stinks of human and automotive waste. And so that never again can we have the chance to see ourselves single, separate, vertical and individual in the world, part of the environment of trees and rocks and soil, brother to the other animals, part of the natural world and competent to belong in it. Without any remaining wilderness we are committed wholly, without chance for even momentary reflection and rest, to a headlong drive into our technological termite-life, the Brave New

World of a completely man-controlled environment. . . . Not many people are likely, any more, to look upon what we call "progress" as an unmixed blessing. Just as surely as it has brought us increased comfort and more material goods, it has brought us spiritual losses, and it threatens now to become the Frankenstein that will destroy us.

David Brower would be the cattle prod for another environmentalist. After Paul Ehrlich gave a speech on population at the Commonwealth Club in San Francisco, Brower pressed him for a book. The result: the best-seller, *The Population Bomb*. It sold three million copies over the next decade. The ever-increasing population would be our undoing, Ehrlich said, not later but sooner. He was roundly attacked and contradicted by those who felt the planet—with the help of technology—could sustain far greater numbers. Ehrlich, a scientist, is no antitechnologist, but he is concerned that technology may have inadvertent consequences. Eventually he modified his views. Population growth was simply one of three factors—faulty technologies and growing affluence being the other two—that "when multiplied together threatened the quality of life for us all." But this book, whether the point was arguable or not, increased awareness of ecological—and technological—issues. It was technology that was enabling population growth and shifting the responsibility for stabilizing population (a role previously played by harsh, challenging conditions and disease) to the average couple, and it was too much of a burden to bear.

But if one single book could be said to have been aimed directly at the technologist, in particular the chemical industry, it was *Silent Spring*. Surely there are few who do not recognize its title and feel they must have read it, whether in fact they have or have not. It is that kind of book.

It was mired in controversy even before its publication. Thoroughly researched and well documented, it was a brutal indictment of the effect of the overly enthusiastic use of pesticides on the natural world, and of the engineering mentality itself, which failed to understand the importance of a complex and diverse environment. It also revealed the cozy relationship of industry and university that both then and now brings the independence, objectivity, and reliability of industry-sponsored research into question. Rachel Carson, a marine biologist turned writer who had already published several very successful books on sea life, intended that the chemical industry be caught off guard, and it was. She had been working virtually in secret,

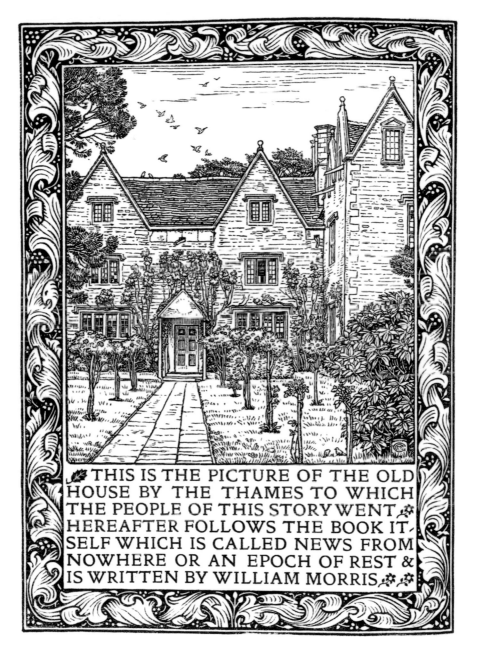

The nineteenth century designer, poet, and publisher William Morris used the courtyard of his own Kelmscott Manor as the frontispiece for his utopian novel, *News From Nowhere* (Kelmscott Press, 1892). The beautiful and peaceful society he describes in the novel has left much of technology behind. (Photograph reproduced by permission of the William Morris Gallery, London.)

The only contemporaneous drawing of Henry David Thoreau's cabin at Walden Pond is this sketch by his sister, Sophie. (Courtesy of the Walter Harding Collection of The Thoreau Society, and of The Thoreau Institute at Walden Woods.)

Although a bit larger than Thoreau's cabin, this equally simple cottage on Placentia Island, Maine, was the home, for forty years, of Art and Nan Kellam. They retreated there to live without the distractions and complications of modern society after his earlier career as an engineer for Lockheed. (Photograph by David Graham.)

The Lackawanna Valley by George Inness was commissioned by the railroad's owners in 1855, just as the impact of the train was beginning to be felt. The thrusting of the locomotive into the center of the bucolic Pennsylvania landscape, coupled with the graveyard of stumps in the foreground, illustrates the ambivalence toward technology that the painter likely felt. (Gift of Mrs. Huttleston Rogers, Photograph © Board of Trustees, National Gallery of Art, Washington, D.C.)

The train, in *The Railway* by Edouard Manet (1872–1873), is represented by nothing more than steam. The woman, with loose, flowing hair, book, and dog, has her back to technology, but it remains a powerful draw for the young girl grasping the fence. (Gift of Horace Havemeyer in memory of his mother, Louisine W. Havemeyer, Photograph © Board of Trustees, National Gallery of Art, Washington, D.C.)

Nineteenth Century critic John Ruskin applied his close observation not simply to nature, but to gothic ornament (here, in a watercolor of the Entrance to the South Transept, Rouen Cathedral). The careful exercise was part of his attempt to understand ornament's role—what it represented about the carvers themselves, what it revealed about the nature of medieval life and art, and what lessons industrial England might learn from it. (Fitzwilliam Museum, Cambridge.)

When *Mariana* (1851) stretches, or leans back in ecstasy—either interpretation is possible—she is emphasizing, in this painting by John Everett Millais, what it means to be human. The leafy pattern of the tapestry, the medieval costume, and the gothic-inspired interior represent the importance of the past and the link to nature, an idea echoed by the real leaves that have blown inside. The machine has been banished. (Tate Gallery, London/Art Resource, NY.)

Hull House, the Chicago social settlement house founded by Jane Addams and Ellen Gates Starr, incorporated literature, as well as art and craft programs, in an attempt to make work a creative experience. (Jane Addams Memorial Collection, The University Library, University of Illinois at Chicago.)

Bookbinders are at work at The Roycroft Shop in East Aurora, New York, around the turn of the century. Founder Elbert Hubbard imported ideas from England's progressive workshops to create Roycroft, a commercially successful application of Arts and Crafts, which began as a reaction to the increasing industrialization of production and the loss of craftsmanship in the nineteenth century. (Elbert Hubbard – Roycroft Museum.)

Charlie Chaplin's 1936 film "Modern Times" drew upon the common fear (if only to judge by the response to his film) that one might become engulfed and entrapped by the machine. (MODERN TIMES Copyright © Roy Export Company Establishment.)

Modern "Benders" in Cornwall, England, have taken to the road precisely to avoid entrapment by technology, with the additional aim of living, as they put it, "lightly on the earth" in their temporary homes of bent hazel sticks. (Photograph, Nicols Fox.)

anticipating a strong counterattack. But "when the attack came," says Paul Brooks, who wrote the introduction to the 1987 paperback, "it was probably as bitter and unscrupulous as anything of the sort since the publication of Charles Darwin's *Origin of Species* a century before. Hundreds of thousands of dollars were spent by the chemical industry in an attempt to discredit the book and to malign the author—she was described as an ignorant and hysterical woman who wanted to turn the earth over to the insects."[25] It was an intentionally misleading argument. Carson offered many suggestions for how insects could be controlled using nonchemical means.

Though hers is clearly a landmark book, there were other writers saying similar things at around the same time, and it is likely the confluence of a number of factors that transformed *Silent Spring* into the classic it has become. If Carson had simply examined the dangers to birds, insects, and animals from chemical use, the book might not have resonated so intensely with the reading public. Instead she examined the human dangers of pesticides and herbicides as well, bringing the matter home, so to speak, and "with that significant addition," says Fox, "conservation started to evolve into environmentalism."[26] Certainly the title itself deserves credit. The working title had been *Man Against the Earth*, which wasn't bad, but *Silent Spring* touches on a primal fear that the eternal cycle of seasons would one day fail to begin anew. Surely the memory of thousands of years of sacrifices and offerings to the gods to ensure spring's return lurked not far beneath the surface of the contemporary psyche. And sales benefited from chemical industry attacks, which brought publicity as well as sympathy. The industry inadvertently created a martyr—a lesson it would remember. (Today its approach is generally to ignore, rather than attack, critical books.) But finally, Carson's fine writing played an important role.

She ends her book:

As crude a weapon as the cave man's club, the chemical barrage has been hurled against the fabric of life—a fabric on the one hand delicate and destructible, on the other miraculously tough and resilient, and capable of striking back in unexpected ways. . . . The "control of nature" is a phrase conceived in arrogance, born of the Neanderthal age of biology and philosophy, when it was supposed that nature exists for the convenience of man. The concepts and practices of applied entomology for the most part date from that Stone Age of science. It is our alarming misfortune that so primitive a science has armed itself with the most modern and terrible weapons, and that in turning them against the insects it has also turned them against the earth.

Carson had discovered that critical balance between science and art. There was more than enough science to satisfy the dubious and establish credibility, and there was just enough art to make the book both accessible and pleasurable. *Silent Spring*, as Brooks points out, "will continue to remind us that, in our over-organized and over-mechanized age, individual initiative and courage still count: that change can be brought about, not through incitement to war or violent revolution, but rather by altering the direction of our thinking about the world we live in."[27]

With the rise of the environmental movement, there has been a shift away from identifying the technological cause of devastation to considering possible technological solutions. Looking too closely at technology had always presented problems. Environmentalists, after all, drove cars, flew in airplanes, used computers—in fact, were themselves a part of the problem, depleting resources and creating additional pollution as they went, and this presented a dilemma that was difficult to resolve. Today an army of wildlife specialists tags and tracks and maps the natural world, many spending more time at computers than in the field, substituting statistics and measurements for the kind of experience that Wordsworth and Ruskin had recommended; the kind of experience that Muir and Brower and Leopold and Stegner and others had translated with such effectiveness into prose.

Perhaps in response, a philosophy emerged that did not expressly mention spirituality but seemed to have the force of a religious conviction, yet was possessed of toughness, a refusal to accommodate itself to the modern world quite so easily. And that was the newly defined concept of deep ecology.

In logic it was an extension of ideas found within Muir's and Leopold's writings: the notion that usefulness to humans wasn't the only way to measure worth in the natural world; that other life on the planet had value that demanded a certain respect. But initially the strongest voices for this new variety of environmentalism emerged from a number of European philosophers writing about the human relationship to nature. Among them, Arne Naess stands out.

The Norwegian philosopher was born in 1912 and studied in Paris and

Austria. Even before taking a teaching position at the University of Oslo, he had built a small hut on the side of a steep mountain between Oslo and Bergen. This small dwelling, which he called Tvergastein, served both as his point of intimate contact with the natural world and as a laboratory for exploring the extremes of simple living. The careful and calculated use of fuel to achieve the maximum useful energy for his needs seemed to shape his life in that environment, which became an exercise in the appropriate use of natural resources. In the late sixties, when his philosophical focus had shifted to consideration of environmentalism, he contrasted the two approaches, which he characterized as deep ecology and shallow environmentalism. The latter tends to concern itself with technological fixes to problems technology has created. It attempts, among other things, to solve pollution by spreading it more thinly; to accept without question the necessity of growth; to conserve wilderness with human interests uppermost in mind, to ameliorate rather than limit the effects of growth, to encourage population growth at the national level for short-sighted economic reasons; to support industrialization of less developed countries as a way of raising living standards; and to regard water resources, oceans, and lakes as proprietary units rather than as parts of a whole.

Deep ecology, on the other hand, is concerned with resource, habitat, and diversity for its own sake. It considers that the present level of population is already putting excessive strain on the planet. It believes that nonindustrial cultures need active protection from penetration by industrial interests when local, soft technologies can suffice, and from the imposition of Western ideas, which implies a lack of respect for cultural differences. It considers that pollution must be viewed not only from the perspective of human health effects but from its effect on the well-being of plant and animal life. And finally, it states flatly that the earth does not belong to humans, that we merely inhabit the land and must use it to satisfy only vital needs.

Although this line of thinking seems to be a natural progression of earlier ideas, it has resounded as a radical notion for the past three decades. What had been hinted at in Carlyle, Thoreau and Emerson and had slipped into the writings of Muir and Leopold, muted by the sense that they represented only individual opinion, was now laid out as a carefully considered and clearly articulated philosophy. It was no longer possible to dismiss the ideas as individual and eccentric. Arne Naess's papers on environmentalism became the text for a new paradigm, albeit a highly controversial one.

Within the deep ecology philosophy, human needs no longer take priority but are placed in the context of the needs of the planet. Luddite in spirit, deep ecology questions the assumptions and domination of the technological culture; defends low-tech cultures against the imposition of these technologies; and encourages soft and appropriate technologies that require fewer resources and less energy and that produce less environmental, social, and cultural damage. From every perspective it remains a challenging alternative.

Damaging technology can be identified and protested, but can it be controlled, its development halted, its use curtailed? Albert Schweitzer said, "Man has lost the capacity to foresee and forestall. He will end by destroying the earth."[28] It is not clear that humans ever had the capacity to "foresee and forestall." That role is instead allotted to natural forces from which we have intentionally and increasingly distanced ourselves using technology. For all our assumptions of control, it would seem, in fact, that we have very little.

CHAPTER EIGHT

Going to Ground

ASK THE AVERAGE LAPTOP-TOTING, BEEPER-WEARING, cell phone–addicted technotron what he is most dependent upon, and he is likely to say, after a moment's thought, "Batteries." Or, if he thinks more broadly, "Electricity." And he will be wrong. Beyond the complex surface clutter of our contemporary lives, one thing remains unchanged. We are dependant upon the land.

That has a quaint ring to it. But brush aside the technological sophistication of our era, and we are still human beings who need to be fed—regularly. The local supermarket appears to be the source of food, but by whatever complicated route or by whatever travels over whatever distances, our nourishment—the substances that sustain us, without which we could not survive beyond a few weeks—comes from the land. For all that most food today seems divorced from anything living, for all the promises of futuristic soilless, high-tech laboratory food production, the reality is that food today has the same source as it did a thousand years ago. In a corn-chip, soy-burger, chicken-nugget, prepackaged, vacuum-sealed-for-your-protection, microwavable world, the relationship between what we eat and the actual process of working the soil is so obscured, so indirect, so complex, so convoluted as to be invisible. Yet it remains, a fact that ultimately cannot be forgotten, and our health, in the end, depends upon the health of the land. Not the wilderness land, although that sustains us in a way, but agricultural land. Or as Lady Eve Balfour, author, farmer, and one of the founders of the British soil conservation movement, put it in the early 1940s, "The health of soil, plant, animal and man is one and indivisible."[1]

The farm we depend upon, however, may look nothing at all like the one we imagine. Almost gone is the picture-perfect farmhouse set in a grove of trees, the red barn with silo, the cows in the green field, the chickens clucking happily about the yard; and yet I suspect that what we imagine—that image of farmhouse, with lush, cultivated fields and meadows, barn, and assorted animals—is too important to be dismissed as mere nostalgia. Since so few of us have genuine memories of such farms, the persistence of this image has significance in other ways. It is no accident, I believe, that we invent or demand it as the source of our nourishment, if only in our own minds. At some intuitive level, we understand that healthy food comes from healthy sources (a concept increasingly supported by the scientific literature[2]). Whatever the reality today of where our food is raised and how it is processed, the advertising and marketing world understands well our need to believe that it comes from the farms of our dreams. It almost goes without saying that the reality of industrialized farming or dairying or raising animals for slaughter would be distinctly unappetizing. The whirring and churning and plucking of the mechanical Leviathans in our fields today do not make for mouth-watering images.

We can look back on the twentieth century as the one in which the few inches of topsoil that stand between human well-being and general starvation were generally squandered, abused, depleted, ignored, neglected, tainted, fouled, or allowed to wash away down the rivers and into the sea. There are exceptions, of course—there are farmers who have nurtured and cared for their land—but anyone who knows anything about the soil knows with a sinking heart that we have lost more of the topsoil under cultivation than we have retained. That it has been allowed to happen represents the kind of collective insanity that makes one believe the human species harbors a barely concealed death wish. Never mind looking for the genetic flaw responsible for some obscure disease. What is the genetic flaw that allows us to continue practices—and poor farming is only one—that virtually ensure our eventual extinction? Is this some species-encoded sunset law? Are we programmed to self-destruct? If so, in the twentieth century we could watch it happening; we could watch the soil blowing and washing away, watch the fields eroding, watch as levees were built that actually halted the flooding that renewed the land even as they increased the force of flooding that stripped the soil—all as if our lives didn't depend upon its presence. And not all, by any means, but a good part of the blame could be laid, once again, on our cursed inventiveness, a trait that increasingly seems to be our undoing. Perhaps inventiveness alone is not all bad; perhaps it only needs to be coupled with arrogance to be truly dangerous.

In 1909, an official announcement of the U.S. Bureau of Soils proclaimed, "The soil is the one indestructible, immutable asset that the nation possesses. It is the one resource that cannot be exhausted; that cannot be used up." We could imagine Hugh H. Bennett, the first chief of the Soil Conservation Service and the father of American soil conservation, shaking his head in disbelief as he responded, "I didn't know so much costly misinformation could be put in a single brief sentence."[3] If the twentieth century was the age of erosion, it was also the age of new concerns about soil conservation, as awareness of the terrible consequences of continuing as we were began to sink in. And yet, even decades later, despite years of effort, tests by the Georgia State Agricultural College on one acre of conventionally farmed land under cotton cultivation in the 1930s found that it lost an average of 127 tons of topsoil a year. Bennett would estimate in the forties that "if the soil lost annually by erosion in the United States was placed in ordinary railway gondola cars, it would fill a train reaching four times around the earth at the equator,"[4] It didn't need to happen. There were ways to control erosion, but every time a tractor drove up a hill, it left a small rut that could become a larger and larger rut as the days went by. Every time a farmer failed to contour plow, every time the soil was left bare to the wind and rain, a little more—or a lot more—was lost.

By then the American conservation movement was already twenty-five years old, but progress was slow. The infamous years of the Dust Bowl occurred even as awareness of the need for soil conservation grew. The country's birthright was being squandered.

What had happened in America was nothing new or unique. Soil depletion began with agriculture, and agriculture is very old indeed. Erosion has been a problem virtually everywhere humans have tilled the soil. But North

America had been a vast stretch of almost virgin soil, rich and productive. It was astonishing how quickly such vastness could be put to the plow; it was equally astonishing how quickly that richness could be exhausted.

It began so simply. In his lovely book, *A Prairie Grove: A Naturalist's Story of Primeval America,* Donald Culross Peattie in 1938 wrote about the early settlers and seems to capture in his wistful tone their thinking, which far from being evil or even greedy, was so simply human.

> In the year when the Goodners broke prairie, the public found northern Illinois. Goodners were pioneers, but the public means everybody. It means preachers and lawyers and landsharks, and landsuckers and idealists and knaves. These people were only a few of them fitted to a wilderness life, and they did not come intending to lead one. They came with a rush to found villages—though of course they called them cities—to edit a newspaper before the subscribers got there. And the women came. . . . Whether you blame them or admire them for the domesticity of their souls, you have to remember that they were all propelled between the shoulders by predestinarian forces. Thrust west, or running to outstrip the thrust, they saw and thought and acted as they were accustomed to do.
>
> So would you. You like to think that if you had to live in Basutoland you would still be a good American and never let down decent standards of living or rational thought processes. This is just the way people felt when from the prairie sea they raised the island groves on the horizon, and brought to them a Pennsylvania Dutch mentality, a 'way down [east] Maine mentality. Herkimer County Shakers, Chester County Quakers, Baltimore Catholics, people who knew Emerson by sight on the streets of Concord and thought their judgments permanently elevated as a result—all these pietists knew God wanted them to get first into virgin prairie and sow the only good seed.[5]

The land was a gift; it was rich and fertile; there was plenty of it; and it was farmed, for the most part, as if there were no tomorrow. When concern about the state of the soil grew early in the twentieth century, Dr. F. H. King turned to agriculture in China, Korea, and Japan in an attempt to discover how they managed to feed such a dense population. His book, *Farmers of Forty Centuries,* written in 1911, described holistic farming techniques, some of which were incorporated into later conservation methods. But as Tom Dale and Vernon Gill Carter wrote in their 1955 book, *Topsoil and Civilization:*

The early Americans were following a pattern as old as civilization and should not be unduly criticized for their waste in settling the country. They caused more waste and ruin in a shorter time than any people before them because they had more land to exploit and better equipment with which to exploit it. Some ruined their land because they knew no better, and others destroyed out of greed for immediate profits, but most of them did it because it seemed the easiest thing to do. The federal and state governments actually encouraged exploitation and waste in some instances, but more often they simply permitted it.[6]

It was a question of scale, and here the machine played its expected leading role. But of course nothing is ever that simple. Some writers have pointed out that part of the blame lies in farming techniques imported from Europe that were not suited to the American land. The prairies were buffeted regularly by severe weather of a kind that was seldom if ever seen in Europe, where frequent soft showers and persistent drizzle were more common. And that sounds reasonable. But if agricultural land could be exhausted and eroded using traditional farming methods, the process was accelerated when farm machinery was introduced. Just as human activity had to reshape itself to the demands of the machine in the factory, so, too, farming practices had to accommodate themselves. Problems were exacerbated. The machines wanted larger, more regularly shaped fields. They didn't like hedges, or copses of trees, which seemed only in the way. Ponds, marshes, and streams were an intrusion, an irritation unless they were corralled. Drainage ditches were installed, streams were irrationally straightened. To fly over the Midwest is to see the domination of the machine on the map, on the face of the land itself: the land squared off as if it were plastic. The square itself is an unnatural shape; no natural substance ever took on such a form. The right angles—mathematically efficient, alien to life—dominate the land, regardless of its natural contours, its creeks and rivers, the nature of the soil. It was an imposition of unnatural order that could not help but end badly. It was going against the grain. The topsoil seemed rich, it still seemed to be present, but as Bromfield notes of the eroding soil, "You cannot see it go; evidence of the change might never occur to a farmer until he begins to plow up his drainage tiles and even then he will try to persuade you and himself that this is not because the soil is wearing off but because the frost or the 'working of the soil' has brought the drainage tiles to the surface."[7] The

Depression and the Dust Bowl merged in the public mind, and the country remained in the grip of denial.

England had no dust bowl, but a movement to elevate the importance of healthy soil was under way. In 1942, Lady Eve Balfour published *The Living Soil*. It was, as she said, a book that built substantially on the writings and work of others, but her particular gift was in painting a broader picture of the importance of healthy soil. It affected not only productivity, in the long run, and the health of the plant itself, but the health of the individuals who ate the plants, she was convinced. There was no real scientific evidence of that at the time, but she felt certain it was true. Good, healthy soil possessed a vitality, that same essence of life that healthy plants and produce exhibited. How could this not translate into vitality in the humans who consumed the produce? Her contribution was to look at the matter of agriculture holistically. Cartesian logic, which had dominated for so long, had been disastrous for farming, she felt. The world that had been taken apart needed to be put back together. It was crucial to the health of society. The Soil Association developed out of her leadership and is the leading organization for organic growers in Britain today.

Edward Faulkner's controversial *Plowman's Folly*, written in 1943, focused the American public's attention on the plight of the soil. He proposed, instead of conventional farming practices, a system of heavy incorporation of organic material to restore soils to a friable consistency that needed no plowing. He considered plowing itself an unnatural act. It did not take place in nature, where plants grew well. Decayed organic material on the ground was gradually incorporated into the soils by earthworms and other creatures. It was the organic material that mattered. In his definition, if you can't reach over and grab a handful of it easily, it isn't soil. The book is seriously flawed, and yet it not only sold well but had a powerful and helpful effect on a generation of farmers and gardeners in the curious way that bad books sometimes do. Faulkner attempted to correct some of the flaws in his next book, *A Second Look*. (He realized, for instance, that his no-plow approach was suitable only for sandy soils and not for clay.) But he was not all wrong. With mechanical plowing, the heavy machinery compacts the soil and prevents root development beyond a certain level. (Lady Eve Balfour had suggested that a return to plowing with horses would be infinitely preferable.) And his ideas about building the soil through composting were echoed by the books—a stream of them—produced by the Rodale Press in Emmaus, Pennsylvania.

J. I. Rodale was a successful manufacturer who was converted to natural farming practices by the books of Sir Albert Howard. In 1931 Howard, with Yeshwant Wad, wrote a book called *The Waste Products of Agriculture: Their Utilization as Humus,* which touted the advantages of composting. In 1943, in *An Agricultural Testament,* Howard wrote about his experiences on a tea plantation, among other things. It is this book that is credited with inspiring the organic farming movement. But in 1942, even before Howard's *Testament,* Rodale had already begun publishing the magazine *Organic Gardening and Farming.* He would go on to reprint Howard's book and many other key texts. Rodale's own works, *Pay Dirt: Farming and Gardening with Composts* (1946) and *The Organic Front* (1948), are both classics.

But even before Howard and Rodale, in 1924, the Austrian scientist and philosopher Rudolf Steiner had outlined in a lecture to a group of farmers in Germany an innovative form of agriculture that would come to be called biodynamic farming. The depletion of the soils through the use of chemical fertilizers was already apparent there as well—as was the declining health and quality of livestock and crops. Steiner—whose work formed the basis for anthroposophy, a movement that blends science, spiritual cognition, and mystical vision—conceived of the farm as an organism or self-contained unit. Biodynamic farming emphasizes the integration of crops and animals, using manures and recycling nutrients through composting, and the health and well-being of everything on the farm, including the farm family. Thinking in this holistic way leads to a set of management practices that look not just at the financial aspects of farming but at the environmental and social aspects. What most clearly differentiates biodynamic farming from other organic farming methods is its emphasis on the spiritual science of anthroposophy. Balance must be achieved between the physical and the non-physical or spiritual realms, Steiner said. Thus biodynamic farming should take into account the influence of cosmic forces to encourage the presence of life-energy or vitality in animals, crops, and the farm family—a different approach to that same vitality that Lady Eve Balfour would look for. In essence, biodynamic farmers believe that there are forces other than chemistry and physics that affect plants and animals and that sensitive individuals can intuit plant needs.

Steiner was profoundly influenced by Goethe, and in its blend of the physical and nonphysical realities, his approach to the challenges of agriculture is the most antimechanical of all; and yet Steiner thought of himself as a scientist. Obviously, anyone who attempts to blend what science today would consider the "unblendable" will be considered out of the mainstream. And yet the appeal of Steiner's methods is strong. The individual willing to expend the energy and diligence necessary to apply them properly, however, is rare.

For many years organic farming techniques were considered radical and controversial, questioning—and indeed challenging—much of the conventional advice of farm experts at a time when "expert," implying the imprimatur of the scientific establishment, garnered a lot of respect. Indeed, some techniques, such as biodynamic farming, are still considered quite strange—although a taste of biodynamically grown produce is apt to convince one otherwise.

Rodale's work has been important in extending the concepts of organic farming to a wide public. Many of the basic practices of today's organic gardening and farming were developed at the Rodale farm in Emmaus, Pennsylvania, and the publishing house continues to print a wide selection of books on gardening and health.

The mechanical approach to farming had taken the view that the soil was an inert base that required only the addition of chemical nutrients to support plant growth successfully. For this new breed of soil conservationists, however, the soil was a living substance. The aim of Rodale, Steiner, and others—though their approaches might differ—was to recreate the richness of virgin soils through the incorporation of organic materials. When they applied science to the process, as Lady Balfour and the Soil Association did in their twenty-five-year Haughley Experiment, a side-by-side comparison of conventional and organic methods revealed significant results. Perhaps the most interesting discovery, totally unanticipated and unsuspected, was that measurements of available minerals in the well-composted and organically nourished soil rose seasonally—at precisely the time that the plants needed these nutrients. "It was clear, from the fact of the closed cycle," said Lady Balfour in her 1977 lecture "Towards a Sustainable Agriculture," "that this seasonal release of minerals could only have been brought about by biological agencies, and it appears to be a natural action-pattern of a biologically active soil." It was, indeed, "living soil." The Romantic poets and Goethe would have appreciated and felt extremely comfortable with this blending of tradition and science with overtones of the intuitive and the mystical.

Between the 1930s and the 1950s, the same decades that many of the seminal works of organic farming were being published, a new genre of sympathetic books recording and lamenting the changes that were taking place on the American farm began to appear. Clearly many traditional American farmers looked at the new technologies and understood that a way of life that had continued without much change for hundreds of years was about to be transformed and perhaps lost, and they hurried to document what they feared might disappear forever. Some of these testaments to traditional farming practices were self published, and finding them today is usually a matter of chance. This memorializing of times-gone-by is inevitably called "nostalgic", but there is nothing foolish about yearning for a past that is preferable, as these farmers felt it was. Too many people have good memories of life on the farm for it to have been some sort of collective fantasy. Perhaps the best of the "country" books took care to document the old but to include the new—when it worked well. There is scarcely a farmer's wife, for instance, who would agree to give up her freezer, as it has made the preservation of food for the winter so much easier. Of course, when the electricity goes out for a long period, the farm that doesn't have a generator can lose a winter's worth of food and a summer's worth of hard work. As interest in getting back to the land increased, books describing how it had been done or how to do it—*This Country Life* and *How to Grow Food for Your Family*, both by Samuel R. Ogden, are examples—increased in popularity. Ogden, too, focuses on modern agricultural practices as a cause of lost soil:

> Rich virgin soil can be mined, lusty and profitable crops can be taken from the soil year after year, but eventually, if nothing is returned not only will a profitable crop be impossible, but the land poor and sour will not support enough natural growth to prevent erosion, so that the very soil itself is lost. On the other hand soils which have been depleted by greed or ignorance, may, if they are not too far gone, be brought back to profitable tillage. So it is that a good farmer may spend years and money working his land up to the point where it may produce its maximum capability, while on the other hand a poor farmer, working his farm factory for all it's worth, with the aid of farm subsidies and commercial fertilizers, may extract a decent profit,

year after year, depleting the humus and the bacteriological resources all the while. In fact I will go so far [as] to state that the profit motive as applied to farming is responsible for our depleted soils, and further, that it is the very essence of the farm-factory point of view.[8]

What is interesting about many of these superficially charming books—Ogden's are filled with appealing photographs of covered bridges, fields of shocked corn, mill ponds, sugaring with oxen, and barrel-making—is that their radical vehemence comes as a surprise. Ogden, writing in 1946, was not alone in his scathing opinion of what he calls the "religion" of "progress."

> To question it is heretical. This becomes apparent if for the purpose of discussion one raises the question of the reality of progress in any intelligent and well informed group. The theology of progress resolves itself to a struggle between an evil called superstition and a good called science. Pareto in his book *The Mind and Society* has established this religious nature in the belief in progress. Because of the religious nature of the belief it is impossible to discuss the subject rationally.[9]

The religion of progress demands that every backward glance must contain a good measure of criticism of what *must be* the harsh reality of the past. It is a given that farm life must be harsh and unpleasant. Amish farmer and author David Kline, in the introduction to his 1990 book, *Great Possessions,* says, "Not too long ago, the editor of a back-to-the-land magazine asked me to write something on small-scale diversified traditional farming—on the advantages of such a way of life, he suggested, and also the disadvantages. This bothered me all summer. Quite honestly, I couldn't think of any disadvantages."[10]

But perhaps Kline's preferences can be dismissed; perhaps the reluctance of the Amish to abandon their old ways puts them in a different category where objectivity cannot be assumed. And yet the farmers and naturalists writing in the first half of the century had spent lifetimes working the soil, and who better to know whether things were actually improving or not? Clearly they felt that many of the older ways were preferable, whatever the labor-saving advantages of the new. The new mechanical techniques were faster and more efficient, but they took a person away from the soil, increased debt, and transformed the farmer into a technologist and a tender of machines. "The tangible manifestations of the belief in progress are mechanization and centralization,"[11] said Ogden, and neither one was inherently attractive. Farming became work, as opposed to a way of life. The farmers looking back with justified nostalgia were pointing out that traditional farming had been about more than efficiency. They remembered the lost past with yearning for a simpler life, with fewer material goods, no doubt, but filled with family, traditions, good food, and the pleasures of well-deserved leisure. As had the Luddites, they were saying, with pens instead of hammers, that the machine was destroying a culture.

Today there is a sharp division between those who want to protect what has come to be called "the environment" and those who do not. One conservative columnist has referred to environmentalists as "the enemy." But in the early and mid-twentieth century, the division was not so sharp nor so political. There was a much larger rural population; many people had grown up on farms and knew the countryside intimately; indeed, many urbanites had begun to return to their rural roots seeking some sort of balance, hoping to restore what they felt was missing. If the logging, mining, and oil industries saw "conservationists" as the opposition, the distinction had little meaning for the general population—who, if they could not actually retreat to the woods, could read and dream about it. From the 1930s to the 1970s, naturalist writers such as Hal Borland and Edwin Way Teale brought their experiences in the countryside—they can be positioned somewhere between the naturalist and the country genre—into suburban American living rooms (suburbs were invented around the turn of the century) across the nation. Both were hugely talented and hugely popular, and their books remain good reading today. There is certainly romance in their depictions of the countryside, but there is close observation as well, and the blend satisfied the longing that many already felt to recapture the lost relationship that might have been imagined but might also have been remembered.

Although the average suburbanite could indulge a pent-up longing for the bucolic by reading the popular nature writers, for others the frustrations brought about by change could not be so easily soothed. Progress, as routinely defined, was inevitably accompanied by the growing domination of industrial standards in everyday life, the continuing loss of the pastoral landscape, and the rapid decline of rural family and small-town values. For a group of Southerners, the situation called for a more active response.

Four poets—John Crow Ransom, Allen Tate, Robert Penn Warren, and Donald Davidson—already well known as the Fugitive Group, joined eight other writers to compile a collection of essays called *I'll Take My Stand: The*

South and the Agrarian Tradition, published in 1930. For these Southern Agrarians, as they came to be called, more than nature was at stake, and this document was nothing less than an antimodernist, anti-industrial manifesto filled with the urgent passion of men who saw before them the specter of a second defeat at the hands of a new enemy.

It could not be denied that industrialization held the tempting promise of an economic renaissance for the beleaguered South. As the introduction to the collection acknowledged, whatever the determination in the 1920s to retain a regional character, "there is the melancholy fact that the South itself has wavered a little and shown signs of wanting to join up behind the common or American industrial ideal."[12] Having little idea just how easily the South would, in fact, waiver and succumb to the lure of Progress, they warned that the danger of a revitalized "new South" was the loss of its particular character and of its becoming nothing more than "an undistinguished replica of the usual industrial community"[13]—a prediction that would prove more or less correct, as the endless suburbs of Richmond and Atlanta have come to look exactly like their counterparts elsewhere.

However indelible the stain of slavery on the Southern legacy, its now endangered agrarian way of life still—in 1930—had elements worth preserving. The leisurely nature of living was part of a tradition—perhaps over-romanticized, but nevertheless fondly recalled. But whatever the special flavor of the Southern agrarian life, these writers knew that they were not alone in thinking that industrialization was bound to undermine social patterns that were not only agreeable but healthy. The introduction to the book acknowledged that there were "many other minority communities opposed to industrialism, and wanting a much simpler economy to live by. The communities and private persons sharing the agrarian tastes are to be found widely. . . . Proper living is a matter of the intelligence and the will and does not depend on the local climate or geography, and is capable of a definition which is general and not Southern at all."[14] Thus, the manifesto was issued not only to encourage support in the South but to promote alliances with sympathetic communities everywhere.

Of course the effort failed utterly. The Old South became the New South, virtually unrecognizable as a distinct cultural region, and industrialization triumphed. And yet, *I'll Take My Stand,* despite the racism of some of the thinking, continues to fascinate readers.

Historian Dan Carter, now at the University of South Carolina, recalled in a speech given several years ago how, in a class at the University of Wisconsin on twentieth-century radical movements, he had, on a whim, assigned *I'll Take My Stand,* which he described as a "right-wing radical text." The reaction surprised him:

> The students which I had in that class were mostly liberal to radical. I assumed they would be appalled and disgusted. But to my amazement they were more fascinated with this book than any of the other eight that I assigned. No, they assured me, they didn't like the implicit racism. Yes, the essays were unrealistic and hopelessly romantic in their view of the South, but they responded to the authors' outspoken anti-materialism, their reflections on spiritual values, even wrongheaded spiritual values, their search— their desperate search—for community, and their criticism of what these students saw as their own parents' embrace of bourgeois comforts. An embrace bought at the cost of the worship of the dehumanizing machinery of the modern age.[15]

What should really come as a surprise is Carter's surprise. The document is much more than a right-wing diatribe. It includes, after all, essays by some of the great writers of the period, and what would today be called racial stereotyping plays a minor role. This is a passionate book about connections—to the soil, to a shared tradition, to community, to a cultural history. It is a book about values—values on which the right wing has no monopoly—that are concerned with how people live their lives. It is about getting at the root of what is really important to a society organized around people instead of machines. It is about culture, which can be defined as a connection to the past . . . and to the future, for without a past and a future, life is meaningless. Materialism and consumerism, on the other hand, rely on the present moment of pleasure and satisfaction, within which the past and the future become merely vague marketing tools. These students in the sixties, Carter now says, "were in a struggle against the Leviathan. I expected them to be hostile." This is Hobbes's *Leviathan,* of course, a complex mechanical political structure for a mechanical man. Carter feels that during the eighties and the nineties the public accepted certain aspects of the machine—now grown to huge proportion—"without question."[16] Now, once again, a growing number of students are awakening to the reality of the new Leviathan—or at least its new faces and new names—and they too, I suspect, would understand *I'll Take My Stand.*

The goal of the new agrarian was simply to encourage circumstances in which an "imaginatively balanced life [could be] lived out in a definite social tradition."[17] The relationship of this ideal to farming is not obvious at first, but nature is the link. This "imaginatively balanced life" would include art and religion as well as the now-neglected human "arts" of conversation, manners, hospitality, sympathy, family life, and romantic love, "in the social exchanges which reveal and develop sensibility in human affairs."[18] None of these fares well in an industrialized society, and a source of that deprivation is the severing of the link with nature that industrialization seems to demand. Industrialism has encouraged the illusion that materialism and consumerism offer suitable substitutes for these lost or sacrificed qualities, but their ability to satisfy these basic human needs is superficial. The population has been duped and remains vaguely dissatisfied, exhausted by meaningless labor with stingily allotted free time spent in aimless, unproductive, and ultimately unfulfilling activity.

Nature was the key element in much that was important to human society. Religion, say the agrarians, "is our submission to the general intention of a nature that is fairly inscrutable; it is the sense of our role as creatures within it,"[19] and a return to agrarianism has the potential of reestablishing that link. "Inscrutability" or mystery is an important part of the relationship. Too much understanding—demystification, in other words—has a deadening effect on the vitality of living, in the agrarian view. Art too, "depends, in general, like religion, on a right attitude to nature," and in particular "on a free and disinterested observation of nature that occurs only in leisure."[20] The agrarians claim that "neither the creation nor the understanding of works of art is possible in an industrial age except by some local and unlikely suspension of the industrial drive."[21] Thus it is hardly an accident that many of the most creative and imaginative individuals have been the least interested in technology.

If the loss of the imaginatively balanced life can be laid at the feet of the mechanization of thought and action that industrialization requires, the solution then must be to reestablish a natural and appropriate relationship to nature. At the core of agrarianism is a link to the soil, and this appropriate relationship is essentially unmechanical. Industrialization is actually another word for control—control of the production process and control of the producers. The Luddites were resisting, in part, this aspect of industrialization. The purpose of mechanical control is to reduce the vagaries and uncertainties of dealing with the natural world.

Explicitly or not, the agrarian way of life also implies an existence divorced from mechanical time. The cyclical pattern of planting, with its link to the natural rhythms of climate and place, allowed society to operate on a time model that was tuned to the natural world. The very idea that not everything can be done at any time during the year or the day—planting and harvesting and milking times are ordered by nature rather than by efficiency—is actually a liberating reality that, while it dictates on the one hand, allows leisure without guilt on the other. The traditional agrarian way of life provided variety in the work experience and periods of enforced leisure, during the winter or when the ground was too wet or too dry. Or even in high summer, when there was nothing to do but watch the corn grow.

The truly interesting thing is not how *much* work was done in traditional agricultural cultures, but how *little*. Providing for oneself at a sustainable and subsistence level is not as challenging as one might suppose, given minimally arable conditions, and it is our love of central air conditioning and refrigerators that spit out ice cubes that keeps the modern nose to the grindstone. As I watched a gardening program on television in which the host interviewed the curator of a gardening exhibition at the Smithsonian, it was almost impossible not to notice that the curator twice mentioned that gardening was "hard work." My own experience over a decade is how little effort it takes to raise a considerable proportion of my summer vegetables and how pleasant that effort is. Who is promoting the "hard work" concept, and why? Is it that it is physical labor? And yet these same people think nothing of expending physical effort at the gym.

This notion of leisure was at the core of agrarianism. The leisurely life could include the vital time for family and community. The question being confronted by the Southern Agrarians (and earlier by those in the Luddite tradition) is: What are we as human beings, and what do we need? What are the fundamental requirements of a healthy, balanced, and pleasant society? The answer is that we are complex creatures whose fundamental needs are for community and family; love and companionship; a continuing association with the natural world around us, of which we recognize ourselves a part; undergirded by spirituality; enlivened by an artistic tradition that allows the exercise of creativity and imagination; enriched by an ongoing and shared cultural heritage. All these are more important than our need for consumer goods and gadgetry, the agrarians understood.

The Southern Agrarians drew attention to something we take for granted, an assumption that is rooted, the agrarians say, in the philosophy of applied science, that "the saving of labor is a pure gain," which is generally translated to mean that labor is something to be avoided by both the economic enterprise and the individual. Says the introduction to *I'll Take My Stand*:

> [L]abor is an evil, that only the end of labor or the material product is good. On this assumption labor becomes mercenary and servile, and it is no wonder if many forms of modern labor are accepted without resentment though they are evidently brutalizing. The act of labor as one of the happy functions of life has been in effect abandoned, and is practiced solely for its reward.[22]

The question of who demonized work is an important one, for as anyone knows, it can give great joy and be immensely satisfying when it is something one genuinely likes doing. Not much mechanized labor today falls into that category, whether it is sitting in front of a computer or tending a machine in a factory. If work is done only for what it achieves or what is earned by doing it, rather than for its intrinsic ability to satisfy and please, it becomes an activity demeaned by association, say the agrarians. If the idea is then lodged in the mind that work is bad and leisure good, and that they are entities that must be kept separate, then what might be a creative and productive activity is handed over to a willing industry. Why have a garden when agribusiness can supply your dinner? Why raise chickens when eggs from the industrialized egg industry are so handy? Why knit a sweater when machine knits are so much cheaper? Why hang your clothes outside when the dryer can do this job for you? It is therefore in the interest of industry to encourage the idea of work as undesirable; to isolate it as a commodity from ordinary life so that leisure, or the machines to create leisure, can be sold.

The demonization of labor created a parallel elevation of leisure that in turn created the leisure industry. Industrialized leisure tends to separate individuals from family, community, tradition, and culture and to impose a standardized, sanitized illusion of experience in an ersatz world—dare one mention Disney World or Carnival Cruise? This sort of leisure was not what the agrarians had in mind. The family together, but clustered gazing blank-eyed at the pale blue light of television, is not what the agrarians had in mind either.

The leisure they envisioned often blended work and relaxation: a celebration after a barn raising or a harvest. In my family, no excuse for leisure was needed. I can remember the all-day-and-half-the-night gatherings of family and friends at my grandparents' country home, where food and talk and sometimes singing went on as the light faded and the crickets played accompanyment. We children chased the lightning bugs in our bare feet as the stars came out and the still of evening settled over voices that quieted to a murmur. In the long pauses we listened to the dark. The commodification of leisure is as alienating and as unnatural as the commodification of work.

It is interesting and perhaps significant that the Southern Agrarians, all of whom were successful writers on other subjects, remained isolated in this way of thinking, and yet they were not the only writers and thinkers to consider the issue of declining rural values. Others just came at it from a different angle.

In 1940, author and editor Russell Lord; his wife Kate, an illustrator; and some of their friends decided to start a magazine devoted to farming and the soil. *The Land* was sponsored by an organization called Friends of the Land, which had as its purpose devotion "to the conservation of soil, rain, and man," and it included essays from some of America's best known writers. Aldo Leopold, Rachael Carson, Wallace Stegner, Paul Sears, Louis Bromfield, and E. B. White all appeared in its pages, as did the recollections and poetry of ordinary farmers, farm wives, and U.S. Department of Agriculture (USDA) extension workers, although there seemed little overlap with the Southern Agrarians.

The aim of the Lords was to collect the best in essays, poetry, fiction, and illustrations on farming and the land, and even in its brief life the magazine made a significant contribution in that regard. But *The Land* managed to document something else, something that was being lost. In talking to older farmers, Wes Jackson, president of the Land Institute in Salina, Kansas, found that many of them remembered the publication. "Their eyes would light up as though they had recognized an old friend. And almost always, a sadness would fall across their faces as they juxtaposed the reality of the modern agricultural world with the hopes and aspirations that filled *The Land* for fifteen years or so."[23]

From the beginning, the publication looked backward as much as forward, extolling the virtues of early conservationists, says Nancy Pittman, editor of *From The Land,* a collection of some of this material. "The Land was informed throughout by a deep nostalgia for the Jeffersonian agrarian ideal," evoking a vision of "small farms, peopled by independent-minded, self-reliant men and women who understood their responsibility to the land."[24] The first issues warned, just as the Southern Agrarians had, that a way of life was being undermined. Although *The Land* was sweetly scented with nostalgia rather than outrage, occasionally a piece of prose would unapologetically take on the source of the undesirable changes that were being imposed on agriculture—although it was careful to balance them with the opposite view. Ralph Borsodi, in his essay "The Case Against Farming as a Big Business," took on the government itself, or at least the USDA and its offspring at the state level:

> Blind leaders of the blind, I accuse them of deliberately commercializing and industrializing agriculture; of subordinating the real interest of agriculture to that of the fertilizer industry, the seed industry, the milk-distributing industry, the meat-packing industry, the canning industry, the agricultural implement industry, the automotive and petroleum industry, and all the other industries and interests which prosper upon a commercialized agriculture.
>
> I accuse them of teaching the rape of the earth and the destruction of our priceless heritage of land.
>
> I accuse them of impoverishing our rural communities, wiping out our rural schools, closing our rural churches, destroying our rural culture, and depopulating the countryside upon which all these are dependent.[25]

The problem, said Borsodi, was in organizing agriculture as an industry and a business, whereas if it were instead understood as a way of life and the land considered a "holy trust to be passed on to future generations,"[26] the result was more likely to be healthy, self-reliant, and freedom-loving people. The leaders of American agriculture, he said, have instead intentionally devoted themselves to the commercialization and industrialization of agriculture, which has been, in effect, to declare war on the rural way of life, which he saw as infinitely healthier and more desirable than urban life.

The questioning of modernism, however, was often indirect. An article by Walter C. Lowdermilk, "Other Lands: Traditional Knowledge," challenges the too-arrogant assumptions of Western medicine by pointing out traditional Chinese cures previously dismissed as superstition that had been proved effective. Dr. Jonathan Forman wrote about the nutritional defi-

ciency in humans that was bound to result as trace elements in soils were
depleted through poor farming practices and not replaced.

The Land represents a pivotal moment in the American experience when
profound concern for soil, health, and culture had not yet been marginalized
as the focus of counterculturists. Writers such as Bromfield, for example,
who wrote not only for the magazine but published the extremely popular
books Pleasant Valley and Malabar Farm, wrote not just of recapturing a farm
tradition but of restoring the soil. In his view, where America was headed as
the Second World War drew to a close required urgent remedy:

> I knew in my heart that we as a nation were already much farther along the
> path to destruction than most people knew. What we needed was a new
> kind of pioneer, not the sort which cut down the forests and burned off the
> prairies and raped the land, but pioneers who created new forests and
> healed and restored the richness of the country God had given us.[27]

The war had changed everything. But the same bomb that led Lindbergh
to think mankind's inventiveness had gone too far, and led Bromfield to set
out to restore the land, was viewed differently by others. The war had
opened the door for a kind of technological exuberance, and writers for The
Land weren't sure where to turn. Said Pittman:

> Nothing was the same after the war, especially after Hiroshima. Mother
> Nature was out of date . . . just a frumpy, old woman, drearily intent on her
> labor-intensive ways. Surely, the reasoning went, the same science that split
> the atom could feed the hungry, replenish the soil, cure erosion, curb
> floods, and halt disease. The Land bravely tried to place its faith in the
> mechanical and chemical improvements. But a curious unease pervaded
> the writing in those last years.[28]

And perhaps that very ambivalence guaranteed The Land's demise. It
wanted to go along; it tried to go along. In effect, it admitted defeat and
quietly died.

Today, clearly, America is feeding her people, regardless of erosion. But
now it is the quality of food from these overworked soils that must be considered. To remove twenty nutrients from the soil and replace them with
three is not to produce foods that will build healthy bodies, but the effects
of this change accumulate slowly and are manifested in ways, such as reduced immunity, that cannot easily be linked to nutritional deficiency.

Industrialized farming practices, especially where animal rearing is concerned, can set the stage for bacterial infections that directly affect consumers.

Farming has always been an unnatural act. Managing plant growth, planting even reasonably sized fields with single crops in rows, selecting for seeds and animals with desirable traits—these are not what nature does on her own. And with any change from the natural pattern inevitably come problems. Monocultures, whether of plants or animals, encourage disease. Animals repeatedly selected for food-production attributes may show unfortunate weaknesses in other areas, such as common susceptibility to infection. But the very smallness of the traditional farm was in itself a kind of control device to circumscribe disease or insect infestation. Whatever went wrong was limited. With today's industrialized agriculture, that cannot be said. Whatever goes wrong is multiplied by the size not only of production (the new name for farming) but of processing and distribution centers. A cow infected with *E. coli* O157:H7 goes into a slaughterhouse with thousands of others and then into a grinding process that may produce hamburger in 70,000-pound lots that are made into hamburger patties that are distributed around the country, and a mistake is multiplied in a way that would have been unimaginable a few years ago. A genetically engineered corn that has not been approved for human consumption is nevertheless planted; combined with human-grade corn; mingled and mixed in grain silos, in trucks, at the factory in the grinding process; and distributed widely to food-production facilities where it is used to make many different food products; and as a result, traces of this potentially dangerous corn are found in a wide variety of foods across the nation. And yet the pressures to farm big and to farm using the latest equipment, technology, and science are fierce. The small farmer, it is widely assumed, is an anachronism; he is on his way out, surviving only because he hasn't sense enough to accept the inevitable. (Only recently has that dangerously mistaken notion come in for revision as the inevitable consequences of industrialized farming—such as the mad cow epidemic—become impossible to ignore.)

But even in the face of change following World War II, the underlying message of writers such as Bromfield, which no reader was likely to miss, was that a kind of balance to life itself needed to be reestablished. A transitional writer, as the country became more distinctly divided into urban, suburban, and rural, with sharper separations between the designations than had been the case when most people remembered some rural experience, is E. B. White, who wrote about nature while playing at rural living on the coast of Maine. In relating his own experiences, White captured the longing for a connection with nature that many felt, and yet he was essentially urban. He understood well enough what the problem was in a world that was changing too fast and not always for the better, and it discouraged him. "I am pessimistic about the human race because it is too ingenious for its own good. Our approach to nature is to beat it into submission. We would stand a better chance of survival if we accommodated ourselves to this planet and viewed it appreciatively instead of skeptically and dictatorially."[29] But his wry tone was well on the way to confirming country life as an eccentric and charming, but certainly not very serious, hobby. Scores of others, unhappy with the alienation of urban life, had already determined that if they couldn't compete with the industrialization of farming on a commercial level, they just might be able, if nothing else, to take care of themselves in the country.

It is difficult to pinpoint the exact moment the back-to-the-land movement began in America, but by 1910 it was in full swing. In England it had been associated with the Arts and Crafts movement. The utopian communities in America in the early part of the twentieth century, as well as the wealthy rusticators—who returned to the simple country life during their holidays, if at no other time—reflected the same mood. My own family is a good example.

My maternal grandmother had grown up on a prosperous farm in the Shenandoah Valley of Virginia. She might question the word *prosperous,* but the house, which stands today, was large, brick, and comfortable. There was a cook to prepare the family meals, and her recollections of the fresh and marvelous food they ate are enough to cause mouths to water. Most of it was raised on the farm, and the animals were slaughtered there as well. Her childhood memories are of intimate relationships to animals, even ones that were eventually to be eaten—she had a pet piglet that she managed to sneak not only into the house but into her bed—and of a warm, extended family. She remembered walking a mile or more to school, but it was not recalled as a hardship, and when the snow was deep her father got out the sleigh to make the trip easier.

She married a man who did not like farming, and the house and land were sold, but their days of town living were short-lived. The draw of rural life was strong. Using logs recycled from an old barn, they built a summer house in a valley filled with sugar maple trees and called it Sugar Tree Hollow. Within a few years, they decided they could live nowhere else. They put in a heating system and moved in permanently.

My grandparents kept chickens and ducks—eggs for those massive breakfasts—and maintained a large garden. Each year they raised a steer for beef, and I think I recall a few pigs as well. My grandmother worked hard—canning and preserving food, making cheese, knitting and hooking rugs—but she also had time for the things she loved. She introduced me to the amazing world of birds and insects, to the pleasures of gardening, and to the delights of wonderful food. But most of all I remember the conviviality, the warmth of a vast extended family of both relatives and close friends. I remember the sense of fun, the joy of living, and I remember the close relationship with the natural world that I was able to develop early on. Playing alone by the creek for hours, undisturbed by overly protective adults; making dams to hold crayfish; watching the busy water bugs; climbing the bluff to gaze out on a peaceful world: these are the memories I treasure. I slept, when I was there in the winter, in an unheated sleeping porch under a pile of quilts, clinging close to my sister for warmth—there would often be snow that had blown through the loosely fitting windows on the sills when we awoke—but in the morning we would scurry to a bathroom that had already been warmed with a portable heater, and the smell of bacon would draw us irresistibly down the stairs.

There was nothing extravagant about the lives my grandparents lived. They watched their pennies carefully. But it was a life that was concentrated on what they valued as individuals. Looking back, it was a golden time when family and friends lived full and joyous lives in a natural setting that was not only splendid but sustaining. When my grandfather died and my grandmother was convinced she could no longer live there, it was, I knew in my eleven-year-old heart, the end of an era. I knew that nothing would ever be the same. And it never was.

My family was hardly unique. But they were not as serious about self-sufficiency as some. Theirs was the ruralism of E. B. White; a pleasant playing at country life, the middle-income version of Marie Antoinette's Petite Plaisance. It was not the earnest, hard-core, unbending, and more or less joyless back-to-the-land migration led by Scott and Helen Nearing.

I met Helen Nearing in the 1980s. She must have been in her eighties then, but she was lively and spry with the habitual coquettishness of the beautiful girl she once had been. She flirted with and seduced everyone she met—or very nearly. I was simply intrigued. But over and over again I heard people tell me how Helen would really like for them to come and live with her. They could sense it, they would tell me with feeling. I thought it unlikely.

Helen was, by that time, the reigning goddess of the back-to-the-land, simple living movement, and she deserved to be. To hear her speak on radio, creating a mood that made it all seem not only reasonable and possible, but crucial, was to be drawn again and again into the Nearing web. One would not be eaten there, but one might well have been consumed. And yet it was a fair trade. The Nearings were unfailingly open and generous in all that they did, sincerely wanting to share what they had learned in a lifetime of ordered, principled, intentional living. Yet it began not with Helen but with Scott, who had died a few years before I met Helen by starving himself to death around his one-hundredth birthday. He had lived a long life, influencing not one but multiple generations. He felt it was time to go. It was a final act of control that seemed completely in character.

Scott Nearing was first of all an economist and teacher, his economic ideas influenced by Karl Marx; John Ruskin ("There is no wealth but life"); Henry George; and his mentor at the University of Pennsylvania, Simon Nelson Patten. And yet he was a disciple of none of them, seeing flaws in all their theories and from the beginning shaping his own unique philosophy. He began as a Christian but became disheartened by the failure of establishment religion to address inequality. He began with an interest in the military but ended as a pacifist. He was a popular and well-published teacher but was fired from the Wharton School because of his agitation on behalf of abolishing child labor and his progressive notions of income distribution. He rejected socialism, then joined the Communist party, then was expelled. He was never a man who could take orders or contentedly swallow a party line. Early on he was a feminist, a vegetarian, and an activist in the causes he espoused; but above all he was a believer in the simple, the strenuous, and the considered life. When he left his first wife, Nellie, to live with the young, beautiful, spiritual, and indulged Helen Knothe (who would be transformed politically under his tutelage), it was 1930. He was broke, unable to find work teaching because of his political views, yet disillusioned with the Left and reduced to lecturing for a small living. Not long afterward he and Helen decided that it would be better to be poor in the country than in the city and moved to Vermont, where they were able to buy a small farm. They set out not to farm for a living but to make a life; not to earn money but to sustain themselves in such a way as to live comfortably and healthily, but with plenty of time for leisure.

The Southern Agrarians realized how crucial the nature and quality of leisure time was as a measure of the quality of life. But Nearing took it further, believing that life was unfulfilled if leisure was not purposeful and occupied. His position echoed that of his mentor, Patten, who felt that "the rich could be rescued from a non-productive life through the pursuit of strenuous, revitalized, constructive leisure," says John S. Saltmarsh, author of *Scott Nearing: The Making of a Homesteader*. For the poor, the problem was the deadening effect of industrialized work that, according to Patten, did not allow individuals to exercise their imagination or creativity; nor did it satisfy the human need for "surprises, varieties and stimulants of life."[30] Industrial capitalism, Scott Nearing felt, had led to "superficial living," "purposeless lives," and "a sterile life pattern." His quest was for a reconciliation with nature and a life experience that was authentic.

Some of Nearing's views had been forged in the fire of religion. Progressive economic ideas about the inequalities and indignities of industrialization and Nearing's views on income distribution blended nicely with a new style of muscular Christianity that emphasized not only the essentially radical (and usually ignored) message of the Gospels but also an energetic interpretation of Scripture that emphasized as an ideal the healthy mind and body employed in righting social wrongs. Nearing quickly discarded the religion, but it suited him to keep the principle. In the country one could test oneself not only mentally but physically. Says Saltmarsh:

> The strenuous life Nearing envisioned included an idealization of country life reflecting the anti-urban bias of progressivism. The basis for the moral economy of a society built upon the values of productive labor would be found in self-sufficient country life offered as a strenuous antidote to a deadening urban-industrial America.[31]

The Nearings were, in fact, following closely on the heels of Ralph Borsodi, a contemporary, whose *This Ugly Civilization* (1929) and *Light from the City* (1933) prescribed the self-sufficient rural life as the antidote to the Depression. Borsodi's communal Dayton Project in the mid-thirties was to fail. The Nearings took the individual approach instead and bought a house in Vermont in 1932. Their success could be attributed to an approach that was disciplined, organized, and rigorous. It was also well-researched, carefully considered, modified by experience, and buoyed by the certainty that they were absolutely right. Self-doubt never bothered the Nearings as they accomplished the impossible time and time again, setting a standard for self-discipline and the principled life that is virtually impossible to duplicate.

For the Nearings, this meant six months of hard "bread work," as they described it, and six months of writing, lecturing, and traveling—the all-important balance of labor and leisure. But they never meant to imply that one was a chore and the other a relief. Work was not just good but healthy and enjoyable if done right. They never ate flesh, kept no animals or pets, saw no doctors, and carefully organized each day to get the very best from it. They were extraordinary organic gardeners; experts in food storage and preservation. They perfected a simple way to build a stone house and applied it time and time again. Were they neo-Luddites? In truth, they are prime examples of the considered approach to technology, which is not unlike the approach of Morris or Ashbee. In their famous book, *Living the Good Life,* they describe their attitude toward machines, which is commonsensical and practical. Discussing the advantages of their refusal to convert their hand cement mixer to a power mixer with a gas engine or electric motor, they noted:

> (1) We saved the time, labor, capital outlay, upkeep and replacement costs incident to the operation of all power tools. (2) We saved the outlay for gasoline or electricity. (3) We avoided the anxiety, tension, frustration and loss of time caused by mechanical breakdowns. Advocates of mechanization do not like to face the fact that a machine gets tired, gets sick and dies during its life cycle, and that a machine tender must be prepared to meet these emergencies in the life of a machine in much the same way that he must meet them in the life cycle of a domestic animal such as a horse or any other slave. (4) Turning the mixer with first one hand and then the other, we got balanced muscle-building, invigorating, rejuvenating physical exercise in the fresh air, under the open sky,—one important ingredient in the maintenance of good health. (5) We had the satisfaction of participating directly in the project, instead of wet-nursing a machine and inhaling its oil fumes and carbon monoxide.[32]

At the same time, they frankly admitted that if they "were building the Hoover Dam," the hand cement mixer would not do. "The machine has its function, especially on gigantic undertakings. Our project was not gigantic, but minute. . . . In such an enterprise machine tools are, on the whole, a liability rather than an asset."[33] And their friends the conservationists would have advised against building the Hoover Dam in any case.

A story was once told to me of the time when Scott and Helen were building their final stone house in Cape Rosier, Maine, in 1971. (Vermont had been overwhelmed by the ski industry, and they had left it some time before for a more isolated spot.) Scott was then in his nineties, and he and Eliot Coleman (of organic gardening fame) were looking over a potential building site. When they agreed on the perfect spot, Scott took out his axe and simply began chopping down a tree. "I would have hired an earth-mover," said Coleman. But Scott believed in accretion, and it was accretion that built a life and a legacy. Theirs is a hard act for mere mortals to follow.

TODAY, AS awareness of the chemical pollution of the environment and of food continues to grow, the organic farming movement is thriving. Much of it is itself industrialized—that is, conducted on a large scale using modern equipment. However, there remains a strong and energetic questioning of common assumptions about the necessity for large-scale agricultural mechanization. To some, farming without the internal combustion engine seems quixotic beyond belief. There are others who are convinced it can work.

One group of farmers that has always maintained a critical view of industrialized farming is, of course, the Amish. It is often assumed that this religious community rejects technology out of hand, but that is incorrect. The Amish position is that religion comes first in their lives. Next in order are their families and their communities. Use of a given technology will be evaluated and reevaluated over time, with different conclusions reached by different sects, to determine whether it contributes to or detracts from the primary values of faith, family, and farm. A phone in the kitchen, for instance, might contribute to a squandering of time and a tendency to gossip. But a phone can be useful, not only in an emergency but to avoid an unnecessary trip to town for something that isn't in stock, for instance. Therefore, a telephone in an open box on the edge of the field is a reasoned compromise. It is useful and available but doesn't encouraging lingering and time-wasting. The logic in the Amish decision-making process on new technologies is not always as clear, and tradition does make a strong contribution, but in general it can be said that the Amish approach is thoughtful and deliberate, and one might wish that the "English" (as the Amish call the non-Amish) approach was half as consciously considered.

David Kline is an Amish farmer whose two books, *Great Possessions* and *Scratching the Woodchuck,* open a window into a way of life that is healthy, satisfying, and close to nature. Nature, not the question of technology, is the topic of Kline's books. But throughout Kline describes the relationship of farmer to bird and animal life when technology is not allowed to come between them. Kline, who plows with a team of horses, makes a good case for the encouragement of wildlife that is the unexpected benefit of low-tech farming. He has strong opinions about the misplaced advice of farm experts who talk of input, output, cash flow, and work-as-drudgery and who assume that the no-till method of soil conservation is preferable to plowing.

> Here it is then, the thorn in my side. . . . I enjoy plowing. Just this past year the SCS [Soil Conservation Service] technician told me, in all seriousness, that if I'd join the no-till crowd I'd be free from plowing, and then my son or I could work in a factory. He insinuated that the extra income (increased cash flow) would in some ways improve the quality of our lives.
>
> I failed to get his point. Should we, instead of working the land traditionally, which requires the help of most family members, send our sons to work in factories to support Dad's farming habit? Should we be willing to relinquish a nonviolent way of farming that was developed in Europe and fine-tuned in America (by what Wendell Berry calls "generations of experience")? Should we give up the kind of farming that has been proven to preserve communities and land and is ecologically and spiritually sound for a way that is culturally and environmentally harmful?
>
> And there are the pleasures of plowing—plowing encompasses more than just turning the soil. Although I can't fully describe the experience, it is like being a part of a whole.[34]

There were non-Amish farmers who understood the impact of mechanization on the farm after the Second World War. In fact, Curtis K. Stadtfeld, in his book *From the Land and Back: What Life was like on a Family Farm and How Technology Changed It* compared the transition to industrialized farming as a war with the environment.[35]

The transition to the mechanical was so innocent, he says: "Like the social revolution that came inevitably to the farm when isolation ended, the technological revolution was so sudden and so complete that no one had time to consider what parts of it were good and which needed a place for the same reasons we go to the moon; we found out we could, and so we thought we must."[36]

Before the petroleum-driven internal combustion engine, the farm itself had generated its own power, even when the source of power was steam. When the transition to kerosene or gasoline was complete, the farmer was dependent upon a supplier for power, and the independence of the farm enterprise had been seriously compromised. Before mechanization, tools and wagons were often shared causally among farmers. "The sharing became so common and so complex that everyone stopped trying to keep track of anything,"[37] says Stadtfeld of the central Michigan area in which his father farmed. Mechanization changed that too. And it brought debt as the size and complexity and cost of the new machines increased. "So . . . we learned a valuable lesson about communal living. It will work only as long as all the members have approximately equal needs, as long as the technology remains roughly static, and while ambitions do not press men to expand their efforts."[38]

Stadtfeld says he also learned something useful about machinery, equipment, and "perhaps even technology":

> It was soon apparent that in many cases the new combines or choppers, or field tillers were not being bought on the basis of calculated economics. A man with 20 acres of grain to harvest each year has no need for a combine of his own, when he can hire a man to do the work for him. . . . Yet the farmers bought them, along with big tractors to run them. For years, I thought they were simply bad managers, not aware of, or at least not making use of, simple management techniques.
>
> But now I see how alluring machinery is, simply in its nature. A man wanted his own combine, partly because it might give him a sense of independence, but also because it is a universal ego satisfaction to dominate a complicated machine.[39]

It is certainly more psychologically complex than that. The shiny red or yellow tractor taps into a myriad individual and social needs. Stadtfeld was writing in the early seventies, when farms, large and small, were getting into trouble. He traveled down the back roads and saw the fine machines rusting beside farms that had been abandoned.

> The men who bought them have left the farm or sold it; they have moved their labor to a factory, and if they live on the farm at all, they may not work

the fields or even walk them on Saturdays, save perhaps with a dog and a gun, hunting for pheasants and rabbits. The machines were a promise, and they kept it only to themselves. They did not give us a better life on the land, only a way to show ourselves that our individual labors, on the small farms we wanted so badly, were no longer economic.[40]

Stadtfeld draws the inevitable conclusion. "We are captives of our technology."[41]

The back-to-the-land movement continues in many forms. Young couples still eye abandoned or neglected farms in America's rural areas with the optimism of youth, but the rural renaissance has evolved. Today there is what Eric T. Freyfogle calls the new agrarianism, in his book of that name. What he detects is a movement that is defined, he says, by a "heightened interest today in land conservation, which has taken on a distinctly ecological cast."[42] It also includes a challenge to materialism and to the dominance of the market. "Yet even with its new shapes and manifestations," Freyfogle says, "agrarianism today remains as centered as ever on its core concerns: the land, natural fertility, healthy families, and the maintenance of durable links between people and place."[43] And in that it is not far from the idealized vision of farming of the Southern Agrarians — or even of the Amish.

Throughout the writings of the authors represented in *The New Agrarianism* there is a consistent questioning of the conventional wisdom of the agricultural experts. Is big really better because it is more efficient? Gene Logsdon, whose books on farming appeal as much to the nonfarmer as to the farmer, as did Louis Bromfield's before him, points out that big is not so much about efficiency as it is about power. Small, manageable farms can indeed compete, he says, because they are small and if they are not burdened with debt. Current economic policies favor large-scale corporate farming — seem, in fact, to be designed to do away with family farms. Making a go of the small holding does means ignoring present-day methods of cost accounting for what he calls pastoral economics. Simply put, this is a different way of calculating value, which can lie in satisfaction rather than in mathematical ways of calculating success. Logsdon quotes the Nearings, who aimed not for a profit but to support themselves and have time left over for leisure, however they wished to spend it. Said Scott Nearing in *The Making of a Radical*, "Price-profit economy presupposes the exchange of labor-power for cash; the payment of a part of the cash in taxes in exchange for regimentation, and the expenditure of the remainder in the market for food, clothing, gadgets and other commodities. The individual who accepts this formula is at the mercy of the labor market, the commodity market, and the State."[44] Pastoral economics is about personal choice as to how one spends one's time.

Logsdon points to the observations of Lord Northbourne in his 1940 book, *Look to the Land,* as the best articulation in the twentieth century of pastoral economics:

> Urban and industrial theories and values have supplanted the truer ones of the countryside. These true ones survive mainly as a sentimental attachment to country life and gardening. Is the romance of country life really only a poetic survival of a bygone age, not very practical because there is no money in it, or is that romance something to which we must cling and on which we must build? Is farming merely a necessary drudgery, to be mechanized so as to employ a minimum of people, to be standardized and run in ever bigger units, to be judged by cost accounting only? Or is the only alternative to national decay to make farming something real for every man and near to him in his life, and something in which personal care, and possibly even poetic fancy, counts for more than mechanical efficiency?[45]

And yet, says Logsdon, to try to think and act outside the confines of industrial economics is to confront the reality of "how embedded in our psyches and our lifestyles are its tenets. . . . Both capitalism and socialism . . . use money to centralize control over society. They differ only in who the central authority should be."[46] The Contrary Farmer, as he calls himself and others who take a variety of unorthodox views, has "no choice but to live and work within the capitalist/socialist economy that society now accepts with such naïveté. But if success is to be achieved on our homesteads, we must separate ourselves as far as possible from that economy."[47]

Pastoral economics means not borrowing money if at all possible. It means working with earned capital and noncash assets "like your muscles." Logsdon points out what seems to be a basic incompatibility between biological systems and borrowed money (when farms are lost, it is inevitably because of overborrowing), but he might have said just as truthfully that there seems to be a basic incompatibility between biological systems and economic systems, for one is full of the unpredictability of life and the other is coldly mechanical, and between them there can be only strife.

Logsdon by no means spurns the mechanical entirely. And yet he finds the distinction between good technology and bad technology difficult to define. "If the use of lever and gear and heat and pressure and gravity, which is all mechanical technology comes down to, makes work truly easier for the laborer without disrupting societal stability or ecological balance, then it is 'good' I suppose. But almost always human behavior runs to excess and that is where the difficulty lies, not in the machine itself."[48]

A good farmer, he believes, must be a good mechanic. But the kind of machine he chooses to use is important. Much resistance to the machine today comes, he says, "from revulsion at the excesses of technology":

Traffic jams. Acres of barrels full of nuclear waste. A 200-horsepower tractor that replaces a hundred rural people and sends them to the cities to compete for jobs with a hundred people already there who can't find jobs. Gargantuan lumber machines that can swallow a tree whole at one end and spit two-by-fours out the other. It is almost amusing to listen to lumber companies hypocritically blame the spotted owl for lost jobs while their machines every year displace more thousands of jobs than a whole decade of environmental reform. If job loss in the timber industry is the issue, one could argue that the chain saw is far more to blame than all the endangered owls in the world.[49]

Realistically, the difficulty with resisting the latest machinery, overloaded with unnecessary gadgetry, comes not simply from economic and social pressures to conform and compete but from the lack of an alternative. Amish farmers have an advantage because they have created their own community support system. When a piece of equipment breaks down, there are people within their communities who know how to repair it; there are replacement parts available. The Amish see little use for education beyond age sixteen but find good use for their most intelligent young people, who can apply their talents and keen minds to perfecting tools and equipment that the rest of the society ignores. Thus, though the horse may pull the cultivator or a more complex piece of equipment, that equipment is the best and most efficient it can be. So "efficiency" is not to be entirely despised in itself but kept in its place. Efficiency can be a helpful factor when not allowed to dictate the show. What is crucial is to create a system in which other values—of community, family, leisure, pleasure—can be factored in.

The individual "English" farmer must confront (unless he lives in Amish territory) the reality of what is available and the difficulty or impossibility of repairing what he attempts to use. Little effort today is put into making new equipment suitable for the small farm. Logsdon found that a company was designing a strong, durable, low-horsepower, crude-looking but low-cost tractor for marketing in Third World countries. He asked why it wouldn't be available here, and the company executive replied that Americans wanted all the gadgets, the "contour seats, cigarette lighters, twelve forward gears and two reverses, headlights, fenders, rubber tires, synchromesh transmission, shift-on-the-go, power steering, rollover bars, cab, gas gauge, front and rear PTO, dashboard lights, quick-mount hitches, gaily painted hoods, electronic fuel injection, four wheel drive, individual wheel brakes, radio, etc., etc., on their garden tractors." Logsdon replied, "The hell we do. We want what you intend to sell to Third World countries."[50] The executive then admitted, only half in jest, that that was precisely what the company was afraid of.

And so farmers who want something simple must resort to reviving old tractors or, in some cases, importing them from the Balkans, an option available to only a few. When one begins to think about the difficulty of avoiding the supertechnological, the superficial, the excessive, and the unnecessary, it begins to feel like tyranny. Something of this is expressed in the resentment Logsdon detects in the "English" farmers against their Amish neighbors, who can grow a bushel of corn for less and pocket the profit. There is a feeling, he says, that "they are not playing fair," because they refuse to subject themselves to the style of farming that keeps their neighbors' costs high and guarantees that they remain in debt. The Amish refusal to submit to this tyranny is not simply an affront, it is seen as a kind of disloyalty to the culture, and this sense that refusing to participate in the wacky system we have imposed upon ourselves represents some kind of treason is common. People who refuse to watch television get this same kind of reaction. On the other hand, there is a fascination with Amish life that supports a vast tourist industry composed of people who just want to get a look at a community that has resisted the pressures of modernization on its own terms and refuses to participate in a race whose goals it rejects.

If there is one person who understands the relationship between what has gone wrong with the land and with agriculture and the imposition of the machine paradigm, it is Wendell Berry, who writes poetry, fiction, and essays from his farm in Kentucky. The first five chapters of his classic *The Unsettling of America* deal with this relationship specifically. Berry understands that the problem is not simply the increasing mechanization and industrialization of agriculture but the state of mind that made it possible—that allowed it to happen. It is a mechanical mind-set that begins with the idea of specialization, that state of being in which no one possesses the big picture and none of the experts is qualified to relate what he or she is doing to what anyone else is doing.

Good agriculture, says Berry, requires a farmer who is "a husbandman, a nurturer." He is created not in college but through generations of experience. He is a cultural product. "This essential experience can only be accumulated, tested, preserved, handed down in settled households, friendships and communities that are deliberately and carefully native to their own ground, in which the past has prepared the present and the present safeguards the future."[51] Instead, farmers—the few that are left—have gradually become businessmen. This has demanded a transformation in the very mind of the farmer. "Once his investment in land and machines is large enough, he must forsake the values of husbandry and assume those of finance and technology. . . . The economy of money has infiltrated and subverted the economies of nature, energy, and the human spirit."[52] Abandoned is the farmer's knowledge of the land and the soil, presumably because it is no longer considered necessary. The great machines can level the growing field, so to speak, correcting the differences in soil chemically, leveling the terrain to suit the machine's needs in a way that does not distinguish between one field and another, doing the work of ten men. But what of those ten men? Berry asks. What of their families and their communities? Don't they count for anything? In a world where power is numbers and time is money, only the quantifiable counts, and the answer is no. And yet impoverished families, broken communities, and insolvent towns are only part of the cost, never factored into any accounting system. The other part—the chemical damage to the environment, the microbial contamination of waterways from the animal wastes inherent in factory farming, the faraway costs of the petroleum "harvesting" that is necessary to run the operation, the cost to future generations of soil erosion and depleted land—these are external costs, not accounted for within modern farm profits, when there are any.

The policies of the USDA bear huge responsibility for the system that has led to the loss of many tens of thousands of small farms, which has, in turn, led to unhealthy cultural changes in the fabric of society, but those policies can in turn be laid at the feet of a shift of metaphor, says Berry:

> Once, the governing human metaphor was pastoral or agricultural, and it clarified, and so preserved in human care, the natural cycles of birth, growth, death and decay. But modern humanity's governing metaphor is that of the machine. Having placed ourselves in charge of Creation, we began to mechanize both the Creation itself and our conception of it. We began to see the whole Creation merely as raw material, to be transformed by machines into a manufactured Paradise.
>
> And so the machine did away with mystery on the one hand and multiplicity on the other. The Modern World would respect the Creation only insofar as it could be used by humans. Henceforth, by definition, by principle, we would be unable to leave anything as it was. The usable would be used; the useless would be sacrificed in the use of something else. By means of the machine metaphor we have eliminated any fear or awe or reverence or humility or delight or joy that might have restrained us in our use of the world. We have indeed learned to act as if our sovereignty were unlimited and as if our intelligence were equal to the universe. Our "success" is a catastrophic demonstration of our failure. The industrial Paradise is a fantasy in the minds of the privileged and the powerful; the reality is a shambles. [53]

Berry is one of the few popular writers—and he is popular—who not only understand the power of metaphor but are not afraid to write about the damage that has resulted, with vigor and a directness that is refreshing—and unusual. Blame can be laid at many doors, but Berry places some of it on the modern American cult of the future, a promised land in which diseases will be cured, social problems will be solved, the poor will be fed, and the streets will be safe. (This sounds a lot like the traditional concept of heaven, and perhaps as participation in establishment religion declined, that particular aspect of faith was replaced by this vision of a perfected future.) Paradoxically, this future, so full of the promise of material blessings, is threatened by shortages of food and energy unless, as the pro-development contingent assures us, untapped fossil fuel resources are exploited even more quickly and less cautiously. Both industry and government use fears of such shortages to make changes, such as removing restrictions on oil and gas drilling and exploring previously protected environments, that serve their interests. The obvious conclusion—that, by whatever math one uses, this fails to compute—is overlooked or ignored. But this yearning for the imagined perfection of the future has allowed otherwise intelligent farmers to make small decisions that have accumulated into ones that may well bring them down, one piece of improved machinery, one loan, one implement at a time.

The translation of the mechanical metaphor at the level of agriculture implies a degree of control that depends upon wishful thinking. Wouldn't it be nice, say the agronomists, if growing things in soil were utterly predictable? And they envision an agricultural future in which the variables are suppressed and a mechanistic order obtains. "The ambition underlying these model farms," says Berry,

> is that of total control—a totally controlled agricultural environment. Nowhere are the essential totalitarianism and the essential weakness of the specialist mind more clearly displayed than in this ambition. Confronted with the living substance of farming—the complexly, even mysteriously interrelated lives on which it depends, from the microorganisms in the soil to the human consumers—the agriculture specialist can think only of subjecting it to total control, of turning it into a machine. But total human control is just as impossible now as it ever was."[54]

The way to exert control is to create boundaries, but boundaries in the natural world are not only disruptive, they are an illusion—and they are permeable. Any attempt to create perfect order out of agriculture predictably affects everything around it, creating opportunities for disorder, which manifests itself in disease. But the effects are even more far-reaching. "It is impossible to mechanize production without mechanizing consumption, impossible to make machines out of soil, plants, and animals without making machines also of people."[55] This infectious nature of the machine model would also seem to imply that the effect of mechanization is order; instead the alienation, the feelings of frustration and loss and a nameless yearning create an unhealthy and destabilizing disorder. The disorder is in the society in which this essential tie between soil and human and food has been severed. It manifests itself in neurosis and desperate acts.

The latest agribusiness vision is of a future of limitless food production using infinite resources exploited by the magic of biogenetics. This future, says Berry, is bound to be totalitarian, whether the food production technology is "publicly" or "privately" owned. "It would overthrow the whole issue of control, for it would be the control. Since everyone would be totally dependent upon it, it would necessarily be everyone's first consideration."[56] Consumer choice would become a marketing illusion; and the right to determine what one puts in one's body, if it ever existed, will vanish. The government agencies that regulate food have refused, for instance, to allow genetically engineered foods to be labeled; thus the consumer will not be allowed to have the information to make choices. This is the ultimate cost of separating ourselves from the production of our food.

At the root of the problem, or at least of its modern manifestation, in Berry's view, is limitless technology without moral constraints on its development. How did this become thinkable? Berry proposes a simple answer: it became thinkable because of the modern separation of life and work. He could just as easily have stopped at the word *separation*—whether it is from work, soil, community; or wildness.

The very word *wildness*—or, from the environmental perspective, wilderness—implies "other." It is what we are not; something distanced from all that we are. But that is not, in fact, true. Our orderliness is an illusion; we are as wild as the rest of nature, but we prefer to think of our lives as under control. All life is disorderly; unpredictability, the essence of variety and diversity, is its most important characteristic, the trait that allows adaptability.

The machine is orderly, but that is because it is dead; any lifelike qualities it may appear to have remain an illusion because genuine disorder (not the artificially produced confusion and animation), which is the essence of life, cannot be programmed. And yet the machine dominates to such an extent in our culture that emulating it has become an admired characteristic. Asks Stephanie Mills in the prologue to *In Service of the Wild*, "Is it perhaps peculiar to cherish difference any more? To resist simplification and homogenization, whether of the landscape or of the human psyche, goes against the grain of industrial civilization. Yet people do have an appetite for variety and rarity in Nature." The appetite is there because wildness is, in fact, vital, in the pure meaning of the word; it is essential to life.

Agriculture has always been an exercise in artificiality. But it is increasingly clear that the degree to which agriculture separates itself from the rest of nature is especially great today. Agriculture needs to work with the ecosystem as something that it is a part of instead of using the natural world merely as calculated raw material.

Today we are facing the ultimate separation of agriculture from life: the new and frightening science of bioengineering. The process of changing or creating new life-forms by inserting genetic material from one organism into another is the ultimate consequence of viewing life from the Cartesian perspective; of considering it nothing more than a machine with interchangeable parts. Bioengineering seems now to be the ultimate consequence of our least desirable traits—our bad habits come back to haunt us. Hubris, intelligence, pride, ambition, self-delusion, and greed have now produced a force so malevolent that it may well—in fact, according to Professor Stephen Hawking, is likely to—destroy us. A virus with the potential to wipe out the human race, Hawking points out, could be produced in somebody's garage. He sees this not as a possibility but as a probability.

At this point, it would seem clear that the machine has won, dominating food production to the degree that most Americans are in thrall to a corporate system for their nourishment, with all that implies in terms of dependence. There are exceptions, of course. The organic food movement is thriving as awareness of the realities of the industrialized process increases. And yet organic growing itself is being industrialized and corporatized at an alarming rate. Within the organic farming community, there is optimism at the growing acceptance of its principles. But there is also discouragement; a sense that—as the domination of powerful international food companies increases; as regulations favoring the biotech industry are put in place; as plants with engineered genes are spread in the environment, contaminating traditional varieties—control over farming and the food supply is slipping away. And with it goes the hope for a saner approach to farming—and perhaps something more. Stadtfeld saw his war metaphor for farming carried to the end: "The danger is that we might conquer so completely that the environment will cease to fight back; it may just lie down and die, and then of course we will too."[57]

It is increasingly clear that the only real potential for change lies with the individual consumer, exercising what few choices he or she has left. Buying foods grown locally from small, sustainable farms is the key. Restoring the small farm will have a ripple effect throughout society that will, I am absolutely certain, leave it collectively healthier and happier. We remain, for all our technological sophistication, more dependent than we realize on the ground beneath our feet, and the extent to which that ground remains healthy will determine the health not only of our bodies but of our culture.

CHAPTER NINE

Writing Against the Machine

P ERHAPS WALLACE STEGNER PUT IT MOST CLEARLY
in his "Wilderness Letter": "There has hardly been a serious or important
novel in this century that did not repudiate in part or in whole American
technological culture for its commercialism, its vulgarity, and the way in
which it had dirtied a clean continent and a clean dream."

Did he really need to use the word *American?* Anti-industrialism as manifested in literature that examines the lost, the frustrated, the alienated, the
bewildered, and the angry follows industrialism as determinedly as the
migrant follows the harvest. The link with Luddism can be direct, as it is in
Glyn Hughes's historical novel, *The Rape of the Rose,* published in 1987, or
the more recent *The Lady and the Luddite,* another historical novel, written
by Linden Salter and published in 2000. Both are writing from the United
Kingdom. Hughes's chief character is an educated and thinking man—a
part-time teacher—whose wife and children work in the mill yet still do not
earn enough to feed themselves without poaching. His bright and talented
son brings conflict within the family when he challenges the oppressive and
dangerous factory system, and the rebellion draws them in. Salter's novel

refers directly to Brontë's *Shirley*—he has Brontë's heroine, Shirley Keeldar, who has inherited a mill, drawn into a relationship with Tom Mellor, one of the rebellious workers. The name is not chosen by accident. George Mellor led one of the first Luddite raids.

The Luddite story has obvious appeal for the novelist. *Ben o'Bills, the Luddite: A Yorkshire Tale,* was written in 1812 by D. F. E. Sykes and George Henry Walker. But more recently, in 1932, Phillis Bentley, a Canadian, wrote *Inheritance,* a passionate story of love and conflict within and between families over the support of the rebellious mill workers. She, too, introduces George Mellor, whose story she fictionalizes. Her second chapter is titled "Machines and Men."

But beyond the obvious, what counts as an expression of Luddism? Not all nature writers are in the Luddite camp, but those who bring passion to their exploration of the nonhuman world, linked to a fierce disdain for the technological and the mechanical, certainly deserve to be included. Those who address the issues of job displacement, child labor, or the exploitation that can accompany industrialization—to the extent that they refuse to replace one mechanical system with another—are candidates. I am thinking of some of Theodore Drieser, John Steinbeck, and Upton Sinclair's novels.

There is a certain body of literature that questions or expresses fears about technology and science in general and raises the specter of totalitarian control that operates with mechanistic efficiency. It establishes a kind of paradigm of horror, life and society completely dominated by what Jacques Ellul calls the technological imperative. These are fictional futuristic societies where humans are increasingly separated from nature and from themselves, history, culture, and experience; living soul-destroying, alienated lives. The dystopian tradition is a persistent one. There are also writers who express a longing for a return to a less technological approach to life. There is an entire modern genre, in fact—usually in popular fiction, but sometimes in more serious fiction, and often in nonfiction—in which the chief character finds peace or salvation or is restored to sanity on an island, at ferry's length from civilization, in touch with nature, and usually with a minimum of technology around, where he or she begins to appreciate simplicity. And there are writers who, more subtly perhaps, imply what they don't like by writing about what they do, about simpler lives where technology seldom rears its head. On the other hand, there are writers in whose books technology tends to come between humans and their relationship with the world around them. One could, in fact, include works that voice an appreciation of the natural, of the whole over the parts; a preference for the simple; a certain nostalgia for elements of living that have been lost to mechanization; and a validation of the sensual, the subjective, and indeed, the irrational. Or consider the novels in which urban man leads an aimless, alienated life—those too could be included. Once tuned to this frequency (to use one of the many mechanistic references that pepper our speech, unnoticed), I suspect the breadth of this stream of thinking will be obvious. A sampling—nothing more—of literature in which resistance to technology makes an appearance illustrates the point.

A feeling for things Luddite can be as direct as Frank B. Gilbreth and Ernestine Gilbreth Carey's *Cheaper by the Dozen,* the funny story, circa 1948, of the real-life adventures of their parents, both efficiency experts, who applied efficiency and time-motion studies to life at home with twelve children. The difficulties of reconciling machinelike efficiency with real human behavior created an American classic. But long before the Gilbreths' adventure, E. J. Rath's novel *Too Much Efficiency* had plowed the same ground. Efficiency expert H. Hedges (the first name reduced to an initial for efficiency and a reduction in printing costs) offers to take over the extravagant family of a wealthy widowed New York industrialist while he takes an extended holiday. The story line is as lacking in subtlety as the title, but it is a very amusing revelation of the inevitable *inefficiency*—not to mention confusion and chaos—that results when mechanical principles are applied too thoroughly to human activities. (Philip K. Howard makes the same point in his 1994 nonfiction book, *The Death of Common Sense.* The inability to make common-sense decisions in a world ordered by forms, studies and surveys, and multiple layers of organizational responsibility; and the unwillingness to take initiative; has left us in thrall to machine-based inefficiency.)

But a quick survey of some of the best examples of what one might call the Literature of Luddism should begin with *Erewhon* by the English writer Samuel Butler, also known for his autobiographical *The Way of All Flesh.* Writer John Fowles called *Erewhon,* published in 1872, "one of the most famous manifestations of this suspicion of the machine, and especially of the arch-machine of Darwinian theory."[1] I include it here, despite my unspoken intention to focus on the twentieth century, because it represents a distinct shift from the antitechnological thinking of John Ruskin and

William Morris, who were concerned with the immediate impact of the machine on craftsmanship; on social order; on the nature of work; and, to a lesser degree, on the environment. Butler's vision was more focused, and, in the longer term, more ominous. He saw the machine as frankly dangerous, with the clear potential, even then, to take over. *Erewhon* is an open attack on modern life, but it is also an attempt to point out the disadvantages of carrying a mechanical rationality to its ultimate irrational conclusion— something Erewhonians have consciously sought to avoid.

Higgs, the exploring hero of the story, discovers a hidden population, beautiful, healthy, and peaceful, but with odd customs. They have, for example, given up all things mechanical. Higgs is made to give up his watch, which he contributes to a vast collection of broken mechanical objects: a museum, of sorts, for errors.

Various critics see "The Book of the Machines," the chapter in which the reason for the abandonment of technology is spelled out, as a discussion of evolution and a reference to Butler's ambivalence about Darwinism. It could easily be interpreted this way, except that the chapter goes far beyond any possible allegorical reference. Critics (Fowles is an exception) appear to be reluctant to see it for what it is: a direct and profoundly critical attack on the effect of the machine on humans—a direct warning about where all that clever technological inventiveness might lead. And yet the questioning of the machine is a logical progression from what Higgs has previously discovered in the Erewhonian educational system: namely, a distaste for reason and logic.

> Life, they urge, would be intolerable if men were to be guided in all they did by reason and reason only. Reason betrays men into the drawing of hard and fast lines, and to the defining by language—language being like the sun, which rears and then scorches. Extremes are alone logical, but they are always absurd; the mean is illogical, but an illogical mean is better than the sheer absurdity of an extreme. There are no follies and no unreasonablenesses so great as those which can apparently be irrefragably defended by reason itself, and there is hardly an error into which men may not easily be led if they base their conduct on reason alone.[2]

With such thinking, can rejection of the machine be far behind? The explanation for how the transformation came about is spelled out in the same chapter. The abandonment had taken place some five hundred years before my arrival: people had long become thoroughly used to the change, although at the time that it was made the country was plunged into the deepest misery, and a reaction which followed had very nearly proved successful. Civil war raged for many years, and is said to have reduced the number of the inhabitants by one half. The parties were styled the machinists and the anti-machinists, and in the end, as I have said already, the latter got the victory, treating their opponents with such unparalleled severity that they extirpated every trace of opposition.[3]

The machine had vanished; the population had survived and thrived. Machines were no longer of any real interest, and technological artifacts could be placed in museums without raising a desire for them in any viewer. They were simply curious objects from the past, like a tomahawk or a cherry-pitter that no one today really wants to use.

In the book, Butler was able to anticipate some of the more recent trends in technology by speaking not as the hero Higgs but through the writer of the Erewhonian treatise explaining the antitechnological revolution that had taken place, which Higgs is allowed to read. It is a kind of sacred text of antitechnology.

Anticipating miniaturization, the treatise writer had predicted that machines would continue to get smaller and smaller. Blending Descartes's notions of the body as a machine with Darwinian theory, the writer sees a kind of mechanical evolution that mirrors the one Darwin described, with the machines themselves adapting to perform optimally. But are humans far behind in becoming more machinelike themselves, merging with technology? He foresees the day when machines speak to one another (as they do now) and when children won't bother to learn English but will converse in mathematical terms instead. Machines are certainly not useless, the treatise writer acknowledges; they can help humans by enhancing vision, for instance, or calculating more accurately. Will the machine eventually take over? he asks.

A machine that doesn't do its job well will naturally be allowed to die, but the Erewhonian treatise suggests that there is nevertheless a danger. Will the machine allow itself to die? Will humans be able to let it die? The job of the machines is ostensibly to serve, and yet the servant can, if one is not watching carefully, become the master. "The servant glides by, imperceptible approaches into the master; and we have come to such a pass that, even now, man must suffer terribly on ceasing to benefit the machines."[4] Without even noticing, we have become dependent. In fact it is quite likely, the writer of the treatise says, that humans have become so dependent that terrible suffering and misery would result if machines were done away with. The machines do dominate. "They have preyed upon man's groveling preference for his material over his spiritual interests," the author of the treatise writes. Control is an illusion:

> The machines being of themselves unable to struggle, have got man to do their struggling for them: as long as he fulfils this function duly, all goes well with him—at least he thinks so; but the moment he fails to do his best for the advancement of machinery by encouraging the good and destroying the bad, he is left behind in the race of competition; and this means that he will be made uncomfortable in a variety of ways, and perhaps die."[5]

If some of these ideas *could* be standing in for Butler's argument with Darwinism, it is quite clear as he goes along that he is, indeed, talking about machines themselves. The lives of individuals have begun to shift from using the machines to caring for the machines:

> How many men at this hour are living in a state of bondage to the machines? How many spend their whole lives, from the cradle to the grave, in tending them by night and day? Is it not plain that the machines are gaining ground upon us, when we reflect on the increasing number of those who are bound down to them as slaves, and of those who devote their whole souls to the advancement of the mechanical kingdom?[6]

At last he questions whether machines of the future will, in fact, be able to reproduce. The Erewhonian document suspects this is the next step: the takeover will be complete. But perhaps the new machine-masters, he muses, will treat humans at least as kindly as humans treated their dogs.

There were arguments to be made in favor of the technology, the narrator writes, but they were not compelling, and on the basis of this writer's argument, the Erewhonians had banished machines. And so long had it been since they were allowed to exist in the society that the people had quite forgotten that they were ever so entirely dependent upon them. They had, in fact, regained their freedom—in some ways. In other ways they lived curious lives.

The people of Erewhon, the hero Higgs notes, have the seemingly odd practice of punishing and imprisoning people who become ill. Illness is a great crime. But it is the reasoning behind this practice that reveals Butler's prescience. Of course, as he notes ironically, every society punishes people for their misfortunes, whether it is acknowledged or not, and the system of justice is inevitably revealed to be manifestly unfair and unjust if too closely examined. But the Erewhonians' rationale for punishing the ill has to do not only with examining the notion of justice but also with discouraging physicians—who, if allowed to practice unchecked, could amass too much power in the society. Butler's protagonist listens in as a judge sentences a man dying of tuberculosis. Not only is he guilty of being ill, says the judge,

> But independently of this consideration, and independently of the physical guilt which attaches itself to a crime so great as yours, there is yet another reason why we should be unable to show you mercy, even if we were inclined to do so. I refer to the existence of a class of men who lie hidden among us, and who are called physicians. Were the severity of the law or the current feeling of the country to be relaxed never so slightly, these abandoned persons, who are now compelled to practise secretly and who can be consulted only at the greatest risk, would become frequent visitors in every household; their organization and their intimate acquaintance with all family secrets would give them a power, both social and political, which nothing could resist. The head of the household would become subordinate to the family doctor, who would interfere between man and wife, between master and servant, until the doctors should be the only depositaries of power in the nation, and have all that we hold precious at their mercy. A time of universal dephysicalization would ensue; medicine-vendors of all kinds would abound in our streets and advertise in our newspapers[7]

This sounds uncomfortably close to modern medicine, where great storehouses of personal medical information, and thus control, have been amassed by the computerized health care and insurance industries, a situation Ivan Illich documented in 1976 in *Medical Nemesis: The Expropriation of Health*. Today illness is punished quite overtly when medical conditions can prevent one from being hired, obtaining insurance, changing jobs, or even moving from one state to another, for fear of losing insurance coverage.

The machine itself is simply an example that confirms the point Butler makes again and again: there *is* a great danger in carrying reason and logic too far. Logic can become illogical. Higgs relates what nearly happened when someone in the Erewhonian past began to think too much about the nature of the life force and the unity of humans with the animal world—

which logically led to the elimination of meat from the diet. That, in turn, prompted the question, How different, really, is a plant from an animal? He enumerates the similarities and concludes that eating plants is likewise offensive. All that can really be eaten, he says, if one follows this train of thought to its ultimate conclusion, are yellowed cabbage leaves and windfall apples—not a very healthy diet. In fact, this reasonable and logical population was in danger of starvation.

To maintain a healthy balance and to avoid the consequences of carrying reason too far, therefore, Erewhon has Colleges of Unreason and Professors of Inconsistency and Evasion, vital to a smoothly functioning society. At the core of Higgs's (Butler's) message is the validity of that old friend, common sense, and the need to maintain the illogic, inconsistency, and unpredictability that is the essence of what it means to be human.

The plot is irrelevant; little more than a device for Butler to put forth his ideas about technology and the need to consider its effects. Higgs will get to know the people, discover the basis for their rejection of the mechanical, fall in love, and escape with his love back to an ordinary London life in a balloon he has constructed. There, he slips easily back into his old ways, Erewhon having had little apparent impact. His opinion, ironically, is that the Erewhonians need converting to Christianity. (Butler was an avowed atheist.) The message: that humans are unlikely to perceive the truth even when it is laid out before them with helpful labels attached. They will, instead, return to their illusions.

In 1944, the novelist E. M. Forster wrote an essay entitled "A Book That Influenced Me;" the book was *Erewhon*. He prefers opinions presented obliquely, he says, and Butler is a master of the oblique. But perhaps more to the point was the congeniality of what Butler had to say. "I lapped it up. It was the food for which I was waiting."[8] Forster thinks he might have written *Erewhon* himself "if the idea of it had occurred to me."[9] Surely that is clue enough that what we are looking for might well be found in Forster's writings.

Today he is newly popular because several of his books have been turned into films, among them *A Room with a View*, *Maurice*, and *Howards End*. The first and last (*Maurice* has a homosexual theme) are the gentle sorts of tales favored by fans of public television and Merchant Ivory films, being mannered and Edwardian in tone. In general, his stories are characterized by restraint. Social conventions create an enviable illusion of order. But it is an illusion. Forster values tradition, family, a sense of flowing history, a feeling for place, and a respect for countryside. The modern is perpetually being

undermined by something older, something slightly mysterious yet powerful
—or if it doesn't undermine, it threatens to. There is a sense in Forster's
work, as Frederick Crews put it, that rural traditions need to be cherished
in the face of "the levelling force of urbanization."[10] But most of all, perhaps,
there is a sense of the importance of the individual and a related distrust of
institutions. The nation is not an entity but a collection of individuals, families, and communities. Commonality is an illusion on this scale, and the
state is shortsighted and arbitrary.

Forster considered himself a liberal, but of a different sort from the Benthamite utilitarians. He understood the Benthamite goal of the greatest
good for the greatest number to be little more than a rationale for free trade
and economic expansion. A strong believer in the rights of the individual to
freedom of choice and a diversity of opinion, he saw the democratic principle of majority rule as simply another way of stifling the minority view.

There is a religious element in Forster's novels, but it is unconventional,
having to do with the sense of a higher power rather than any established
theology. This religious feeling is expressed in a sense of mystery, the
unknown, the presence of something that cannot be defined; but it lurks in
the passageways, just offstage, more pagan or pantheistic than Christian.

Forster likes to pit the logic and rationality of social convention against
periodic brushes with uncontrollable wildness, irrational behavior that is
sometimes brought on by the sensuality of luscious, fecund nature itself—
the countryside, infused with the vitality of a barely tamed paganism. The
hold of rationality is then revealed as tenuous, an illusion.

However much Forster's characters long for the assurances of order and stability; desiring to separate themselves from the unruliness of the natural world,
they are often reminded how exciting and liberating the brush with wildness
can be. The experience feels dangerous. It is tension-filled, perhaps even hurried and regrettable, or even imaginary, yet nevertheless a tear in the fabric of
propriety long and deep enough to let in the flickering light of impulse and
unreason. Conclusion: the carefully woven fabric of conventional society will
not hold. The life force (the essence of the anti-mechanical) cannot be contained. Whatever it is that escapes must be forced back or can be simply
accepted and enjoyed. The choice is the individual's. And finally, there is that
quintessentially Luddite impulse to "only connect," (boldly written on the title
page of *Howards End*): to preserve those linkages to family, community, and
nature that are so vital. That, of course, is the theme of *Howards End,* but it is
a sentiment felt throughout much of Forster's work—sometimes clearly

expressed, at other times a faint plea, but always at the core of his writing.

In *Howards End,* all these themes can be found. Two unmarried and independent sisters meet the Wilcoxes on holiday and are invited to visit them at their country home, Howards End. Only one sister goes, and she yields to a fleeting moment of life-shattering impulse. The reader suspects later that it is the house itself that has brought it on. It is ancient; a wych-elm looms near its doorway; and it is inhabited by the mysterious, congenial, and infinitely wise Mrs. Wilcox, a woman of a slightly older generation, whose feet seem hardly to touch the ground. She glides instead of walking. But with straw in her hair from feeding the animals, and flowers in her hand, she is linked to the world around her as the Mother Goddess figure. She is destined to disappear—to die, in fact—and things begin to fall apart. Or rather, for a while they become very practical, very efficient, very directed—and very unhealthy. Passion is thwarted and the ordered life boringly prevails, until passion reexerts itself and unconventionality triumphs. The theme is really quite simple and direct: those who do well in the long run are linked to and respectful of tradition; have a connection to nature, family, and community; are intuitive and commonsensical; and are capable of feelings. It is a statement of priorities: what is human over what is mechanical. The things that money can't buy triumph. Thus the prevailing order of materialism and utilitarianism is reversed. Things are not quite that clear-cut, of course, or they would be boring. One of the sisters—the more intuitive of the pair—directs her energies to saving a poor young man with literary aspirations. (He reads Carlyle and Ruskin, of course.) Her efforts go badly wrong, and he ends up being killed. She, however, is carrying his child. There is the sense that the "enlightened" way will be littered with traps and snares, and that failures are inevitable but the spirit will endure in some form.

Is this linking of Forster with the Luddites a bit contrived? To banish all doubts, consider his novel, *The Machine Stops,* a short work now out of print.[11] Written in 1909, a year after *Howards End,* it is set in a barren future. The planet has been devastated. Very little plant life has survived. The air is cold and inhospitable. The human race lives below ground in small cells where every physical need is satisfied by a button or lever. Communication is by electronic means with video images. It has expanded to such a degree that a single individual may be in contact, electronically, with a thousand people. Life is a series of constant distractions from urgent communications unless one chooses to isolate oneself for a time, after which the problem is to catch up with all the messages that have arrived in the interim.

The central figure, Vishta, never having moved a muscle or seen daylight, is pale and fat, a blob of a person who never leaves her cell with its many comforts and gadgets. Face-to-face communication and direct experiences with other individuals are so unknown that they are unsettling. The citizens of this underground world can travel in airships from one enclave to another, but only out of necessity, not desire, for all places are alike, so there is no point in going anywhere. It is as if Forster had imagined a world where globalization has triumphed and all distinctive cultures have given way to blue jeans and burgers. Personality is frowned upon; the most desirable people are those whose behavior has become the most machinelike.

(Stewart Brand, founder, publisher, and editor of the *Whole Earth Catalog* and author of *Clock of the Long Now*, described our own techno-dependent future in similar terms in an article in *Civilization* magazine in 1998. Referring to the huge interlocking computer systems that futurists think will eventually become one large global computer, he noted that "It could easily become The Legacy System from Hell that holds civilization hostage —the system doesn't really work; it can't be fixed; no one understands it; no one is in charge of it; it can't be lived without; and it gets worse every year.")[12]

Vishta's son, however, is a different sort. For that reason he has been refused permission to breed. He is recognized as having a personality that is too curious, too challenging to the complete devotion that the machine demands. He wants to see the outer world, and he attempts to escape. He makes it out but is forced back inside, yet he realizes that there are those who have escaped and survived. His mother is horrified. But he alone appreciates what is happening. He knows that the machine, which by now is worshiped but not understood, is on the verge of stopping.

As the machine gradually begins to fail, there is adaptation and resignation. Denial keeps the population going. Eventually life-support systems begin to malfunction, and people realize that the end is near. The final sentences, in light of the destruction of New York's World Trade Center, are chilling:

> As he spoke, the whole city was broken like a honeycomb. An air-ship had sailed in. . . . It crashed downwards, exploding as it went, rending gallery after gallery with its wings of steel. For a moment they saw the nations of the dead, and before they joined them, scraps of the untainted sky.

And yet, what one does not feel in Forster is any real anger at humans, even in the aftermath of a ruined, uninhabitable planet. There is a certain quiet resignation to his telling of the tale. Human foibles and failings are only to be expected; humans are, after all, frail and subject to error. The end is predictable and unavoidable. Unless? Unless what?

What prevailed in Forster was the pull of the ancient, mysterious past, but its strength was waning and uncertain. Where the past has been plowed over, paved, and obliterated, what might substitute? It could be passion. It was held in check in Forster's writing, its escape startling and periodic, but a contemporary of his was all passion; all passion all the time.

David Herbert [D. H.] Lawrence stands out sharply in the Luddite tradition. The son of a collier and the fourth of five children, he was born in 1885 in Eastwood, near Nottinghamshire. This was the heart of the Luddite triangle, the center of the counties where the original rebellion had taken place. He had a keen sense of place. Of his birthplace, he says, it was a

> village of some three thousand souls, about eight miles from Nottingham, and one mile from the small stream, the Erewash, which divides Nottinghamshire from Derby. It is hilly country, looking west to Crich and towards Matlock, sixteen miles away, and east and north-east towards Mansfield and the Sherwood Forest district. To me it seemed, and still seems, an extremely beautiful countryside, just between the red sandstone and the oak-trees of Nottingham, and the cold limestone, the ash-trees, the stone fences of Derbyshire. To me, as a child and a young man, it was still the old England of the forest and agricultural past; there were no motor-cars, the mines were, in a sense, an accident in the landscape, and Robin Hood and his merry men were not very far away.[13]

If he felt kinship with the Luddites, he didn't say. What he does say is how much he resents what industrialism has made of this countryside. He blames a culture of materialism. Looking back at the labor of his father and other colliers, he observes that it wasn't so much the work that wore them down—in the bowels of the earth, a warm, physical, satisfying, and compensating camaraderie developed—but the demands of the world above; the wives always wanting more, as they were trained to want by the commercial and acquisitive culture; and, perhaps worst of all, the hideousness of it all.

> The men are beaten down, there is prosperity for a time, in their defeat— and then disaster looms ahead. The root of all disaster is disheartenment.

And men are disheartened. The men of England, the colliers in particular, are disheartened. They have been betrayed and beaten.

Now though perhaps nobody knew it, it was ugliness which betrayed the spirit of man, in the nineteenth century. The great crime which the moneed classes and promoters of industry committed in the palmy Victorian days was the condemning of the workers to ugliness, ugliness, ugliness: meanness and formless and ugly surroundings, ugly ideals, ugly religion, ugly hope, ugly love, ugly clothes, ugly furniture, ugly houses, ugly relationship between workers and employers.[14]

This passage is from the essay "Nottingham and the Mining Country," but the powerful feelings of revulsion appear elsewhere in Lawrence's writing. In fact, similar phrasing turns up in *Lady Chatterley's Lover*.

The car ploughed uphill through the long squalid straggle of Tevershall, the blackened brick dwellings, the black slate roofs glistening their sharp edges, the mud black with coal-dust, the pavements wet and black. It was as if dismalness had soaked through and through everything The utter negation of natural beauty, the utter negation of the gladness of life, the utter absence of the instinct for shapely beauty which every bird and beast has, the utter death of the human intuitive faculty was appalling. The stacks of soap in the grocers' shops, the rhubarb and lemons in the greengrocers', the awful hats in the milliners' all went by ugly, ugly, ugly, followed by the plaster-and-gilt horror of the cinema with its wet picture-announcements, "A Woman's Love!" and the new big Primitive chapel, primitive enough in its stark brick and big panes of greenish and raspberry glass in the windows. . . . Just beyond were the new school buildings, expensive pink brick, and gravelled play-ground inside iron railings, all very imposing, and mixing the suggestion of a chapel and a prison. Standard Five girls were having a singing lesson, just finishing the la-me-doh-la exercises and beginning a "sweet children's song." Anything more unlike song, spontaneous song, would be impossible to imagine: a strange, bawling yell that followed the outlines of a tune. It was not like savages: savages have subtle rhythms. It was not like animals: animals mean something when they yell. It was like nothing on earth, and it was called singing. Connie sat and listened with her heart in her boots, as Field was filling petrol. What could possibly become of such a people, a people in whom the living intuitive faculty was dead as nails, and only queer mechanical yells and uncanny will-power remained?[15]

What indeed? Lawrence's understanding of the growing dangers of mechanical thinking, of mechanical living, of the gray sordidness of it all, is not an underlying theme but is central to his work, for he sees in the technological, in the worship of science and the machine, the source of estrangement of humans from their bodies, their emotions, their history and traditions, their proper religion, and the natural world around them.

The essence of Lawrence is indeed passion, a strength of feeling freely expressed not simply in his writing about love and lovemaking—which is why most of us first picked up his books—but in virtually everything he wrote. It is in his writing about place, about nature, about literature. It is in the strength and energy of his words themselves. It is a powerful protest against the suppression of feeling and expression that Lawrence identified with mechanical thinking. Passion, which is really that love of what makes us human, is also the essence of Luddism. It is an overt rejection of what is not full of life.

As Mark Schorer points out in his 1957 introduction to *Lady Chatterley's Lover,* Lawrence has two major themes: "the relation of men and women and the relation of men and machines. In the works as they are written, the two are one, and his most subtle and penetrating perception, the knowledge that social and psychological conflicts are identical, is so firmly integrated in the structure of his books that it is almost foolhardy to speak of his having two themes when in fact he had one vision." [16]

It is easy enough to say what Lawrence is against, because he never hesitates to tell us. As were Carlyle, Morris, Butler, and others, he is against the elevation of reason to the exclusion of other human faculties. And with that comes a resistance to emotionless science. If it has its place, it is not in art, and it is an unsuitable model for human behavior. Writing about the works of John Galsworthy, he says of literary criticism, for instance:

> [It] can never be a science: it is, in the first place, much too personal, and in the second, it is concerned with values that science ignores. The touchstone is emotion, not reason. We judge a work of art by its effect on our sincere and vital emotion, and nothing else. All the critical twiddle-twaddle about style and form, all this pseudo-scientific classifying and analysing of books in an imitation-botanical fashion, is mere impertinence and mostly dull jargon. [17]

The critic "must be able to feel the impact of the work of art." [18] The observer of the countryside must feel nature. The novelist must feel. Everyone must feel, and must do so at the very core of being. And yet, Lawrence attacks some of those whom we think of as emotionally expressive in literature. Walt Whitman, for instance. He dismisses as false and "mechanical."

He is scornful, especially, of Benjamin Franklin and his list of virtues. Franklin, he insists, established an efficient and democratic code of behavior that was particularly American and served to sever America from old and mysterious Europe, which had another, darker side. Lawrence himself represents that side. His own creed, he says, would read as follows:

> That I am I
> That my soul is a dark forest.
> That my known self will never be more than a little clearing in the forest.
> That gods, strange gods, come forth from the forest into the
> clearing of my known self, and then go back.
> That I must have the courage to let them come and go.
> That I will never let mankind put anything over me, but that I will
> try always to recognize and submit to the gods in me and the gods
> in other men and women.[19]

It is not, therefore, simply Lawrence's writing that is antimechanical but his very concept of self. There is something within him that is ancient, only half-civilized by purpose, in touch with the wild and unpredictable and mysterious, relying on an order that is as old as the universe.

Lawrence brings our attention to certain violations of what he saw as the natural order, just as Forster did. Among them are social conventions and class differences, the separation from the wildness of nature, the cleavage of people from the past and tradition, the degradation of the landscape by the brutalization of industrialism, and the stifling of normal and natural passions. These themes repeat themselves in all his works, but they are virtually all present in *Lady Chatterley's Lover,* arguably his most popular novel.

Constance Reid has married Clifford Chatterley, the son of a baronet, and enjoyed a month's honeymoon before her husband is shipped off to war. He returns six months later "more or less in bits." The bits are pieced together, but he remains paralyzed from the waist down (not too subtle, pointed out some of Lawrence's friends), and Connie finds herself trapped in a marriage that is unsatisfactory physically and, increasingly, emotionally and intellectually.

The setting is Wragby, the Chatterley family's estate in "the utter soulless ugliness of the coal-and-iron Midlands."[20] The park around it is beautifully laid out, but just beyond and always intruding is a mechanistic horror, which Lawrence paints as a technological apparition:

> From the rather dismal rooms of Wragby she heard the rattle-rattle of the screens at the pit, the puff of the winding engine, the clink-clink of shunting trucks and the hoarse little whistle of the colliery locomotives. Tevershall pit-bank was burning, had been burning for years, and it would cost thousands to put it out. So it had to burn. And when the wind was that way, which was often, the house was full of the stench of this sulphureous combustion of the earth's excrement. But even on windless days, the air always smelled of something under-earth: sulphur, coal, iron, or acid. And even on the Christmas roses the smuts settled persistently, incredible, like black manna from skies of doom.
>
> Well, there it was: fated, like the rest of things! It was rather awful, but why kick? You couldn't kick it away. It just went on. . . . On the low dark ceiling of cloud at night red blotches burned and quavered, dappling and swelling and contracting like burns that give pain. It was the furnaces.[21]

Connie finds relief, first by taking a lover (nearly as unsatisfying as her husband) then in the outdoors, walking far afield, flinging herself on the wild bracken, venturing more and more frequently into the woods: dark, ancient, mysterious, and melancholy; seemingly, from Lawrence's hints—he mentions John's Well—a lingering remnant of Nottingham Forest, home of Robin Hood. And here, eventually, she finds Mellors, the gamekeeper. The relevance of Nottingham Forest with its Luddite link is confirmed in Lawrence's choice of a name for his hero, only a single letter away from (George) Mellor, who, as previously noted, led an early Luddite raid.

Lawrence has set up a series of appositions. The village with its working people is psychologically distant and cut off from Wragby, with no communication possible between the classes. The orderliness of Wragby itself— "All those endless rooms that nobody used, all the Midlands routine, the mechanical cleanliness and the mechanical order!"[22]—is set against the disorderly wildness of the woods in which anything can, and does, happen. And then there is the juxtaposition of Clifford and Connie and Mellors: Clifford increasingly finds satisfaction in the scientific and the industrial, while Connie lets down her guard and allows herself to explore her sensual, imaginative, and intuitive nature, even as Mellors is portrayed as an echo of Rousseau's natural man, intuitive and deep.

The woods have a certain sanctity, but they can be penetrated. Clifford violates this sanctity with his mechanical chair. Mellors's former wife, coolly revengeful, intrudes. And the industrial world is not far off. Connie leaves Mellors after making love and turns into the dark woods. Mellors hears the noises of the engines at Stacks Gate, the traffic on the main road. He climbs a denuded knoll and sees the bright rows of lights

> on Stacks Gate, smaller lights at Tevershall pit, the yellow lights of Tevershall, and lights everywhere, here and there, on the dark country, with the distant blush of furnaces, faint and rosy, since the night was clear, the rosiness of the outpouring of whitehot metal. Sharp, wicked electric lights at Stacks Gate! Undefinable quick of evil in them! And all the unease, the ever-shifting dread of the industrial night in the midlands![23]

Mellors, toughened by life, can take care of himself, but he is afraid of what the world will do to Connie. "Poor thing," Mellors says, "she too had some of the vulnerability of the wild hyacinths, she wasn't all tough rubber-goods-and-platinum, like the modern girl. . . . But he would protect her for a little while . . . before the insentient iron world and the Mammon of mechanized greed did them both in, her as well as him."[24] In fact, Mellors himself must be hounded—not just because he was suspected in the neighborhood of having a woman in his cottage in the wood, but because he represents something more dangerous: the forces of nature that cannot be quelled, something old and tenacious that seems not to have found its place —or perhaps no longer has a place. He is a living violation of rigid convention. He will not bend to the pressures that keep society organized and its people compliant. He thinks for himself.

Connie must, in the end, decide between the two, and it is a decision that is clearly defined in the novel. Science and industry, cool and efficient, on one side; warmth and passion on the other. There is, for her at least, no contest.

If Lawrence's intentions were not clear, he spells them out in an essay, "A Propos of 'Lady Chatterley's Lover.'"[25] Lawrence explains and justifies the open sexuality of the novel, mocking the British for their lack of passion. This is a lengthy apology, but suddenly it takes a sharp turn. It isn't just the lack of pleasure in pure sensuality that is a particularly English flaw, says Lawrence, but the demystification of life and the world by Protestantism and science, linked as uncomfortably, yet as tightly, as two men in a three-legged race.

If poor "sexless England" is to be regenerated, it will be in "relationship to the rhythmic cosmos" which is something "we cannot get away from, without bitterly impoverishing our lives." Protestantism had dealt "a great blow to the religious and ritualistic rhythm of the year" by eliminating ancient feasts and festivals, and "nonconformity [dissenting Protestant sects, such as Methodist] *almost* finished the deed."[26]

> Now you have poor, blind, disconnected people with nothing but politics and bank-holidays to satisfy the eternal human need of living in ritual adjustment to the cosmos in its revolutions, in eternal submission to greater laws.[27]

A few pieces from this lengthy essay give a sense of the riff of Lawrence's thinking.

> It is a question, practically, of relationship. We must get back into relation, vivid and nourishing relation to the cosmos and the universe. The way is through daily ritual, and the re-awakening. We must once more practise the ritual of dawn and noon and sunset, the ritual of the kindling fire and pouring water, the ritual of the first breath, and the last. This is an affair of the individual and the household, a ritual of day. . . . Then the ritual of the seasons, with the Drama and the Passion of the soul embodied in procession and dance, this is for the community, an act of men and women, a whole community, in togetherness. . . .
>
> The universe is dead for us, and how is it to come to life again? "Knowledge" has killed the sun, making it a ball of gas, with spots; "knowledge" has killed the moon, it is a dead little earth pitted with extinct craters as with small-pox; the machine has killed the earth for us, making it a surface, more or less bumpy, that you travel over. How, out of all this, are we to get back the grand orbs of the soul's heavens, that fill us with unspeakable joy?. . . .
>
> We've got to get them back, for they are the world our soul, our greater consciousness lives in. The world of reason and science, the moon, a dead lump of earth, the sun, so much gas with spots, this is the dry and sterile little world the abstracted mind inhabits. . . . This is how we know the world when we know it apart from ourselves, in the mean separateness of everything. When we know the world in togetherness with ourselves, we know the earth, hyacinthine or Plutonic, we know the moon gives us our body as delight upon us, or steals it away, we know the purring of the great gold lion of the sun, who licks us like a lioness her cubs, making us bold, or else, like the red angry lion, slashes at us with open claws. But the two great ways of knowing, for man, are knowing in terms of apartness, which is men-

tal, rational, scientific, and knowing in terms of togetherness, with is religious and poetic. The Christian religion lost, in Protestantism finally, the togetherness with the universe, the togetherness of the body, the sex, the emotions, the passions, with the earth and sun and stars. . . .

The sense of isolation, followed by the sense of menace and of fear, is bound to arise as the feeling of oneness and community with our fellow-man declines, and the feeling of individualism and personality, which is existence in isolation, increases. . . . Class hate and class-consciousness are only a sign that the old togetherness, the old blood-warmth has collapsed, and every man is really aware of himself in apartness. Then we have these hostile groupings of men for the sake of opposition, strife. Civil strife becomes a necessary condition of self-assertion.[28]

And the Luddites had picked up their hammers and aimed them at the machines.

Lawrence connected repressed sexuality, loss of ritual and cosmic context, with the alienation of the industrialized, technological society.

FOR C. S. LEWIS, who wrote thirty books, most of which were either directly concerned with Christianity or contained obviously allegorical Christian themes, repressed sexuality played a very minor role. Most of his work focuses on what the machine is not; it is an affirmation of life. A professor of medieval and Renaissance literature at Oxford and Cambridge universities, he was profoundly concerned by the increasing domination of reason and logic, when employed without the tempering influence of more human values. What would a society be like without love, respect, consideration, which had nothing to do with logic and reason? Rationality and atheism were a dangerous combination, leading to a cool pragmatism divorced from principles and values and untempered by any hint of the mysterious other. Where might it lead? His answer is found in the novel *That Hideous Strength*, the third of a Space Trilogy that includes *Out of the Silent Planet* and *Perelandra*. It is, for the greatest part, set firmly on the ground rather than in space, although the universe does have a role to play.

Writing in the early forties, Lewis, like so many of his fellow writers, was overwhelmed by the horrors of war, which had played out with the atomic bomb as the ultimate technological misadventure—all that cleverness and ingenuity turned to destruction and death. And it had all been done so efficiently.

His story begins with a young couple whose marriage is in trouble. Jane longs for something more than the shallowness her relationship with her husband, Mark, has become. He is a university fellow, preoccupied with his work; her own thesis on Donne, for which she has lost enthusiasm, remains unfinished. One night she has a curious dream about a prisoner, under sentence of death, whose head was removed—simply unscrewed. But then, in the confused manner of dreams, the head became a different head, with a flowing beard covered with earth. "It belonged to an old man whom some people were digging up in a kind of churchyard—a sort of ancient British, druidical kind of man, in a long mantle."

"Look out," she cries. "You are waking him up. But they did not stop. The old buried man sat up and began to talk in something that sounded vaguely like Spanish."[29] In the morning, she sees in the newspaper the face of the prisoner in her dreams. He was a brilliant scientist who had poisoned his wife and had now been executed.

Lewis's preferences and priorities are laid out in the first chapters. Jane's husband Mark, who will become the chief character, reveals his essential humanity at once in small ways. He prefers the town they live in to the larger academic centers of Oxford and Cambridge. "For one thing it is so small. No maker of cars or sausages or marmalades has yet come to industrialise the country town which is the setting of the University, and the University itself is tiny."[30] The university is not, however, exempt from greed nor immune to academic politics, where the sins of pride and ambition are played out, and the entanglement of the two leads to the sort of disaster that the reader, with growing dread, can see coming. Mark, eager and ambitious, is sucked into an alliance with a new enterprise that has been proposed by "The Progressive Element" at the college, which he has perceived as the most desirable clique and is flattered to be drawn into. At stake is the selling of Bragdon Wood, land belonging to and adjoining the college where an old well is thought to have mysterious "special properties." Lewis, himself an academician, is masterful at recreating the psychology of long, tortuous business meetings where the skillful manipulation of language, information, and ambiance can lead a group to vote for what might otherwise be defeated. Those whose predisposition might have been to preserve Bragdon Wood would come to find that they had instead unknowingly voted for it to be sold, for an astonishing sum, to an organization called N.I.C.E., the National Institute of Co-ordinated Experiments, which would build on the site a structure that would "make quite a notable addition to the skyline of New York"[31] and would have some difficult-to-define relationship to the college.

Jane, on the other hand, will find refuge in an ancient farmhouse, otherworldly and mysterious, with a small group of carefully selected individuals, all with inherent qualities of goodness, and the conflict is set up. N.I.C.E. is revealed to be a monstrous operation. It "marks the beginning of a new era—the really scientific era. Up to now, everything has been haphazard. This is going to put science itself on a scientific basis,"[32] says one of its supporters. The guiding light will be a mechanical notice board called a Pragmatometer. Mark is taken in. "The real thing is that this time we're going to get science applied to social problems and backed by the whole force of the state, just as war as has been backed by the whole force of the state in the past."[33] Lewis's aim, of course, is to demonstrate where even good intentions can lead, especially when the ruling model is efficiency, practicality, and outcome.

The visionaries of the project are quite explicit about what they intend. Humanity is at a crossroads. The question of the moment: whether one is on the side of obscurantism or order. "It does really look as if we now had the power to dig ourselves in as a species for a pretty staggering period, to take control of our own destiny. If Science is really given a free hand it can now take over the human race and re-condition it: make man a really efficient animal,"[34] says Lord Featherstone, who seems to be some sort of leader of the effort. There are only two problems, he tells Mark. The first is interplanetary—which he doesn't care to go into. "The second problem," he says, "is our rivals on this planet. I don't mean only insects and bacteria. There's far too much life of every kind about, animal and vegetable. We haven't really cleared the place yet."[35] And a third problem is man himself.

> Man has got to take charge of Man. That means, remember, that some men have got to take charge of the rest—which is another reason for cashing in on it as soon as one can. You and I want to be the people who do the taking charge, not the ones who are taken charge of.[36]

This entails, not surprisingly, "sterilization of the unfit, liquidation of backward races (we don't want any dead weights) selective breeding. Then real education, including pre-natal education. . . . We'll get on to biochemical conditioning in the end and direct manipulation of the brain."[37]

Mark's job, it appears, will be to create news stories that precondition the public to the logic of these ideas. How things are phrased is the key. It wouldn't do to talk of experimenting on criminals: "You'd have all the old women of both sexes up in arms and yapping about humanity. Call it re-education of the mal-adjusted, and you have them all slobbering with delight that the brutal era of retributive punishment has at last come to an end. Odd thing it is—the word 'experiment' is unpopular, but not the word 'experience.'"[38]

One job of N.I.C.E. would be to liquidate anachronisms, and there were plenty about, especially in the small English villages around the university. Mark is startled to find the village characters agreeable, but they must go.

> All of this did not in the least influence his sociological convictions. . . . [H]is education had had the curious effect of making things that he read and wrote more real to him than things he saw. Statistics about agricultural labourers were the substance; any real ditcher, ploughmann, or farmer's boy was the shadow. Though he had never noticed it himself, he had a great reluctance, in his work, ever to use such words as "man" or "woman." He preferred to write about "vocational groups," "elements," "classes," and "populations": for, in his own way, he believed as firmly as any mystic in the superior reality of the things that are not seen.[39]

Mark becomes sucked into a giant institution where power is exerted by the careful rationing of information and contrived confusion. The principles behind the transformation N.I.C.E. plans to implement are revealed gradually. They serve as a means for Lewis to explore the distance between theory and reality, between intellect and emotion, between science and the senses. The cost of value-free modern education is clarified. When Mark is physically threatened, he is without resources.

As the full horror of the N.I.C.E future is beginning to reveal itself, the forces of opposition are gathering in that ancient farmhouse. Lewis is so skilled as a storyteller and the development of the tale is so compelling that to reveal the climax would be cruel, but one point is made clear throughout. The "hideous" and inevitable consequences of the relentless pursuit of rationality and efficiency will not be pleasant for either man or beast; but within such a plan, which represents pure evil, reside the seeds of its own collapse, which appears inevitable when finally confronting the forces of good.

Although Lewis is considered to be the quintessential Christian writer, it seems clear that what he promotes is not simply Christianity, but mysticism. What is vital, he seems to be saying, is a sense of something outside ourselves, some tradition with continuity that serves as a moral force for good. It is not clear at all in this book that it needs to be Christian in the conventional sense.

EQUALLY STEEPED in mythology, tradition, and ritual is Robert Graves, poet, novelist, mythographer, critic, and historian, well known as the author of *I, Claudius* and *The White Goddess*. Less well known is his 1949 novel, *Watch the North Wind Rise* (published in England as *Seven Days in New Crete*), a charming and compelling story and a good read, if it can be found It, too, is out of print.

In it, Edward Venn Thomas is taken from his dreams and summoned two thousand years into the future to visit a society on the island of Crete where machines have been outlawed. As he and those who have summoned him get to know one another, the reader learns more about each culture. Venn-Thomas is interested to see how pleasant, solid, and well-proportioned is the room in which he finds himself. "I see that you still burn wood in your grates," he says. "Prophets of my epoch have promised a future in which atomic energy will supersede wood, coal and electricity in domestic heating." His New Crete host replies, "That was a very temporary future and, according to the Brief History, not at all a happy one."[40]

New Crete, he is told, had begun as one of several experiments when the world realized that the industrial-technological paradigm wasn't working. Its model was the late Iron Age, before the invention of gunpowder, and this experiment proved to be the most successful. A pre-Christian, nature-based religion evolved; traditional farming methods made the land fertile; and the community's handicrafts were in demand on the mainland. The challenge was warding off illegal landings on the island. Some immigrants were accepted, others destroyed. Understanding the key to their success,

> the limitations on the use of mechanical contrivances which had been imposed for historical reasons on the original colonists were jealously preserved by their descendants Never having had a chance to become used to explosives, power-driven vehicles, the telephone, artificial light, domestic plumbing and the printing press, they had no need to legislate about their destruction, as (speaking of Utopias) Samuel Butler's Erewhonians did; and

their view of the quays of Corinth [where they traded]—where they were not permitted to land—did nothing to recommend a more advanced form of living. In fact, the sailors made the voyage with increasing distaste; they called Corinth "the terrible city," objecting to it on moral and aesthetic grounds. Eventually it was arranged for all trading to take place at Stalin-nopol, a small port some distance from Corinth, and at the quietest hour of the night, when they would not be exposed to the whir of dock machinery, the unceasing blare of amplified dance music, the ugly outlines of waterside buildings, and the garish, raucous, three-dimensional cartoon comedies telecast every hour in mid-air over the harbour.[41]

No money is exchanged—there is no money, in fact, in New Crete itself. One simply offers what one has produced and takes what one needs from other vendors. There is no measure of material value, therefore no attempt to make trades fair and equitable. It will all work out in the end, because there is no greed. The premier value in New Crete is love:

> They elevated this regard for their sensibilities into the religious principle "nothing without the hand of love"; meaning that no product or process was acceptable unless love had a part in it. No product, for example, turned out by a machine, however harmless it might appear, whether a jam pot, a screw driver or a box of chocolates, had love in it, and neither had any hand-made goods produced for commercial ends only.[42]

In New Crete, common sense rules in the social order that has been created. There are five estates: the captains, the recorders, the commons, the servants, and the magicians. Children who are born into one estate can easily be sent to another when their talents and disposition indicate that it is more suitable.

Graves appreciates that humans are by nature imaginative and inventive and that things mechanical are fascinating and tempting. He recognizes also the dark side of human nature, and New Crete provides outlets for these less desirable impulses in a controlled setting. Wars are fought, but they are symbolic games—no one is killed. And yet death, even murder, does occur. But with reincarnation immediate, it is not especially feared.

As with all utopian visions, Graves's purpose was simply to make us think more seriously about the realities of our own culture and to consider that there might be alternatives to some of our most persistent ideas. Like Forster's, Graves's tone was more philosophical than angry.

The mood among American novelists between 1900 and 1940 was entirely different. They were critical of the hardships imposed on the workers by industrialism but did not translate their criticism as boldly into a rejection of the machine. The strongest voices—those of Upton Sinclair, Henry Roth, John Steinbeck, and Theodore Dreiser—were focused on the human factor, the inherent injustice of the industrial system, rather than on the larger implications of the machine or its impact on the environment and culture. And Dreiser, in *Sister Carrie,* was willing enough to concede the strong appeal of machine-made consumer goods and the materialistic culture they created. In fact, this appeal would be hard to deny. Consumers themselves, though, managed to separate their purchasing habits from the realities of industrialism, and the success of the economy depended upon their ability to do that. With growing consumerism, resistance to the machine grew fainter in literature. Instead, the machine itself became a source of consolation in an alienated world where the drama of life took place either within or before the soft glow of the sickly blue light of the ubiquitous television.

But Lawrence's angry voice could still be heard in poetry. Robinson Jeffers, for instance, who lived and wrote on the California coast from 1914 until 1962, is determinedly anti-modernist both in style and subject. His poetry is filled with a defined loathing for his own species and what it has managed to do (a position that limited his popularity). If other poets managed to draw a shaky line between their explicit agrarian views as expressed in their political writings and those expressed in their literary work, Jeffers did not. His "nature" was not simply a sentimental background against which humans acted out their dramas, as it was for the Romantics; it was at the center of his life. His is a frankly impassioned voice for nature and against its exploitation by humans. He mourns "the broken balance, the hopeless prostration of the earth under men's hands."[43]

In the poem "Salmon-Fishing," he contrasts the living cycle of the salmon run with the actions of the heartless anglers:

> *The days shorten, the south blows wide for showers now,*
> *The south wind shouts to the rivers,*
> *The rivers open their mouths and the salt salmon*
> *Race up into the freshet*
> *In Christmas month against the smoulder and menace*
> *Of a long angry sundown,*
> *Red ash of the dark solstice, you see the anglers,*

Pitiful, cruel, primeval,
Like the priests of the people that built Stonehenge,
Dark, silent forms, performing
Remote solemnities in the red shallows
Of the river's mouth at the year's turn,
Drawing landward their live bullion, the bloody mouths
And scales full of the sunset
Twitch on the rocks, no more to wander at will
The wild Pacific pasture nor wanton and spawning
Race up into fresh water.[44]

Jeffers gathers his full-blown passion for nature and flings it at the pitiful humans who exploit it so mindlessly. His poems are filled with a terrifying violence. In "Original Sin," he imagines the "man-handed ground-ape" capturing a woolly mammoth in a pit, unable to kill it with sticks and stones and inventing a new and different way—a fire that will burn it to death.

Jeffers is quintessentially Luddite in his favoring of the unconscious over the conscious, his reliance on the intuitive, his fear of what technology will do, and his preference for nature unsullied by humankind. Like William Morris, he was fully prepared to leave no gap between his principles and his lifestyle. His house is called Tor for the craggy knoll on which it was built, then a treeless headland almost empty of structures. It is low to the ground, Tudor-like. Oil lamps and candles were the only means of illumination until electricity was installed in 1949. Later he built Hawk Tower as a retreat for his wife, then the cottage was enlarged with a dining room and later another wing. Embedded into this house and wall were stones from all over the world that he, his wife, and his children had collected, which he felt represented a kind of sacred continuity.

Jeffers, along with John Muir, would become a strong influence on the deep ecology movement. Edward Abbey and Wallace Stegner, two of the strongest of the literary defenders of Western wilderness in the twentieth century, are direct descendents of Jeffers, and they both had an impact on the ideas of the deep ecologists as well.

Abbey, noted as one of the most irascible, contrary, and passionate literary figures of our time, died in 1989 but remains a cult figure. His novel *The Monkey Wrench Gang* (1975), in which an odd assortment of nature defenders attempts to dismantle in various unorthodox and illegal ways the infrastructure of modern civilization—roads, bridges, and mines—is credited with inspiring the radical EarthFirst! organization. The link with the

Luddites is explicit; an epigraph at the front of the book includes the Byron quote: "Down with all kings but King Ludd."

The book plays on common frustrations, but Abbey's unlikely characters do something about them. Confronted with a classroom filled with stale air, unopenable windows, and students who docilely explain that opening a window messes up the air conditioning, Doc picks up a chair and smashes one open. One of the motley crew dreams of a world when technology has been destroyed:

> When the cities are gone, he thought, and all the ruckus has died away, when sunflowers push up through the concrete and asphalt of the forgotten interstate freeways, when the Kremlin and the pentagon are turned into nursing homes for generals . . . why then, why then by God maybe free men and wild women on horses . . . can roam the sagebrush canyon lands in freedom . . . until, he reflected soberly, and bitterly, and sadly, until the next age of ice and iron comes down, and the engineers and the farmers and the general motherfuckers come back again.[45]

His mad team of saboteurs forms a plan out of their passionate hatred of technology:

> "I hate that dam," Smith said. "That dam flooded the most beautiful canyon in the world."
>
> "We know," Hayduke said. "We feel the same way you do. But let's think about easier things first. I'd like to knock down some of them power lines they're stringing across the desert. And those new tin bridges up by Hite. And the goddamned road-building they're doing all over the canyon country. We could put in a good year just taking the fucking goddamned bull-dozers apart."
>
> "Hear, hear," the doctor said. "And don't forget the billboards. And the strip mines. And the pipelines. And the new railroad from Black mesa to Page. And the coal-burning power plants. And the copper smelters. And the uranium mines. And the nuclear power plants. And the computer centers. And the land and cattle companies. And the wildlife poisoners."[46]

It's easy to see the subversive strength of this kind of writing, but don't expect a happy ending.

It is, however, Abbey's intensely powerful essays in such books as *Desert Solitaire* that have enthralled two generations of environmentalists. It is the authenticity of his writing that makes the strongest impression. He is in the desert and part of the experience, never the bystander. With vivid language and minute and accurate observation, the desert is felt through the pain it can inflict and the awful loneliness it can produce. The desert and its flora and fauna maintain an independence that resists penetration or even comprehension, and it is that quality that Abbey feels is sacred and should not be violated. His disgust at the Park Service for making wild places more accessible, which he spells out in _Polemic: Industrial Tourism and the National Parks,_ is powerful reading for the more radical in the environmental movement. Abbey is a true revolutionary in that it is virtually impossible to read _The Monkey Wrench Gang,_ with its extraordinary mixture of anger, humor and passion, and emerge unmoved.

The Luddite Rebellion began with passion—against the machines that were destroying the livelihoods and way of life of craftsmen and skilled laborers. The poets of the time linked industrialization to the threat to nature. As technology and industrialization proceeded, compromises were made with organized labor, which gradually grew docile and compliant. Nature had no unions and its supporters few weapons. Today many of those who continue to see technology as a threat have shifted the focus to nature and, with the passion of the original Luddites, direct their outrage and occasionally their violence upon the chain saws and all-terrain vehicles and feller-bunchers and bulldozers of the world, standing up and standing in for a part of the world that is defenseless in the face of mindless mechanization.

Elements of neo-Luddite thinking—often of a barely repressed anger against the Leviathan of technology, at other times simply a stinging awareness of the heavy human footprint—are not hard to see once the eye is conditioned to look for them.

The same powerful commitment to the environment seen in Abbey, with a similar ability to express outrage—although without the obvious incitement to violence—is evident in the work, among others, of such contemporary poets as Gary Snyder and W. S. Merwin. Snyder's poem, "Front Lines," for instance, has a clear sense of violation, doing much more than hinting at the impending rape of the landscape by developers. In Merwin's poem "The Last One," the arrogance and thoughtlessness of the human relationship to nature, which amounts to a technologically-enhanced cult of appropriation and wanton destruction, is expressed with a subdued ferocity.

It is as if these poets have picked up the Luddite bludgeons, substituting words for weapons.

CHAPTER TEN

The Clockwork God

NOT LONG AGO, A FRIEND OF MINE MOVED INTO the house that had belonged to her parents. It is an old farmhouse, respectfully restored, filled with books and antiques. Over the mantle hangs a lovely old clock that long ago had stopped. It never occurred to her that it might actually run until her brother in law asked about it; then, out of curiosity, she found the key and gave it a wind. It keeps good time.

Each day my friend must wind her clock, and the ritual has become an important part of her life, she tells me. Winding it puts the day in order. If she is distracted and forgets, the clock stops, and when it does she feels unsettled; out of sync. The day no longer feels as promising; a certain balance has been lost.

Listening to her tell this story, I could see how it expressed much of our ambivalence toward machines and technology. It has probably always been a confused relationship. Some technologies we prefer in one form but not in another. In others the clear advantages overcome any disadvantages. Some we clearly struggle with. Mostly, we don't think about the relationship at all. We know technology has transformed what we do, but seldom do we give much thought to the subtle ways in which it has changed how we think. But my friend has made the rare connection between a particular kind of mechanical device and its effect on her mood. Technology is stealthy. It becomes a part of society, of our lives, sometimes an extension of our own bodies. It has the potential to change subtly what we do and how we feel. We adjust our living to the pace and demands of the machines, often without realizing it.

Historian and philosopher Lewis Mumford, writing in the 1930s, paid particular attention to the role of mechanical timekeeping in preparing humans for the transition from what he called the ecotechnic to the paleotechnic and neotechnic periods of technological development.[1] Each phase is distinguished by the raw materials it employs; by the energy it uses; by the relationship of the worker and the consumer to the product; and finally, by the degree of complexity of the system that creates the phase. Each of these factors, he proposes, has a direct impact on the society in which the technology appears and to which it is applied. He uses the example of the quill pen to illustrate the ecotechnic. It is a somewhat crude device, cheap, shaped by the user, with close links to agriculture. And yet it is easily adapted to personal preferences: individuals once created their own pens from feathers using a sharp knife. The steel pen, the next step, represents the paleotechnic stage: still cheap, uniform, and durable, but clearly the product of someone else: a mine, a steel mill, and a factory. Although it may come in a half-dozen points in an attempt to accommodate itself to the style of the user, it is, in fact, the user who must now adapt his own style and preferences to the points available. He can no longer fabricate his own pen to this new standard of uniformity and is thus dependent upon the system, from miner to shop owner, that provides the pen. Should the system fail for some reason, he may find it difficult to obtain a replacement pen. Thus his independence and individuality have been sacrificed for convenience and standardization—the trade-off being the assumption, whether correct or not, that the pen will always be available. There is an element of faith in this relationship that is seldom considered. Faith is there when we reach for the light switch.

The fountain pen, Mumford says, with its automatic action and durable tip, is a typical neotechnic product. Its various parts might have been invented at different times, and it is the assembly of these complex inventions—not the inventions themselves—that creates the device. And so we have moved from the simplicity of the tool to the potential complexity of the machine. To put it simply, he says, the ecotechnic phase is a water and wood complex, the paleotechnic phase is a coal and iron complex, and the neotechnic phase is an electricity and alloy complex.

Technology has now taken on something of a life of its own in society to become what Mumford called The Machine, a system so entrenched, so influential, so much a part of our living and our thinking that it has become virtually invisible. We are conditioned to machine expectations in unsuspecting ways. In December I notice the rows of Christmas trees lined up in the lot managed by the Boy Scouts. They are perfect, every one, with a perfection never or seldom found in nature. They have been clipped and groomed into the machine version of a tree, uniform and standardized, which we have all come to expect, with small variations in height to satisfy individual needs. They are the products of a tree farm, and they come via trucks. They are paleotechnic trees. Everywhere one looks, there are example of machine standards. Zoning restrictions have typically been shaped not to people and their needs but to the car. Tomatoes are bred not for taste but to be picked by machine, transported by truck, and stored in refrigerators, capable of withstanding a bounce or two in the process. The computer-written letter now has such dominance that a business letter written by hand might as well come stamped KOOK. The machine has shaped our expectations of everything, creating a pattern to which we are now obliged to conform ourselves, and we do so unconsciously. And it all began so benignly.

The transition from one phase to another was neither so dramatic nor so abrupt as schoolbooks might lead one to believe. The evolution of societies that sought simple mechanical means of performing tasks more easily to our present machine-dominated world was gradual. Inventions built on earlier inventions, and the origins of our modern technical age are found in developments that began at various points from the tenth to the eighteenth century nor did the ecotonic stage end abruptly. The clipper ship, one of its finest manifestations, appeared in the nineteenth century. The Amish are still improving horse-drawn farm equipment.

Nor was the early ecotechnic phase as primitive as one is lead to believe. Although its politics were complex and certainly not always just, the Middle

Ages—roughly from the fifth to the fifteenth century—was a time when great cities were built, landscapes were cultivated, the visual arts were highly developed, costumes and social customs were elaborate, and human thought was innovative. Thus, in many ways, says Mumford, the Renaissance did not represent the dawn of a new age, but its twilight; for as the mechanical arts advanced, the humane arts declined and receded. What he meant was that certain particularly human activities, customs, skills, crafts, and traditions were about to be sacrificed to the machine. In the seventeenth century, a long history of progressive invention was coming to a climax. The future would be based on mathematics, fine manipulation, exact measurement, and accurate timing. Accurate timing, in fact, involved the first three.

Today most clocks run automatically on small batteries so efficient that their eventual failure comes as a surprise. There is no predictability or ritual to replacing a clock battery, as clock-winding once represented. It is just necessary maintenance of the machines that keep us ticking, for clock time has replaced the sun, abolished the seasons. The clock is now ruler of the universe, ordering the march, playing the tune to which we step—all of us very nearly, the entire developed world, tuned to the opening bell, the noonday whistle, the last train, the evening news. And so accustomed to living by the clock have we become that we scarcely give it a thought; can hardly imagine what it must have been like when the sunrise or the rooster started the day and the evening's darkness ended it, when the stomach set mealtimes, the baby was suckled when it cried, and the news arrived when it arrived. Then there was a natural rhythm to the day, tied to the world around us. Now time is completely artificial, imposed by the clock and transformed abruptly when it is arbitrarily changed twice a year to the confusion of cows and chickens and my dog, who now must wait for her dinner or have it (to her delight) an hour early, according to the season when the change occurs. We humans just reset our clocks and march on.

Another friend tells me that the clock is her favorite invention and refers me to Daniel Boorstin for a description of its virtues. If Boorstin recognizes that the clock is probably the most profound technology ever created in terms of its long-term effects on culture, he isn't saying. He is a techno-enthusiast, content to look at the obvious rather than the subtle changes wrought by technology. In *The Discoverers*, he says:

While man allowed his time to be parsed by the changing cycles of daylight he remained a slave of the sun. To become the master of his time, to assimilate night into the day, to slice his life into neat, usable portions, he had to find a way to mark off precise small portions (not only equal hours, but even minutes and seconds and parts of seconds). He would have to make a machine.[2]

What can Boorstin be thinking? "To become the master of his time"? Even casual reflection on the nature of our relationship to time would reveal that the invention of the clock made *other people* the masters of our days, whether it's the boss, the dentist, the hairdresser, the stationmaster, or the last mail pickup. Our lives are counted out not in T. S. Eliot's coffee spoons but by a relentless ticking that gives urgency to every moment, which in turn becomes a constant reminder of the brevity of life and the inevitability of death. The world before the clock had a natural rhythm, an infinite quality; each dawn a new chance, each season a promise of tomorrow. Now the century, the decade, the year, the week, the day, the hour, the minutes, the seconds are ticking away, in a measured, finite day, in a measured, finite life; each tick a lost opportunity; all the unfulfilled promises giving birth to endless, inevitable frustration. And this frustration is now the universal disease, for with this division and redivision came the concept of saving time and adding time and, of course, wasting time. And yet, "in time-keeping," Lewis Mumford points out in *Technics and Civilization,* "men counted numbers; and finally, as the habit grew, only numbers counted."[3]

Only numbers counted: That sounds like hyperbole. But think of the test grades, the measured gallons, the pennies, the miles; the two cups of this and the four sheets of that. Consider the polls, the ratings, the numbers of dead, the pounds of flesh, the pages typed. Think of decisions based on cost-benefit analysis; lives valued by age, by bank balance; safety pitted against profits and cleanup costs. Think of the drinking age, the driving age, the senior-citizen discount age. Counting is much of what we do, and it was the clock that propelled us down that path. It marked a turning point in human civilization that set the stage for further mechanization.

There are any number of acknowledged experts on technology who have looked at the darker side of mechanization, and my aim here is to look more closely at some of their ideas, incorporating them into a brief survey of where we began and where we have ended up. There is Jacques Ellul's *The Technological Society,* Siegfried Giedion's *Mechanization Takes Command,*

Friedrich Georg Juenger's *The Failure of Technology,* Albert Borgmann's *Technology and the Character of Contemporary Life,* E. F. Schumacher's *Small Is Beautiful,* and Langdon Winner's *Autonomous Technology,* to name only a few. More recent books include Neil Postman's *Technopoly,* Edward Goldsmith's *The Way,* Carolyn Merchant's *The Death of Nature,* Chellis Glendinning's *When Technology Wounds,* Stephanie Mills's *Turning away from Technology,* and Jerry Mander's *In the Absence of the Sacred.* But among them, Lewis Mumford stands out for the breadth of his thinking.

Today, in the era of specialization, the vastness that Mumford tackled is breathtaking. He wrote decisively, often brilliantly, about technology, but also about philosophy, literature, art, culture, and architecture, among other subjects. *Technics and Civilization* set the stage for a larger work focused on the impact of technology that he called *The Myth of the Machine,* which would include *The Conduct of Life, Technics and Human Development* and *The Pentagon of Power.* He remains the quintessential Luddite philosopher not simply because he was critical of the ends to which technology had been put but because, in his words, his books "did not regard scientific discovery and technological invention as the sole object of human existence; for I have taken life itself to be the primary phenomenon, and creativity, rather than the 'conquest of nature,' as the ultimate criterion of man's biological and cultural success."[4] *Life,* that simple yet all-encompassing term. It was what Ruskin and Morris and Thoreau were after, that reification of what it means to be human, living in the real world.

Mumford focuses on the clock because it was the first instrument to take what was a natural and organic occurrence, the day, and divide it into artificial increments that had little relationship to what was actually occurring. Order was being applied.

The appeal of order had always been strong in the human species. Long before the clock, there were social groups that superimposed an artificial structure on the lives of their members, but the clock was especially important for monasteries, for the military, and then for commerce. The clock was well suited to the regimentation of monastic life even before the thirteenth century, when the cities, with their bankers and traders, began to demand an organized routine.

This dependence on timekeeping, Mumford says, "helped to give human enterprise the regular collective beat and rhythm of the machine; for the

clock is not merely a means of keeping track of the hours, but of synchro-
nizing the actions of men." As humans began increasingly to gather in
towns, "The bells of the clock tower almost defined urban existence." By the
fourteenth century, the first truly modern clock had been invented, and
"time-keeping passed into time-serving and time-accounting and time-
rationing."5

To look more closely not at the discovery but at the actual use of the clock
is to discover, along with Mumford, that its product is seconds and minutes,
a division of life into increments. The rule of the clock bears little relationship to a reality in which days have different lengths, pulses different beats,
the year its own seasons; to the agricultural rhythms we lived by when we
were closer to the land. "The shepherd measures from the time the ewes
lambed; the farmer measures back to the day of sowing or forward to the
harvest," says Mumford. And so the clock, "by its essential nature . . .
dissociated time from human events and helped create the belief in an inde
pendent world of mathematically measurable sequences: the special world
of science."6 The very artificiality of timekeeping laid the foundation for
other artificial ordering devices. It presented a reliable, if awkward and illu-
sionary, model for ordering a disorderly universe.

The clock was well suited to enhancing the authority and power of those
already in control; to imposing order for those enterprises that required
order. It was a managing device. And as a consequence of its invention, the
way humans related to time, and thus the way they thought about and inter-
acted with the natural world, and with one another, was transformed.

"That man until recently got along well enough without measuring time
precisely," says Jacques Ellul, "is something we never even think about, and
that we do not think about it shows to what a degree we have been affected
by technique."7 What has been surrendered is what Ellul calls the "psychological and biological tempo" of life. Nature's time had been concrete. Now
it became abstract. And although time can be reduced to increments,
controlling and studying the increments creates the illusion of power and
understanding—yet, stripped of context, the increments tell us nothing
at all.

Ellul's thoughts echo Mumford's: "Time, which had been the measure of
organic sequences, was broken and dissociated. Human life ceased to be an
ensemble, a whole, and became a disconnected set of activities."8 Sepa-

rated from real life, time became mere quantity. It was the quantification of the universe—the breaking down into numbers, increments, isolated pieces and parts—that would bring us to where we are today, struggling with an alienating world of our own creation.

What took humans so long to invent the clock? Was it not needed before? Was it perhaps not wanted? The patterns of different cultures demand different devices. A society will invent what it requires. There have been societies, although rare, that resisted inventions—or even outlawed them—until they were imposed on them by stronger cultures. There have been artificial restraints put on certain technological changes by guilds that wanted to protect their members from job loss, in fact. But there does appear to be a certain inevitability to the "relentless march of progress," a phrase that has been repeated often enough to feel like dogma. Human beings are inventive, imaginative, curious, and love a challenge. One thing leads to another. Humans are contrary. Forbidden is an exciting place.

Ellul suggests that the Greeks intentionally resisted technology not out of blind technophobia but because they had something to protect: a balanced, harmonious way of life based on moderation and self-control. Technological innovation, says Ellul, represented brute force.[9] (Nor would relying on slaves for unpleasant or heavy work, as the Greeks did, have been an incentive to the development of labor-saving machines.) And yet Mumford would argue that in this very search for a precise balance between extremes, in the focus on the mean and on perfection, the Greeks were introducing a mathematical element and thus laying the groundwork for future mechanization. Perhaps both were right.

The Romans were more obviously inventive, building their roads and aqueducts straight across the countryside, covering the shortest distance in the shortest time, the concept of efficiency metaphorically conquering nature. "Roman law, Roman administration, Roman sanitation, Roman engineering were everywhere," says Mumford. Order and system triumphed and, for a period, reigned. "But the inner logic that held all these parts together, the structure of meaning, collapsed: as life became mechanically disciplined it became spiritually incoherent."[10] A great civilization crumpled in on itself. (In Mumford, there are always allusions to the balance between the mechanical and the spiritual; between the concrete and the metaphysical, hinting always that in this balance lies satisfaction.)

Technology's roots extend even further into the human past, though. The desire to control the world around us connects us to the past as an enduring fantasy: If only we could wave a wand and the rains would come, or the grasshopper plague would go away, or the lead would turn to gold. Perhaps the idea that humans could in some way control nature rather than always be controlled by it developed as early as fire. From then on, the idea was compelling. The origins of smithing, weaving, brick-making, tanning, brewing, and dying lie thousands of years in the past. Well before the Romans, the Egyptians had used the waterwheel; and China had paper, the magnetic needle (by way of the Middle East), and gunpowder. The ideas from these cultures spread from one to another with the ease of windblown seeds, nourished when they fell on fertile ground. What we think of as the modern machine age of European and American industry was actually a long, unbroken tradition of inventiveness encouraged by need. And yet there was a difference. "They had the machines," says Mumford, "but they did not develop The Machine."[11]

At a certain point, the process of inventiveness and the exchange of ideas, the complexity of the inventions themselves, and the synergy among them increased dramatically. The explanation for the quickening pace of invention in fifteenth-century Europe lies in the confluence of certain ideas and trends. The role of Christianity in the process cannot be overlooked. It was itself more orderly (or ordered) than the cultures of the East, where nature gods prevailed and the links to nature remained more compelling. At the same time, the church almost always clung to older ways and looked upon some technological innovations with suspicion, but there is no reason that both cannot be true. It is perfectly possible to support a concept that is in fact undermining what you believe in.[12]

It would be the people of Western Europe who would develop the "physical sciences and exact arts to a point that no other culture had reached, and to adapt the whole mode of life to the pace and the capacities of the machine," says Mumford.[13] The sorcerer and the alchemist were the first scientists. Science was the eternal appeal of magic. It was, says Mumford, "the bridge that united fantasy with technology, the dream of power with the engines of fulfillment. . . . No one can put his finger on the place when magic became science, where empiricism became systematic experimentalism, where alchemy became chemistry, where astrology became astronomy."[14]

But eventually it happened. Each passing invention—the telescope, the microscope, the printing press—added to the sense of control until anything seemed possible and everything could be improved. Today the human body itself is a candidate for genetic improvement, as if the old model hadn't proved itself sufficiently clever and adaptable. And yet the reality is that at some point—and it came fairly early, perhaps beginning with the printing press—humans actually began to relinquish control and to become tenders of the machine. If on the one hand the printing press allowed the democratization of ideas and encouraged literacy, it would on the other begin to reshape the concept of what a book is, dictate the nature of the illustrations, and impose a new order—and with it, a new way of thinking.

In *The New Industrial State* (1967), the economist John Kenneth Galbraith warned, "I am led to the conclusion, which I trust others will find persuasive, that we are becoming the servants in thought, as in action, of the machine we have created to serve us."[15] And yet, the effect of the machine on the social order and on human thinking had far greater impact than simply ordering the day—or even transforming the exterior world into numbers, or encouraging the cold-hearted side of capitalism, or turning us into techno-tenders. It would change the way humans thought about themselves. And it would take on something of a life of its own. The German philosopher Martin Heidegger would see the development of technology as something out of control and unstoppable. There was a depressing resignation to the view. Technological advance, he would observe,

> will move faster and faster and can never be stopped. In areas of his existence man will be encircled ever more tightly by the forces of technology. These forces, which every minute claim, enchain, drag along, press and impose upon man under the form of some technical contrivance or other— these forces . . . have moved long since beyond his will and have outgrown his capacity for decision.[16]

We have, unwittingly, been taken over by a system because we have made small yet cumulative decisions to trade independence and health for the comfort and convenience the megamachine provides. Denying the risks makes the decisions possible.

The foundation for the shift in perspective from the tool-using artisan, in control of his own mechanics, to the victim (if sometimes a comfortable one) of a centralized, remote-controlled, power-driven modern technological machine, was laid early on by the thinking of a series of luminaries from Copernicus and Kepler to Galileo, Descartes, Leibnitz, and Newton. New concepts of time, motion, space, mass, and gravitation transformed the pre-vailing view of the natural world into one in which mathematics ruled. The legacy of these thinkers was a universe composed of units, a quantifiable reality.

Ideas were the key to change; a shift in the way one looked at things. The German astronomer Johannes Kepler (1571–1630) had said, in his first volume of *Opera,* "As the ear is made to perceive sound and the eye to perceive color, so the mind has been formed to understand not all sorts of things but quantities."[17] Numbers again. Earlier still, the English philosopher Roger Bacon (1214–1294) had come up with a similar notion: that without mathematics there could be no exact knowledge of things. Galileo, the Italian astronomer, mathematician, and physicist who lived from 1564 until 1642, picked up on these ideas. The universe, he said, could only be understood by deciphering its code, which was written in the language of mathematics. The world was geometric—circles, triangles, squares—and it could be ordered by viewing it through the lens of time, motion, mass, and quantity. In his own words:

> As soon as I form a conception of a material or corporeal substance, I simul-taneously feel the necessity of conceiving that it has boundaries of some shape or other; that relatively to others it is great or small; that it is in this or that place, in this or that time; that it is in motion or at rest; that it touches, or does not touch, another body; that it is unique, rare, or common; nor can I, by any act of imagination, disjoin it from these qualities. But I do not find myself absolutely compelled to apprehend it as necessarily accompanied by such conditions as that it must be white or red, bitter or sweet, sonorous or silent, smelling sweetly or disagreeably; and if the senses had not pointed out these qualities language and imagination alone could never have arrived at them. Therefore I think that these tastes, smells, colors, etc., with regard to the object in which they appear to reside, are nothing more than mere names. They exist only in the sensitive body, for when the living creature is removed all these qualities are carried off and annihilated, although we have imposed particular names upon them, and would fain persuade our-selves that they truly and in fact exist. I do not believe that there exists any-thing in external bodies for exciting tastes, smells, and sounds, etc., size, shape, quantity, and motion.[18]

Curiously, in an era of new eyeglasses and microscopes, when the senses had never been used as well, they were being devalued unless observations could be quantified and thus verified. Abstraction and isolation are undeniably useful in the process of scientific observation, but when an organism is removed from its setting, seen not as part of a whole but as an isolated object, it tends to die or to act in an unnatural manner. The mechanical view created a universe that Kepler and Galileo saw as consisting of dead matter. And yet, in the living organism, the elements that Galileo rejected because they could not be quantified would eventually emerge as crucial. Mathematics has its obvious uses and is vital in comprehending the universe, but the subjective elements were dismissed far too easily precisely because they were difficult or impossible to quantify.

The real world, as Mumford and scores of others have pointed out, is one of great complexity and extraordinary richness, only a small part of which consents to be measured, counted, or weighed. Says Mumford:

> Form, color, odor, tactile sensation, emotions, appetites, feelings, images, dreams, words, symbolic abstractions—that plenitude of life which even the humblest being in some degree exhibits—cannot be resolved in any mathematical equation or converted into a geometric metaphor [although many have tried] without eliminating a large part of the relevant experience.[19]

What Galileo was doing, with the best of intentions, was devaluing the totality of human experience for that fraction that can be measured or validated quantitatively in terms of mass, weight, and motion. And Kepler, notes Neil Postman, had separated moral and intellectual values. By divorcing the authority of the church's model of the universe from the one that reason told him existed, Kepler was taking another small but necessary step toward mechanization. If morality, whether it was the church's or the individual's, had no place in the development of science and the machine, there were potentially no limits. The machine was on its own. Nothing was sacred.

Not even the human body. As if his mechanical, mathematical worldview were not damaging enough, Galileo began dismembering (metaphorically) the human body; treating each part—eye, ear, brain—as if it operated independently instead of in concert with the rest of the body. This is ridiculous, of course, but it is startling how persistently the concept remained viable, how long it endured: tainting experiments, enabling studies carried out on the "perfect" dead organ or organism, allowing it to speak for the living, laying the groundwork for future collective dehumanizing practices, and distorting medicine.[20]

"With his exclusive preoccupation with quantity, Galileo had in effect disqualified the real world," says Mumford.[21] If what was real was only what could be counted and measured, the optimal model was mechanical, and the human was encouraged to conform to the new standard. With Galileo's model, "to be redeemed from the organic, the autonomous, and the subjective, man must be turned into a machine," says Mumford, "or better still, become an integral part of a larger machine that the new method would help create."[22] As a legacy, we live today in a world ordered by the blind, the deaf, the soulless, and the senseless machine model—the counters and the measurers deny reality, and it is no wonder that life has become a struggle against something that can be felt and sensed and yet remains difficult to define or explain or escape. The machine throbs away in an artificially ordered universe.

This was all theory. Galileo himself was cultured, passionate, religious, and sensual, every bit a real human being; never suspecting that "the ultimate consequence of the mechanical world picture would be an environment like our present one: fit only for machines to live in," says Mumford.[23] But this curious tendency to separate idea from reality has always caused problems.

Shall we, for what evolved from their ideas, condemn these early thinkers?

Seen in context, Galileo and those who followed him were shaking off the medieval view of the world, which was theologically based—the only truths being those established by divine revelation illuminated by dialectic exchanges—alongside of which coexisted a murky underworld of ignorance and superstition. Careful observation and well-planned experiments were valuable contributions to understanding the world. Eventually these approaches to study and experimentation would bring great respect to the vocation of the detached, objective scientist who pursued essential truths free from self-interest or dreams of patents and profits—a rare and endangered species today. And interestingly, the murky underworld of ignorance and superstition remains—with some of the nonsense perpetrated by science itself, cloaked in the white-coated disguise of authority.

The trouble was, the mathematical view made examining the world so much easier. Quantifications enabled quick comparisons, and if they weren't always accurate or realistic, the ease of the comparison could override any qualms about inaccuracy. Error, in various forms, was tolerated for the sake of convenience—a practice that continues today, whether it is in the "rounding off" to the tidy millions of this or that or in ideologically generated estimates or in results blatantly ignored and assumed to be incorrect because they do not fit the theory. Here was "information" that could be transmitted, bypassing some of the dangers of interpretation. How could it not appeal to someone who wanted to apply new standards to the study of the real world? Yet today, as narrowly designed studies contradict one another with bewildering frequency, we might well wonder just what has been achieved. The public, schooled to expect the certainty of numbers, finds that numbers alone fail. Today there is good science, bad science, and bought-and-paid-for science. The average person is confounded by contradiction while the knowledgeable know simply to be wary.

René Descartes was to take this mathematical vision of the world and fuse it to a mechanical model of reasoning, and in the process leave an indelible mark on Western thinking. Both he and Francis Bacon saw the possibility that self-determination could be achieved through the appropriate application of human reason. Descartes's solution to avoiding the dangers of subjectivity, that supposed nemesis of reason, was beautifully spelled out in his *Discourse on Method*, which established a system for experimentation. The strong pull of curiosity that finds satisfaction in the discovery of relationships, systems, and underlying patterns is among humanity's great strengths. Applied with appropriate restraint within a structured approach, it would attempt to unravel the mysteries of the natural world. Thinking was intentionally systematized. But along with curiosity, there was an irrepressible urge to control and change. Descartes made clear that his goal of "knowing the force and action of fire, water, air, the stars," was to "render ourselves the Lords and possessors of nature."[24] This was not a power-hungry urge to dominate but a desire simply to challenge disease, hunger, and hard work; yet it's easy enough now to see where this could lead. Control would eventually overtake the effort to improve the human condition and would become the paramount goal. In addition, the urge to dominate nature fit in rather too neatly with seventeenth-century ambitions to explore, colonize, rule and then to develop a commercial and manufacturing base. Developing the full human potential, an early goal, took a backseat as well. But without knowing exactly where it would lead, decoding natural systems clearly seemed a desirable goal, even a laudable one. Now even the method appears to be problematic. Descartes's famous "I think, therefore I am," seemed a harmless enough acknowledgment of the prodigious power of the human brain; and yet, just as Galileo had, Descartes was neatly severing one part of the body from every other and from its environment. The brain without sensual input cannot, in fact, function. And the "I" part of that famous observation, alone and isolated with brain, neatly abandoned the history of human enterprise and tradition. Yet a decontextualized, isolated human thought, bereft of personal experience and a collective history, is only a momentary, indescribable experience. To function best, the brain is connected to an individual in a rich environmental context associated with a tradition, linked to history, and capable of envisioning a future.

The appeal of the mechanical model is, in some ways, easy to understand. The machines of Descartes's age were relatively simple. One could look at them and see how they worked fairly easily. It was a short hop from there to assuming that the natural world must operate in a similar, if theoretically more complex, way; and from there it was but a step to thinking, as Descartes did, that the working of living organisms might be understood and explained if they were approached as if they were mechanical. Descartes noted that the basic physical functions of the body bore a striking resemblance to the "variety of movements performed by the different automata, or moving machines fabricated by human industry."[25] To understand them meant taking them apart. The impact of the clock on society and thought is evidenced by Descartes's description of the functions of the human body:

> I want you to regard these functions as taking place naturally in this machine because of the very arrangement of its parts, neither more nor less than do the movements of a clock or other automaton from the weights and wheels, so that there is no need on their account to suppose in it any soul vegetative or sensitive or any principle of life other than blood.[26]

What was the human body, he suggested, other than "a machine made by the hand of God"? But perhaps the most consistently unhelpful of Descartes's many ideas was his model for examination, which was to isolate, take apart, and separate out what could be counted and measured down to the smallest possible particle. By knowing and understanding the parts, the whole system could be comprehended, he felt certain.

As Mumford says, "Unfortunately, isolation and abstraction, while important to orderly research and refined symbolic representation, are likewise conditions under which real organisms die, or at least cease to function effectively."[27] Disassembly had demystified life. A clocklike ordering was a natural result.

Practical results benefited from this approach; and yet, as a method for understanding the world, taking things apart is less important than putting them back together. The part is now understood to look different; to act different; and, in fact, to be different when this disorganization is applied, but to correct Cartesian thinking would take centuries. In fact, it is still being applied regularly and consistently. What is genetic engineering but the direct descendant of Cartesian thinking?—an approach that operates on the assumption that a bit of DNA will perform the same function in a new setting that it performed in the old, as if it were not influenced by what surrounds it.

Mumford proposes a simple example to show the fallacy of causality. If the clock had been unknown in Descartes's time but had suddenly fallen from the sky, whereupon it was disassembled and every part examined in a diligent, objective, reductionist manner, each part might become known, even to the molecular level, "but meanwhile the clock itself disappeared. With this disappearance, the design that held the parts together vanished, along with any visible clue to the function each part performs, how the assembled mechanism interlocks, and for what purpose the clock once existed."[28]

The clock can be understood, in fact, only as a working whole. If somehow by chance it were reassembled without a subjective knowledge of its ultimate purpose, "the dead mechanism would remain mysterious and its purpose baffling. Even the twelve numbers on the dial would mean nothing in a culture that had never divided the day into twice twelve hours," says Mumford.[29]

The progression of mechanical thinking can be illustrated nicely by looking at the development of the book itself. Early books were written to be read in their entirety. The intention of the writer was to relay the essence of his thoughts and his being as a single whole. Then the convenience of page numbers was instituted. Then chapters. Each allowed the book to be read in parts, rather than taken as a whole. Footnotes are a fairly recent addition. One contemporary writer uses both ordinary and boldface type. The individual in a hurry need only read the boldface to grasp an overview of the book; the leisurely reader who wants more can read both. The book becomes something of a buffet dinner, with its parts able to be picked up and consumed as desired, and in this vision, the whole is no longer important. Computer hypertext takes us further down the path toward a concept of knowledge as nothing more than the accumulation of isolated increments of information. Hypertext no longer accords any value to the whole.

It is easy enough in hindsight to see where this incrementalization would lead. Looking at the world in ever smaller divisions and parts resulted inevitably in specialization. Out of specialization emerged the expert. If only the experts have correct information, the ordinary individual is no longer entitled to an opinion. Experience, observation, tradition, and common sense were all devalued in this process. The ordinary individual is thus deprived of the ability to make judgments and decisions without the assistance of experts and, at the same time, relieved of responsibility. The result is irresponsibility. Everything can be left to someone else. There is a certain comfort in this, but there is also an enormous forfeiture of control and autonomy.

And yet the specialists themselves, focused by definition on the minutia of their specialty, typically lack any larger picture. They have no vision of the whole, no notion of how their information or invention might affect the larger world—which leaves decision-making in the hands of managers, who need to know nothing except how to manage the information received from experts. The death of individuals with a larger vision has meant the absence of adequate ways of dealing with the complex questions presented by the new technologies, such as cloning and bioengineering. And this lack leaves society vulnerable to those who have a monopoly on information and the most to gain by implementing it.

To be fair, there was in the Cartesian method a healthy rejection of misguided conjecture and ignorance. Coupled with Francis Bacon's contribution to science of inductive reasoning, the ground was prepared for modern thinking. We can see what an advance this was over rank superstition and misinformation. And no doubt the world had much to gain from Bacon's conviction that the principal aim of work was "to advance the happiness of mankind" and Descartes's belief that human benefits of health and well-being would accrue from knowing the basic laws of nature. The thoughts of the two philosophers were complementary, and a new age had begun.

The new age would continue to change, because the tenets of science and technology assumed that there were no real limits to the expansion of knowledge, material goods, or environmental control, says Mumford. And Langdon Winner, who has examined in depth the question of an out-of-control technology as it relates to political thought, points out that Bacon, in setting new power for humans as his goal, made a "direct comparison between the powers and goals of his new science and the powers and goals of politics"—a relationship that would come to have significance. But although the goals are similar, Bacon hoped to prove, science is superior.[30]

Eighteenth-century Europe saw enormous political change that was due, in no small part, to the expanded use of the printing press, with its ability to facilitate the spread of ideas and encourage independent thinking. But along with the new politics came a new abundance of consumer goods and greater expectations of improved living standards by the middle and upper classes. The new inventions—improved looms, the blast furnace, the steamboat—really had utility and practicality in mind, says Ellul. The aim was the "easing of human life," with the additional goal of bringing more pleasure into it and simplifying labor. There was a new sense of possibility, he says, when it "seemed evident that the problems of life would be resolved when men were able to work less while consuming more."[31]

As the nineteenth century began, there was no dramatic change in thinking. Technology still drove science, and the systematic development of inventions was not yet possible. Yet even though the conditions of the previous century favored technological advance, Ellul says, that alone could not have explained the sudden burst of activity that was about to occur. There was certainly optimism in the air. But there was also what he calls "a kind of good conscience on the part of scientists who devoted their research to practical objectives."[32] Their intentions were the best. "They believed that happiness and justice would result from their investigations, and it is here that the myth of progress had its beginning."

Ellul feels there were five conditions that contributed to the inventive renaissance that followed. The basic structure had been well and soundly laid in terms of theory and method; now it could be built upon. The population had greatly expanded. The economic climate was healthy. There was movement within society from one class and one profession to another. And there was clear technological intention: people wanted to invent. There was a frenzy of activity among scientists, but technology was at a stage where invention might come not simply from a laboratory but from anywhere—from someone's shed or barn or cellar. Possibility, progress, and individuality merged. The idea of perfectibility was also in the air—it had become a realistic possibility in all this enthusiasm for getting on—and a related notion that limits were no longer applicable or appropriate. One could, ergo, one should. A certain inevitability accompanied each new invention—there were machines for kneading dough and for rearing chicks; an exercise machine; a perpetual oven that used a chain conveyer; and, of course, the infamous shearing frames the Luddites so hated—and there was no holding back. It began to feel as if invention had a life force of its own, and in fact, it did—but that is to leap ahead of the narrative.

As the industrial revolution progressed, conflict developed between the classes that *used* the new technologies and the class that *was used by* those technologies. If the industrial revolution was raising the standard of living for some, improvement had not yet reached the workers. They were, as Ellul says, reeling from "a loss of equilibrium in their lives brought about by a too rapid injection of technique," but they had not yet felt the "intoxication of the result."[33] In *Wealth of Nations,* Adam Smith had contributed to a movement that was already in progress and was now picking up speed; he developed a theory that would give it authority and relevance. The "unseen hand" that hovered over Smith's "economic man" would regulate markets, rewarding those who produced desirable goods most cheaply. The incompetent, the slow, the principled, the least machinelike would be eliminated—although it was never spelled out just where they should go or why they had to be redefined and evaluated by this new standard. But by this standard, a man such as Richard Arkwright, the developer of the first successful cotton-spinning mills and by his death, in the last decade of the eighteenth century, the owner of 25 mills, triumphed and was celebrated—except by those who worked in his mills, many of them children, trained to conform "to the regular celerity of the machine."

All the difficulties of the transition from the agricultural to the industrial economy were borne by the workers, yet they had seen no real benefit. But that would change. The last significant Luddite uprisings of workers against machines took place early in the twentieth century (although there are sporadic attacks even today); as finally, during the second half of the nineteenth century, the effect of increased productivity and consumer goods began to be felt throughout the ranks of society. The surprising thing, perhaps, is how easily much of the working population was consoled by the cheap socks and pretty ribbons of the marketplace.

To be fair, for all the oppression of factory workers, the wholesale pollution, and the deplorable living and working conditions these workers endured, the nineteenth century was also the period when public education and literacy was extended significantly. With increased literacy, a new consideration of the value of the individual emerged—which encouraged more literacy. Postman calls this period of inventiveness and mechanical development a technocracy. With the idea of Progress now firmly entrenched, "technocracy filled the air with the promise of new freedoms and new forms of social organization," says Postman. "We could get places faster, do things faster, accomplish more in a shorter time. Time, in fact, became an adversary over which technology could triumph. And this meant that there was no time to look back or to contemplate what was being lost."[34] Somewhat ironically, the attempt to control time had resulted in the common feeling of not having any or of not being in control of what we had. In a world reoriented to numbers, where time had been commodified and only the quantifiable had value, the things that had once seemed important—an older set of values—could no longer be justified. The simple truth now began to dawn: if it couldn't be counted, it didn't count.

Time itself was being transformed. The railroad was one of the most revolutionary developments of the nineteenth century, and it reordered the lives not only of those who used it, as Thoreau noted, but of society in general, for which it set a new pace. In *Dickens: From Pickwick to Dombey,* author Steven Marcus points out how conscious Dickens was of the rapidly changing nature of the world and the role of both the railroad and clock time in that change:

> *Dombey and Son* is full of clocks which do not work, or work incorrectly, or work precisely but somehow tell the wrong time. Dombey's "very loud ticking watch" (Ch.1) or Blimber's monstrous clock only emphasize that something is wrong with their owners' relation to time. And even Sol Gills with all his faith in his "tremendous chronometer" can only learn from it that he has "fallen behind the time, and [is] too old to catch it again." (Ch. 4) In a sense it is a clock that ticks backwards into past time, for with every tick Sol feels he is carried further and further away from the present.[35]

The railroads actually changed time, applying standards that hadn't existed before, and in the process "altered the nature of reality," says Marcus. A radical transformation had occurred, which Dickens revealed by demonstrating how "space and time contract and expand relative to the motion of the train."[36]

Still, it remained possible, in the midst of advancing industrialization in Europe and America, to conform to the old world; to cling to traditions, rituals, and myths; to retain a sense of community and family life, of regional pride and social responsibility; even to respect age-old wisdom and common sense. Possible, Postman says—but not easy. For all these "represent a thought-world that stands apart from technocracy and rebukes it—rebukes its language, its impersonality, its fragmentation, its alienation. Technocracy disdains such a thought world."[37] And yet technocracy could not entirely destroy it. That world endured—out of favor, under constant attack—yet as persistent as a backyard dandelion.

The competition between the old, comfortable, reassuring values and the appeal of the new inventions is played out in nineteenth-century literature, as we have seen: a clue to its resonance with readers. But most people were as yet unaware that the two were incompatible, at least from a philosophical perspective. The machine demands the sacrificing of other values. Efficiency begins to triumph over pleasures or satisfactions that cannot be quantified. Some reconciliation was possible in daily life, obviously, but the fit between the machine and those other values has always been awkward. Nevertheless, in nineteenth-century America, says Postman, though "one can hear the groans of religion in crisis, of mythologies under attack, of a politics and education in confusion . . . the groans are not yet death throes. They are the sounds of a culture in pain, nothing more."[38] Science and technology were not yet a real substitute for religion and philosophy, and the new inventions, as clever and as appealing as they were, remained servile and obedient.

Not everyone was blinded by the brilliance of the new consumer age, however, as we have already seen. "With the nineteenth century," says Waldo Frank in *The Rediscovery of Man*, "industrial capitalism stepped up its rate [of production] to the geometric; the hegemony of things began, the ethos of things, threatening to weave mechanism into human life." Reaction came from "the sensitive men of the West [who] shrunk from mechanism in horror and were crying out against it. These were the Romantic rebels: Rousseau, Blake, Proudhon, Novales, Bakunin, Tolstoy, Kropotkin, Rimbaud, Ruskin, Nietzsche, Emerson, Thoreau, Whitman and many others, [Goethe and Morris, he could have added] whose unifying trait was that they feared one 'enemy.'"[39] There is a certain desperation in these voices that resonates today, for they could see clearly what was being sacrificed for superficial gains. Yet while their transcendental and spiritual escapes and simple retreats were important as art, and "as lyrical projections of man's nature against the darkening scene,"[40] says Frank, they took too little notice of the long tradition of capitalism and ignored basic elements of human nature. It was wishful thinking, he implies, to believe that ordinary people could see beyond ease and comfort, novelty and delight, abundance and possibility to evaluate carefully the true cost of this new prosperity. And there was tremendous social pressure to conform to the acquisitive model.

Ellul points out that the domination of the bourgeoisie in the nineteenth century "excluded all romantic enthusiasm."[41] Nevertheless, the bourgeoisie not only submitted willingly to this new order but compelled everyone else to submit as well, he says. But both the bourgeoisie and the working classes were consumed by the system, whether it manifested itself in the bourgeois focus on money and goods or in the alienation of the workers. The point, says Ellul, is that no one escaped from this industrial-technological nexus. Not even the wealthy and well-educated. Everyone was affected by technology, like it or not. The changes wrought by the machine were perhaps more keenly felt in America, which had embraced the new technologies and where the pull of tradition was weaker than in Europe.

The Education of Henry Adams, the autobiography of the grandson of American president John Quincy Adams and the great-grandson of President John Adams, is not only a literary masterpiece but a powerful record of the pressures placed on individuals to adapt to the new technological and economic realities of the nineteenth and twentieth centuries. With both brilliance and every social advantage, one would think that, of all people, Adams (1838–1915) should have been able to weather the transformation—yet even he had difficulty. His own education, he felt, had prepared him not for the century he was living in, but the previous one. Returning from five years in England in 1868, he discovered "how much its character had changed and who was being left out":

One could divine pretty well where the force lay, since the last ten years had given to the great mechanical energies—coal, iron, steam—a distinct superiority in power over the old industrial elements—agriculture, handwork, and learning; but the result of this revolution on a survivor from the [eighteen] fifties resembled the action of the earthworm; he twisted about, in vain, to recover his starting point, he could no longer see his own trail, he had become an estray; a flotsam or jetsam of wreckage; a belated reveler, or a scholar-gipsy like Mathew Arnold's. His world was dead. . . . One comfort he could enjoy to the full. Little as he might be fitted for the work that was before him, he had only to look at his father and [John] Motley to see figures less fitted for it than he. All were equally survivors from the [eighteen] forties . . . They could scarcely have earned five dollars a day in any modern factory.[42]

As the twentieth century dawned, maintaining traditions, art, cultural heritage, social mores, religious faith, and links to nature was becoming ever more challenging. The abundance and variety of goods available would have been astounding to someone from the previous century. Insidiously, however, that great insatiable giant called The Economy had awakened. Adam Smith had provided support and credibility for this direction. It was no longer land but money that was the key to wealth, a shift that was having enormous social and cultural repercussions. When more goods became available, the very availability demanded that more goods be purchased. Consumerism became first desirable and, finally, something of a patriotic duty by the last quarter of the nineteenth century. In the developing language of obfuscation, notes Ellul, "the crisis of over-production is explained as a crisis of under consumption."[43] If need did not exist, it now had to be created. This represented a distinctive shift, and technology stood by to lend a hand.

And yet, this was still Postman's technocracy. Beyond the abundance, the flood of new inventions, the demanding nature of the new consumerism, even the domination of the factory system, there was still no systematic application of technology. It had not yet completely reshaped government, or the banking system, or education; these institutions, although changing, were still recognizable from an eighteenth-century perspective. Science, says Ellul, was not yet enslaved by commerce and industry; efficiency was a concept but not yet a god. Put simply, humans still had some measure of control. "Big business" in the sense of the large corporation—despite Arkwright's twenty-some cotton mills—did not exist as we know it today; but as Adams points out, it had begun to.

Between 1850 and 1914, the development of industrial technology brought enough real improvement in Europe and America for the great mass of people to become convinced that progress was now a realistic possibility. Both Mumford and Ellul note the neat fit between capitalism and technology, and the clock set the stage for this marriage of convenience. It was not inevitable. Technology could, and did, exist without capitalism and capitalism without technology, but together they formed a formidable alliance and one was reshaped by the other. During the last decade of the nineteenth century, Adams found himself, to his great surprise, unwillingly caught up in a banking crisis and in the debate between the silver and gold standards, a turning point in economics. Adams, who always uses the third person in referring to himself, said, "He had, in a half-hearted way, struggled all his life against State Street, banks capitalism."[44] In 1893 that struggle reached a crisis. Two events were pivotal: the Chicago Exposition, which offered a taste of the technological wonders to come, and the money crisis. Banks were on the verge of closing, and yet the men who owed them money could not pay. There was a momentary and frightening impasse. Eventually the matter was resolved and the storm blew over, but not without leaving damage behind. A certain blind faith in the monetary system had been shattered.

But the Exposition had an even more lasting effect on Adams. Seeing what lay ahead—the uses to which "force," as Adams calls sources of power, whether electric or steam, could be put—frankly unsettled those who had shaped their lives according to other assumptions. The certainties about the nature of the world and the shape of the future were transformed by the marvels revealed. What was there to do after seeing such things "but to sit down on the steps and brood as they had never brooded" on the errors of their prior thinking, "ashamed of the childlike ignorance and the babbling futility of the society that let them" make such assumptions.[45] Adams is unusually prescient in perceiving the nature of the machine long before the effects of technology had been analyzed by academics. He refers to political machines, to "thinking like a machine," to the "mental machine." In fact, he seems conscious of the systemic effect of technology on society very much in the tradition of Carlyle, Ruskin, Morris, and Marx; but what is interest-

ing is that he speaks of this effect with such clarity and in the context of
writing about his own life.

The question of the silver or gold standard, as obscure as it seems to
those not economically minded, and I include myself, focused Adams's
attention on the nature of the economic system and how it was changing in
the face of the new technologies. He draws the important distinction
between the old industrialized society of the eighteenth and early nineteenth century and what it was now becoming, and he makes the clear connection between technology and not simply capitalism but the corporation,
with all that implied.

He had hugged his antiquated dislike of bankers and capitalistic society
until he had become little better than a crank. He had known for years that
he must accept the regime, but he had known a great many other disagree-
able certainties—like age, senility, and death—against which one made
what little resistance one could. The matter was settled at last by the people.
For a hundred years, between 1793 and 1893, the American people had hes-
itated, vacillated, swayed forward and back between two forces, one simply
industrial, the other capitalistic, centralizing, and mechanical. In 1893 the
issue came on the single gold standard, and the majority at last declared
itself, once for all, in favor of the capitalistic system with all its necessary
machinery. All one's friends, all one's best citizens, reformers, churches,
colleges, educated classes, had joined the banks to force submission to capitalism. . . . A capitalistic system had been adopted, and if it were to be run
at all, it must be run by capital and by capitalistic methods. . . . The rest
was a question of gear; of running machinery; of economy; and involved no
disputed principle. Once admitted that the machine must be efficient,
society might dispute in what social interest it should be run, but in any
case it must work concentration. Such great revolutions commonly leave
some bitterness behind, but nothing in politics ever surprised Henry Adams
more than the ease with which he and his silver friends slipped across the
chasm, and alighted on the single gold standard and the capitalistic system
with its methods; the protective tariff; the corporations and trusts; the
trades-unions and socialistic paternalism which necessarily made their
complement; the whole mechanical consolidation of force, which ruth-
lessly stamped out the life of the class into which Adams was born, but created monopolies capable of controlling the new energies that America
adored.[46]

Industrialized nations were now, at the turn of the century, facing the Leviathan that Postman calls technopoly, Ellul calls "la technic," and Mumford calls simply The Machine. What precisely is this "thing"? Technopoly, says Postman,

> is a state of culture. It is also a state of mind. It consists of the deification of technology, which means that the culture seeks its authorization in technology, finds its satisfactions in technology, and takes its orders from technology. This requires the development of a new kind of social order, and of necessity leads to the rapid dissolution of much that is associated with traditional beliefs.[47]

Ellul's translator, John Wilkinson, has a neat definition of Ellul's "la technic" that bears repeating. (Ellul himself is nowhere near as succinct.) It is, Wilkinson says,

> a description of the way in which an autonomous technology is in process of taking over the traditional values of every society without exception, subverting and suppressing these values to produce at last a monolithic world culture in which all nontechnological difference and variety is mere appearance.[48]

Adams understood what was happening in the 1890s. Mumford began writing in the 1930s; Wilkinson was writing in the 1960s, Postman in the 1970s. The transformation was glaring to Adams, clear to Mumford, and more difficult to explain as time went on precisely because the technological force has been so successful. Today the machine has penetrated the culture and dominates to such a degree that only a few perceive its presence; fewer still understand its nature. Criticism of the machine is generally viewed as heresy and protest as a frankly subversive activity. We now live in a culture not simply dominated by the machine but completely in thrall to the machine.

The point at which technocracy became technopoly, to use Postman's term, or the machine took over, is hard to define precisely. Adams had sensed the impending transformation at the Chicago Exposition of 1893. By the time of the Great Exposition of 1900, he perceived that the change had taken place. The chief emphasis, as he describes it, was on the new uses of force. There was the prototype of the airship, and the "astonishing complexities of the new Daimler motor, and of the automobile, which, since

1893, had become a nightmare at a hundred kilometers an hour, almost as destructive as the electric tram which was only ten years older; and threatening to become as terrible as the locomotive steam engine itself."[49]

Adams was fully aware of that seminal moment when his own allegiance shifted from a theological construct of the world, from God to machine, from religion to science. He describes this transformation from his personal perspective as he felt it happening within himself. The dynamo had the potential to transform coal into heat into power, a reasonable, understandable, homely use,

> but to Adams the dynamo became a symbol of infinity. As he grew accustomed to the great gallery of machines, he began to feel the forty-foot dynamos as a moral force, much as the early Christians felt the Cross. The planet itself seemed less impressive, in its old-fashioned, deliberate, annual or daily revolution, than this huge wheel, revolving within arm's length at some vertiginous speed, and barely murmuring—scarcely humming an audible warning to stand a hair's-breadth further for respect of power. . . . Before the end, one began to pray to it; inherited instinct taught the natural expression of man before silent and infinite force.[50]

Adams was already certain that the development of force would now go beyond the calculations of those who saw a finite limit to the development of coal or steam. There were new forces abroad, and they were ominous in their potential.

> [Samuel P.] Langley [inventor of the unmanned flying machine and director of the Smithsonian, with whom Adams visited the Exposition] seemed to be worried by the same trouble, for he constantly repeated that the new forces were anarchical, and specially that he was not responsible for the new rays, that were little short of parricidal in their wicked spirit towards science. His own rays, with which he had doubled the solar spectrum, were altogether harmless and beneficent; but Radium denied its God—or what was to Langley the same thing, denied the truths of his Science. The force was wholly new. . . . The rays that Langley disowned, as well as those which he fathered, were occult, supersensual, irrational; they were a revelation of mysterious energy like that of the Cross; they were what, in terms of medieval science, were called immediate modes of the divine substance.[51]

Adams wrestles with the contest between religion, which he represents as the Virgin, and technology, represented by the dynamo. He reckons that the Virgin, also a stand-in for metaphysics in general, never had much of a chance in practical, go-getting America anyway. And so by the turn of the century, the road to technopoly had been graded and paved. The new forces waited only to be exploited, the economic system had been designed with the needs of business in mind, the corporations and trusts had been given legal authority, the allegiance had shifted from god to science, the potential of invention seemed unlimited, and the consumer was waiting. But something more was required.

Both Giedion and Postman locate the turning point with Frederick W. Taylor's publication in 1911 of *The Principles of Scientific Management*. An American industrial engineer and the father of scientific management theory, his goal was to increase production and decrease working hours by the application of time and motion studies. Efficiency was the goal, and science —careful and systematic analysis of job and worker—would determine the means. However well-intentioned, the result was profound and ultimately disastrous, for at once the balance between man and machine shifted dramatically. Mechanical man would replace economic man. Efficiency was not a new idea, but now it would be undertaken systematically, using assumptions that were, indeed, novel, and that included a redefining of the purpose of expending effort of whatever sort. Now effort would be defined in terms that were instantly translated into profit. There could no longer be the slightest doubt who was in control, for the essence of Taylor's message was, as Postman sums up so admirably, that the

> primary, if not the only, goal of human labor and thought is efficiency; that technical calculation is in all respects superior to human judgement; that in fact human judgement cannot be trusted, because it is plagued by laxity, ambiguity, and unnecessary complexity; that subjectivity is an obstacle to clear thinking; that what cannot be measured either does not exist or is of no value; and that the affairs of citizens are best guided and conducted by experts.[52]

Taylor's extraordinary success in promoting these ideas—and the degree to which, however misguided and flatly mistaken, they have penetrated the thinking of the twentieth century—is that they do not seem all that outrageous. The degree to which they are now accepted as realistic assumptions accurately reflecting the way things are is clear evidence of the infiltration and domination of the machine in human thinking and behavior. Taylor assumed that his concepts were to be applied only to industry. They would, instead, transform everything from the way the cow was milked to the way the dishes were washed to the way the child was reared. They would change thinking. By 1933, at the World's Fair in Chicago, the sign above the entrance read, without apology or conscious irony, "Science explores, Technology executes, Man conforms."[53]

A PERFECT CONTEMPORARY example of the domination of the machine is the confused vote in Florida in the presidential election of 2000 and the reactions to it. It would be difficult to find an event in which the rule of the machine was better illustrated. The American voter—and indeed much of the world—remembers the details: the poorly computer-designed ballot in one county that led people to vote for candidates they did not want; the punch-card ballots with their "hanging chads"; the vote-counting machines that were famous for rejecting ballots that failed to meet their standards; the undercounted overvotes where people voted twice for the same candidate because of failure to read instructions, failure to understand instructions, or simple enthusiasm.

What was particularly fascinating were the reactions to this situation. Of course each side might be expected to support a position with regard to the acceptability or unacceptability of these votes according to their perception of advantage, and yet a cultural picture of our relationship to the machine emerged that went beyond partisan politics. There seemed to be a general assumption that machine counts were preferable to human counts, presumably because machines do not possess the subtle ability to discriminate that humans do. Emotionless and indiscriminate, they are preferred, even if they are wrong—that is, if they eliminate as nonvotes indications of preference that would be obvious to human beings, this is acceptable because they are presumed (whether this is true or not) to be consistent. The fact that voting procedures failed—whether because computer-designed ballots were difficult to comprehend, or because perforated card openings were difficult to push out, or because pieces were left attached that confused the machine—was seen by many not as an indication of failure of the process but of failure of the voter.

Not long after the election, two groups did studies to find out the best and most accurate method of tabulating votes. When representatives of these groups appeared on a national news program, they both had to admit that humans did the best job of counting. Yet so ingrained is the notion that machines do a better job that both groups had some obvious hesitation and apparent reluctance to admit what their own studies revealed. It was the wrong answer. And, in fact, it was not the recommended solution. It is now an article of faith that a new and better machine must be found and its errors overlooked. This blind faith in machines represents an effect of technopoly. Doing something by hand has taken on the quality of primitivism and to return to it would be to take a step backward. Accuracy is a casualty, a sacrifice that must be made to our vision of mechanical man.

THE POTENTIAL for technology to allow economies of scale and increased efficiency proved equally irresistible to commerce and industry. As mechanization began to dominate industry, the point was not that the machine produced a better end product than the artisan or craftsperson—many times it didn't—it was simply that it turned out a product more quickly and thus more profitably. Thus began a relationship that defied common sense —at least from the standpoint of quality and culture. The goal might just as easily have been to improve working conditions and the quality of goods produced; instead it was simply to spend less to sell more.

Does it matter that old skills have been irrevocably lost? Do handcrafted goods retain any intrinsic value? The short answer is yes. Just as thousands of unidentified insect and plant species of potentially great importance are wiped out in the destruction of a rain forest, so we simply cannot know how the careless squandering and neglect of the store of human knowledge and skill will blight our future. Diversity in human culture and experience is just as important as diversity in the natural world. Indeed, just as plant and animal life needs no human usefulness to justify its right to exist, neither should these precious lost skills require justification. The loss of culture and tradition and artistry is a loss to all humanity. The handcrafted object retains that all-important imprint of humanness that is vital to remembering who and what we are. Yet efficient production trumped everything else. Handwork is almost exclusively reserved now for the discriminating few within an upper-income minority.

Because it was so closely linked to efficiency, speed became a highly desirable quality as well. Improving the pace of the machine became a preoccupation of capitalism. Change was overstimulated—that is, it began to occur at a faster pace than it would have without the driving energy of capitalism—and the rate of acceleration became artificial and unsettling. Change proceeded at a pace that made adaptation and assimilation difficult if not impossible, thus creating a level of stress that has now become a given of developed societies. As Sven Birkerts says, "Our era has seen an escalation of the rate of change so drastic that all possibilities of evolutionary accommodation have been short-circuited."[54] (Note his perhaps unconscious use of the mechanical metaphor.) We have been outpaced by the machine, which now seems to be running the show, and we struggle just to stay in the race.

By the end of the nineteenth century, promoting the machine in its various manifestations to the public as if its function were to improve society, rather than simply to increase profit and consolidate power, became vital. It was important to the growing mechanized culture around the turn of the century that the machine be viewed as part of a March of Progress that became a cult. Who is opposed to Progress? Who dares even now to admit misgivings? Very few, although Ogden Nash is supposed to have said, "Progress was alright once, but it's gone on too long."

Adams's story is of a man who sought to observe and analyze his own relationship to the rapid technological changes experienced in one lifetime. His experience with Progress was personal and poignant; he saw the contradictions that we struggle with today, so much splendor and beauty; so much power and potential, so much being lost and destroyed. Nearing the end of his life—he died in 1915—he approached New York City and found it

more striking than ever—wonderful—unlike anything man had ever seen—and like nothing he had ever much cared to see. The outline of the city became frantic in its effort to explain something that defied meaning. Power seemed to have outgrown its servitude and to have asserted its freedom. The cylinder had exploded, and thrown great masses of stone and steam against the sky. The city had the air and movement of hysteria, and the citizens were crying, in every accent of anger and alarm, that the new forces must at any cost be brought under control. Prosperity never before imagined, power never yet wielded by man, speed never reached by anything but a meteor, had made the world irritable, nervous, querulous, unreasonable and afraid. All New York was demanding new men, and all the new forces, condensed into corporations, were demanding a new type of man—a man with ten times the endurance, energy, will and mind of the old type—for whom they were ready to pay millions at sight. . . . The Trusts and

Corporations stood for the larger part of the new power that had been created since 1840, and were obnoxious because of their vigorous and unscrupulous energy. They were revolutionary, troubling all the old conventions and
values, as the screws of ocean steamers must trouble a school of herring.
They tore society to pieces and trampled it under foot. . . . The single problem before [government] was not so much to control the Trusts as to create
the society that could manage the Trusts. The new American must be either
the child of the new forces or a chance sport of nature. The attraction of
mechanical power had already wrenched the American mind into a crab-
like process . . . .The mechanical theory, mostly accepted by science,
seemed to require that the law of mass should rule. In that case, progress
would continue as before.[55]

And so technology had managed to undermine or eliminate traditions,
cultures, skills, quality, and communities and had inflicted growing insult
on the environment and on human health in the form of toxic chemicals. It
was changing the way humans thought, reordering their priorities, causing
them to doubt their own abilities and to set inappropriate, inhuman standards. It had created weapons of great destructive power—even ones such
as the automobile or train, which for all their convenience could cause accidents and bodily harm of new intensity and proportion. It is worth considering that the machinelike efficiency of modern medicine is directed in
large part to the efficiency of the machine itself in producing bodily harm.

But what of the special ire Adams directed at the corporation? Others
had pointed out the natural affinity between technology and capitalism, but
with the invention of the corporation, defined and privileged by law, that
affinity was transformed into a union that furthered the least desirable qualities of both technology and capitalism. Adams was not speaking of the privately owned company, which can do what it likes, but of the very nature of
the corporation and its public ownership. His dislike of the corporation was,
it seems, intuitive. He had not yet analyzed completely what it was that he
so disliked, although he could describe it well enough. Something larger
was at stake, and he knew what it was.

The corporation could use all these new "forces" to run roughshod over
everything that Adams valued. And in the end it comes down to values, for
the corporation has none in the sense that we think of them. Or rather, it has
only one—that of profit. Beyond that the corporation has no conscience. By
law it must consider its shareholders first—not individually, but the return

they receive on their investment. And every decision must be made with that return in mind. There is no room in corporate thinking, therefore, for sentiment, for morality, for considering the social or historical or cultural impact of what it does—even of considering the environmental impact, unless it appears that not considering it might have a negative impact on the bottom line. The "do-good" corporation is a carefully constructed illusion. Painting itself green, for instance, can be justified to shareholders only because studies have shown that consumers favor products from corporations they consider environmentally responsible. And so responsibility counts only when it can be counted—as profit. To do good for any other reason would, in fact, be seen by analysts and shareholders alike as irresponsible, if not illegal. The corporation is thus nothing more than an instrument for counting. It is the perfect reflection of the efficient, cold-blooded, emotionless machine, however it may attempt to disguise this fact.

A television ad for a computer features an old-fashioned sepia image of children playing in a garden, swinging, doing the things that children once did in freedom and with joy, when what it is selling is precisely the opposite: a machine that will tie them to a chair in front of an electronic screen where none of the real stimulation of interaction with imagination, nature, and other children will occur. It plays shamelessly upon the consumer's longing for the old values, the traditions, the simple pleasures in order to sell something quite different. And yet even as it plays on nostalgia, it dismisses it with a sneer. But what is nostalgia but the longing for what we know to have been better? Yet what we long for can be used to sell its nemesis, and the longed-for images are so powerful that the absurdity of the association escapes us. The corporation is the machine, and a duplicitous one at that.

This is what Adams understood. This was the reality then, and it is now. A corporation will, in the end, sweep away anything of value unless it can find a way to transform that value into profit. Unless the corporate charter can be rewritten, unless some way can be found to incorporate values other than profit, we are in thrall to a system that will finish us off—or at least finish off the world that we know and love. It is only in that niche where the longed-for can be translated into profit that a small window of satisfaction remains. Some of these things can be sold—the old-fashioned board game, the garden bench, the fireplace—and so they survive. Others cannot: the extended family, which represents the accumulation of years of tradition and love; the sense of oneness with the world around us; the joy of sitting down to eat with people we care for; the freedom to play in a healthy, untrammeled outdoors; the satisfaction of producing something with our hands or of a job well done. Intangibles, they are called—as if they weren't crucial to a healthy life and a healthy community. But valueless to our present economic structure, now, except as a lure.

STANDING ON the brink of the twentieth century, Adams recognized there was more to come from science and technology: "The man of science must have been sleepy indeed when, in 1898, Mme. Curie threw on his desk the metaphysical bomb she called radium. There remained no hole to hide in."[56]

Adams was prescient in his technological qualms, but he had also identified in Mme. Curie's discovery the very thing that would, fifty years later, galvanize the notion that progress had most assuredly gone on too long. The dropping of atomic bombs on Hiroshima and Nagasaki in 1945 reverberated powerfully in the scientific community. Those working on new technologies were forced to stop and consider where their work might lead and whether they had any control at all over the eventual uses to which their discoveries might be put. The terrible power of the bomb forced a reevaluation of the assumption under which they had been working: the basic notion that innovation was good. There had always been a strong association between innovation and military needs. There was constant pressure to gain advantage by devising more effective means of killing. But The Bomb was something else. Suddenly the potential was there not just to gain territory or vanquish a foe, but—unintentionally, for it could not be a part of any nation's strategy—to destroy the planet.

Hitler's minister of armaments and war production, Albert Speer, shifted some of the blame for Nazi horrors on to runaway technology and warned, at the Nuremberg trials, what might lie ahead:

> The more technological the world becomes, the greater is the danger. . . . As the former minister in charge of a highly developed armaments economy it is my last duty to state: A new great war will end with the destruction of human culture and civilization. There is nothing to stop unleashed technology and science from completing its work of destroying man which it has so terribly begun in this war.[57]

"Technology made us do it," in other words. It was a poor excuse, no excuse at all, for what had taken place. Still, there is truth enough there to make us pause. We should not underestimate the potential damage the mechanized mind can do.

A pall settled over the scientific world—briefly. During that period, attention was devoted anew to looking at the history, role, and effect of technology. How, precisely, had we gone from the reasonable practicality of McCormick's reaper and Marconi's clever transmitter to the devastating possibilities of atomic weaponry? The promise of Progress had been shaken along the way. Siegfried Giedion was one of the several writers, along with Juenger, Mumford, and Ellul, who took up the topic of technology and its effects. His *Mechanization Takes Command* is a tome of a book that tracks the lineage of selected forms of mechanization, sometimes from early medieval prototypes, looking at the way in which technical advances reflected—and changed—the culture. Writing in 1947, looking at the wreck that was Europe and sniffing the lingering trails of whatever The Bomb had left on the wind, he expressed the disillusion that was in the air. At that point he could say, with some seriousness, "Now, after the Second World War, it may well be that there are no people left, however remote, who have not lost their faith in progress. Men have become frightened by progress, changed from a hope to a menace. Faith in progress lies on the scrap heap, along with many other devaluated symbols."[58]

Of course, we know now how mistaken he was; how—rather in the way nature's anesthetic blurs the memory of childbirth until the act of procreation once again seems appealing—the horror of those first post-Bomb years faded. Faith, if not precisely in progress (for it was easy enough to see that peace, justice, and prosperity did not lie in everyone's future regardless of how advanced mechanization became), then in the sorts of technological advancement that might prove useful to those who could pay for them, lived on. In fact, the definition of Progress has shifted. Once it implied a final perfectibility. Now we call that a utopian fantasy. Today the belief in progress seems to have evolved into belief simply in more ease and comfort. Progress, for some, comes down to biological or chemical solutions to the diseases and disasters technology has created, although the irony of that has not quite sunk in or is intentionally overlooked. If scientists in the lab were tinkering with DNA and microchips and planning great things, ordinary individuals had their faith restored in technology and progress by automatic garage-door openers; clap-on, clap-off Christmas tree lights; and the far-away promises, hardly more real than the claims of old patent medicine men, of cancer cures. Hope is a hard thing to kill, and the fog of fantasy and delusion is as thick now as it was in the murky medieval past. As Giedion had said in 1944, the world had become a

> vast storehouse, bursting with inventions, new discoveries, potentialities, all promising a better life. . . . But the promises of a better life have not been kept. All we have to show so far is a rather disquieting inability to organize the world, or even to organize ourselves. Future generations will perhaps designate this period as one of mechanized barbarism, the most repulsive barbarism of all.[59]

Giedion was not the only one to use the term *barbarism*. Observers of the new technology noted that people now lived with sources of heat, light, and communication that they could adjust without any awareness of how they worked. These were, in truth, the new urban barbarians, possessed of a fragmented knowledge base but without any real concept of how their world operated. Theirs was, in fact, a more profound ignorance than that of the supposed Dark Ages. One pull of the plug and society—the great bulk of the population—risked being plunged into a deep primitivism where the average individual would be unable to meet his or her most basic physical needs. Chicken nuggets, they would discover, do not grow on trees, and the thermostat on the wall does not generate heat. "Society is composed of persons who cannot design, build, repair, or even operate most of the devices upon which their lives depend," said Winner.[60]

Hints of the new barbarianism appeared briefly in New Zealand in 1998 when the electricity in Auckland went out and could not be reestablished for weeks. Chaos was the result: lights failed, water didn't flow, toilets didn't flush, air conditioning stopped, televisions were blank, elevators didn't work, electronically controlled doors didn't open, cash registers and computers were useless. Security devices didn't work, and shopkeepers were left defending their stores themselves, sleeping in the dark with weapons. And it went on and on. Business couldn't operate; people couldn't cook, had no sanitation, couldn't open the windows in the climate-controlled buildings, couldn't function. Society broke down, and the downtown became a ghost town plagued by gangs and graffiti until electric power was restored only after many attempts some six weeks later. The system had become so complicated and interdependent that restoring it proved more challenging than anyone could have imagined. It was a warning to the rest of the developed world that was like the whisper of a dream. It went ignored. We have an astonishing and irrational optimism that the systems that support this dependent life will eternally remain in place. Call it faith.

Mohandas Gandhi had noticed the ability of technology to breed an unhealthy dependence. In India's case it threatened the independence he envisioned. Gandhi hated the machine. He was very clear about that. India was being "ground down, not under the English heel, but under that of modern civilization," he wrote in his *Critique of Modern Civilization*. And the machine, whose evils he could enumerate, was at the heart of the problem. "I cannot recall a single good point in connection with machinery," he said.[61]

India was in thrall to those non-Indians who controlled the factories that produced one of the essentials of life: the very cloth in which the people clothed themselves. The solution was to encourage the concept of *swadeshi*, roughly translated as the mutual support of community—and that meant encouraging the use of locally made goods. There were other examples of the domination of outsiders in Indian life; but Gandhi, who had read and absorbed both Thoreau's and Ruskin's ideas well, seized upon the importation of cloth or the production of cloth in local factories using imported thread. He understood that the act of spinning cotton to produce garments that were truly indigenous would have great symbolic value. The small spinning wheel was revived; the tradition was taught; and the image of Gandhi himself using this simple device was unforgettable. But he also knew how difficult it would be to wean people from their technologies. For one thing, the opposition was strong:

> Those who are intoxicated by modern civilization are not likely to write against it. Their care will be to find out facts and arguments in support of it, and this they do unconsciously, believing it to be true. . . . A man labouring under the bane of civilization is like a dreaming man. What we usually read are the works of defenders of modern civilization, which undoubtedly claims among its votaries very brilliant and even some very good men. Their writings hypnotize us. And so, one by one, we are drawn into the vortex.[62]

Although *swadeshi* may well have contributed to Indian independence, technology—on a world scale, reinforced by those sometimes good yet intoxicated men—marched on, now coupled with corporate globalization.

None of this has gone unnoticed. Economist E. F. Schumacher in his classic, *Small is Beautiful,* examined the role of technology and proposed "an economics as if people mattered." Technology, he observed, possesses no natural controls as does everything else in nature, which "knows where and when to stop." Technology, by contrast, "recognizes no self-limiting principle—in terms, for instance, of size, speed or violence." And here he may have hit upon the core problem. "It therefore does not possess," he says, "the virtues of being self-balancing, self-adjusting, and self-cleansing."[63] Humans must take on that task, and so far it seems one they are either unwilling or unable to manage.

Kirkpatrick Sale not only described the history of the Luddites but examined, in *Rebels Against the Future,* aspects of the role of technology and the evolution of neo-Luddites. Jerry Mander's *In the Absence of the Sacred* made an eloquent case for a thorough reevaluation of technology and a restoration of vital links to the natural world. The myth of the computer was challenged by Clifford Stoll in *Silicon Snake Oil* and by Sven Birkerts in several books, beginning with *The Gutenberg Elegies.*

There was an audience for this message, and perhaps it was growing, but it remained small. The environmental movement was split over the issue of technology. If part of it saw technology as the problem, another branch hoped that the computer and quantitative methods could be used to save what was left of the natural world. Both sides found computer technology difficult to avoid. The antiglobalization movement was larger, drawing a younger crowd freshly awakened to the monolithic nature of the global corporate culture, the ubiquitous presence of fast-food franchises and trademarked products around the world that—by sheer force of marketing, advertising, and a relentless focusing on the lowest common denominator of taste preferences—undermined local traditions, cultures, and even health. Native cultures that switched from local, traditional diets to commercialized, processed foods found health decline, as study after study confirmed. Promoted as a way of spreading the wealth, it was obvious that the real result of the globalization effort, intentional or not, was to make rich nations richer and poor nations poorer, as even Nobel Prize winner and former World Bank chief economist Joseph Stiglitz recently began pointing out. As America took on Afghanistan for its support of terror in late 2001, one began to suspect that the secondary goal of liberating Afghani women had to do not simply with getting them out of their *burqas* but with getting them into Calvin Kleins and Nikes.

With bomb testing now infrequent and underground, the memory of the mushroom cloud that had been imprinted on an earlier generation slipped back into some seldom-accessed part of the collective brain. The computer seemed useful enough, the fax was something of a miracle, and e-mail was convenient and relatively cheap. The cell phone transformed every grown-up kid's Dick Tracy dream into reality. There was no doubt of its handiness, and the possible dangers of radiation exposure and brain tumors were downplayed by industry and pushed to the back of the mind, perhaps literally, by the enthusiasts. It was one more trade-off—humans are adept at thinking that they are individually immune to ill effects or accidents to which others might fall prey—and the exchange was deemed "worth it." Individually, we have become highly skilled at rationalizing potential hazards from the appealing convenience of technology.

The new goal was not a chicken in every pot, but a cell phone in every hand—which law enforcement, newly alert to terrorist threats in the early years of the twenty-first century, planned to tap and envisioned loaded with tracking devices. The law-enforcement fantasy of a bar-code personal identifier implanted somewhere on every individual moved closer when, as 2002 dawned, the first commercial data implants became available from a company in Florida.

Just as critics had imagined, technology, with all its potential applications, was rapidly becoming a dystopian nightmare realized, taking on the qualities only the fiction writers had entirely foreseen. The excuse was a common enemy in the developed world, and the increasing loss of freedom was justified by playing good against evil, just as Ellul had suggested it might be as technic triumphed. In 1954, he had laid out in *The Technological Society* an outline of how the machine would finally triumph over personal freedom, and in 2002 we seemed on target. Identify the evil, maintain a steady flow of propaganda, use fear to rationalize limitations on liberty. He outlined the game plan, but who was reading Ellul?

Every device, every tempting toy, had its dark side. But few consumers made the link between these amusing toys or handy gadgets and the more ominous uses of technology that their purchases supported. Whatever else the computer was, it had quickly been transformed into an information-collecting nightmare. Illusions of personal privacy were rapidly disappearing as individuals could be known through the ubiquitous collectors of market data down to their toothpaste preference, every lick of an envelope could leave an identifiable genetic trail, and the potential was there for it all to be accessed with a few clicks of a computer mouse. DNA itself could be transformed into minute living computers that could be injected into the bloodstream to cure diseases, so the creators claimed—or to do what else? To be injected by whom, where, when? The questions were unanswerable or classified. The limits would be defined by those holding the needle. The future did not look good, and the technologists knew it. Forty years earlier, "radical" critics of the technological society in both Europe and America, noted Winner, "insisted that what deserves our attention is not the rate of technological innovation and its effects, but rather the very existence of advanced technology . . . as a source of domination that effectively rules all forms of modern thought and activity—whether by an inherent property or by an incidental set of circumstances, technology looms as an oppressive force that poses a direct threat to human freedom."[64] That notion no longer seemed so radical. Now even the computer gurus themselves were concerned.

In late 1999 Bill Joy, one of the founders of Sun Microsystems, made something of a splash by speaking out against the very system he represented. In April of 2000, an article called "Why the Future Doesn't Need Us" appeared in *Wired* magazine. The development of nuclear weapons in the twentieth century had created the potential to wreak havoc at the least and poison the planet at the worst. The technologies of the twenty-first century—genetics, nanotechnology, and robotics (GNR)—because they could be carried out more clandestinely than the development of atomic weapons and because they had the potential to self-replicate, presented even more danger. The creation of an organism, perhaps a virus or bacterium, with undesirable traits and the potential to spread throughout the environment, selecting for certain victims, could be created in a converted garage, undetectable by any known means. "My own concern with genetic engineering," Joy says, "is . . . that it gives the power—whether militarily, accidentally, or in a deliberate terrorist act—to create a White Plague," an infectious disease, resistant to antibiotics. He gives credibility to the worst nightmares of those knowledgeable about the potential of nanotechnology, such as Eric Drexler, author of *Engines of Creation,* who envisions the creation of self-replicating "plants" that could outcompete real plants, "crowding the biosphere with an inedible foliage," or masses of "uncontrolled replicators able to obliterate life" a phenomenon called "the grey goo problem."

Joy admits to having put aside his early worries as unrealistic and unlikely—to having skimmed over the potential for disaster—only to be made aware a few years later that nanoscale molecular electronics were now practical and presented a new and acute danger:

> As with nuclear technology, it is far easier to create destructive uses for nanotechnology than constructive ones. Nanotechnology has clear military and terrorist uses, and you need not be suicidal to release a massively destructive nanotechnological device—such devices can be built to be selectively destructive, affecting, for example, only a certain geographical area or a group of people who are genetically distinct. An immediate consequence of the Faustian bargain in obtaining the great power of nanotechnology is that we run a grave risk—the risk that we might destroy the biosphere on which all life depends.

How could this situation have developed without the public being aware of it and understanding the dangers? The information had been available for years, he said, but there "is now profit in publicizing the dangers."

But the media bear responsibility as well. There is a perceptible pro-technology bias in the press. It has become a voluntary cheering section for innovation, seldom questioning the information that comes from the innovators. Before the summer of 1999, when a field of genetically engineered corn was destroyed in Maine, the press gave little attention to the question of the safety of genetically engineered foods, although the topic of "Frankenfoods" had been on the front pages of European newspapers for a year or more and public pressure had managed to keep much of the food off grocery shelves. In the United States, the media coverage of the issue, when it finally appeared, generally supported the industry line. Dangers were inevitably downplayed. The news that traits from genetically engineered corn had been found in native Mexican strains, a country that had banned the planting of the genetically engineered corn, was reported in some papers; but it is doubtful whether the public spotted the reports or understood the ominous implication: that the spread of these engineered traits was uncontrollable and the results unpredictable.

Bill Joy had raised the alarm, but even this questioning by so respected an insider had little lasting effect. The article was profoundly alarming; and yet, although widely discussed, it had the curious quality of a symphony that climaxes in the second movement, only to be quietly resolved in the third. Its very form was the effective neutralization of its message. The problem, so eloquently articulated, could be resolved, Joy calmly implied. It was simply a matter of will; of scientists agreeing not to pursue anything dangerous (as if that were likely, given the incentives to do whatever was required); of treaties being agreed upon (even as, in real time, treaties were being abandoned). Throughout, he carefully denied having Luddite tendencies, virtually a requirement in those who wish to be taken seriously. He would continue to try to develop perfect computers, he said, even as he feared that GNR technologies would destroy the planet, and all without any apparent awareness that he is a part of the system that has made GNR possible. But Joy also bravely acknowledged the wisdom of his mother, who "had an awareness of the nature of the order of life, and of the necessity of living with and respecting that order." He confirmed the necessity of applying common sense, something now in short supply, and he suggested that we listen to the wisdom of the Dalai Lama, who "argues that the most important thing is for us to conduct our lives with love and compassion for others, and that our societies need to develop a stronger notion of universal responsibility and our interdependency." Good advice, yet hardly equal to combating the forces that bring the sheer cliff of our annihilation ever closer.

Still, the questions had been raised. The religion of science, technology, and capitalism had developed its cathedrals, its organization, and its priesthood. And yet Joy, a member of the priesthood, had raised questions within the cathedral itself by suggesting the unthinkable, a suggestion that only one of the priests could be allowed to utter: "The only realistic alternative I see is relinquishment: to limit development of the technologies that are too dangerous, by limiting our pursuit of certain kinds of knowledge." Brave words, and yet impractical.

Two things prevent the halt of GNR technology: First, the military will not be able to resist the temptation to achieve power through superior technology and so will develop whatever is possible. Second, the idea that limits will be imposed on biotech companies is unthinkable in the present economic climate. When the president places restrictions on the cloning of human cells, remember, it applies only to federally funded projects. Nothing restricts the private sector. And nothing prevents other countries from developing these technologies.

Joy, true technophile that he is, cannot bring himself to reject GNR. He would support the technologies if they were used in positive ways, he says, buying into the illusion that such a distinction can be made. But who will decide? There is presently no structure that would allow the questioning and control of private research in that way. Every new technology is promoted to the public with the claim that it will lead to greater safety or represent a health breakthrough. Determining whether claims are genuine, exaggerated, or entirely false is difficult, if not impossible.

Resistance to technology at the beginning of the new millennium had become heresy, and who doubted that a kind of ongoing electronic Inquisition was but a hairsbreadth away? The implantation of identifying chips was already being proposed for prisoners, patients, and foreign visitors; human cells were being cloned; people were dying from a superior grade of anthrax that conceivably might have come from the U.S. government's own stock; the government was looking into ways of tracking the individual mouse clicks on the computers of those suspected of terrorist thinking; and terrorism was being broadly defined.

Even challenges to the new global economy, the one that supported the biotech industry, appeared likely to be curtailed. "Countries that resist globalization will be where we will look for new enemies," a government official said on a National Public Radio program as 2001 ended, and it didn't take much imagination to translate that into a warning to individuals who oppose corporate globalization—Stiglitz included. He was asked to either mute his criticism or resign from the World Bank, and he chose to resign.

Looking back, Giedion could see how it all "began so marvelously":

> How was it possible for the foundation and very core of nineteenth-century thought and action [with its great faith in progress] to collapse so hopelessly? Without a doubt it was that mechanization was misused to exploit both earth and man with complete irresponsibility. Often it penetrated domains that were by nature unsuited to it. . . . The way in which this period handled mechanization is no isolated phenomenon. It has occurred practically everywhere. Means have outgrown man.[65]

Adams noted the problem of acceleration, the increase in the rate of change, the exponential increase in the numbers of goods, of inventions. Old ideas of limits would be upset at every turn; the concept of finite resources, even of satiation, had to be abandoned. There were no limits, it seemed— not even to the amount individuals could consume once the ball got rolling. Just as the Romans leaned over the vomitorium in order to consume more, today's American children have gone beyond need or even pleasure to celebrate the actual act of consuming. The owner of a small candy store tells me that she really hates to tempt the children. "They come in and buy everything in sight. They'll spend $10 on more candy than they can eat. I'll tell them, 'Don't waste your money.' And they tell me, 'I want to waste my money.'" The consumer society gone mad.

Says Giedion,

> The idea of progress faded because it stepped down [from more noble visions] to the lowest reaches of materialistic interpretation. Before our eyes our cities have swollen into amorphous agglomerations. Their traffic has become chaotic, and so has production. . . . With unbelievable speed atomic energy sprang from the worksheets and laboratories into reality . . . threatening human culture with annihilation.[66]

Today many would suspect that the culture has been annihilated without the bomb, and it is a toss-up as to whether the world will end with a bang or a whimper.

And yet . . . and yet. As Giedion correctly points out, while capitalism was taking the hand of mechanization and running with it, science itself was acknowledging the faults in the Newtonian, Baconian, and Cartesian principles. Giedion lists the changes that had begun at the very same time that Adams was despairing over the domination of the machine, the new sciences that were beginning to acknowledge the reality of the holistic view. Ecology would be one of them. And within the disciplines of the older sciences, new more balanced approaches were challenging prior assumptions. There are ongoing attempts to look at the whole, rather than simply the parts.

Does technology really have a life of its own? Is it unstoppable? Or is technology today simply another word for greed? Once invention had as its goal the improvement of human life. Now, tied to corporations and patents, the purpose of most scientific advance is economic advantage. Nothing else —not morality nor human values nor common sense—appears to stand a chance. Body parts will eventually be bought and sold; humans will be cloned; whatever creatures commerce can envision will be coaxed out of DNA; and at the heart of every Frankensteinian endeavor will be found a corporation, legally and psychologically aloof from every concern except its bottom line.

But neither will resistance be stamped out. Every one of the writers we've discussed proposed some kind of solution; some more serious, better defined, and more practical than others. There is a certain repeating theme to possible responses. The first is surely to understand the essential changes in human life affected by the machine and to appreciate that they are not healthy for either the short-term well-being or the long-term survival of the human species. The next step is to envision a more harmonious and healthy way of life, connected with nature, community, and tradition. There are such things, as Schumacher and Gandhi knew, as "appropriate technologies" that do not damage the environment or relationships or communities. The final step is to make changes in our individual lives. And around the globe, in quiet rebellion, there are individuals, families, communities who continue to do just that.

My friend with the clock is an environmental activist with both a woodstove and a computer, a flock of chickens, a large garden, a freezer, and a dishwasher; and her life represents the compromises thoughtful people make. She does not hate the clock—not her clock with its sturdy, labored tick. It tells the time, it even establishes a kind of ritual and rhythm, but it does not control her day. It is an older technology with a crucial difference: she is in charge. She holds the key. And who holds the key turns out to be essential in resolving the alienation and unrest that technopoly has produced.

CHAPTER ELEVEN

Looking for Luddites

SOME TIME AGO, IN 1996, I THINK, A "NOTE" APPEARED in *Harper's Magazine* about a magazine so disciplined in its aversion to technology that it objected to having any reference to itself on the Internet. *Harper's* found that quaint enough to feature.

The magazine was called *Plain,* and its editor, Scott Savage, says that life is "moving at electronic speed. We're finding that people can't live at that speed. We're being crushed by that speed." A plain Quaker who lives in an area of Ohio where there are many Amish, Scott and his family live similar lives and dress in traditional plain clothes that his wife makes. Over the years, they have given up their computer, their television, their radio, and even their car. They have a horse and buggy instead. His reaction to the news of the Internet posting:

> If any of our subscribers have access to the Internet and come across a listing or discussion of *Plain,* would you please post the following statement from us?
>
> "We the editors of *Plain* respectfully request that information about our magazine and the articles appearing in it not be referred to or used as top-

ics on any of the interactive data networks. You have the right to speak freely; hence this is a request, not a demand. We don't expect everyone to agree with our intent, which is to keep the discussion of our approach to living out of the daily diet of information-consuming elites. We merely ask that our little corner of reality be left alone. We are confident that we can reach people and discuss the issues we are raising entirely and exclusively through the offices of the real world."

I was intrigued. *Plain* was so principled that it didn't even have a phone—at least not one listed in the directory. I tracked it down with a loosely addressed envelope sent with the hope that small-town post offices are still staffed with humans who know their communities and can apply their common sense—an optimism that proved justified when I received a reply I sent them a check to see what they were up to—they didn't take credit cards, of course.

The publication, when I first subscribed, was still being printed by the offset method, but it was working toward a goal of using the now-obsolete letterpress method, where type is actually set for each page. Even at that stage its graphic design was simple but carefully considered and its woodcut illustrations striking, and its pages contained articles by writers I recognized, such as Wendell Berry, Gene Logsdon, Wes Jackson, and Jeff Robbins. The first issue, which I later obtained, laid out the principles that would dictate the tone. Savage selected a passage from E. F. Schumacher's *Small Is Beautiful*:

> I think we can already see the conflict of attitudes which will decide our future. On the one side, I see the people who think they can cope with our . . . crisis by the methods current, only more so; I call them the people of the forward stampede. On the other side, there are people in search of a new life style, who seek to return to certain basic truths about man and his world: I call them home-comers.

The first issue was addressed to these "home-comers." The Center for Plain Living, for which the publication would be a vehicle, was founded for the express purpose of questioning the impact of technology:

> Our mission is to develop a new fellowship of people who want to make peace with nature, create viable communities and strong families, and lead spiritually based lives. . . . We seek to open a space where people enmeshed

in contemporary culture can begin to discuss its effects on their daily lives. A space where encounters with simpler, less mediated living can be shared. Where the unity of life, land and spirit can be experienced.

He quotes once more from Schumacher:

The term "home-comer" has, of course, a religious connotation. For it takes a good deal of courage to say "no" to the fashions and fascinations of the age and to question the presuppositions of a civilization which appears destined to conquer the whole world; the requisite strength can be derived only from deep convictions.

Savage is a deeply religious man, but he was starting from a different perspective than the Amish who, as the world changed around them, refused to accept those elements that interfered with their religious focus. Savage was rejecting a world that was already here because it was interfering not only with religion but with every other aspect of human life. He was seeking to unify what had become divided and isolated, to bring people back to older values as exemplified by older ways. He had sampled the new world and was intentionally turning his back on it.

As the readership grew, it was perhaps the letters to the editor that were most intriguing. Here were individuals whose gratefulness at having discovered *Plain* was profound and quite moving. There were, it seemed, thousands who agreed with *Plain*'s ideas, even if they weren't willing to go as far as the Savages. Many felt trapped in the computerized work world and spelled out with passion their longing to be free of it. Others were in the process of creating new and different lives.

Under my lifelong assumption that anything that interests me will interest someone else, I proposed an article on neo-Luddites for the *Economist*. As part of my research, I traveled to New York City in 1996 to a "Teach-in on the Social, Ecological, Cultural, and Political Costs of Economic Globalization" sponsored by the International Forum on Globalization, where I understood neo-Luddites would be well represented. Kirkpatrick Sale was there, as was Jerry Mander, Helena Norberg-Hodge, and Scott Savage, bearded and hot and sweaty in his plain, buttoned trousers and suspenders and flat hat. He'd had an arduous journey sitting up overnight in the coach section of a train, which he'd taken instead of an airplane on principle. (Neo-Luddites generally like to use the least-technological means of travel avail-

able.) He was friendly, helpful, clearly intelligent, and perfectly at ease in
his nineteenth-century garb, which he told me his wife had made.

I emerged from the conference a wiser woman, with an armload of books,
a list of names, and a lot of catching up to do. Not long afterward I received
notice of the Second Luddite Congress, to be held in Barnesville, Ohio, and
knew I was missing the chance of a lifetime when finishing a book on dead-
line meant I couldn't attend. I wasn't the only one. In an issue of *Plain* that
appeared after the conference, Scott printed a passionate letter from a senior engineer at a nuclear power plant who could not attend because he was
working "60–70 hours a week for six weeks" during a refueling process. He
wrote,

> To paraphrase "Star Trek's" Commander Spock, the needs of the machine
> exceed the needs of the people. We spend too much time at work. We earn,
> not to sustain ourselves alone, but to indulge ourselves in too much food,
> too many gizmos, extravagant educations for our children, and overly large
> houses in oft-times impersonal communities. Our fast paced lives separate
> us from our families and our God.

Is a nuclear engineer sincerely contemplating the end of the machine age?
"Absolutely," he says, "for I have seen how the machines steal life and
deaden men's souls." He has imagined, he says, a simpler life "without airplanes, rockets, and satellites," but more imagining is needed. Yet, he says,
"Our souls demand that we find our way out of the labyrinth of this mechanical purgatory."

Reports of the conference appeared in the *New York Times*, illustrated
not with a photograph—cameras were barred from the gathering—but with
a drawing. In fact, the gathering had been contentious and emotional as
well as inspiring. The organizers had planned for much of it to go as a Quaker
Meeting does, with individuals speaking only when they feel genuinely
moved to. The discipline is one that isn't learned in an hour. There were
loud voices of disagreement that left many participants upset. One source
of the conflict was the idea that resistance must always take a nonviolent
form.

Some anarchists are Luddites, but the original Luddites were not anarchists. They eventually were forced into a violent expression of their frustration, but it was not their intention to bring down a system. Rather, it was

to protect a system that existed and was working—if not perfectly, then very much better than what was being introduced to replace it.

Kirkpatrick Sale had already addressed the issue with good sense in his opening talk on the original Luddites. "We are fighting a much more difficult battle now," he told the gathering, "here in the Second Industrial Revolution driven by the omnipotent micro-chip, and we know so much more than they about the awesome power, the awesome destructiveness, of industrialism now that we have seen how it has played itself out in these last two centuries all over the world." Nevertheless, he said, there were lessons to be learned from the original Luddites. Violence was dangerous and counterproductive:

> For example, there comes a time when resistance to machinery is right and just, the only moral act in defiance of an immoral world. Violent resistance, however, quite apart from whatever evil may be inherent in it, will bring down upon you the wrath of governments that have made themselves powerful with the weapons of violence and of corporations that have made themselves powerful with the weapons of social control. Violent resistance escalating to the taking of human lives is, again apart from its inherent evil, misguided and counterproductive—as I tried to warn the Unabomber some time ago and as his demise so readily makes clear—and carries with it the absolutely debilitating contradiction that it is imitating the very world it is acting against.

Yet, he admitted, working within the political process was also futile because it had been established for the protection of the industrial system. And "successful resistance to such an immense socioeconomic phenomenon as industrialization cannot be driven by rage and outrage, however righteous." It needed to be based instead in an understanding of the philosophical and literary tradition and the "whole chorus of contemporary neo-Luddites . . . whose voices have been so sharp and so penetrating in these past years." It needed to spread the Luddite philosophy "throughout this land in the effort to change the fundamental belief-system of this technologized society, to wean it away from the false gods . . . of materialism, rationalism, and humanism that tell us that amassment of personal riches is the highest goal of life, and the attendant deities of exploitation, dominance, profit, progress, and growth." And finally, these false gods needed to be replaced with those that "have proven to be reliable, trustworthy, and inspi-

rational for human societies since the earliest." They are the "forces, config-
urations, systems, and organisms of the natural world, the whole grand,
sacred, precious, and numinous biosphere upon which all life depends."

This would mean, says Sale, restoring Ned Ludd to life, not as a general,

> but as our brother, our comrade, our colleague in the enterprise of peaceful
> resistance." It would mean . . . that we start here and now to be orators and
> activists against the energetic genius of destruction around us: to name the
> enemy, which is technology, and its gods, and tell the baffled public out
> there, quite aware that the new technologies are overwhelming them—in
> Newsweek's words, "outstripping our capacity to cope, transforming our
> mores, reordering our priorities, and shifting our concept of reality"—tell
> those baffled, battered citizens that the problem is not one political party or
> another, one President or another, not the lack of family values or the rise of
> the welfare state or the erosion of community or decline in religious beliefs,
> not any one of the –isms that beset our nation today, not even the strangle-
> hold of corporate power and the ascendancy of corporate greed, but rather
> the technology in service to false gods that has made all the rest of it pos-
> sible, that is in fact behind all those other ills and evils. Technology—
> high, computer-driven, corporate-wielded, government-sponsored, nature
> destructive technology.

I was intrigued by his reference to the false god of humanism. I had
thought the rejection of humanism to be a preoccupation of the far-right
fundamentalists, and Sale was certainly not that. Humanism had created a
man-centered universe that left out the rest of the world. But there were
certainly those who would argue—Lynn White's voice being one of the
strongest that Christianity had done the same thing. Luddism was being
defined, I could see, but slowly and tortuously. The second draft statement
for the Congress, presented the next day, said simply:

> Technology is out of control and is unraveling society.
> We are in an ecological, social and spiritual crisis.
> The needs of people exceed the needs of machines.
> There are signs of hope—we are building bridges to people who are "in" the
>   machine.
> We must stand with others, serve others, build community with all people
>   and with all creation.

Savage apologized for the conflicts and reminded the delegates that they
had come because they had something in common, and that the draft was a

starting place. But he was clearly shaken, says a delegate who was present. He had one view of what a neo-Luddite was, and clearly there were others.

It was several years before Savage contemplated another gathering, and in the meantime he had published an anthology, *The Best of Plain,* and his own book, *Walking My Beliefs.* When the Second Luddite Congress II finally rolled around a few years later, I wouldn't have missed it for the world. I like to think I was the first one to send in a deposit, although I doubt it. And by that time I had not only discovered the wealth of literature on the topic, I'd begun to look for modern-day Luddites wherever they seemed likely to be—which was everywhere, as it turned out. Although they weren't always that easy to find.

I live in Maine, along the coast, but the woods around here have always been filled with back-to-the-landers and technology resisters of varying degrees of intensity. Half the people I know heat their homes either totally or partially with wood, and folks who live, or have lived, off-the-grid are almost as common as duct tape. What accommodations they make to civilization vary from individual to individual and from year to year. Sometimes the goal is to avoid certain technologies, sometimes it is independence, sometimes it is to live more lightly on the earth for environmental reasons. Other times it has nothing to do with the environment. Saturn Press on Swan's Island, Maine, a letterpress publisher of fine cards and writing paper using old designs has no computer, no web page, and an unlisted phone number, but it claims not to be intentionally Luddite so much as simply perverse. The end result is the same. Some individuals who live quite extreme lives even think—all evidence to the contrary—that they appreciate technology. They are not immune, it would seem, to the possibly enforceable law that an early twenty-first century individual *must* appreciate technology or be shunned for heretical thinking. Social pressure is strong to be on technology's side, at least publicly.

Intentional livers—those who shape their lives to their principles— understand that living always represents compromise and accommodation to one degree or another. It is the attempt that is important, and the degree that is crucial.

I set off with friends, Robert and Diane Phipps, one early winter day to visit Bill Coperthwait, otherwise known as "the yurt guy." The Phipps live in the Acadia Friends Community, housed in a rambling building Robert owns in Bar Harbor. It varies, he says, from being an intentional community to simply being a boardinghouse, but the arrangement is always interesting. They had never been to Coperthwait's land, either.

Coperthwait is, in fact, director of the Yurt Foundation—a yurt being a structure of circular construction used traditionally by Mongolians. There is something satisfying about being in a yurt; perhaps it is the circular form itself that creates that particular sense of well-being. I had seen one of his yurts at the Nearings' Good Life Center, and I'd been interested in meeting him for some time.

We set off for "down east" Maine, a section of the coast that is still not heavily populated. When we reached the general area east of Machias, we stopped for lunch at the home of a couple who practice biodynamic farming. The method evolved from the writings of Rudolf Steiner and involves the preparation of compost using herbal solutions to strengthen its dynamic qualities. We had a wonderful lunch of organic foods, some from the farm, and inspected the livestock (the chickens they keep are old varieties of Buff Orpington and Delaware) and what remained of the gardens—we were long past the first frost. With the help of an intern, Dan and Iris plant a vegetable garden an acre in size, which they work with hand tools. They harvest hay for their livestock with scythes.

I know nothing about anthroposophy, which they practice, but get the sense that it is more than a philosophy but less than a religion, a belief that the natural world is animated and full of energies waiting to be tapped by those who know how. Dan explains that there are energy lines running across the earth and that new lines can be created and made to cross. We are shown a grove of trees near where Dan and Iris plan to build a house one day. He calls it magical, and the word has a certain resonance. We are shown a tree, one side of which has been packed with an herbal mixture. There are others up and down the coast, Dan tells us, each setting up a protective biodynamic field that can extend five hundred miles; creating, he hopes, overlapping fields of good vibrations—perhaps against the forest of communication towers the navy has set up across the water on a distant but visible point, a rather ominous techno-intrusion in this otherwise benign landscape.

As we pass the field where the cow grazes, we see a young one still nursing. Unlike most modern dairy arrangements, the calf is allowed to continue nursing for six to eight weeks, then is gradually weaned as Iris begins to milk. Many older farmers shared with their animals in this way, and the calves were undoubtedly better off. (In the "other" dairy world, calves are taken away at once and bottle fed if they are female. If they are male, they are usually left to die or are killed; if a bit luckier, they are sold for a few dollars.) We dawdle on the farm, reluctant to leave, but the early winter days are short, and finally we get on our way.

Bill Coperthwait doesn't have a phone. If you are planning a visit, you have to write ahead, but you also need to know that he only picks up his mail once a week, so you have to plan ahead and think ahead. Those are two things that reliance on technology has meant we don't have to do as often. Not so when you live as Coperthwait does, which involves discipline but also a certain letting go of the very modern idea of control.

Leaving the farm, we follow the directions we've been given, take a paved road to its end, then a dirt road, then park in a turnoff and set off down a footpath. There are no markings—just general directions to take the left fork when there is a choice and to follow the sawdust. Bill, we were told, takes it out with him (from his carpentry projects) when he ventures into the world, spreading it on the path where it is soggy.

I don't think any of us were prepared for the distance. The trail was said to be a mile and a half, which is a good walk on a smooth surface. This is a rough walk, over roots, around puddles, through boggy areas. The worst areas have been improved with logs or stones, but being unfamiliar and uncertain, it is slow work.

Soon we are deep in a mixed woodland, no longer hearing traffic noises or, indeed, any noises of the outside world. I wish there was time to stop and listen to the silence, but it is already after two and the winter sun is low. We cross a beaver pond over which Bill has built a walkway with a railing. Beside the planks the water is smooth and black, frozen now perhaps until spring. There are a few faint signs of human presence from time to time: a gate made of rough wood; a bit of blue tied to a tree (for what reason no one can say); and finally, on a stump, an animal skull with the back of the head turned to us. Is this a sign? Does it mean "Come in" or "Go away"? We cannot say and tramp on. Finally we hear the sound of hammering ahead and know we must be nearly there.

The yurt appears suddenly, three stories high, exotic and beautiful, rising out of an open field behind a clump of birches and scattered pines. It is substantial and an impressive sight. I stop to take a picture and am left alone for a moment; I look around. There are smaller yurts scattered about—sheds, perhaps.

The ground floor of the yurt is a carpentry workshop. All around are signs of work in progress, pieces of wood still carrying the shape of the limb, stripped of bark and polished, ready to be the arm or back of a chair. Trailing behind the others, I climb the broad stairs to the next level and finally meet Bill Coperthwait. I had expected a wild man, an unkempt loner, eccentric and antisocial. Instead Bill is neat in wool tweed trousers, blue shirt, and red vest and is very civilized. He looks to be in his mid-sixties, with an open, interested face and healthy good looks. I sense reserve, but not secretiveness.

He hadn't gotten our letter saying we were coming, but he was glad to see us anyway, and we'd brought a few offerings to make sure: some fresh yogurt from the farm and some other small treats.

The upper level is a warm living space outfitted by a man with a keen sense of utility and beauty. Everything I see has both. There is no electricity, of course. No running water. And yet there is a simple elegance. The kitchen area is different from standard expectations because it is applianceless. It is merely a shelf outfitted with several old metal bread-boxes, obviously found at yard sales or junk shops, arranged on a mellow wooden shelf. They are attractive, and undoubtedly useful in thwarting the mice that must find the yurt an appealing retreat. There is a sense of complete order, but there is also warmth in the use of natural materials and the occasional carefully selected visual image. The seating platform has both exotic hand-woven throws and animal skins. The chair I am sitting on is wood, built to exploit the natural curves of found pieces, with a seat woven of leather strips. There are built-in bookcases and along one outside wall, beneath the windows, a long desk unit. Walking in the opposite direction around the circle I come upon a library area and a bank of perhaps a hundred small drawers fitted into a cabinet. Each has a small leather pull. Door handles are polished pieces of wood. Everything speaks of a certain patience: the ability to wait for the right piece of wood, the perfect object; the strength to spurn the unnecessary, the inferior, the ugly. Selectivity is key to this life.

After a cup of tea, we walk down the hill to Bill's first yurt. The sea is a surprise. Until now I hadn't realized how close we were to the shore. His property is on a cove, and he can bring in materials by water. He lived in this smaller yurt until he realized that in winter, there beneath the hill, he got very little sunlight. Now the first yurt is used for workshop attendees who come in summer to learn his techniques. In the cliff overhanging the sea, he has constructed a bathing pool out of rocks, and the summer yurt kitchen is nearby. Yurts are everywhere—the by-products of the workshops.

"I tend to like architecture to be harmonious," he says. "I believe in using common materials. In this locale it made sense to build round with cedar shingles." The upper level of the big yurt is all windows. Now, having lived for a long time in a circle of windows, he is accustomed to having light pouring in.

Of traditional Western architecture, he says, "We've been building rectangles because it seemed to use materials better. Now we understand that we can build round and not waste materials. Still, a yurt has some magic about it." That word again; the antithesis of science, technology, the twentieth century.

Coperthwait began building yurts because he was searching for simple, low-cost housing. Today, in the workshops, he uses yurt-building to teach other things: a way of life, simplicity, cooperation, a worldview. "That way we can have discussions on social design, the way we have to live—what we're going to have to do if we're going to have a decent planet to live on."

He is not antitechnology, he says, in that fierce way that so many neo-Luddites use—as if it were vital, after all, to establish that fact. No, this man who lives without running water, electricity, or a telephone, who saws by hand and hammers by hand, says he is merely choosy. "Pipes were invented by the devil," he says, a bit grimly. "Imagine having an electric can-opener." He chooses to have a solar panel for lighting.

We return to his yurt, share book titles, look at reading materials, select some to take home. "Don't leave yet, you have plenty of time before the light goes," he says, and looking at the fading sunlight I wonder if I can believe him. It is almost dark when we set out.

"Watch out for the giant beaver," he calls out as we leave. He had shown no signs of humor until now. It is a nice surprise. We wave and start down the path more quickly than we came up it. The moon has risen, thankfully, as we concentrate to avoid roots and holes and marshy places, walking as quickly as we dare over single planks laid across rivulets, smiling as we cross the narrow footbridge beside the beaver's den. The moon is behind the trees, the woods silvery and mysterious and quiet and seemingly empty— until a buck crashes out of our way.

The sight of the car is a bit of a relief. On the way home, we pull off the road to eat a supper of bread, cheese, dried fruit, and avocado and drink coffee from a thermos. From where we are parked, we can see that vast forest of navy communication towers on the opposite shore, lit red now, above the silvery water.

Not far down the road is a potter still working in a tradition that had its roots in the Arts and Crafts movement, as filtered through Bernard Leach. We pass his sign. He and his wife were both professionals in the sciences until they abandoned that for something more fulfilling. That story is told over and over again, especially here in Maine where living costs are low—if you don't mind chopping wood. I try to stop in when I'm down this way to see what they've produced, but it's too late today. Another time.

MAINE IS a good place to look for Luddites, but so is England. A few years ago I spent six weeks there and let my friends know what I was interested in. "My brother's a Luddite," my Surrey friend told me on my first stop. But the brother lived on the Isle of Man, and I doubted I'd get there. "And the choirmaster at the church," said my friend's wife. "He hates anything technological." But the choirmaster was busy or didn't want to talk to me. Luddites tend, on the whole, to be shy and a bit wary.

Cornwall, my next stop, was a gold mine—or a tin mine, a least, for tin mining was, for many years, the chief activity of the Penwith Peninsula, where I was visiting. I stayed with friends who were gradually renovating a stone cottage nestled against a hill outside of Penzance. They had friends they were eager for me to meet, and on a Sunday we set out to visit Andrew Lanyon and his wife Jacquie Levin. Finding them was the first challenge. My friends had been several times—Andrew and Jacqie hold an open house every Sunday—but locating the turnoff to their place is a challenge. It involved spotting a shed with a blue door, as I remember, but the blue door was open and thus not visible. Finally a local resident on a tractor pointed us in the right direction, and we descended a dirt road that eventually became a lane—a track, really—so narrow and grassy that hedge flowers brushed against both sides of our small car. At the end there was a small clearing where we could park alongside a tethered horse.

The walk to the house was weedy and unkempt. We passed what appeared to be an Elizabethan cottage. My friends knew enough to keep going. Jacqie, Andrew, and their children only sleep there. We meandered—

struggled, actually—up a path, past a small camper trailer where food is pre-pared and consumed—chickens scattering with irritation before us—and entered one of the two polythene tunnels, the kind usually used as green-houses. We were in a residence, clearly, although an unusual one. (The other tunnel serves as Andrew's studio and workshop.)

There were grape vines meandering across supports and laundry drying on poles. But as we wound past these obstacles, a sitting area came into view. Here was a circle of sofas and chairs already filled with people. Jacqie and Andrew seldom know who is coming. Most bring food or wine. Some bring guests.

Andrew Lanyon makes what are known as artist's books. He writes them, creates the illustrations, then has the book typeset and letterpress printed. The illustrations, printed separately, are tipped in (affixed as an insert) by members of his extended family. The books are funded mostly by sub-scribers, who pay a discounted price in advance to support the work. Those who wait for the actual book pay the full price. The major books are pub-lished in limited editions of around three hundred, come in protective slip-cases, and are extraordinary treasures, unique expressions of one individ-ual's curious and fascinating vision of the world. From time to time there are other, more modest volumes in paper wrappers.

Time is hard to pin down in Andrew's stories of the Rowley family, as is everything else in these fusions of the fantastic and the real—including place and identity. Vera Rowley, it is revealed in *Room to Maneuver*, has invented her relatives, Walter and Mervyn. They are manifestations of Vera herself, yet are too well established socially to be abandoned. And Vera is the medium through which Lanyon himself speaks. In a subsequent book, *Dying for Eternity*, Vera is revealed actually to be the invention of Walter and Mervyn, who have gone to great lengths to convince people that she really exists.

The three (or two, or one) are searching endlessly for the Holy Grail of total comprehension. What, for instance, is the source of art? Walter finds "the very spot where a single seed had been flung ashore on a seventh wave" —art's beginning. Yet understanding, we learn, is found not simply in the measurable and the quantitative but in the space between—a nether world where gold and silver are rivals, for instance, and Vera feels a thin vein of fine gray in her own mind and takes it as a sign of silver's desire to anthro-pomorphize.

Lanyon's illustrations, like his prose, are beautiful; brilliantly wacky;

surreal; and, above all, subversive. Vera, a scientist of many disciplines, discovers late in life that art or "decoration" can influence the outcome of a scientific experiment. Her beakers and flasks begin to take on fantastical shapes as a result of this realization. She had flung open the window and allowed nature to enter the lab, whereupon it began to affect the purity of the previously controlled studies—no doubt for the better. Vera—as Vera and as Walter and Mervyn—has an effect on machinery, causing it to malfunction. Thus civilization begins to avoid Vera, perhaps also because she is in the process of knowing and understanding everything.

There is always a sense of play in the fantastic adventures of the Rowleys, yet in the absurdity and wildness of his stories Lanyon is questioning or mocking the assumptions and traditions not just of technology but of psychiatry, history, sociology, and art and science. "Today in this silent cemetery of Science, the only movements are of shadows circling wolf-like, undulating over uneven ground like mounted engineers riding round a castle to site trebuchets," reads a line in *Room to Maneuver*.

Lanyon's life is one of quiet but intense rebellion against expectations and the predictable. He blends invented history with real history, an implicit questioning of what we "know" and what we do not. Always enigmatic references remain to be explored further. Understanding for the reader is a work in progress. And, of course, that's half the point—and half of the fun.

Their real lives, Lanyon says, are purposeful but capitalize on the accidental, "allowing the accidental to happen, particularly when filming, writing and painting." They are, he tells me, "suspicious of technology but make use of much of it. Jean Gimpel [who wrote *The Cathedral Builders*] believed the hoe was the high point of technology. I sort of agree."

They are not antisocial. "We keep a good (I mean effective) distance from society [but] being gregarious we go out a lot." Both of their children were first educated at home, Sam not going to school until he was sixteen; Rosa beginning when she was ten. They decided when they were ready. It wasn't that they were formally taught at home, he says, "we just talked and did." Today both are doing well academically.

Andrew and Jacqui's greatest challenges have been located within a mile of home. They have fought proposed power lines ("major ones with pylons"), a fireworks factory, the loss of a large wood to time-shares, a gas pipeline across their land. When not defending their land and the environs against techno-predators, they say that their lives are not hard. "We do not do what we do not want to do." What they have spurned is the consumer culture. They manage nicely with the flotsam from the flood of consumer goods. At their Sunday gathering, Andrew hears something he wants to make a note of and grabs his "notepaper," a yellowed roll of old adding machine tape. He probably bought a whole boxful of these rejects for pennies.

In Cornwall, I hear much talk of Benders. It is a new word to me. It refers to a shadowy group of people, I am told, who travel about with bent hazel sticks from which they build temporary shelters. As we are driving out to dinner, I spot a string of carts making their way alongside a narrow road: a handcart, a bicycle cart, and one pulled by a mule. On the top of the mule cart are piled a clutch of bent poles. I call out to my friends to stop the car and I rush over. I can only imagine what they thought of an American woman, not young, dressed to go out to dinner, waving them down and asking if they were Benders. "Some people call us that," a young woman told me.

They seemed to take me at face value, and when I told them what I was up to, they invited me to come for a visit at Madrun Holy Well, an ancient site in the middle of the peninsula, where they planned to camp. The next morning, one of my friends and I started down the worn trail leading from the parking area of the often-visited well. At the well there are hundreds of bits of colored cloth, torn from clothing. They flutter from the overhanging branches, tied there by people who believe the waters will heal. I would never have spotted the Bender camp had it not been for their mule, his nose visible through the underbrush as he grazed. The older footpath, which ran parallel to the trail I was on, had been made within a hedge of hawthorn that now was overgrown, the rough trees meeting overhead to form an arch. It was within that ancient green cathedral that they had made their camp.

There were four of them, all in their twenties or early thirties. Two had been playing their musical instruments down by the well; another struggled sleepily from the hut. But they welcomed us and put a heavy iron kettle onto the struggling fire of smoking new wood built in the traditional circle of stones. There was no tea, someone apologized; and Lisa, a beautiful young woman with a mass of curly reddish-blond hair, answered "Never mind," dashing off into the brush with the animation of a wood nymph. She came back with elder flower blossoms. One in each cup of boiling water from the well made a sweet and fragrant drink. I talked to one or another as they began to break up camp.

They were not Gypsies—nor were they "travelers," whose reputation is not the best. Three had attended university; one had a graduate degree. Their group—they, and the eighteen others that they would rejoin that evening—had grown out of a protest against the building of a motorway through an ancient site on Twyford Down. "It was a magical place with a long, involved history that made it significant in different times. There were ancient and important sites. It was so beautiful. You'd never see the point of destroying anything like that. Obviously it was the wrong thing to do in every way," Steph told me, still clearly caught up in the passion and pain of that failed endeavor. "We felt the best way to defend it was to be there. It began with thirty-four people. We set up permanent camps." There had been people there before they came, going through official channels, but it wasn't working. Their encampment didn't work either.

They had been ousted and the road had been built, but some of the group, feeling a deep loyalty, had stayed together. They called themselves the Donga People, an African name for the place where the roads came together, I am told. The group had changed—some dropping out, some joining in—but it continued to travel together. For a time they were in Brittany. Cornwall, with its mild climate, was attractive. It was also filled with sacred sites. They see themselves as having pagan roots, wanting to live as simply as possible—without electricity.

In an effort to end such protests, Lisa says, the government passed a Criminal Justice Bill in 1994 making it an offense for six or more vehicles to be gathered at an ancient site. It also allows the police to use force to break up protests. They have been evicted from their camps and made to move on, but they continue their traveling and their gatherings, "celebrating the wheel of the year." They earn money by playing and singing—pub gigs, engagements to entertain in old people's homes. Inge shows me a photograph of the group sitting around a beautifully laid table with linen cloth and silverware, surrounded by smiling elderly people. "Us," she says. "Can you believe that's *us* sitting there?" She is so pleased. She imagines the dinner to have been the good fortune of the blessed.

As we are talking, a young man is taking down the Bender hut, and I see how ingeniously it is constructed. A metal circle at the top is welded round with pipes the size of the hazel poles. (They are taken from pollarded trees, so the tree does not have to be cut and will grow new poles. The idea is that nature can be used without being destroyed.) One end of the pole is put into the ground, the other into the wheel. A tarp covers the hut. There is a small wood-burning stove inside.

They had various reasons for living as they did, far more primitively than even the Kellams. But Lisa summed it up: "We want to live lightly on the earth." And for that they were willing to forgo almost every comfort that people have come to expect, even of having a permanent roof over their heads. "It's surprising, but you find you don't need much," says Lisa as she loads up her cart. But even when you travel in a cart you accumulate things. "I still feel I have loads of tat," She says. "That's my issue: my tat"—(British slang for stuff).

The question of technology is clearly a major one for the Benders. "It's an endless cycle," says Inge, who is expertly harnessing the mule as we talk. "You've got to work to keep up with technology, but you can't keep up." Echoing Thoreau's idea that we end up working for the machine, Inge says, "You end up providing for technology."

Lisa, who has been on the road for five years now, suspects that "the people who make the decisions must never get out of their cars." They no longer have any idea—or very little—of what the real world around them is like. She likes living outside, close to nature. The communal living aspect is important to her. Then, of course, there's the cold and the wet, and that's when spirits falter. But they trudge on. That's what living on this planet is all about.

Their lives are not without patterns and rules about how to live. They make it a point—a rule, actually—to gather each evening, to play music, tell stories, sing. The community and the connection to the land are what is vital.

I saw them off, watched them set off down the road and wished I had the commitment and endurance—and the youthful energy—to join them. There was no satisfaction in leaving the well and getting back into our car.

A few days earlier, a side trip had taken me to the Isles of Scilly, a group of islands fairly far out to sea, reached by way of ferry (or helicopter) from Penzance. In St. Mary's, the largest town, the most casual inquiry directed me to a man the locals defined as a Luddite who lived on the island of St. Martin's. Of course, everyone had lived without electricity on St. Martin's until fairly recently, when a cable was laid, but Richard Morton and his family did so out of principle. I took the boat out to the island one morning with no idea how I would find him but perfectly certain that I would. The day was gloomy and wet. We were dropped off at one end of the island and were expecting to be picked up at the other in late afternoon. The day was mine. I had a rudimentary map, and the sensible thing seemed to be to walk from one end to the other looking for "signs," by which I don't mean anything mysterious. In fact, I didn't know what I meant. The island was beautiful, wild and windblown, with long views of the narrow fields banked with high hedges to shelter the daffodils that grow there. The climate is so mild that they begin blooming in December. But no signs of any sort appeared. Finally I reached the village at the other end and started into the post office to inquire. Just as I was entering, I saw a tall young man with a straight posture, healthy and fit, and a curiously alert look. His self-possession was striking. He was smiling cheerfully. "That's his son," I said to myself, and thinking myself absurd, went inside to ask directions. The postmistress told me generally how to find Morton, and then pointed to the young man, now disappearing down the road. "That's his son," she said.

What I had heard about Morton was this: That he and his large family lived rather primitively. That when his children needed shoes, he had learned to make them himself and now sold shoes. That when his children needed a school he had started one. It was all true. And there was a sign in the end, a real sign—reading "Organic food." The direction was right and I took off down an overgrown path between two cottages, and at the bottom found the small stone house where Richard serves freshly baked goods and sandwiches to the island's "day trippers," like me. I ordered something to eat and talked to him between customers.

He is, indeed, passionate about the issue of technology. His biggest concern is the loss of skills that technology has allowed. Machine tools have done away with craftsmanship. Calculators leave children unable to do math. Literacy is declining as more information comes in a visual format. "Technology is used for laziness, not for raising standards," he says. He could never be violent against technology, however. "You've got to look at your own situation and decide what's best for you. It's about living in harmony. It's about finding a right livelihood." When he began making shoes, he knew he could make them faster, but he also knew he had to make them as well as he could. "You have to look to your own actions, and not to what others do." When he first began cobbling, he got the leather from a small tannery in Cornwall. Now he has no idea where it comes from. Some things are now beyond control.

He has lived eighteen years without a telephone. In twenty-two years of living on the island, he has been off it twice. The counter he is serving from is wood, mellow and soft. There is a table inside where I sit, so that I can talk to him as he works. Outside on the terrace are a few others, all covered with red and white checked cloths. All have fresh flowers. People place their orders, then take their food outside where, among flowers, you can look at the sea.

His farm sits up against a hill. From the beach you can look back and see the lay of the land—the fields, the stone house with its red roof and smoke curling from the chimney, the barn, the orchard, the extensive gardens. Young people are doing things—working in the garden, cutting brush, working with the animals. The pace seems unhurried.

"Think healthy," says George. "Live healthy. Keep away from stress." His family—there are seven children—has had no major medical care—no diseases. He has had fights with his wife—the local gossips tell me that, too. Nothing is perfect.

From Cornwall, I headed to northern England where I also had friends who were interested in my project. My friend, Malcolm Whiteside, picked me up at the train station. The Appleby Horse Fair, where the Gypsies come each year to trade horses, was to begin the next day. On the way from the train station, we saw a caravan pulled to the roadside and on impulse we stopped. The couple, friendly and hospitable, made us coffee from a kettle over an open fire and showed us the neat and artful interior of their tiny home as the horse that pulled it grazed nearby. It is the perfect freedom of the life that they love and for which they were willing to give up what others consider essential. The pouring rain for the next few days might have discouraged anyone. It discouraged me from even going to the fair, although I admired the caravans, ranged on the hillside, from a distance.

Another friend, Terry Doherty, designated herself my guide to things low-tech. She had managed to accumulate a folder-full of references to old-ways devotees before I arrived, and we set out on a fine day to talk with an iron worker, a miller, a baker, a traditional cabinetmaker, and a blacksmith. Almost all used selective technologies—electric lights, for instance—even as they adhered to traditional crafts. They had found some middle ground where they could please themselves and still provide for themselves.

Our first stop was the Watermill at Little Salkeld in Cumbria, which sits almost at the bottom of a hill, nearly hidden in the curve of the road, the entrance enticing. The long, low building is a soft, dark, and dusty pink color, which seems not at all exotic but completely fitting. There are flowers everywhere, spilling from boxes and growing up between the cracks in the pavement. The door-trim is blue, with some window frames picked out in white and others left in stone. Huge rosebushes are in flower; pears are espaliered up the side walls; and to the left, along the road, there is a "laid," or woven hedge, created by weaving the shoots of the hedge plants together when they are young to create a growing, impassable barrier—a traditional skill that is now seldom seen. You notice the café before the mill—it's here you purchase your ticket to see the mill, which produces wonderful flour but also attracts people who want to see how it works.

The smells inside are of baking bread and good soup. The floor is tiled, the curtains cotton, the chairs comfortably old, and behind the glass counter there is an array of wholesome-looking food to choose from. Kathryn, the cook, likes to use what is in season. "Why should we have melon in the winter or leeks in the summer?" she asks, as if that were not a question others rarely ask themselves in the seasonless supermarket world of eternal availability. She doesn't plan menus in advance, she says, but responds to what's growing at the time. She might choose something from the garden or something she has foraged from the hedgerows, such as nettles or elder flowers. She believes that the care she puts into what people eat determines what they get out of it. "You have to have respect for what you are doing and for the person that gets it," she says. Her attitude toward technology is to use it to make life simpler, but to be selective. She uses a vacuum cleaner, for instance, but not an electric mixer. "I find doing things by hand much more satisfying."

The Watermill is owned by Ana Balfour and her husband, Nick Jones. Ana is a craftsperson, too, designing hand-knit sweaters and hats made from wool from her own sheep, dyed with plant materials—her studio is a jumble of hand-dyed hanks of yarn. Her designs reveal a fully developed, uniquely personal and confident style. Her very personal taste is evident wherever you look, in the choice of flowers and vines, in the colors, in the hand-printed wallpaper and the handmade spreads and rugs throughout the house. Shades of pink and peach unify everything. Life is what this is all about; the pure and simple joys of living with respect for the land, for human beings and what they can do; for simple pleasures; for the pleasure of the senses and the work of the hand.

Derek Martindale, who runs the mill, is usually dusty with flour from head to toe. The Watermill doesn't produce a great deal—a ton in a day compared to the hundred tons a day commercial mills produce—but it is an impressive thing to see, the huge wheel turning from the water, directed from the "beck" or stream into the mill race and then onto the wheel. The original millstones are still in use. Different ones are used for different grains: local red sandstone for oats and French hard stones for wheat. There are actually two stones, the top stone turning against the bed stone, which is fixed. The grain is fed down between them. They never actually touch; in fact, it is a cardinal sin, he says, ever to let them run dry. The water turns the wheel, which turns the gears, which turn the drive spindle that comes up through the gears, through the floor, and through the stone to the block. A hopper stores the grain, which is fed into the eye. The stone itself has a slightly concave dressing, which, with centrifugal force, allows the grain to move out and across the stone. Flour comes out of the edge. The tun, a wooden case, is a very close fit to the stone. It sets up a suction drag effect—sometimes assisted by a leather or metal sweeper—to collect the flour.

"Engineering wise," says Derek, "It's crude. It's so simple, and yet it works." He explains to me the workings of the central shaft; the meshing of the pit wheel with the crown wheel. The swing of a lever changes everything.

There are smaller gears that could drive other stones if they were needed and if there were enough water. The system seems beautifully adaptable. The energy of the water can be used for different purposes; the flour can be sent to different places. Finally, the simple moving of a piece of metal can divert the water entirely and bring the wheel to a halt. The water has to be carefully watched. Too much water would be as much of a problem as too little.

But the stream never runs too low to mill. If the water level drops, it simply means that things slow down and Derek works longer hours. "I take whatever water I can. I open the sluice gates, adjust the feed of grain to the amount of water." A change in the angle from the hopper to the shoe increases the rate at which the grain moves across the stone. You can adjust the fineness of the flour by lifting the stone up or down. He checks upstairs at the throat to gauge the fineness. The whole process can be greatly affected by the dampness of the day—the amount of moisture in the air. The noise of the mill tells him how things are working. The chatter tells him how fast the damsel is feeding the grain into the shoe.

Listening to Derek explain the workings of the mill, realizing that I can understand it myself; can comprehend what makes it work and how it can be adjusted in different ways, I begin to see what Derek likes about his work. There is something exciting about this expression of human ingenuity. This is technology, but it is comprehensible, it is adjustable. It is not in charge—Derek is in charge. All of his senses are employed in getting the most from the mill. His training and experience make all the difference in the quality of the product. You wonder how we got from here, which seems such a natural and reasonable expression of human cleverness, to the computer chip, which to look at tells us nothing; allows no participation.

"It's a lot of satisfaction," he says. "There are no dials or meters to read. In my opinion you can't turn a dial to produce fine flour."

When not at the mill, Derek works with horses. He is interested in preserving Cleveland Bays. They were once common in the Yorkshire dales where they worked the land or were hitched to wagons—maybe they went hunting on Saturdays. "They're rare. I try to keep them going. I don't believe in change for change's sake."

I followed the flour to the end, learning about the bolter, the rotary sieve, the reel, the "silks" for screening. I learned about the different sorts of flour for different purposes, what middlings are (once these leftover bits were eaten by the peasants—now they are added to rye, which is heavy and dense, to make a lighter bread). I learned about rollers, the carriage, the sieves and riddles and the reject mat where the tailings land. I emerged with an appreciation for flour—for real flour—not the sad, overly refined poor excuse for flour that comes from the supermarket. And I know I love this mill.

It is really hard to describe the feeling you get spending time at the Watermill. It is a sense of exhilaration, the certain feeling that life can be good and healthy if people care enough to make it so. And there is the impression that the effort put out to do so flows back in abundance.

I ask Ana to make a sweater for me, and we work on the design together over many months. She sends me a swatch of colors, I make small suggestions that she implements, and together (my contribution is minuscule, but I feel involved) we create a work of art that carries with it all that good feeling of beauty and health and joy.

The Watermill is clearly not simply a business but a means of demonstrating what is possible if care and consideration are applied to the acts of living and working. The last year has been hard. First there was a deluge, more rain than anyone needed, and then there was the horror of foot and mouth disease, when millions of healthy animals were destroyed. "It was like a war. You couldn't help being depressed."

Ana Balfour managed to keep her sheep. They were healthy, and she fought for their survival and won. Now things are looking up again.

IN ALL OUR visits to those preserving the old crafts, the one thing that came across loudly was the importance of independence, the feeling of satisfaction that individuals have when they can "effect" something. The tool is not a bad thing. It is a wonderful thing when used properly, but the crucial factor in whether it is healthy or unhealthy seems to be who is in charge. An individual may *feel* in control at a computer or in front of a dial or standing before a gauge, but it is a complete illusion. The numbers on the gauge are only that. They reveal nothing about the character of the machine—nothing like the clatter Derek listens to. Disconnected from reality, they leave the machine in charge; the people who made the machine, the system that needed and wanted the machine—that's who is in charge.

Wendell Berry has made up a list of questions that need to be answered before buying a new tool:

> The new tool should be cheaper than the one it replaces.
> It should be at least as small in scale as the one it replaces.
> It should do work that is clearly and demonstrably better than the one it replaces.
> It should use less energy than the one it replaces.
> If possible it should use some sort of solar energy, such as that of the body.
> It should be repairable by a person of ordinary intelligence, provided that he or she has the necessary tools.
> It should be purchasable and repairable as near to home as possible.
> It should come from a small, privately-owned shop or store that will take it back for maintenance and repair.
> It should not replace or disrupt anything good that already exists, and this includes family and community relationships.[1]

Berry made a good beginning when he first wrote this in 1987. It can be improved upon. Tools ought to be enduring in the first place—they ought to be strong enough not to break easily. Buying old tools is a good option as well. There are plenty about if you want to look for them.

The question of what tools do to a community is one that Schumacher had already addressed. What precisely is appropriate or "intermediate" technology? Schumacher was an economist. What seems to have started his contemplation of technology was the problem of underdeveloped nations and the question of how developed nations could lend a hand. The question of technology was a vital one. Did you transfer something high-tech, train individuals, and hope that the industry would pull the rest of the country up to its standard? Schumacher thought this unlikely. The technology would typically employ few people, and it would be isolated in the culture, not really helpful at all. Far better, he said, to set up intermediate technologies that were perhaps less efficient but employed more people and could be integrated into the existing culture. The question of which technologies are most appropriate to developing countries is an argument that continues. But Schumacher created standards for methods and equipment, asking that they be

> cheap enough so that they are accessible to everyone.
> Suitable for small-scale application; and compatible with man's need for
>   creativity.[2]

"Out of these three characteristics," Schumacher says, "is born non-violence and a relationship of man to nature, which guarantees permanence. If only one of these is neglected, things are bound to go wrong."[3]

Again, other criteria could be added. These tools should not be toxic to produce nor to use. They should be recyclable. Everyone can work out his or her own standards, based on certain unifying goals, but they will probably sound similar if human values are incorporated.

When Schumacher contemplated where we had gone so wrong, it came down, in the end, to a basic error, a basic misconception, a misunderstanding right at the start. It always does. Look for something that has gone badly awry, and inevitably, right back there at the beginning, is a bad idea.

> The strength of the idea of private enterprise lies in its terrifying simplicity.
> It suggests that the totality of life can be reduced to one aspect—profits.
> The businessman, as a private individual, may still be interested in other
> aspects of life—perhaps even in goodness, truth and beauty—but as a busi-
> nessman he concerns himself only with profits. . . . [T]he market . . . is the
> institutionalization of individualism and non-responsibility.[4]

Schumacher did not mean that private enterprise had to be abandoned but that certain underlying concepts had, at the very least, to be identified and questioned. We need to consider seriously how other values can be incorporated into our economic system. Frankly, I believe that Schumacher overstated his case. An individual who owns a business can operate however he or she chooses. If one pays oneself and one's workers, profit is an option that need not be pursued at all, or the amount of profit can be weighed against the importance of other goals. Values can be incorporated into the business plan. It is the corporation that is stymied, that is subjected to the profit imperative, that does not have the freedom to incorporate values into its decision-making process. And it is there we should begin: in redefining the corporation. Or perhaps in outlawing it, certainly in the form it takes today, for just as Adams suspected, ruin is inherent in its present structure.

Our society today operates under certain other assumptions that have been incorporated into economic theory as basic principles. One is that the "standard of living," measured by how much a person consumes, is a valid measure of well-being. The culture or society that consumes more is considered better off.

If consumption is the goal of economic activity, then other assumptions, some of them incorrect, inevitably follow. That efficiency is a primary goal, for example; that faster is inevitably better. That one must produce as much as possible in the least time, with quality a secondary consideration, in order to create the maximum profit. That the economies of scale make this possible—the assumption that bigger is better.

Schumacher would argue that these are not only false assumptions, but dangerous ones. What is left out of this equation is whether anyone living and working is actually happier for increased consumption and whether the environment can sustain the economic system developed along these lines. Consumption—individual acts—drives technology. Schumacher puts it bluntly: "It is the sin of greed that has driven us over into the power of machine."[5] That is not an idea that many of us want to confront. And, in truth, part of our greed as a society is not simply encouraged but almost compelled by the relentless pressures of the consumer culture in which individuals are bombarded night and day with advertising and marketing whose primary function is to fire up that basic human desire to "have more." Somehow we have to put "thinking" back into "buying." Or, perhaps into "not buying." And perhaps the most important word is "thinking," whether about consumption or technology or way of life.

One context in which it is possible to do all that is Schumacher College, where Satish Kumar is program director. The college offers both short and long courses in ecological studies. His Holiness the Dalai Lama, a patron, says in the brochure, "Schumacher College is founded upon the conviction that a new vision, inspired by concern with what is sacred in nature and human nature, is needed to sustain the earth." You do not leave there unmoved.

My stay was brief—only a day to speak with Satish—but it was a full one. Everyone—the students, who are all ages and from all walks of life—participates in the domestic needs of the college, doing something: sweeping, cleaning the bathrooms, preparing food. The participation eliminates what Anita Roddick has called "the servant class" and expresses the prevailing philosophy of complete egalitarianism. Meal preparation is a collaborative venture under the supervision of whomever is cooking that night. The menu is vegetarian, and caffeine addicts are in trouble, although it is possible to find a neglected jar of instant coffee if one really searches.

Satish was in charge that night, and as he prepared Indian food, quietly directing his helpers—I was one—in such tasks as crushing twenty cloves of garlic, dicing thirty tomatoes, chopping bunches of cilantro in the food processor as he worked at the other end of the kitchen, stirring lentils and cooking rice, it became not work but an event. A cookbook called *Gaia's Kitchen* gives a good idea of what the process is like. After dinner we walked along the footpath to the pub, I doing the impossible: scribbling frantically and trying to walk as quickly as this man who once set out to walk around the world for peace and managed half a world at least.

Satish was once a Jain monk, an Indian religious discipline so respectful of life that believers sweep the ground before them to avoid inadvertently crushing an insect. His journey from India to Schumacher College and the editorship of *Resurgence* magazine with his wife, June, is a story he tells in his book *Path Without Destination*. I had not heard of him nor of *Resurgence* before someone suggested, a few years ago, that I read *Conversations Before the End of Time* by Suzi Gablik, an art critic whose work I have always admired. Her book is a series of interviews with an unusual collection of people from the ultraconservative art critic Hilton Kramer to the Gorilla Girls. After reading the interview with Satish, I immediately subscribed to *Resurgence*, a magazine that blends ecology, art, poetry, organic growing, antiglobalization, intermediate technology, craft, food, and spirituality. Shortly afterward I put him on the list of people I needed to talk to.

The college is part of the Dartington Hall Trust in Devon, England, housed in a medieval manor house surrounded by a landscape that includes both flower gardens and agricultural use. On the lawn in front of the college is an ancient tree whose massive convoluted trunk and broad limb spread make reverence the only appropriate response. Before it one understands the veneration in which older cultures held such giants. The atmosphere is familial, pleasant, beautiful, and efficient yet unhurried.

The trust was established in 1925 by Dorothy and Leonard Elmhirst, who were inspired and encouraged, Satish tells me, by the Indian poet, educator, and social reformer Rabindranath Tagore. Education is the fundamental purpose, but a rural revival and the appropriate use of the 1200 acres around Dartington Hall are important as well. In 1995 its farming operation was converted to organic methods. The trust is perhaps best known for its sponsorship of art and craft: the potter Bernard Leach worked there, as did the painters Mark Tobey and Cecil Collins. Gregory Bateson, Benjamin Britten, Peter Maxwell Davies, Aldous Huxley, R. D. Laing, Witold Lutoslawski, Bertrand Russell, Henryk Skolimowski, Igor Stravinsky, Michael Tippett, and Arthur Waley are among the list of visitors or residents on the estate. Dartington offers, in its own words, "an exceptional setting for radical experiment." The college was started when Dartington Hall School, a rather famous progressive boarding school, closed. From the beginning, the idea was to combine ecology and the arts with Schumacher's ideas of appropriate technology and appropriate scale. Now the speakers include such writers and thinkers as Bill McKibben, Fritjof Capra, James Lovelock, Kirkpatrick Sale—virtually my entire bibliography of neo-Luddite thinkers and writers. The criterion, says Satish, is that one think in a holistic and integrated way. The program—three-week courses, with an M.S. offered for a year's residence—provides inspiration in a setting of intimacy and simplicity. "It is not just for information," says Satish, "but for transformation." Participation in the work is part of the program. "To create a sense of belonging you begin in the kitchen," he says.

The idea is to model a lifestyle that is sustainable; that can be learned and practiced. After beginning with meditation, a certain calm permeates the day. The work is organized by groups, which change tasks daily. The study is from ten in the morning to one in the afternoon. But equally important is the building and maintaining of a feeling of community. The college is international in scope, combining the wisdom of traditional societies. The emphasis is on concepts of complexity; chaos; systems thinking; deep ecology; and Gaia, James Lovelock's theory that views the planet as a living organism. This sustainable worldview favors the local over the global, the organic over the inorganic. Courses in ecopsychology create a sense of the sacredness of nature. "Earth, water, air, fire are sacred elements," says Satish. "Without clean and healthy sources of these elements, life cannot be nourished." The program combines influences of east and west, north and south, and is influenced by the philosophy and writings of Tagore, a Nobel Prize–winning poet.

I continue to trudge along behind Satish, who has a light and rapid step, scribbling madly and almost illegibly, feeling like an inferior disciple as he lets flow a torrent of ideas that I try to capture: "All our actions need to have consideration of nature. We can criticize the system until the cows come home, but real change will come when we start constructing good projects."

In the English village where he lives, the school was fifteen miles away. "That's not good. A school should be a part of the community," he says. He and others started one, and it is still going today. "We should have education that is holistic, spiritual, artistic; that emphasizes the relationship with nature; that nourishes mind, body, soul and spirit. A school should have a kitchen at the center—cooking should be part of the curriculum. Arts and crafts should be taught."

Satish was very much inspired by William Morris, he says. "The industrial society is producing ugliness. The soul and spirit are dry and hungry. Beauty is the food of the soul."

Satish, Schumacher College, and *Resurgence* magazine are not entirely opposed to technology. They use a computer, there are electric lights; but if there was a television on the premises I didn't see or hear it. There was a food processor in the kitchen, but no microwave oven. There was the sound of a broom, but I didn't hear a vacuum cleaner. I don't believe many people appreciate how much stress can be reduced by eliminating the noise of motors. There may well be something uniquely irritating to the human system about these manufactured and unnatural sounds. The people at Schumacher College have clearly thought carefully about what they use and what they do not. Says Satish:

> Appropriate technology is what we need. Not having it for the sake of having it, but using what truly aids us. Washing up [in the kitchen] takes time, but there are interesting conversations. Work is essential for sanity. Only

through work do we manifest the spirit. What is important is to serve others and to maintain good companionship. The machine cannot respect matter. We respect matter through work. . . . In making choices we can apply the BUD principle: Something must be beautiful, useful or durable. All three is best.

Every once in a while Satish holds a session for businesspeople. In the courses, they explore how to change the models. What shape would a post-corporate world take? "Institutions are the most difficult to change. Industry is in the grip of institutions. The present system may last twenty or thirty years," he says. "Then it will collapse under its own weight" Unless it changes. "Individuals are moving," he says, "institutions are not."

Satish himself helps me with my bag the next morning. I object. "I believe a person should carry his or her own baggage," I say, trying for something a bit deep. "A person should learn to accept help," he says, and I smile. He drives me to the train station, where we say goodbye and he wishes me well. I feel transformed after only one day. Work, meditation, learning, community, beauty, and nature come together under Satish's orchestration, just as they did at the Watermill. He has perfected the formula for achieving a more satisfying and a fundamentally more sustainable lifestyle. Still, it is isolated from the daily life where most of us find ourselves, since we mainly depend upon others to supply our needs, as consumers. And that role needs to be addressed.

I am convinced that individuals exercising discrimination in every commercial transaction can transform the world using the economic system we have. A small caveat: the vitally important ingredient is information, and when it is missing, choice becomes impossible. That is certainly the case with genetically engineered foods; the biotech food industry has tried very hard, by lobbying successfully against labeling, to make certain that consumers do not have the option to refuse them.

The new personal economics begins with a revitalization of self-respect. I don't mean the kind of "I'm worth it" that justifies a hundred-dollar facial, but a respect for what we are as human beings, what we need, what we can do, and what gives us the most deeply sustained pleasure over a lifetime. As an exercise, it really involves thinking seriously about our lives, what is truly important, what is truly satisfying, truly beautiful, truly healthy, and then realizing that we are—each of us—important enough to have those things. It may involve not consuming more but consuming less. Being "choosy," as

Bill Coperthwait explained, is about saying no as much as it is about saying yes. It means having a clear idea of who we are and how we want to live our lives.

Too many people today are wasting their lives, working at jobs they hate, enduring terrible stress, in order to accumulate what advertising has defined for them as the measure of success. Sven Birkerts, in his essay "Against the Current," finds the pressures of modern life increasingly frustrating, the pressure to accommodate to the machine standard painful. "We are living in a new condition, one of overload and acceleration. Our lives are crammed with stimuli, and the time available for absorbing and processing new information seems to shrink by the day. We respond to this by moving faster, by doubling up when we can . . . and editing away things that seem superfluous." Poignantly, he finds that "Just sitting in the park while our kids play on the swings feels like truancy."[6]

It is time to take back the power of defining for ourselves what the satisfying life looks like—as many of the people I visited have clearly done. Each has, in his or her own way, established his or her own, unmediated, measure of success. I know of a young woman who has vowed to buy nothing at all new, and it's easy enough in an affluent society such as ours to live well on its castoffs. I know people who *seem* to be truants who are in fact living full and considered lives shaped to personal preferences.

I feel a certain urgency in this enterprise, this effort to decide for oneself. The pressures to conform to the commercial standards of society intensify every day. It is increasingly difficult not to have electricity, not to have a car, not to have health insurance. City dwellers are at the mercy of technology, their choices limited. Perhaps that is why a Native American tribe being filmed by a friend of mine defined urban dwellers as "they who are mistaken." Yet wherever one chooses to live comes with its own challenges. To own property comes with certain other obligations. To build a shelter requires that one meet standards set by law. In some cases, to live an independent life involves becoming, like the Benders, outlaws. And yet, one does not need to be a libertarian or a survivalist to see that the pressure society applies to make us conform to a consumption standard has already become onerous—sometimes by law and sometimes in other ways. Individuals clinging to older crafts and traditions, making objects on a small scale in a small way, find themselves in a tangle of regulations imposed by the demands of industrialized standards. Will small traditional cheese makers in France be able to survive new regulations? Will traditional potters be able to support themselves? Will organic farms be able to compete—or even, in the face of spreading pollen from genetically engineered crops, be able to protect what they produce from contamination? Will children ever again know the delights of playing outside in a green and pleasant land, or will their days be filled with ersatz experiences via a computer-mediated or television world? Will hanging up the clothes in the backyard rather than using a dryer be forbidden, as it is now in many gated communities? Will we be able to make a phone call without assuming that someone is listening; buy a book without wondering if someone is keeping a log? Will the delights of life be overwhelmed by the pressures of the machine—conformity often justified by exaggerated claims of increased safety in a mapped, graphed, charted, numbered, tracked, videotaped world?

Fear is the weapon that enables tyranny. It is used to install and operate the machine at a repressive and intrusive level. As technology itself enables more control—surveillance of bank accounts; tracking of individual movements; instantly accessible information databases that reveal every vital fact about an individual; the awareness that every communication is vulnerable and that privacy is no longer a guarantee anywhere—it appears to me that the situation is now at a crucial point. The ability to live out individuated lives, such as I have described, becomes more and more difficult as society imposes a consumption-ordered conformity. In my worst nightmares I envision a society that *requires* a certain level of consumption, in which, just as a country-club member is charged for a certain number of meals whether he chooses to eat them or not, an individual will be required to spend a certain amount each month or have it deducted from his or her personal account. Perhaps it will even be decided how we spend that money, with choice reduced to the inconsequential—as it is today, when there are five brands of orange juice, all reconstituted; ten choices of dog food, all made with rendered animal protein and thus suspect; chicken cut up in ten different ways, but all likely contaminated with bacteria that can make you sick—which is, in fact, no choice at all.[7]

There is urgency, then, to acting now: to assuming some control over our lives before it is too late; to reexerting the authority of the individual to make real decisions. It will begin with self-discipline. It will begin with the ability to say no, by individuals examining their lives and determining their personal set of values: what they need and don't need, what they want and don't want. Applying them can be challenging.

Almost every day for years, a woman rode by my house on a bicycle. "Betsey Bicycle," everyone calls her. But it was a long time before I realized that her mode of transportation and recreation represented a principled lifestyle choice, and it was even longer before I finally arranged to sit down and talk to her about it. Betsey Holtzmann doesn't have a car. She owns a white frame house on a quiet, tree-lined street in a Maine seacoast town where she can walk or ride to just about everything she needs to do. She also has a boat, and when she can't ride, she sails. The trouble with cars, she says, is that they go too fast. The speed is all wrong for us humans, she says. It gives us a false sense of reality. Betsey has electric lights in her house but no television, and as we sit in her kitchen eating grapes and homemade cookies, it's some time before I notice that there is no refrigerator either. The quiet, when you become aware of it, is wonderful.

She doesn't need one, she says. Out in back of her house is a large, well-tended vegetable garden. She and her son are vegetarians, and it's really meat and milk you need a refrigerator for. Her son eats yogurt, but you can buy that fresh daily. (Anyway, as the French taught me, it will keep perfectly well in a cool spot, such as a windowsill.) If you took everything out of the refrigerator that didn't really need to be in there, it's a good bet there wouldn't be much left, and you'd begin to realize that the refrigerator supports the supermarket, which feeds the refrigerator. The consumer just becomes the tender in the process.

To the great interest of the town, Betsey rode her bike the entire time she was pregnant, becoming, as time went on, an ever more impressive sight. The baby was soon on the bike with her, and when he was old enough to walk she would take him with her to town, not on the bike but on foot. She was patient, walking at his pace, but she wanted him to strengthen his legs and get in the habit of walking, which he did. He is a wonderfully healthy child who seems to play outside more than inside.

But motherhood, which came somewhat late in Betsey's life, has begun to force a number of compromises. There is a local school, but she preferred another, farther away—beyond biking distance on the other side of the harbor. For a while she picked him up every day in her boat. Then a Waldorf School (operated on the principles established by Rudolf Steiner) opened in another town, and that presented a new dilemma. She wanted her son to attend—which meant finding transportation (the boat wasn't a reasonable option)—and now he wants to participate in activities that can't be reached by bicycle. She still doesn't drive, and so she has to depend on other people to get him there. She wants him to take tennis lessons in yet another town, and she has to find rides or pay people to drive them to the facility.

She was able to make sacrifices when she was the only one involved, but now things look different. And part of her ability to lead this principled life is certainly a result of her having the financial independence to do so. Still, she's searching for a comfortable middle ground, which is not uncommon. Technology resisters today have to find that middle ground, and it's always going to involve intensely personal decisions based on individual values and principles. There is, frankly, no way to avoid technology entirely. Certainly city dwellers have fewer options, other than to resist computers or refuse to have a telephone answering machine. They can, however, survive more easily without a car than can country dwellers, who have few if any public options for transportation. Resisting can be more challenging when you have a child, because the local welfare office, if you don't stay out of their line of vision, may decide that not having a telephone or an indoor toilet or even a refrigerator is a new, institutionalized form of child neglect. The pressure to conform should not be underestimated. Not everyone can live on St. Martin's Island way out in the Atlantic Ocean or at the Watermill or in the rarified air of Schumacher College—although it would be everyone's wish that they could if they chose to. We must recreate our lives where they are: there is certainly no other option.

Taking control of one's life can be threatening to others. Curiously, people for whom technology is not an issue seem to insist on a kind of all-or-nothing approach. To do without television intentionally can be threatening to those who are addicted to it—and I believe it does have the potential to addict. In fact, any principled stand seems to have the capacity to annoy. And quite commonly (and oddly), some people demonstrate an attitude that says you have no business protesting or resisting any sort of technology unless you are willing to give it all up and live in the proverbial mud hut. "Ah ha," they say, upon discovering that a neo-Luddite writer has an answering machine or that an Amish boy has a transistor radio. There is a curious demand for purity; any use of technology is evidence of fraud. "You see, you can't get along without it." And indeed, it would be extremely difficult today to avoid all modern technology, because of the way the world is arranged. There is a certain tyranny to modernity.

Scott Savage can give up his car because he lives in Amish country where it's not that difficult to buy a cart horse and find someone to shoe it, or to buy a carriage and find someone to repair it. There is a support system for people who want to avoid technology, and Amish lives are made immensely easier because they have a community that contributes support. There are skilled Amish who have perfected the low-tech choices made by the community's members. And businesses have found a niche supplying the needs the Amish community can't meet on its own. Lehman's Non-Electric in Kidron, Ohio, has parts for oil lamps and hand pumps and new blades for scythes. They found themselves with a lot of new business as concerns about Y2K grew. Some of it never went away.

Living in a mud hut isn't the point for technology resisters in any case. Thinking about technology is. Finding one's own comfort level is essential; working out for oneself what is acceptable and what is not is part of the process of leading a considered life. The compromises may seem arbitrary and artificial to others, but that doesn't matter. In the considered life, we must find ways of incorporating subjectivity; we must find a place for the people and the things we love; we must make time for inefficiency.

I drove to the Second Luddite Congress II—drove by myself even, rather than finding a carpool, because I wanted the independence, staying at motels along the way, not watching the scenery so much as listening to books on tape, yet conscious of the irony. If there is a tyranny to technology, there can be a neo-Luddite tyranny as well. Scott Savage's wife, Gail Leiser, calls him "plainer than thou." It's important to put judgment aside and not make a contest of who is pure and who is not. The fact is, purity is not possible. Life is a compromise.

I got to Barnesville in time to visit the farmer's market where an Amish woman was selling her baskets. Her horse and carriage were tied under a nearby shade tree, and as she and her children climbed in at the end of the day and drove off, I was conscious of how unskilled and inadequate I would have been at that simple task. How fearful, even, of the unpredictability of the horse; the fragility of the carriage driving down a country road among the cars and trucks.

The conference was held at the Stillwater Friend's Meeting House, an old brick structure of simple yet noble design. It sits under massive shade trees high on a grassy knoll near the Olney School. It is as inviting as any place could be. A powerful, tangible feeling of tranquility hung in the atmosphere that hot summer afternoon. Car sounds were few; there were no motor sounds, no radio sounds—nothing but the whisper of trees moving in the breeze, of birds, and people. They were already gathering and registering, and some were clearly old friends. But it was the great mix of individuals that was interesting. There were Mennonites and other plain people there, but there was also a girl with Rasta locks and a ring through her nose. The great bulk of attendees looked like the great majority of Americans. But something had brought them here. They had come from California, Florida, and Maine, from the far reaches of the country, to gather with other people who shared their concerns. Some admitted to having arrived by plane. Most drove. A number were sleeping in tents under the great trees, and I wished I'd known enough to do that.

It was hot, but the tall windows in the high-ceilinged meetinghouse were open, and the breezes stirred as we gathered to listen to a variety of speakers and, perhaps most important, got to know one another. The food was good and the presenters inspiring, yet Scott's vision remained incomplete. Some of the scheduled speakers had canceled at the last minute. Scott would stop publishing *Plain* magazine and devote himself to writing other things, he said. He offered the surplus copies to anyone who wanted them. He wanted to form a community now. He invited others to join. The Second Luddite Congress had come together one more time. It had been worth it. But there was the sense that it might not happen again. The narrowness of Scott's religious perspective denied the possibility of the holistic vision that Satish described. The difference between the negative and the positive approach became apparent. Success is in creation more than in abstention; in love rather than anger; in openness rather than exclusion; in choice rather than rejection.

I find it hard to accept that the fight for appropriate technologies is over. My own approach has been to change my life through attrition. The clothes dryer stopped working and was not repaired. Instead, I line-dry my clothes, and it actually becomes a pleasure to be outside and aware of each day. I gave up call waiting on the telephone and found that life went on. There is no caller ID on my personal telephone, no answering machine either. I have a small television for emergencies, shoved into the back of a closet, but no cable. The two channels I receive on the rabbit ears are more than enough.

The coffee grinder broke, and I replaced it with a hand grinder from Germany and banished that horrible noise that tore into the peace of the morning. I don't use a cell phone. I'm forced to use a computer, and I dislike every moment of it. When the washing machine goes, I'm not sure what I will do. It will be a moment of truth. The process is illuminating, however. What technologies do we really need? What do we really want from life? How can we take back our power; find the strength to shape our own lives to our own values? These are questions we have—most of us—forgotten to ask in the mad rush to have it all. But we can begin to ask them now.

Notes

PROLOGUE

1. Berry, Thomas, *The Dream of the Earth* (San Francisco: Sierra Club Books, 1990), 8.

CHAPTER ONE. THE KELLAMS AND THEIR ISLAND

1. Fukuyama, Francis, *Our Posthuman Future* (New York: Farrar, Straus, and Giroux, 2002), 218.
2. Glendinning, Chellis, "Notes toward a Neo-Luddite Manefesto," *Utne Reader,* March–April 1990, issue 38.
3. Birkerts, Sven, *The Gutenberg Elegies* (New York: Fawcett Columbine, 1994), 4.
4. Sale, Kirkpatrick, *Rebels Against the Future: The Luddites and Their War on the Industrial Revolution,* (Reading, Mass.: Addison-Wesley Publishing Company, 1995), 16 (hereafter cited as *Rebels Against the Future*).

CHAPTER TWO. THE FRAME BREAKERS

1. Sale, Kirkpatrick, *Rebels Against the Future,* 3.
2. Paine, Thomas, "Rights of Man," *Collected Writings,* ed. Eric Foner (New York: Library of America, 1995), 554.

3. Thompson, E. P., *The Making of the English Working Class* (New York: Random House, 1966), 62.
4. Ibid., 63.
5. Ibid., 485.
6. Ibid., 495.
7. Ibid., 528.
8. Ibid., 529.
9. Quoted in Thomis, Malcolm L., *The Luddites: Machine Breaking in Regency England* (New York: Schocken Books, 1972), 50.
10. Sale, *Rebels against the Future*, 73.
11. Quoted in Thompson, *The Making of the English Working Class*, p. 559.
12. Brontë, Charlotte, *Shirley* (London: Penguin Books, 1985) 62.
13. Ibid.
14. Sale, *Rebels against the Future*, 5.
15. Sale, *Rebels against the Future*, 190.
16. Sale, *Rebels against the Future*, 3.
17. Noble, David, *Progress Without People: In Defense of Luddism* (Chicago: Charles H. Kerr, 1994) 4.
18. Thompson, *The Making of the English Working Class*, 548.
19. Ibid.
20. Quoted in Thompson, *The Making of the English Working Class*, 548–549.
21. Thompson, *The Making of the English Working Class*, 549.
22. Sale, *Rebels Against the Future*, 201–202.
23. Sale, *Rebels Against the Future*, 191.

CHAPTER THREE. ROMANTIC INCLINATIONS

1. Wordsworth, William, *The Prelude*, (1850) bk 9, 1.108.
2. Shelley, Percy Bysshe, "Queen Mab," *The Poetical Works of Percy Bysshe Shelley edited by Mrs. Shelley with a Memoir* (Boston: Houghton, Mifflin and Company, 1855), 30.
3. Shelley, Percy Bysshe, "The Mask of Anarchy: Written on the Occasion of the Massacre at Manchester," stanzas XXXIX–XLI, *Major British Poets of the Romantic Period*, ed. William Heath (New York: Macmillan Publishing Company, 1973), 888.
4. Blake, William, "Jerusalem: Chapter 1," plate 16, line 18.
5. Muggeridge, Malcolm, *A Third Testament* (Boston: Little Brown, 1976), 85.
6. Wordsworth, William, "The World is too Much with Us."
7. Barzun, Jacques, *From Dawn to Decadence* (New York: HarperCollins, 2000), 468.
8. Muggeridge, 100.

9. Stettner, Fran, personal interview, January 1998.
10. Blake, William, "Auguries of Innocence," line 125.
11. Blake, William, "Milton," plate 41, lines 15–17.
12. Muggeridge, 57.
13. Blake, William, "Milton," plate 41, lines 1–6.
14. Hume, David, *A Treatise upon Human Nature*, bk. 2, pt. 3.
15. Barzun, 468.
16. Wordsworth, William, "The Tables Turned."
17. Wordsworth, William, Letters to Charles James Fox, 1801, cited in Heath, William, *Major British Poets of the Romantic Period* (New York: Macmillan Publishing Company, 1973), 415.
18. Ibid.
19. Blake, William, "Jerusalem: Chapter I," plate 19, lines 1–12.
20. Thompson, E. P., *Witness Against the Beast: William Blake and the Moral Law* (New York: W. W. Norton, 1993), 191.
21. Blake, William, "Jerusalem: Chapter I," plate 20, line 16–18.
22. Quoted by Kirkpatrick Sale in *Rebels Against the Future*, 89.
23. Ibid., 97.
24. Ibid., 98.
25. Ibid., 89.
26. Shelley, "Queen Mab," 41 and 45.
27. Ibid., 37.
28. Cited in Sale, *Rebels Against the Future*, 183.
29. Cited by David Pirie in *The Romantic Period* (London: Penguin, 1994), 342.
30. Thompson, E. P., *The Making of the English Working Class*, 686.
31. Ibid., 345.
32. Pirie, *The Romantic Period*, 352.

CHAPTER FOUR. THE MECHANIZED HAND

1. Carlyle, Thomas, *Selected Writings* (London: Penguin Books, 1986), 65.
2. Quoted in Kirkpatrick Sale in *Rebels Against the Future*, 199.
3. Dickens, Charles, *Pickwick Papers* (London: Chapman & Hall, LD., 1897), 361, Vol. II.
4. Quoted in Jacques Barzun, *From Dawn to Decadence*, 554.
5. Wordsworth, William, "The Excursion," *British Poets: Wordsworth* vol. III (Boston: Houghton, Mifflin and Company, 1854), 324.
6. Carlyle, Thomas, "Sartor Resartus," *Thomas Carlyle: Selected Writings* (London: Penguin Books, 1986), edited with introduction by Alan Shelston, 103.
7. Thompson, E. P., *William Morris: Romantic to Revolutionary* (New York:

Pantheon Books, 1977) (hereafter cited as *Romantic to Revolutionary*), 29.

8.   Carlyle, "Sartor Resartus," 103.

9.   Carlyle, "Chartism," *Thomas Carlyle: Selected Writings* (London: Penguin Books, 1986), 157.

10. Ibid., 64.

11. Ibid., 64.

12. Ibid., 70.

13. Dickens, Charles, *Hard Times* (London: Penguin Books, 1969), edited with introduction by David Craig, 65.

14. Dickens, Charles, *Hard Times* (Harmondsworth, Middlesex, England: Penguin Books, 1969), 159.

15. Ibid.

16. Dickens, *Hard Times,* 52.

17. Ibid., 223.

18. Ruskin, John, *Unto This Last* (London: Penguin Books, 1997), 171.

19. Johnson, Edgar, *Charles Dickens: His Tragedy and Triumph* (New York: The Viking Press, 1977), 387.

20. Engles, Friedrich, *The Conditions of the Working Class in England,* ed. Victor Kieran (London: Penguin Books, 1987), 87–89.

21. Disraeli, Benjamin, *Sybil,* ed. Thomas Braun, intro by R. A. Butler (Harmondsworth, Penguin Books, 1984), 96.

22. Brontë, Charlotte, *Shirley,* eds. Andrew and Judith Hook (London: Penguin, 1974), 62.

23. Ibid., 62.

24. Ibid., 62.

25. Ibid., 156–157.

26. Ibid., 598.

27. Ibid., 599.

28. Ibid.

29. Ibid.

30. Pevsner, Nikolaus, *Pioneers of Modern Design* (Harmondsworth: Penguin, 1974), 217.

31. Quoted in Peter Fuller's *Theoria: Art and the Absence of Grace* (London: Chatto and Windus, 1988), 143.

32. Hilton, Tim, *John Ruskin: The Early Years, 1819–1859* (New Haven: Yale University Press, 1985), 75.

33. Ruskin, John, *Selected Writings* (London: Dent, 1995), 45.

34. Ruskin, John, *Selections and Essays,* ed. Frederick William Roe (New York: Scribner's, 1918), 302.

35. Ruskin, *Unto This Last,* 167.

36. Ruskin, *Selections and Essays*, 178.

37. Ibid., 180.

38. Ibid., 180–181.

39. Ibid., 187

40. Ibid.

41. Ibid., 203.

42. Ibid., 209.

43. Ibid., 226.

44. Ibid., 227.

45. Ibid., 228.

46. Ruskin, John, *The Storm Cloud of the Nineteenth Century* (Philadelphia: Reu Wee, Wattley & Walsh, 1891), 392.

47. Fuller, Peter, *Theoria: Art and the Absence of Grace* (London: Chatto and Windus, 1988), 141.

48. Carlyle, Thomas, *Selected Writings*, 83.

CHAPTER FIVE: GOLDEN BEES, PLAIN COTTAGES, AND APPLE TREES

1. Marx, Leo, *The Machine in the Garden: Technology and the Pastoral Ideal in America* (New York: Oxford University Press, 1967), 3 (hereafter cited as *The Machine in the Garden*).

2. Mumford, Lewis, *The Golden Day* (New York: W.W. Norton, 1926), 58, 59.

3. Marx, Leo, *The Machine in the Garden*, 18.

4. Hawthorne, Nathaniel, *The American Notebooks*, ed. Randall Stewart (New Haven: Yale University Press, 1932), 102–105.

5. Thoreau, Henry David, *Walden* (New York: Milestone Editions), 105.

6. Quoted by Leo Marx's *The Machine in the Garden*, 17.

7. Thoreau, *Walden*, "Spring."

8. Beverley, Robert, *The History and Present State of Virginia*, ed. Louis B. Wright (Chapel Hill: University of North Carolina Press, 1947), 17.

9. Marx, Leo *The Machine in the Garden*, 87.

10. Thoreau, Henry David, *Walden*, 106–107.

11. Ibid., 37.

12. Ibid., 105.

13. Drinka, George Frederick, *The Birth of Neurosis: Myth, Malady, and the Victorians* (New York: Simon & Schuster, 1984), 121.

14. Quoted by Robert D. Richardson Jr. in *Emerson: The Mind on Fire* (Berkeley: University of California Press, 1995), 93.

15. Quoted by Octavius Brooks Frothingham in *Transcendentalism in New England* (New York: G.P. Putnam's Sons, 1876), 55.

16. Quoted in Richardson, 141.

17. Ibid., 141–142.
18. Quoted in Carlos Baker's *Emerson Among the Eccentrics* (New York: Penguin, 1997), 162.
19. Mumford, Lewis, *Golden Day* (New York: W.W. Norton, 1926), 103.
20. Ibid., 104
21. Ibid., 100.
22. Carruth, Hayden, *Selected Essays and Reviews* (Port Townsend: Copper Canyon Press, 1995).
23. Thoreau, *Walden,* "Economy."
24. Ibid.
25. Thoreau, *Walden.*
26. Ibid., "Conclusion."
27. Ibid., "Economy."
28. Ibid.
29. Ibid., "Where I Lived, and What I Lived For."
30. Ibid., "Sounds."
31. Ibid.
32. Ibid.
33. Ibid., "Ponds."
34. Ibid., "Economy."
35. Ibid.
36. Ibid.
37. The essay by Thoreau that has come to be known as "Civil Disobedience" originally appeared in the short-lived periodical *Aesthetic Papers* in 1849 where it was listed in the Table of Contents as "Resistance to Civil Government; a Lecture delivered in 1847." Precisely when Thoreau spent his night in jail is not known.

CHAPTER SIX: SIGNS OF LIFE

1. Gablik, Suzi, *Has Modernism Failed?* (New York: Thames and Hudson, 1984), 12.
2. MacCarthy, Fiona, *William Morris: A Life for Our Time* (New York: Alfred A. Knopf, 1995), 454–455 (hereafter cited as *A Life for Our Time*).
3. Ibid., 16.
4. Thompson, E. P., *William Morris: Romantic to Revolutionary* (New York: Pantheon Books, 1977), 29.
5. McHale, John, *The Future of the Future* (New York: Braziller, 1969), 31.
6. Thompson, *William Morris: Romantic to Revolutionary,* 18.
7. Ibid.
8. MacCarthy, *A Life for Our Time,* 58.

9. Ibid., 56

10. Ruskin, John, *Selected Writings* (London: J. M. Dent-Everyman, 1995), 202.

11. Mullins, *A Love Affair with Nature* (Oxford: Phaidon, 1985), 32.

12. Quoted in MacCarthy, *A Life for Our Time,* 435.

13. *Clarion,* November 19, 1892, Quoted in E. P. Thompson's *William Morris,* 603.

14. Carlyle, Thomas, *Past and Present,* Book III, chapter 4.

15. Ibid., Book III, chapter 12.

16. Thompson, *Romantic to Revolutionary,* 34.

17. Ruskin, John, *Selected Writings,* "The Stones of Venice," 196.

18. Ibid., 199.

19. Marx, Karl, *Capital: A Critique of Political Economy* (New York: Modern Library), 388–389.

20. Mill, John Stuart, *Principles of Political Economy* (London: John W. Packer and Sons, 1848), ii, iv, vi.

21. MacCarthy, *A Life for Our Time,* 152–456.

22. Ibid., 453.

23. From *The Dream of John Ball,* quoted by E. P. Thompson, *William Morris,* 722.

24. Morris, William, *News from Nowhere and Selected Writings and Designs,* ed. Asa Briggs (London: Penguin Books, 1986), 263.

25. Coleman, Stephanie and Paddy O'Sullivan, *William Morris and News from Nowhere: A Vision for Our Time* (Hartland, UK: Green Books, 1990), 97.

26. Morris, William, *News from Nowhere,* ed. A. L. Morton (London: Lawrence and Wishart, 1973), 367.

27. Coleman and O'Sullivan, *William Morris and News from Nowhere: A Vision for Our Time,* 98.

28. Ibid.

29. Ibid., 127.

30. Ibid., 130.

31. Morris, William, *Works,* Vol. XVI, p.p. 71–72, first quoted in Paul Thompson *The Work of William Morris,* 2nd edition (Quartet Books, 1997), 278, cited by Colin Ward, *William Morris and News from Nowhere,* 133.

32. Ibid., 169.

33. Cited by O'Sullivan, *William Morris and New from Nowhere,* 170.

34. Ibid., 171.

35. Cited by Wendy Kaplan, *The Art That is Life* (Boston: Museum of Fine Arts, 1987), 306.

36. MacCarthy, Fiona, *The Simple Life: C. R. Ashbee in the Cotswolds* (Berkeley: University of California Press, 1981), 21.

37. Ibid., 19.

38. Ibid.

39. Ibid., 21.

40. Ibid.

41. Ibid., 22–23.

42. *Ashbee Memoirs,* November 1902. Quoted by MacCarthy in *The Simple Life,* 61.

43. Ibid.

44. Quoted in Tim Hilton's *John Ruskin, The Later Years* (New Haven: Yale University Press, 2000), 470.

45. Clark, Robert Judson, and Wendy Kaplan, "Arts and Crafts: Matters of Style," *The Art That Is Life: The Arts and Crafts Movement in America, 1875–1920* (Boston: Bullfinch Press, 1998), 97.

CHAPTER SEVEN: THE NATURE OF DISSENT

1. Wolfe, Linnie Marsh, *Son of the Wilderness: The Life of John Muir* (New York: Alfred A. Knopf, 1945), 79 (hereafter cited as *Son of the Wilderness*).

2. Ibid., 80.

3. Quoted in Fox, Stephen, *John Muir and His Legacy* (Boston: Little, Brown and Company, 1981), 5.

4. Wolfe, *Son of the Wilderness,* 147.

5. Quoted in Fox, Stephen, *John Muir and His Legacy,* 51.

6. Quoted in Fox, Stephen, *John Muir and His Legacy,* 52.

7. Muir, John, *Mountains of California* (Golden, CO: Fulcrum, 1988), 301.

8. Quoted in Linnie March Wolfe, *Son of the Wilderness.*

9. Fox, *John Muir and His Legacy,* 107.

10. Ibid., 109.

11. Muir, John, *The Story of My Boyhood and Youth* (Boston: Houghton Mifflin Company, 1913), 1.

12. Fox, *John Muir and His Legacy,* 142.

13. Quoted in Fox, Stephen, *John Muir and His Legacy,* 145.

14. Johnson, E. D. H., ed, *The Poetry of the Earth: A Collection of English Nature Writings from Gilbert White of Selborne to Richard Jefferies* (New York: Antheneum, 1966), 388.

15. Fox, *John Muir and His Legacy,* 52.

16. Ibid., 159.

17. Ibid., 229.

18. Quoted in Fox, Stephen, *John Muir and His Legacy,* 236.

19. Fox, *John Muir and His Legacy,* 238.

20. Leopold, Aldo, *A Sand County Almanac* (New York: Ballantine Books, 1970), 101.

21. Benson, Jackson J., *Wallace Stegner: His Life and Work* (New York: Penguin

Books, 1997), 204.

22. Ibid.

23. McPhee, John, *Encounters with the Archdruid* (New York: Farrar, Straus and Giroux, 1971), 138.

24. Lawrence, D. H., "New Mexico," *Selected Essays* (Harmondsworth, UK: Penguin Books, 1960), Richard Aldington, introduction, 187.

25. Carson, Rachael, *Silent Spring,* ed., Paul Brooks (Boston: Houghton Mifflin, 1994), xii.

26. Fox, *John Muir and His Legacy,* 296.

27. Ibid., xiii–xiv.

28. Quoted by Rachael Carson in her dedication of *Silver Spring* to Albert Schweitzer.

CHAPTER EIGHT: GOING TO GROUND

1. Quote by HRH The Prince of Wales, speech given on the 50th Anniversary of the Soil Association, The 1996 Lady Eve Balfour Memorial Lecture, The Banqueting Hall, London, September 19, 1996.

2. Fox, Nicols, *Spoiled: Why Our Food is Making Us Sick and What We are Doing About It* (New York: Penguin, 1998). This book gives many examples of how industrialized production methods can actually encourage and sustain the presence of disease-causing organisms.

3. Pittman, Nancy P., ed., *From The Land* (Washington, D.C.: Island Press, 1989), 4.

4. Cited by Bromfield, Louis, *Pleasant Valley* (New York: Harper and Brothers, 1945), 105.

5. Peattie, Donald Culross, *A Prairie Grove* (New York: Simon and Schuster, 1938), 245.

6. Dale, Tom, and Vernon Gill Carter, *Topsoil and Civilization* (Norman: University of Oklahoma Press, 1955).

7. Bromfield, Louis, *Pleasant Valley* (New York: Harper & Brothers, 1945), 100.

8. Ogden, Samuel R., *This Country Life* (A. S. Barnes & Company, 1946), 79.

9. Ibid., 149.

10. Kline, David, *Great Possessions* (San Francisco: North Point Press, 1990), xv.

11. Ogden, Samuel R., *This Country Life,* 149.

12. Twelve Southerners, *I'll Take My Stand: The South and the Agrarian Tradition* (Baton Rouge: Louisiana State University Press, 1995), xxxviii.

13. Ibid., xxxix.

14. Ibid.

15. Carter, Dan T., "What Would Mr. Gingrich Have Said?" *Journal for Multi-Media History* 2 (1999).

16. Carter, Dan T., telephone interview, 2001.

17. Twelve Southerners, *I'll Take My Stand: The South and the Agrarian Tradition*, xliv.
18. Ibid., xliii.
19. Ibid., xlii.
20. Ibid., xliii.
21. Ibid.
22. Ibid.
23. Pittman, Nancy P., ed., Wes Jackson, intro., *From The Land* (Washington, D.C.: Island Press, 1988), x.
24. Ibid., xiii.
25. Ibid., 87.
26. Ibid., 92.
27. Bromfield, Louis, *Pleasant Valley*, 48.
28. Pittman, Nancy P., ed., Wes Jackson, intro., *From The Land*, xiii.
29. Quoted by Rachael Carson, *Silent Spring* (Boston: Houghton Mifflin, 1994), epigraph page.
30. Saltmarsh, John A., *Scott Nearing: The Making of a Homesteader* (White River Junction: Chelsea Green, 1998), 21.
31. Ibid., 54.
32. Nearing, Helen, and Scott Nearing, *Living the Good Life: Helen and Scott Nearing's Sixty Years of Self-Sufficient Living* (New York: Schocken Books, 1989), 49.
33. Ibid., 47.
34. Kline, David, *Great Possessions* (New York: North Point Press, 1990), xviii–xix.
35. Stadtfeld, Curtis K., *From The Land and Back* (New York: Scribner's Sons, 1972), 153.
36. Ibid.
37. Ibid.
38. Ibid.
39. Ibid.
40. Ibid., 154.
41. Ibid.
42. Freyfogle, Eric T., *The New Agrarianism: Land, Culture, and the Community of Life* (Washington, D.C.: Island Press, 2001), xvii.
43. Ibid.
44. Scott Nearing quoted by Gene Logsdon in *The Contrary Farmer* (White River Junction, VT: Chelsea Green, 1994), 17.
45. Northbourne, quoted in Logsdon, Gene, *The Contrary Farmer* (White River Junction, VT.: Chelsea Green, 1994), 17–18.
46. Ibid., 18.

47. Ibid., 19.
48. Ibid., 177.
49. Logsdon, Gene, *The Contrary Farmer,* 176.
50. Ibid., 181.
51. Berry, Wendell, *The Unsettling of America: Culture & Agriculture* (San Francisco: Sierra Club Books, 1977), 45.
52. Ibid.
53. Ibid., 55–56.
54. Ibid., 70.
55. Ibid., 75.
56. Ibid., 78.
57. Stadtfeld, Curtis K., *From the Land and Back: What Life Was Like on a Family Farm and How Technology Changed It* (New York: Charles Scribner's Sons, 1972), 153.

CHAPTER NINE: WRITING AGAINST THE MACHINE

1. Fowles, John, Introduction to Richard Jefferies, *After London, or Wild England* (Oxford: Oxford University Press, 1980), vii.
2. Butler, Samuel, *Erewhon* (New York: New American Library, Signet, 1961), 162.
3. Ibid., 170.
4. Ibid., 180.
5. Ibid., 181.
6. Ibid.
7. Ibid., 93.
8. Forster, E. M., *Two Cheers for Democracy* (New York: Harcourt Brace and Company, 1951), 222.
9. Ibid.
10. Crews, Frederick, *E. M. Forster: The Perils of Humanism* (Princeton, N.J.: Princeton University Press, 1962), 38.
11. *The Machine Stops* can be found on the Internet: plexus.org/forster/index/html.
12. Brand, Stewart, *Civilization* (Library of Congress, 1998).
13. Lawrence, D. H., *Selected Essays* (Harmondsworth, UK: Penguin Books, 1960), 114.
14. Ibid., 119–120.
15. Lawrence, D. H., *Lady Chatterley's Lover* (1928) (New York: Penguin, 1994), 132.
16. Lawrence, D. H., Mark Schorer, introduction, *Lady Chatterley's Lover* (1928) (New York: Grove Press, 1959), xxi.
17. Lawrence, D. H., *Selected Essays,* 218.
18. Ibid.

19. Ibid., 238.

20. Lawrence, D. H., *Lady Chatterley's Lover*, 13.

21. Ibid.

22. Ibid., 17.

23. Ibid. p 119.

24. Ibid.

25. Ibid., 305.

26. Ibid., 328.

27. Ibid.

28. Ibid., 329–332.

29. Lewis, C. S., *That Hideous Strength*, (New York: Scribner, 1996), 15.

30. Ibid., 16.

31. Ibid., 23.

32. Ibid., 38.

33. Ibid.

34. Ibid., 41.

35. Ibid., 42.

36. Ibid.

37. Ibid.

38. Lewis, C. S., *That Hideous Strength*, 43.

39. Ibid., 87.

40. Graves, Robert, *Watch the North Wind Rise* (1949) (New York: Farrar, Straus, and Girous, 1976), 4.

41. Ibid., 43–44.

42. Ibid., 44.

43. Quoted by Louis Untermeyer in *Modern American Poetry/Modern British Poetry* (New York: Harcourt, Brace & World, Inc., 1962), 357.

44. Jeffers, Robinson, ed., Tim Hunt, *The Selected Poetry of Robinson Jeffers* (Stanford: Stanford University Press, 2001), 19.

45. Abbey, Edward, *The Monkey Wrench Gang* (1975) (New York: Perennial Classics, 2000), 107.

46. Ibid., 68.

CHAPTER TEN: THE CLOCKWORK GOD

1. The latter two first defined by Patrick Geddes.

2. Boorstin, Daniel J., *The Discoverers: A History of Man's Search to Know His World and Himself* (New York: Random House, 1983), 36.

3. Mumford, Lewis, *Technics and Civilization* (New York: Harcourt Brace, 1934), 22.

4. Mumford, Lewis, *The Myth of the Machine: The Pentagon of Power* (New

York: Harcourt Brace Jovanovich, 1964), Preface (no page number) (hereafter cited as *Pentagon of Power*).

5. Mumford, Lewis, *Technics and Civilization*, 14.

6. Ibid., 15.

7. Ellul, Jacques, *The Technological Society* (New York: Random House, 1964), 328.

8. Ibid., 329.

9. Ibid., 29.

10. Mumford, Lewis, *The Condition of Man* (New York: Harcourt, Brace and Company, 1944), 39.

11. Mumford, *Technics and Civilization*, 4.

12. In one of his last articles, Christopher Lasch pointed out how conservatives bemoan the loss of values and yet support the kind of free-market capitalism that undermines the values they want to protect. Hollywood operates in the free-market mode, and what sells most enthusiastically is not what most conservatives say they want.

13. Mumford, *Technics and Civilization*, 4.

14. Ibid., 39.

15. Quoted in Winner, Langdon, *Autonomous Technology: Technics-Out-of-Control as a Theme in Political Thought* (Cambridge, Mass.: The MIT Press, 1977), 14 (hereafter cited as *Autonomous Technology*).

16. Ibid.

17. Quoted in Mumford, Lewis, *Technics and Civilization*, 25.

18. Ibid., 48.

19. Mumford, *The Pentagon of Power*, 54.

20. Ibid., 54.

21. Ibid., 55

22. Ibid., 58.

23. Ibid., 57.

24. Descartes, Rene, *Discourse on the Method of Rightly Conducting the Reason and Seeking the Truth in the Sciences* (1637) (London: Penguin Books, 1999), 44.

25. Quoted in Mumford, Lewis, *Technics and Civilization*, 41.

26. Quoted in Mumford, *The Pentagon of Power*, 85.

27. Quoted in Mumford, Lewis, *Technics and Civilization*, 50.

28. Quoted in Mumford, *The Pentagon of Power*, 88.

29. Ibid., 89.

30. Winner, Langdon, *Autonomous Technology* (Cambridge: The MIT Press, 1977), 21–22.

31. Ellul, *The Technological Society*, 46.

32. Ibid., 47.

33. Ibid., 54.

34. Postman, Neil, *Technology: The Surrender of Culture to Technology* (New York: Vintage Books, 1993), 45.

35. Marcus, Steven, *Dickens from Pickwick to Dombey* (New York: W. W. Norton, 1965), 332.

36. Ibid., 3333

37. Postman, Neil, *Technopoly: The Surrender of Culture to Technology*, 46.

38. Ibid., 47.

39. Frank, Waldo, *The Rediscovery of Man* (New York: George Braziller, 1958), 161–162.

40. Ibid.

41. Ellul, *The Technological Society*, 220.

42. Adams, Henry, *The Education of Henry Adams* (New York: The Modern Library, 1999), 238.

43. Winner, Langdon, *Autonomous Technology*, 284.

44. Adams, Henry, *The Education of Henry Adams*, 335.

45. Ibid., 342.

46. Ibid., 343–344.

47. Postman, Neil, *Technopoly: The Surrender of Culture to Technology*, 71.

48. Wilkinson, John, translated for Jacques Ellul's *The Technological Society*, x.

49. Adams, Henry, *The Education of Henry Adams*, 380.

50. Ibid.

51. Ibid., 381.

52. Postman, Neil, *Technopoly: The Surrender of Culture to Technology*, 51.

53. Mumford, *Pentagon of Power*, 213.

54. Birkerts, Sven, *The Gutenberg Elegies: The Fate of Reading in an Electronic Age* (New York: Fawcett Columbine, 1994), 15.

55. Ibid., 500–501.

56. Adams, Henry, *The Education of Henry Adams: An Autobiography* (1906/1918) (New York: The Modern Library, 1999), 452.

57. Winner, Langdon, *Autonomous Technology*, 15.

58. Giedion, Siegfried, *Mechanization Takes Command* (New York: Oxford University Press, 1948), 715.

59. Ibid., 715.

60. Winner, Langdon, *Autonomous Technology*, 284.

61. Gandhi, Mohandas, ed., Rudrangshe Mukkerjee, *The Penguin Gandhi Reader* (New York: Penguin Books, 1996), 60.

62. Ibid., 60.

63. Schumacher, E. F., *Small is Beautiful*, Paul Hawken, introduction (1973)

(Point Roberts: Hartley & Marks, 1999), 120.

64. Winner, Langdon, *Autonomous Technology*, 3.

65. Giedion, *Mechanization Takes Command* (New York: Oxford University Press, 1948), 716.

66. Ibid., 717.

CHAPTER ELEVEN: LOOKING FOR LUDDITES

1. Berry, Wendell, *What Are People For* (New York: Farrar, Straus and Giroux, 1999), 171–172.

2. Schumacher, E. F., *Small is Beautiful: Economics as if People Mattered* (London: Blond and Briggs, 1973), 35.

3. Ibid.

4. Ibid., 272.

5. Ibid., 38.

6. Birkerts, Sven, *Readings* (St. Paul: Graywolf Press, 1999), 116–117.

7. Note: In Sweden it is possible to buy a chicken labeled "Salmonella Free," and European consumers still have choices about genetically engineered ingredients; but in the United States choice is eroding, and if it is not to become an illusion, consumers must exert their power.

Bibliography

Abbey, Edward. *The Monkey Wrench Gang*. New York: Avon Books, 1992.

Adams, Henry. *The Education of Henry Adams: An Autobiography*. 1906/1918. New York: Modern Library, 1999.

Baker, Carlos. *Emerson Among the Eccentrics*. New York: Viking, 1996.

Berman, Marshall. *All That Is Solid Melts into Air*. New York: Simon and Schuster, 1982.

Berry, Thomas. *The Dream of the Earth*. San Francisco: Sierra Club Books, 1988.

Berry, Wendell. *The Unsettling of America: Culture & Agriculture*. San Francisco: Sierra Club Books, 1977.

———. *What Are People For?* New York: North Point Press, 1999.

Birkerts, Sven. *The Gutenberg Elegies: The Fate of Reading in an Electronic Age*. New York: Ballantine Books, 1995.

———. *Readings*. St. Paul: Graywolf Press, 1999.

Borgmann, Albert. *Technology and the Character of Contemporary Life*. Chicago: University of Chicago Press, 1984.

Brontë, Charlotte. *Shirley*. 1849. London: Penguin Classics, 1985.

Brooks, Van Wyck. *The Life of Emerson*. New York: E. P. Dutton & Co, 1932.

Broomfield, Louis. *Pleasant Valley*. New York: Harper & Bros., 1945.

Butler, Samuel. *Erewhon*. 1872. New York: New American Library of World

Literature, 1960.

Carlyle, Thomas. *Selected Writings.* Harmondsworth, England: Penguin
Classics, 1971.

Carson, Rachel. *Silent Spring.* New York: Houghton Mifflin, 1962.

Coleman, Stephen, and Paddy O'Sullivan. *William Morris & News From
Nowhere: A Vision for Our Time.* Bideford, England: Green Books, 1990.

Daiches, David, and John Flower. *Literary Landscapes of the British Isles.*
Harmondsworth, England: Penguin Books, 1981.

Dickens, Charles. *Hard Times.* 1854. Harmondsworth, England: Penguin
English Library, 1969.

Ellul, Jacques. *Propaganda.* New York: Random House, 1973.

————. *The Technological Society.* New York: Random House, 1964.

Emerson, Ralph Waldo. *The Selected Writings of Ralph Waldo Emerson.* New
York: The Modern Library, 1992.

Engels, Friedrich. *The Conditions of the Working Class in England.* 1845.
London: Penguin Classics, 1987.

Fox, Stephen. *John Muir and His Legacy: The American Conservation Movement.*
Boston: Little, Brown and Company, 1981.

Freyfogle, Eric T. *The New Agrarianism: Land, Culture, and the Community of
Life.* Washington, D.C.: Island Press, 2001.

Frothingham, Octavius Brooks, *Transcendentalism in New England: A History.*
New York: G. P. Putnam's Sons, 1876.

Fuller, Peter. *Art and Psychoanalysis.* London: Writers and Readers, 1980.

————. *Theoria.* London: Chatto and Windus, 1988.

Gandhi, Mohandas K. *Gandhi An Autobiography: The Story of My Experiments
with Truth.* Boston: Beacon Press, 1993.

Gaskell, Elizabeth. *Mary Barton.* 1848. New York: Penguin Books, 1979.

————. *North and South.* New York: Oxford University Press, 1998.

Gladwell, Malcolm. *The Tipping Point.* Boston: Little, Brown and Company,
2000.

Glendenning, Chellis. *My Name Is Chellis and I'm in Recovery from Western
Civilization.* Boston: Shambhala, 1994.

Giedion, S. *Mechanization Takes Command.* New York: Oxford University Press,
1948.

Goethe, Johann Wolfgang von. *Goethe on Science: An Anthology of Goethe's
Scientific Writings. ed. Jeremy Naydler.* Edinburgh: Floris Books, 1996.

Goldsmith, Edward. *The Way: An Ecological World-View.* Athens: University of
Georgia Press, 1998.

Graves, Robert. *Watch the North Wind Rise.* 1949. New York: Farrar, Straus,
Giroux, 1976.

Henderson, Bill. *Minutes of the Lead Pencil Club.* Winscott, N.Y.: Pushcart
    Press (W. W. Norton), 1996.
Hewison, Robert. *John Ruskin: The Argument of the Eye.* London: Thames and
    Hudson, 1976.
Hill, Christopher. *The World Turned Upside Down: Radical Ideas During the
    English Revolution.* 1972. Harmondsworth, England: Penguin, 1991.
Hilton, Tim. *John Ruskin: The Early Years.* New Haven, Conn.: Yale University
    Press, 1985.
———. *John Ruskin: The Later Years.* New Haven, Conn.: Yale University Press,
    2000.
Hobbes, Thomas. *Leviathan.* New York: Macmillan, 1962.
Hostetler, John A. *Amish Society.* 1963. Baltimore: The Johns Hopkins Press,
    1981
Hobsbawm, Eric J. *Labouring Men: Studies in the History of Labour.* London:
    Weidenfeld & Nicolson, 1964
Hughes, Glyn. *The Rape of the Rose.* New York: Simon & Schuster, 1987 .
Illich, Ivan. *Tools for Conviviality.* New York: Harper and Row, 1973.
Jeffcries, Richard. *After London: Wild England.* 1885. New York: Oxford
    University Press, 1980.
Juenger, Friedrich Georg. *The Failure of Technology: Perfection Without Purpose.*
    Hinsdale, Ill.: Henry Regnery Company, 1949.
Kaplan, Wendy. *"The Art That Is Life."* 1987. Boston: Little, Brown and
    Company, 1998.
Kimbrell, Andrew. *The Fatal Harvest Reader: The Tragedy of Industrial
    Agriculture.* Washington, D.C.: Island Press, 2002 .
Kline, David. *Great Possessions: An Amish Farmer's Journal.* San Francisco: North
    Point Press, 1990.
Lawrence, D. H. *Lady Chatterley's Lover.* 1928. New York: Grove Press, 1957.
———. *Selected Essays.* Harmondsworth, England: Penguin Books, 1960.
Lewis, C. S. *That Hideous Strength.* 1943. New York: Simon & Schuster, 1996.
Lindsay, Jack. *William Morris.* London: Constable, 1975.
Logsdon, Gene. *The Contrary Farmer.* White River Junction, Vt.: Chelsea
    Green, 1994.
Lord, Russell. *The Care of the Earth: A History of Husbandry.* New York: New
    American Library (Mentor), 1963.
MacCarthy, Fiona. *William Morris: A Life for Our Time.* London: Faber and
    Faber, 1994.
———. *The Simple Life: C. R. Ashbee in the Cotswolds.* Berkeley: University of
    California Press, 1981.
McHale, John. *The Future of the Future.* New York: George Braziller, 1969.

Mander, Jerry. *In the Absence of the Sacred*. San Francisco: Sierra Club Books, 1991.

———. *Four Arguments for the Elimination of Television*. New York: William Morrow, 1978.

Marcus, Steven. *Dickens from Pickwick to Dombey*. New York: W. W. Norton, 1965.

Marx, Leo. *The Machine in the Garden: Technology and the Pastoral Ideal in America*. 1964. London: Oxford University Press, 1979.

Mills, Stephanie. *Epicurean Simplicity*. Washington, D.C.: Island Press, 2002.

———. *In Service of the Wild*. Boston: Beacon Press, 1995,

———. *Turning Away from Technology*. San Francisco: Sierra Club Books, 1997.

Morris, William. *News from Nowhere and Selected Writings and Designs* London: Penguin, 1984.

Muggeridge, Malcolm. *Chronicles of Wasted Time*. Vol. 1 & 2. New York: William Morrow & Company, 1973, 1974 .

———. *A Third Testament*. Boston: Little, Brown and Company, 1976.

Mumford, Lewis. *The Conduct of Life*. New York: Harcourt, Brace and Company, New York, 1951.

———. *The Golden Day: A Study of American Literature and Culture*. New York: W. W. Norton & Company, 1926.

———. *The Pentagon of Power: The Myth of the Machine*. New York: Harcourt Brace Jovanovich, 1970.

———. *Technics and Civilization*. New York: Harcourt, Brace & World, 1934.

Myerson, Joel. *Transcendentalism*. Oxford: Oxford University Press, 2000.

Nearing, Helen, and Scott Nearing. *Living the Good Life: How to Live Sanely and Simply in a Troubled World*. 1954. New York: Schocken Books, 1990.

Noble, David. *Progress Without People*. Toronto: Between the Lines, 1995.

Ogden, Samuel R., *This Country Life*. A. S. Barnes & Co., 1946.

Peattie, Donald Culross. *A Prairie Grove*. New York: The Literary Guild of America, 1938.

Pichaske, David R., ed. *Late Harvest*. New York: Smithmark, 1996.

Pirie, David B., ed. *The Romantic Period*. The Penguin History of Literature, vol. 5. Harmondsworth, England: Penguin, 1994.

Pittman, Nancy P., ed. *From The Land*. Washington, D.C.: Island Press, 1988.

Postman, Neil. *Technopoly: The Surrender of Culture to Technology*. New York: Vintage Books, 1993.

Richardson, Robert D. Jr., *Emerson: The Mind on Fire*. Berkeley: University of California Press, 1995.

Rousseau, Jean-Jacques. *A Discourse on Inequality*. London: Penguin Books, 1984.

Ruskin, John, *Selected Writings*. London: Everyman Library, J. M. Dent, 1995.

————. *Unto This Last and Other Writings*. London: Penguin Classics, 1997.

Sale, Kirkpatrick. *Rebels Against the Future: The Luddites and Their War on the Industrial Revolution*. Reading, Mass.: Addison Wesley, 1995.

Saltmarsh, John A. *Scott Nearing: The Making of a Homesteader*. 1991. White River Junction, Vt.: Chelsea Green Publishing Co., White River Junction, 1998.

Saul, John Ralston. *Voltaire's Bastards: The Dictatorship of Reason in the West*. New York: The Free Press, 1992.

Schumacher, E. F. *Small Is Beautiful: Economics as if People Mattered*. New York: HarperPerennial, 1989.

————. *Small Is Beautiful: Economics as if People Mattered*. New York: Perennial Library, 1989. Prefaces Kirkpatrick Sale and John McClaughty.

Scott, Stephen, and Kenneth Pellman. *Living Without Electricity*. Intercourse, Pa.: Good Books, 1990.

Stadtfeld, Curtis K. *From the Land and Back: What Life Was Like on a Family Farm and How Technology Changed It*. New York: Charles Scribner's Sons, 1972.

Stross, Randall E., ed. *Technology and Society in Twentieth Century America*. Chicago: The Dorsey Press, 1989.

Thoreau, Henry David. *Walden and Civil Disobedience*. 1854. New York: Viking Penguin, 1983.

Thomis, Malcolm I. *The Luddites: Machine Breaking in Regency England*. New York: Schocken Books, 1970.

Thompson, E. P. *The Making of the English Working Class* New York: Vintage Books, 1966.

————. *The Romantics: England in a Revolutionary Age*. New York: The New Press, 1997.

————. *William Morris: Romantic to Revolutionary*. New York: Pantheon Books, 1977.

————. *Witness Against the Beast: William Blake and the Moral Law*. New York: The New Press, 1993.

Thompson, Paul. *The Work of William Morris*. London: Heinemann, 1967.

Twelve Southerners. *I'll Take My Stand: The South and the Agrarian Tradition*. 1930. Baton Rouge: Louisiana State University Press, 1995.

Walls, Laura Dassow, ed. *Material Faith: Thoreau on Science*. Boston: Houghton Mifflin, 1999.

White, Gilbert. *The Natural History of Selborne*. 1789. New York: Penguin Books, 1997.

Widmer, J. Wesley. *Life in the Country*. New York: Vantage Press, 1978.

Williams, Raymond. *Culture and Society: 1780–1950.* 1958. New York: Columbia University Press, 1983.

Winner, Langdon. *Autonomous Technology: Technics-Out-of-Control as a Theme in Political Thought.* Cambridge, Mass.: The MIT Press, 1977.

———. *The Whale and the Reactor.* Chicago: University of Chicago Press, 1986.

Acknowledgments

This is a book that relies upon the work of others. I am indebted, for instance, not simply to the works of Blake, Ruskin, Morris, and Muir, to name but a few, but equally to those who have written about Blake, Ruskin, Morris, and Muir—to those scholars and historians who put these individuals into context. I am most grateful, therefore, for the work of E. P. Thompson, Fiona MacCarthy, Kirkpatrick Sale, John Saltmarsh, Carlos Baker, Robert D. Richardson, Jr., Stephen Fox, Leo Marx, and Tim Hilton, among others. I want to thank Richard Parker, who knows a great deal about this topic, not only for pointing me in the right direction, and lending me books from his personal collection, but for reading the manuscript and offering valuable advice. I sincerely appreciate all those many individuals who gave me encouragement along the way, especially Beverly Gologorsky and Tom Engelhardt, who mysteriously made things happen. But most of all, I am thankful to have had a wonderful editor, Jonathan Cobb, whose diligence, wisdom, skill, good humor, and patience, are, apparently, without limits. My sincere gratitude goes, as well, to editorial assistant Kathryn Jergovich, who went way beyond what was expected in helping to pull together the necessary bits and pieces, and who remained unfailingly cheerful in the process. And finally, a word of thanks to Lehman's Non-Electric in Kidron, Ohio, where I was able to find a hand-cranked coffee grinder, oil lamps, and other low-tech items as I tentatively tackled my own addiction to technology.

Index

About the Author

The articles, essays, and book reviews of author Nicols Fox have appeared in a wide range of publications, including, most recently, the *New York Times,* the *Washington Post,* and the *Ruminator Review*. She has also written regularly for *The Economist*. She is the author of *Spoiled*, a journalistic perspective of emerging foodborne diseases, and *It Was Probably Something You Ate*. She lives on the coast of Maine.